D1083018

COLOR AT HOME AND ABROAD

COLOR AT HOME AND ABROAD

BY

GEORGE MALLISON

AMS PRESS, INC.
NEW YORK

Reprinted from the edition of 1929, Boston
First AMS EDITION published 1970
Manufactured in the United States of America

International Standard Book Number: 0-404-00198-X

Library of Congress Catalog Card Number: 72-132388

AMS PRESS, INC.
NEW YORK, N.Y. 10003

This work is dedicated to the White American who is working for the preservation of the integrity of his race and for the preservation of American Democracy, and to the American Negro who will work for an opportunity to give expression to his awakening national consciousness in a country of his own and who will try to carry the message of civilization to the natives of his Fatherland.

CONTENTS

PART I

PART II

PART III

8 CONTENTS

INTRODUCTION.

This work is undertaken with the hope that some impetus may be given to serious consideration of race matters, both as a domestic and as an international question. The stage, since the World War, has been occupied by organized industry and organized labor, the only organized bodies that know what they want and are going after it. Aside from propaganda in behalf of these two, the extra numbers on the stage have been devoted to prohibition under the management of Mr. Wheeler; the daily diversions of the bootleggers; the psychology of the latest crime, or is it safer to kill the husband or the wife or to rob the mails; the reservations for entrance into the World Court; and a few other matters of manufactured interest. It may be unduly optimistic to hope that it is about time for us to emerge from the war mists of passion and emotional insanity and the haze of gasoline, and appear again in our right mind; but it does seem that the time has arrived when we should stop drifting and formulate constructive plans of some ethical value to the race and show that we still live and possess virility.

That our race problem is one of serious domestic concern is conclusively shown by the numerous authorities who have taken it as a theme in recent works. That there is a larger aspect of the race question, the solution of which is the healing of the breaches in White Solidarity in the face of a world-wide anti-white sentiment, has also been brought forcibly to the public attention by numerous writers. That these writers have not succeeded in arousing public sentiment is evidenced by the fact that in our domestic problem we are drifting along gradually into a worse condition without any effort toward a solution; and that in its international aspects progress is still blocked by politicians who yet preach the doctrine of hate and talk about responsibility for the war—war guilt—as a camouflage for aggression upon others' rights. That I should hope to change this—a task that could not be viewed with complacency by genius—would pronounce me an unspeakable egotist or fit subject for a home for feeble-minded;

9

but that I should fail to protest against the neglect of these most important matters would be inconsistent with my interest in public affairs and the maintenance of my own self-respect.

Americans are as old as the oldest and as young as the youngest Europeans; for the roots of our race are embedded in the sources from which sprang the races of Europe—the whites. Therefore, our traditions are as rich as those of any power of Europe and much more so than some; for the blood of our people knows no one source in Europe but includes them all. It is true the tongue we speak was brought to this country with the colonists from England, and that our laws and civil institutions were in their inception based upon the common law of England and her institutions; yet, the development and growth of our language and of our institutions, political and civil, have been affected by the mixed sources of blood and environment in the new home to such extent that neither our language nor our institutions are to-day identical with those of England.

Though old as a people, the Americans are young as a political entity; but, as far as relates to government itself, ours is older than any of the governments in Europe aside from that of England, of Switzerland and of Denmark. The first settlers came from a hardy, adventurous stock, whether Cavalier, Puritan, or indentured servant. Some came to enjoy the right to worship God in accordance with the dictates of their conscience, some for a freer political and economic life, and some prompted by the spirit of adventure alone. Even the indentured servant was willing to sell his liberty for a time in order to enjoy and profit by the future, larger, freedom and opportunity in a new land. There was a dissatisfaction with, and rebellion agaist the religious, the political, and the economic conditions with which they were circumscribed; and this in the end, as always, has led to a broader tolerance under better conditions. Rebellion always contains potentially the germ of tolerance. These adventurers came not from England alone, but from Scotland, Ireland, Wales, France, Germany, Norway, Sweden and elsewhere.

Between 1607, when settlement was made at Jamestown, and July 4, 1776, when the United States came into existence as a separate body politic among the nations of the earth, the principal occupation of these people was subduing a wilderness, rendering it fit for occupation, and fruitful of the necessities of life, in the face of opposition by hostile and uncivilized savages. The log hut along the shore of bay or river, from the shelter of which the occupant cleared and tilled the soil or from which he set out on his fishing expeditions, became a social center and in time grew into a village, town or city. The encroachments of the whites were along the bays, sounds and rivers until finally, on the last mentioned date, the domain of the new power extending from Maine to Georgia and westward to the Mississippi, was the home of 2,750,000 people.

On March 4, 1789, the Constitution of the United States became operative, and the first census taken under the new government in 1790 showed a population of 3,929,326 of which number 697,697 were Negro slaves and 59,511 persons of color not slaves. From then until now many immigrants have poured in from Europe and from countries that had not previously furnished them, thus introducing new sources of European blood and extending the traditions and sources of history of our people beyond what it was at the time of Independence.

During the period from the first settlement to Independence, the Americans were busily engaged in making homes and in fitting themselves economically and politically into the new conditions of life with which they found themselves surrounded. That they did not neglect their opportunities is fully attested by the success of the Revolution and the instrument produced as a form of government for the new power—the Constitution of the United States. Whatever may be the opinion at this time as to the merits or demerits of this or that form of government, there can be no question but that this instrument was, when adopted, the greatest charter of human justice and liberties ever produced by man; and the authors of it were proclaimed men good and wise above their generation.

No effort of unfriendly critics to bring ridicule upon these men as rough and uncouth backwoodsmen, because they did not contribute to literature, art and the sciences, will survive a fair investigation of facts or save the critics from contempt. Literature, the arts and the sciences flourish in settled communities where the civic, social and economic life of a people has so shaped itself as to stimulate to efforts along these lines, and where leisure gives opportunity. To convert a great land, covered with forests and inhabited by warlike savages, into a self-sustaining community under a government the most just, liberal and humane ever instituted by man required a high order of genius; and one may rest assured that such people passed on to future generations potential genius in literature, the arts, the sciences, and in all other lines of human endeavor.

Beginning with the inauguration of Washington as President and down to the Civil War, the energies of the people were directed toward the development of the country's resources and the extension of its borders to the Pacific on the west and to the present Mexican line on the south. The Civil War was the great climacteric in the darkest phase of our national life. However dear to us may be the memory of those who gave up life in this struggle, however much we may exalt the patriotism—the love of a cause of their own people—of the victims of this holocaust, however sacred the niche reserved in our hearts for these victims, the fact remains that it was a senseless, brutal war between brothers, the pernicious result of which was a distilled hate that sought to justify measures of repression which, if literally carried out, would have resulted in extermination.

The introduction of the Negro into America as a slave is the greatest crime of modern history, if not of all time; and if the guilty parties are to be indicted and held to answer at the bar of justice, the list of criminals will be a long one. Among them will be found the Dutch, the English who forced slavery on the colonists, the Portuguese, the Spanish, and even the New England Puritan who found profit in the slave trade or opportunity to elevate the slave through instruction in the Gospel. The lowly African, the most degraded of the human species—he who, although in contact with civilization for thousands of years, was utterly incapable of lifting himself from his savage state—was the sport of the greedy who trafficked his body as an article of commerce. The slave trade flourished and slave markets were forcibly, if necessary, created by governmental agencies. In the course of time public sentiment against the slave trade crystallized and expressed itself in an aggressive campaign for its extermination. Among the most active and zealous in the suppression of this traffic was England, formerly one of its most persistent supporters. In the meantime America had become well stocked with African slaves, and gradually conditions shaped themselves to that situation found existing at the outbreak of the Civil War.

The outstanding result of the Civil War was the abolition of slavery through the adoption of the 13th Amendment to the Constitution and the declaration of complete equality in all respects between the blacks and the whites in the 14th and the 15th Amendments.

No one would now have the 13th Amendment other than it is; but many of us do find fault with the false declarations of equality between the races contained in the 14th and the 15th Amendments.

In this work it will be maintained that the following conclusions, bearing upon our domestic race problem, necessarily follow from facts disclosed by history, traditions, and scientific research into the antecedents of civilized man:

(1) That the White race is the initiator, builder and preserver of civilization.

(2) That the Black race is incapable of civilization through any effort of its own, and cannot acquire any degree of it except under duress of a superior civilized people.

(3) That the two races cannot jointly occupy the same territory without amalgamation.

(4) That this amalgamation results in decay of civilization in the hands of the mixed bloods, who are inferior to the pure whites in every respect.

(5) That the outward, apparent differences between the races, the existence of which cannot escape our observation, are indicative of radical differences of the utmost importance, the inexplicable origin of which reaches into the remotest antiquity.

(6) That the White race developed and became a civilized people in Atlantis, and that this view is not inconsistent with any reasonable presentation of the theory of evolution and conforms most closely to our knowledge as to the dispersion of the races. Nor, on the other hand, is it inconsistent with the Biblical account of the Garden of Eden.

(7) That there is nothing in the Bible to justify the contention that the black man descended from Adam.

(8) That the War Amendments (the 14th and the 15th) not only have failed in furthering the solution of the race problem, but have, on the other hand, added to the difficulties to such an extent that the problem exists now in a more aggravated form than it did before slavery was abolished.

(9) That segregation by transportation of the Negro to some country of his own is the only solution; and that this can and should be done in justice to both races.

Up to this time, we in the South have been able to maintain

a line of demarcation upon one side of which are the whites and on the other the blacks and the mixed bloods; and we are, therefore, still of European extraction and the history of Europe to the time when we become an independent nation is our history, and their traditions are ours as well. In so far as the civilization of ancient Greece has influenced modern civilization, we are interested to the same extent as are the European nations; and the same applies to the institutions of Rome, particularly as relates to political or administrative affairs—the law. Likewise we claim a personal interest and right in that list of great names in the arts, letters and sciences, which characterized the revival of learning in that period between the discovery of America and the year of our Independence. But unless we remove the menace of amalgamation due to the presence in our midst of a large number of blacks and mixed breeds not many centuries will elapse before the mottled skin, torpid energies and degenerated mental powers of our progeny will proclaim them as foreign to the clean blood heritage we enjoyed as are the present-day Hindus to that of the conquering Aryans who first entered India; and the world will witness the spectacle of a brown or yellow people doing homage, yearly on the 22'd day of February, to the memory of the great Washington as the Father of Their Country, provided he is then deemed of sufficient importance to cherish his memory. Right reason demands that we pass on to our children that pure blood which is their birthright.

With our entry into the World War the average American thought he was playing the part of a crusader in a holy cause, whereas he had in fact become the partisan of one side in a criminal civil war waged between members of the White race to the great loss of civilization, the responsibility for which must in any candid view be spread out among all European belligerents. As a result of this war we seem to be on the verge of something; on the brink of a precipice and about to take a plunge into the unknown, throwing all our traditions to the winds, and heading for we know not where. America was great and wealthy and powerful before we entered into the war, and no verbal acknowledgement of these facts by our late associates, *during the struggle,* or abuse heaped upon us since, has added anything to alter the facts, or strengthen or weaken our position.

If we *can* remain white and *have left sufficient race pride* to force a solution of our domestic race problem, then are we worthy representatives of our sires; and, safe in the assurance of our own racial integrity, we may well interest ourselves in the wider international aspects of the race problem.

In the concluding part of this work an effort has been made to show that we are so happily situated in many respects that we should be able to view with less passion, and consequently in a more judical and critical attitude of mind, the obstacles to be surmounted in bringing about White Solidarity in the affairs of the world; and that we should exert ourselves to this end.

That we may do this intelligently involves not only a consideration of the League of Nations, and European indebtedness to us: but, above all, a realization of the fact that, being European in extraction and not of the blood of any particular country in Europe, we should avoid, as we would the plague, all partisan action in behalf of any individual power or coterie of powers, and confine ourselves to such measures as will be helpful in bringing about White Solidarity and to this alone.

In so far as what follows lends itself to appropriate division into parts, it seems to fall into the three general divisions adopted as follows:—

Part I contains some comment, from the layman's point of view, as to evolution and the monogenetic theory of creation; also a summary of some of our knowledge relative to prehistoric man in general, and as to prehistoric man in America and in Atlantis, in particular,—all in the belief that these maters have a bearing, direct and indirect, on our race problem. In view of the fact that the economic element in the race problem is generally regarded as adverse to final solution and even opposed to all discussion of the problem, general comment as to this feature is included in this part with the criticism directed against the equalitarian evolutionist and churchman.

Part II contains the general presentation of our domestic race problem in some of its aspects, together with the proposed solution stated in general terms.

Part III contains briefly a general summary of the international aspects of the race problem, and what is conceived to be the desirable attitude on our part with respect to it.

PART I

Color at Home and Abroad

CHAPTER I.

A LAYMAN'S VIEW OF THE MONOGENETIC THEORY OF

EVOLUTION.

Very naturally the question may be asked, "What has either evolution or creation to do with the subject matter of this work?" The answer to this rests in the fact that the future safety of America depends largely upon a correct understanding, by the existing white population, of the history, characteristics and potentialities of the race elements that make up her total population. The generally accepted opinion that all mankind is descended from a common ancestor, the result of evolution or creation, as construed by many who accept either the one or the other origin, fails to take into consideration existing race-values based upon facts easily ascertainable by ordinary observation and research; runs contrary to the facts presented by history; and is instinctively repulsive to the members of the highest existing race. The generally accepted application of this theory of the brotherhood of man, whether based upon evolution or creation, operates only to one end in its practical effects—the utter destruction of the higher race. It is rather startling to find that, through the agencies outlined and others acting with them, we are confronted with the threat of future generations composed of a black or mongrel population of degraded people; and it is, therefore, plainly our duty, in so far as we can do so, to expose the fallacy of these malign influences and fight for the right of fututre generations to be secure in their heritage of pure blood and maintain their place among those who are marching along the path of progress.

The chemist has at his disposal the accumulated knowledge of all chemists who have gone before him, and when, after much labor in his laboratory, he announces a new discovery and proposes a new theory affecting the science, how is this announcement received? Is it at once accepted as true without further investigation? Even though the discoverer may be the leading scientist in the subject matter in which he specializes, the new discovery is subjected to the most thorough and rigorous tests before acceptance as true, and any explanatory theory must likewise conform to and be consistent with known facts before it is acepted even as a tentative explanation.

The astronomer with his telescope, its mirrors and photographic apparatus, gives out information that a new star, a new planet, a new comet, or a new nebula, has been discovered; and, at once, the telescopes of all observatories are directed to the point given for the new body, and the reported discovery is checked in detail.

In all the useful sciences—those of value to mankind in controlling the forces of nature—the greatest exactitude is required; and no alleged new theory or discovery is accepted as true until, after careful investigation, it is found to conform to known facts. It is only when we come to human affairs that imagination is allowed to run riot without check or hindrance. Some industrious and painstaking individual with a peculiar liking for investigations of a certain kind proceeds laboriously and with infinite care to collect and classify data of a certain kind. With these results in hand he further laboriously proceeds to advance a theory as to some matter connected with his classified data; he is declared a scientist and, if his subject-matter relates to the origin of the human race or in any way to pre-historic man, numorous followers flock to his standard and accept his theories without investigation.

If by evolution is meant the orderly sequence of progressive events in the affairs of nature from one stage to another, there can be no question but that the material universe and organic life upon the earth give us many examples around which we may draw finespun theories. When the astronomer looks into the heavens he finds nebulous matter in the process of forming constellations; he finds innumerable suns in comparison with which our own is but a toy; he finds many suns in pairs—binary stars—revolving about their common center of gravity, and possibly in process of forming a solar system similar to our own; he finds an occasional dead sun, or a runaway sun, comets with erratic courses through the heavens, and other wonderful things.

All this indicates that some wonderful, all-pervading, all-controlling Power is directing the affairs of the heavens; that it must be done with some purpose in view; that, despite the fact that some of the phenomena observed appear to be erratic and without the observance of fixed law, there must be a definite method of building and disposition of material. In other words, we had as well admit there is evident a process of evolution in the heavens, and this is nothing more than recognizing and recording as we see them the sequence of events that are in process in different parts of the heavens. No explanation of the ultimate truth is given us by using the term evolution. We merely designate by it the process we observe to be going on. So we may call the Great Architect, the Creator; for, while by so doing we are not any nearer the ultimate truth, this designation is certainly as intelligible and brings us as near the ultimate truth as substituting for the Creator insensate matter operated upon by the Laws of Nature. It is just simply repellent to the human instinct and contrary to the summation of all human experience that the culmination of all, the inexplicable, the unknowable, should be included in something insensate.

Indisputably the earth has been operated on through countless ages by the evolutionary processes apparent in the heavens, and doubtless will be subject to these same laws for countless ages to come; and any theory that has to do with the process by which man appeared on earth should not be inconsistent with known facts and should appear reasonable in the light of all obtainable knowledge. The word process is here used instead of evolution which does not explain the beginning of life but merely affirms that, by certain processes, man was finally produced from an inferior order of being or life.

Most of us are convinced that at one time the earth was in a plastic, molten condition; that, while in this condition, it became somewhat flattened at the poles due to revolution on its axis; that it gradually cooled and, due to shrinkage on cooling, its surface became furrowed and wrinkled; that it went through further and intermediate processes until we find it as it is to-day. These things, generally speaking, are as clearly true as it is possible to demonstrate anything that does not actually occur before us. This general process of evolution as relates to the earth is borne out by the fact that like events are now taking place in the heavens; that it is the only explanation consistent with what we find upon a study of the earth's crust with its different strata, and the condition of the earth at this time with its internal fires.

During the early stages of cooling, when the wrinkled surface began to appear due to contraction of the body, it seems reasonable to assume that the earth was yet at such temperature, as a whole, that the greater part of the water on the earth was held in suspension in the atmosphere; that electric disturbances of far greater magnitude than any with which we are acquainted were almost continuous, and that great quantities of water were being continuously taken into the atmosphere by evaporation about as fast as they fell to the earth on condensation. In time the slight depressions in the earth's surface contained the water precipitation in excess of evaporation, when this condition of excess was brought about by cooling. Futher cooling of the earth resulted in further roughening of its surface, the deepening of a valley here, the greater elevation of a ridge there, or sometimes the appearance of an elevation where there had been a former depression, or *vice versa*. Thus the process continued through the ages until the earth with its oceans and continents is as we find it to-day. Doubtless, innumerable convulsions of great magnitude have shaken and torn the crust of the earth between the time when it was in a plastic state and now, though within the strictly historical period no convulsion of overwhelming magnitude has visited the earth. However, there is much evidence that Atlantis did exist and that its disappearance below the waves was the last great cosmic disaster with which man has been visited.

The generally accepted theory of evolution, so far as relates to man, seems to be based on the assumption that at some remote period there appeared upon the earth a germ of life or possibly a number of like germs; that this primordial form of life was potentially in the earth when the earth assumed its form as such, and when conditions were ripe this organism appeared in full life; that first there was developed from this the fish; that some fish, by process of differentiation, became an amphibian, while the other fishes proceeded to develop along the line of fishes; that some amphibian, by the same process of differentiation, became a reptile, another a bird, another a mammal, while the rest of the family proceeded to develop as amphibians; that the mam-

mal, by process of differentiation, eventually became the ancestor
of the various four-footed vertebrata, including the monkey with
a tail; that, by process of development, the monkey became the
ancestor of a man-like ape who, in turn, became the ancestor of
the first human being; that this human being was of a very inferior type with a small development of brain and without speech;
that this ancestor was probably dark in color, if not black, and
that from this source, by process of differentiation, arose the
different types of men upon the earth at this day. Of course, in
this last, are included only the types produced by differentiation
from the common ancestral type, and not those which are the
result of crossing between the different types produced.

It seems to be generally accepted by those professing to speak
with authority among the evolutionists that all life on the earth
came from this common ancestral germ-cell, including all flora
and fauna. In accordance with these monogenists plants came
before animals; and, though they admit they do not know if
bacteria are plants or animals, they assert that bacteria are
older than either, and their prior existence was necessary to the
appearance of plant life and higher forms of animal life. He who
would hold to the theory of evolution that the existing classes
of living flora and fauna were evolved by direct descent from
different life germs that were, in their plastic age, subjected to
different stimuli from environment and proceeded along different
lines of development until the existing forms were evolved from
these distinct sources, and not step by step from fish to amphibian, to mammal, and eventually to man, is regarded by the elite
of the guild of monogenists as an unscientific layman—a crude
individual with little knowledge.

Let us concede in general terms that the theory of evolution
has much to commend it to the consideration of thoughful people
and search for any convincing data that the monogenist finds in
justification of his stand. This matter would be one of little or
no consequence here but for the fact that much written along
these lines at this time has, apparently, for its object antagonism
to any movement that attempts to consider race values in the
body politic; and while stoutly maintaining the white man, the
Mongoloid, the Negro, and the brown man are the results of
differentiation, through process of evolution from a common type
of man, some of these monogenists maintain this human summation of evolution means but little, after all, because we come

from a common type; that we do not know which is the superior present type and we had as well not worry about the matter, but let nature take its course, and all causes of conflict be removed by a process of amalgamation in the melting pot, thus wiping out all that has been accomplished by this process of evolution of which they are such devout disciples.

One of the latest writers on the subject, after referring to the human germ-cell, the ovum, in the mother's womb, and remarking that its early adaptations are of great interest, says: "But the interest will be increased if we have before us a law of biology which says that *individual* development rehearses or recapitulates the life history of the *species*. This means that our individual prenatal and postnatal growth up to the time of adolescence is a *résumé* of the evolution of the human race. It does not mean that at one stage of development the fetus is a fish, or a reptile; it does say that the ovum develops along the road our ancestors traveled in becoming human."[1]

"During our early prenatal days we live fast; we can be certain of that. In a few days we have developed structures that were evolved only after tens of millions of years."[2]

"One of the greatest steps in evolution was a backbone or vertebral column. Three types were tried out before Vertebrates developed a true backbone. All three types or stages appear in the developing human embryo. The *notochord* or permanent body axis of the lowest fishes appears early; later it is obliterated by the bodies of the vertebrae, but traces of the notochord may persist and lead to tumors in adult life. Our bony vertebrae proper are preceded by cartilage, the only backbone sharks have. This is replaced by bone."[3]

"The nerves of our face moved the gill-covers of our respiratory system when we were fishes."[4]

"At the time the gill-clefts are present the human fetus has a freely projecting tail and four tiny paddle-like limbs."[5]

"As the olfactory nerves alone are connected with the hemispheres of the human brain, it is inferred that the brain itself arose

[1]Professor George A. Dorsey's "*Why We Behave Like Human Beings*," pp. 3-4, Harper & Brothers.
[2]Ibid., p. 6.
[3]Ibid., p. 7.
[4]Ibid., p. 8.
[5]Ibid., p. 9.

in connection with the sense of smell; the original brain was a smelling organ."[6]

"We often wonder where we get our brain; it was standardized a million years ago. From stock such as the gibbon, man also sprang. That life in the trees gave him his start toward his big brain. There was no 'fall'; man climbed down. And that is a story of changing limbs."[7]

"Man's reptilian ancestors had a supplementary smell organ between roof of mouth and floor of nose. With this they could sample odors while eating without having to sniff. We—in common with other mammals—have its vestage in our *Jacobson's organ*."[8]

"The ear also begins as a pocket, in the first gill-cleft. This sinks into the head until its outer opening is closed by the tympanum or eardrum. A rare anomaly is an individual with two, or even three, external ear openings; these represent the second and third gill-clefts. In some fishes the opening remains; their ear is primarily a balancing organ. Our equilibrium sense organ is also located in the inner ear; if our semilunar canals are destroyed, we cannot balance ourselves."[9]

"Our eyes are compound and are made up of the same three parts that are found in fishes' eyes."[10]

"At the fourth month, the embryo begins to show a fine silky hair coat or *lanugo* (down). This begins to be replaced, even before birth, by a second coat of different character. The lanugo may persist as 'down' on the face of girls and women, or even all over the body, as on the so-called dog-faced people of the menageries. The lanugo probably represents our adult ancestral condition. But no satisfactory theory has yet been advanced to account for the fact that man is the least hairy of the primates."[11]

"Hair does not grow on our bodies in haphazard fashion, but in lines and sets of three, four, or five, each set being the hairs that grew beneath one scale of our reptilian ancestors."[12]

---

[6]Professor George A. Dorsey's *"Why We Behave Like Human Beings,"* p. 12, Harper & Brothers.
[7]Ibid., p. 53.
[8]Ibid., p. 12.
[9]Ibid., pp. 12-3.
[10]Ibid., p. 13.
[11]Ibid., p. 15.
[12]Ibid., p. 15.

"Our ancestors went on all-fours. In acquiring the upright gait, the axis of the body changed from horizontal to perpendicular. This necessitated changes in every bone and muscle in the body and a complete overhauling of everything inside—lungs, circulation, abdominal viscera—everything."[13]

Such facts as are included in the above quotations, with others of like character, are assumed to form the premises from which the monogenetic theory of evolution is deduced as a necessary conclusion. Professor Dorsey does not even argue his case. He apparently assumes this pet theory of evolution to have been established beyond cavil and proceeds to explain the wonderful structure of the human body and its functionig from inception to death by reference to this theory as an established fact.

How was the law of biology established under the workings of which "individual development rehearses or recapitulates the life history of the species?"

If there is such biological law, it should apply to all forms of life; and it would be interesting to know if there is to be found any evidence of such law in the lowest forms of animal life or among the flora.

A law is defined to be, in so far as relates to Science, "A statement of an order or relation of phenomena invariable under the given conditions; as, the *laws* of nature." It was pointed out by Darwin and others that the human embryo and that of certain animals were almost identical in appearance at certain stages of development, and that from the fertilization of the egg to birth the development proceeded with a striking similarity as though in obedience to a fixed general law. From this might be deduced the conclusion that the human embryo and that of certain other classes of animal life developed along certain definite lines in accardance with a definite law. One cannot go further than this without indulging in the rankest sort of speculation, even though the uniform operation of this law, together with other ascertainable facts pointing in that direction, might be considered as persuasive in advancing a general theory of evolution as probable. But to hold that this embryonic development establishes a biological law that such development recapitulates in detail the development of the species from primordial life is, to put it gently, beg-

---

[13]Professor George A. Dorsey's *"Why We Behave Like Human Beings,"* p. 26, Harper & Brothers.

ging the question; and to dignify such assumption as a law and vigorously assail all who do not agree with it as ignorant, uninformed persons, is pure effrontery. The most that any reasonable person with a tendency toward such belief might do, would be to advance such proposition as a tentative theory—as a possible explanation of our arrival.

Professor Dorsey seems not to be content with sticking to his subject, but must have his fling at those who maintain that there is such thing as race values. He preaches evolution under the aegis of which all·admit that with development came advancement in the end—progress—despite setbacks here or there or at this time or that; but he would have us believe that no value is to be attached to race types produced by evolution. In other words, that the long process of evolution through which the existing races became differentiated from one another in process of derivation from the common type was simply wasted time and effort and counts for nothing.

There follows some of Professor Dorsey's comments bearing upon race:—

..." 'Race' is a biologic term and has to do with physical characters based on blood relationship. The extent to which environment may alter the physical features we are born with is still an unsolved problem. There is no Aryan or Semitic race, because 'Aryan' and 'Semitic' are linguistic terms and refer to peoples who learn to speak an Aryan or Semitic dialect. In other words, race is the naked body we are born with; language and culture, the duds we learn to wear—often, in civilization, with much discomfort. There are varieties or types of men on the one hand; on the other, groups, tribes, nations, having a common language or a common culture or both. To classify people by language or culture is one thing; to classify man by physical traits is quite another."[14]

"There are Negroes in America of African ancestry; they speak English, are civilized, Christian, American. Transplant them to Africa: they cannot get rid of their physical features; they may forget or retain their English or acquire a new tongue— or a half-dozen; they may retain their 'civilization'; they may

---

[14]Professor George A. Dorsey's "Why We Behave Like Human Beings," p. 39, Harper & Brothers.

become Mohammedans and adopt Arabic culture; or they may become cannibals and found a slave-trading kingdom."[15]

"A man's great-grandmother may have been Indian, his other ancestors mixed Irish, Swedish, Spanish, and Turkish: that man is white, Caucasian, Aryan, and may be 'Nordic.' For 'Indian' substitute 'Negro'; if any of the Negro shows through, he is a Negro! This gives us the emotional element; prejudice is at work. Clothes and the barber go far to make the man, but prejudice trains the eye to detect signs that would otherwise never be noticed. A Negro of Atlanta is often a white north of Dixie."[16]

"Assuming, as every biologist does, that man's ancestor was a monkey before he was an ape, is the blond Caucasian a 'higher' type than the dark Ethiopian? Is one the end, the other the beginning, of human evolution? In other words, are there *higher* and *lower* races? Common sense says 'yes.' Common sense also said: There are ghosts. Witches turn milk blue. Any idiot can see that the earth is flat!"

"If I measure by my foot and weigh by my body, I can grade the whole human race from myself down to the lowest, blackest Pygmy. Man is usually measured and weighed that way, and with the same result: 'high'; 'low.' The 'highest' are the whitest; the 'lowest,' blackest: when the grader is white. It is good psychology—self-love is the first law of life—but not good biology. Imagine dogs graded from 'high' to 'low' by a Pekinese pug, a Mexican hairless, a Scotch collie, an Australian dingo; or pigeons graded by a pouter, a carrier, a fantail, a tumbler, a rock-dove!"

"Color probably has no biologic significance; it may have physiologic value. Nowhere in the plant or animal world is it a mark of high or low, or of progressive or backward. Man's skin color is partly determined by exposure, mostly by an inherited mechanism which regulates pigment. How or why this mechanism works, how it arose and why it varies as it does in man, we do not know."[17]

"Much is known of man's anatomy at the dawn of the human race; the color of his skin and other details are not known. Fos-

---

[15]Professor George A. Dorsey's *"Why We Behave Like Human Beings,"* p. 39, Harper & Brothers.
[16]Ibid., pp. 39-40.
[17]Ibid., p. 40.

sil bones tell a story; they supply 'links'; they may help clothe the skeleton with flesh, but not with skin color."

"Our ancestral skin was probably dark. The amount of pigment increased in the Negroid type, decreased in the Mongoloid. They represent the two extremes. But 'high' and 'low' skin color is as sound biology as grading planets by color would be sound astronomy: Venus 'highest' because whitest!"[18]

"Kinky wooly hair is found in no apes or monkeys; straight black hair is. The kink is the 'highest' type, the straight black the 'lowest.' Where shall we put the red—and the tow-heads?"

"The African's jaws are heavy: they support a first-class set of teeth. The European goes to the dentist to have his jaws stretched; *high*—or merely degenerate? The Negro scores with his thick out-turned lips; no men in the world have such human lips as the blackest Africans. Thin lips are primitive—'low,' apish. Even in the bony ridges above the eyes, most Negroes are among the 'highest' of man. This ridge is extraordinarily developed in the gorilla; also among the blacks of Australia. But in the gorilla it is a secondary sexual character. It is not found in gorilla children, nor at all in gibbons of either sex."[19]

"What is it all about, then? Much of it, convictions; habits of mind; prejudices, emotionally reinforced. There are dozens, perhaps hundreds, of physical types. Some have peculiarly or excessively marked features in one direction, some in another. To have diverged from the parent type means—simply divergence. We read significance into color of skin and other physical traits without knowing the facts behind these traits or the causes of change. There is no known fact of human anatomy or physiology which implies that capacity for culture or civilization or intelligence inheres in this race or that type."[20]

"How about the 'Nordics,' then? How comes it that the Anglo-Saxon is at the top of the heap? Is it not because of his inherited ability that he rides the wave? The answer is to be found in the cultural history of man. What wave did the Anglo-Saxon ride in the days of Tut-ankh-Amen, or of Caesar, or of William the Conquerer? Are his feet riveted to the crest?"

---

[18]It so happens that color in the classification of stars seems to be sound astronomy.

[19]Professor George A. Dorsey's *"Why We Behave Like Human Beings,"* p. 41, Harper & Brothers.

[20]Ibid., pp. 42-3.

"Civilization is young; blood is as old as salt water. Once there was no Anglo-Saxon; but there was 'civilization.' Were there 'higher' and 'lower' races then? How 'low' the savage European must have seemed to the Nile Valley African, looking north from his pyramid of Cheops!"

"Divergence, mixture; in isolated spots more divergence, less mixture; and so, sharply defined types—as the Eskimo. No people have a more distinct physical type than they have. I know of no skull more specialized or more easily distinguishable in a collection of skulls than an Eskimo's. They are 'pure.' Perhaps no people living are purer! No one pretends that there is an Eskimo race."

" 'Pure' types are *extreme* types. Blue eyes, flaxen hair, white skin, is an extreme type. The huge African with kinky hair, black skin, thick lips, high smooth brow, hairless body, is equally extreme. One is as pure as the other; one is as high as the other."[21]

"We know too little yet what environmental change does to physical structure, too little of the permanence of types, too little of the causes of change of type. We have no classification of man based on stature, skin color, hair form, head form, proportions of limbs, etc., so correlated that they fit one race and one only. The original divisions of the human race are not yet known. Possibly they never will be known; possibly there were no grand divisions; possibly only minor types developed from time to time. Some of these types became extinct or left only traces which, through intermarriage, have become so hopelessly mixed that they can no longer be distinguished."[22]

"Nature is not so prejudiced as we are. She says that there is a human race, that all human beings are of the same genus *Homo*, species *sapiens*. She draws no color line in the human or in any other species. Black and white dogs mix as readily as do blacks and whites when the sex impulse is not outlawed, and are equally fertile."

"In biology, fertility is generally regarded as a criterion of species. Using 'race' as synonymous with 'species,' man is of one race. Hence the difficulty in distinguishing even subspecies,

---

[21]Professor George A. Dorsey's *"Why We Behave Like Human Beings,"* p. 43. Harper & Brothers.
[22]Ibid., pp.43-4.

subraces, varieties, and types of men; they overlap. The human species has interbred. There are no biologically pure varieties and certainly no pure races, except, possibly, the Pygmy."[23]

"But the 'racial purity' and the 'racial inferiority' behind such books as McDougall's *Is America Safe for Democracy?* Chamberlain's *Foundations of Nineteenth Century Civilization;* Grant's *The Passing of the Great Race;* Wiggman's *The New Decalogue of Science;* Gould's *America a Family Matter;* and East's *Mankind at the Crossroads,* are bunk pure and simple. If these United States wish to restrict immigration to 'Nordics' or to this or that political group, why not say so and be done with it? To bolster up racial prejudice or a Nordic or a Puritan complex by false and misleading inferences drawn from 'intelligence tests' or from pseudo-biology and ethnology, is to throw away science and fall back on the mentality of primitive Savagery."

"Evolution produced a human brain, our only remarkable inheritance. Nothing else counts. Body is simply brain's servant. Treat the body right, of course; no brain can function well without good service. But why worry more about the looks, color, and clothes of the servant than the service it performs?[24]

The above quotations from Professor Dorsey disclose a remarkable state of mind and a wonderful frankness as to his ignorance in regard to some matters for one so learned. He states as a positive fact that "the nerves of our face moved the gill-covers of our respiratory system when we were fishes," but he doubts if color has any "biologic significance," though he admits, seemingly inconsistently, "it may have physiologic value," and states that "how or why this mechanism (referring to the mechanism which regulates pigment) works, how it arose and why it varies as it does in man, we do not know."

He is sure that our hairs do not grow in a haphazard fashion and that each set of three, four, or five, represents the hairs "that grew beneath one scale of our reptilian ancestors," but he admits "we know too little yet what environmental change does to physical structure, too little of the permanence of types, too little of the causes of change of type."

His admissions in regard to the lack of knowledge concerning

[23]Professor George A. Dorsey's "*Why We Behave Like Human Beings,*" p. 44, Harper & Brothers.
[24]Ibid., p., 119.

certain matters appear inconsistent with his positive information about certain other matters; but there is no doubt in his mind that the "racial puriy" and the "racial inferiority" "behind such books as" those mentioned by him above, "are bunk pure and simple."

We were all taught in our school geographies and histories to divide the human race into different classes and designate each class by name as a distinct race; and this classification still holds in literary productions and other works except in instances where the author adopts some other classification in order to more clearly bring out the views advanced by him. Professory Dorsey, however, says that " 'race' is a biologic term," and that all members of the human family belong to the same race. Presumably all that has been written about the different races of men is a waste of time about something that never existed—"bunk pure and simple." There is no Negro race, no Mongoloid race, no White race, no Aryan race, no Semitic race! We shall have to stop our attempts at classification because it is not biologically correct to do so; and yet the differences that do exist, however they may be described, were the result of differentiation in the process of evolution! It would seem that where writers about the human family have adopted a classification and nomenclature acceptable by the generality of human beings, it is a piece of impertinence for a scientist, or any one else, to apply this nomenclature with a different significance and maintain that he has by so doing refuted all that was ever advanced by such writers under the old appellations. This seems to be a sure case of bunk. He might have said that historically "race" has one meaning, biologically another, and not have attempted to hog a term long in use before biology was thought of as a science. At one time there was a body of people who developed the Aryan tongue. This could have arisen only among a homogeneous people who dwelt in isolation from other peoples; and, therefore, they at one time constituted an Aryan type among the human family to whatever extent they may have subsequently become mixed with other peoples, or the tongue diffused among different races. The same process of reasoning establishes the Semitic race as a type.

Throughout his references to the various divisions of the human family—the races—Professor Dorsey uses a flippant style not appropriate to the subject matter. Even when one may expect him to be serious, he disappoints. He asks himself the question,

"In other words, are there *higher* and *lower* races?" He answers, "Common sense says 'yes.' Common sense also said: There are ghosts. Witches turn milk blue. Any idiot can see that the earth is flat!"

The author quoted is of the fish-ape type of evolutionist, the fundamental basis of whose belief is progress wrought through a process of differentiation in which some types were lost, while others survived specializing along certain evolutionary lines. At one time in the remote past some particular people became civilized in the process of evolution, and these people must have been surrounded by other peoples in a state of savagery. Can it be denied that there was a difference between this civilized people and the degraded savages surrounding them? If it be found that the civilized man has a skin of one color and the degraded savage one of another, is there any reason why we should consult a militant disciple of a new science—Biology—in applying the color scheme to mankind as indicative of type values?

Those of us who believe that the human race can be classified with reference to actual and potential civilization and mental and moral characteristics, deducible from history of the past and actual present conditions, are the victims of "convictions; habits of mind; prejudices, emotionally reinforced." Professor Dorsey is free from the shackles of conviction, habit of mind, prejudices. Like nature he is without prejudice. Nature says: "There is a human race, that all human beings are of the same genus *Homo*, species *sapiens*. She draws no color line in the human or any other species. Black and white dogs mix as readily as do blacks and whites when the sex impulse is not outlawed, and are equally fertile." Whatever may have been the actuating motive in the production of his work, Professor Dorsey seems to be an out and out apostle of amalgamation, a sapper and destroyer of race pride, an internationalist of a more dangerous type than the communist or the trust dollar.

If it be true, as Professor Dorsey says, that "language and culture" are "the duds we learn to wear," then, it would seem, our only recourse to escape such calamitous situation lies in a revision of the dictionary.

The views entertained by Professor Winchell in regard to race differences are in marked contrast to those of Professor Dorsey. He says:

"The old question of the zoölogical value of the intervals separating races has been vacated of all importance. The differences existing are patent to all observation. There they are, beyond all question; call them what you will, that will not alter their value, their significance or their force. Call them varietal, racial, specific or generic in value; that does not affect in the least the nature and the reality of the thing which we contemplate, and its implication as a phenomenon in the course of Nature's processes. Undoubtedly, racial distinctions are as wide as those which we regard of specific value among Quadrumana and other Mammals."[25]

What evidence does the evolutionist produce in support of his monogenetic theory? If it be conceded that man rose from a primordial germ to his present state through the process of evolution, why should we infer that we were once fishes from the fact that certain nerves of our face correspond more or less with those controlling the gills in a fish? Why not once trees; for it has been advanced that trees possess a complete nervous system? What logical potency is there in the conclusion that we were once reptilian from the fact that there appear striking similarities during the incubation of the human egg and that of the reptile? Does the discovery of the fact that the Creator operates along strikingly similar lines in reproducing animate life render useless the ordinary rules of logic in applying the deductive or inductive processes to such premises as we are able to establish? Or, may be, there is some intangible, subtile process of reasoning required to follow the plodding footsteps of man from the fish to the man-ape in buried Lemuria,—the happy hunting ground of the monogenist who ignores the sleeping, buried Atlantis. If the data available is not sufficient to render reasonably clear the connection between alleged biological laws and facts, let us slow up on the laws and grope for more data.

Present day knowledge seems to require imperatively the acceptance of evolution of some kind and in some degree in explanation of earth building and the production of life on it; but glaring inconsistencies should be removed before the general acceptance of any particular theory may be expected. A theory that will even partially explain in a reasonable manner, provided it be free from exaggerated incompatibilities, seems to be preferable to an all inclusive one filled with discords.

---

[25]*"Preadamites,"* pp. 86-7.

We are informed that life appeared on the earth in this order: Bacteria; Algae, forms of plant life; and then the Protozoa, the lowest forms of animal life, consisting of either single cells or groups of cells, from which all animal life is presumably derived. However, we are told that were there any tendency toward the genesis anew of life at this time, it would be defeated through the operations of "primitive feeding" bacteria.[26]

The inconsistency on the face of this may be explainable; but, as it stands, we must conclude the "primitive feeding bacteria" have changed habits, otherwise they should have been destructive of the budding life that arose immediately after them instead of helpful as they have been held to be by some authorities.

The apparent impossibility of identity in likeness in the offspring of parent stock indicates a tendency to variation; and this tendency seemingly aids in the process of adaptation to changed surrounding conditions and results, in time, in the production of different types, the characteristics of which are transmitted by heredity to future generations. Heredity, in conjunction with a long-continued sameness of surrounding conditions, may bring about what evolutionists term an "evolutionary *cul de sac*," resulting in extermination of the type on any marked change in surroundings. It seems to be conceded by all that a long continued sameness of surroundings produces a fixed type transmissible by heredity; and it would seem reasonable that, once developed under such circumstances, a fish should be incapable of ever accommodating itself to life along the shore line where one would naturally expect independently developed types.

The human ovum, from fertilization to birth of young, gives an example of development from the germplasm, parasitic in nature, to an air-breathing food-consuming young human; but to assume that the process here shown recapitulates the evolution of the race and that a fish was among our ancestors, because there here appears embryonic characters in process of construction that resemble the gill-clefts or arches of a fish, is to argue in a circle.

The fundamental conception of evolution might be stated in somewhat the following terms:—

---

[26]"*The Ways of Life*," Professor Richard Swann Lull, p. 23.

(1)   Simple cell life. Reproduced by division, but still simple cell life, however multitudinous the colony.

(2)   Multi-cellular life through union. In which the permutations and combinations, depending upon fortuitous circumstance, brought into existence a multi-cellular organism. That this body assumed functions as an organism, depending upon its reaction as an organism—an individual entity—to its surroundings, and the reactions of the celular constituents of the organism as well. If the organism functioned at all as an entity it was started upon its evolutionary career, and has either fallen by the wayside or is with us to-day in a form totally different from the original one, depending upon adaptability or the avoidance of "catastrophism." This involves direct line of descent, with collateral derivative forms, but no connection with independent primitive forms except such as is implied in a common protoplasmic origin.

If we accept evolution as a possible or probable fact, it must inevitably and irrevocably be based upon two rock-bottom facts or premises:—(1) That the potential, primordial life-germ was made by the Creator with, and impressed upon, the matter from which the earth was made, and remained in this dormant state until congenial surroundings brought forth actual life; or the primordial form of life was specially created when conditions became fit for its activities. (2) The changes thereafter, forming the evolutionary process, were those incident to life adapting itself to the changed conditions in which it found itself.

Let us, accepting these two general statements as true, attempt to visualize something of the process of development that went on. It is not unreasonable to assume that the waters of the earth were first dominant upon the earth and, therefore, became first the scene of life activity. The primordial life-germs, awakening in the waters, must have found the conditions existing appropriate to their awakening, and were started upon their journey of life development by impulses received from their surroundings. Thus through the vast expanse of the earth's waters numerous hosts of life germs appeared. In one place the conditions seemed appropriate to single-cell life, and thus single-cell life congenial to the surrounding water conditions was started upon its course. When it was definitely started along these lines, it was, per force, required to remain a single cell organism changing, if at all, to conform to changed conditions or disappearing altogether. In other parts of the waters, under conditions not identical but varying, multiple cell organisms were formed and started on their life journey. Depending upon the stimuli to which subjected, which differed with different surroundings, these multiple-cell organisms must have been very numerous and many of them unstable, abortive monstrosities; but persistent effort resulted in the production at last of the several and distinct fishes we have with us to-day, those organisms incapable of meeting the changed conditions that came with the aging of the earth having disappeared. The only effect that the process of differentiation could have had upon these fishes was that of making them adaptable to the changed water conditions and enabling them to survive to this day. To imagine that by any process of differentiation a fish might become an amphibian and eventually the father of man, is to introdce a miracle monstrous in design and more difficult, if there may be difficulty in such matters, than would have been a special creation by fiat.

It cannot be conceived that when land appeared above the waters of the earth the primordial life-germs had exhausted themselves in activities throughout the seas, and that none remained for activities along the shore line and on the high and dry land. There must have been some left to start on life's journey under conditions markedly different from those encountered in the water. Although it may be easily conceived that certain general climatic conditions prevailed throughout the earth at this period of its career, there must have been marked differences as to temperature, moisture, physical surroundings, etc., at the different points along the extent of the coast line and throughout the extent of the higher dry land. One distinctive characteristic of the primordial life-germ must have been a marked ability to adapt itself to the range of conditions met with upon the earth at this time. The countless hordes of these germs spread over the face of the earth along the coast line and upon the higher dry land met with markedly different stimuli. Stimulated by the surroundings in which they found themselves, the multi-cellular bodies assumed the bulk, form and character of life consistent with these surroundings, and started on the evolutionary journey that produced man and existing animal life. We do know that there existed pre-historic monsters that have perished because of the fact, in many cases at least it so seems, that there was an over-development in certain directions rendering them incapable of adaptation to new conditions as they arose. It seems far more reasonable than the generally accepted theory, to assume that each form of life on the earth is a direct descendent of some particular ancestral life germs that early received the impress of its destiny; that the fish of to-day was always a fish of some sort; the amphibian, always an amphibian of some sort; the reptile, always a reptile of some sort; the bird, always a bird of some sort; the mammal, always a mammalian of some sort; and man, placing him in a class by himself, always a man of some sort. In fact, if there is anything in evolution, it seems reasonable to conclude that the black man, the white man, and the Mongoloid must have had their origin at different sources where conditions, though markedly alike, were not identical; and these differences must have persisted throughout the ages to produce the marked contrasts we find between these people at the dawn of history. It is reasonable to assume that these differences were developed in isolation, one people from the other; and that no marked amalgamation was begun until civilization had appeared in the near pre-historic times. There may have been in the beginning more distinct types than now appear, but that there is a distinct Black race, a distinct White race with shades from the extreme blond to the dark brunette, and a distinct Mongoloid type, is evident to all who choose to investigate. Nor was the ancient Egyptian a black man or akin to him, though Professor Drosey might wish his readers to believe that this was true when he says: "How 'low' the savage European must have seemed to the Nile Valley African, looking north from his pyramid of Cheops!"

Chemistry teaches that all matter is made of electrons, that the simplest element, hydrogen, is composed of one building unit of electrons, and that step by step the known elements are made by adding a building unit of electrons to some other element. However, we have no evidence that the Creator, in producing the known elements, began with hydrogen and proceeded step by step up the list to the top. In fact, we have in many cases evidence not of building up, but of disintegration, particularly among the radioactive substances. In the heavens we observe certain general laws in operation. There is a general similarity as to process going on, but there is no identity of process or of stage of progress. The law of gravitation is universally accepted and is mathematically correct; for it explains the continuing, persistent motion of the heavenly bodies; but in obedience to the law of gravitation all matter in the universe would be located in some one central mass had not motion been initially imparted to all heavenly bodies. With these facts before us it seems imbecile to insist that evolution shall have its origin in a buried Lemuria and in a fish-ape ancestor.

It is to be regretted that investigators, who have demonstrated their worth by personal contributions to an enlargement of our knowledge as to the origin of life and the antecedents of man and greatly illuminated these subjects in their writings, should permit their enthusiasm or bias to render them neglectful of their immediate surroundings. That one who, through equipment, training, and persistent effort, qualifies himself to see with a fair vision the hidden past, should be unable to see and understand in a measure at least what his eyes behold, is an enigma. We may thankfully accept their contributions to knowledge and sing their praises for this, but we cannot accept their leadership in our daily affairs. To this class belongs the scientist who adds to our fund of knowledge in regard to the origin of man and yet insists we are all one and the same. Great knowledge probably has an intoxicating or hypnotic effect that lifts one to heights from which all human flesh and blood appear the same; and we must eradicate the evil, pernicious, and false teachings of this character before we can view our race problem in its proper proportions.

CHAPTER II.

WHERE DID THE WHITE RACE PASS THROUGH THE STONE AGE?[27]

Before proceeding to say anything in regard to the monogenetic theory of creation let us investigate facts alleged to have been established by scientific research into prehistoric man, and ascertain, in so far as we can, how these facts agree with the conception of the descent of man from a common prehistoric stock. Let us see whether this conception of the monogenist evolutionist follows with reasonable certainty from the facts established in regard to prehistoric man, or whether there must still be postulated as many premises as were before required in order to draw the necessary inference.

In referring to the inhabitants of America, historic and prehistoric, Professor Winchell says: "Dr. Morton, the distinguished American craniologist and ethnologist, insisted upon the racial unity of the American aborigines, and their distinctness from the Mongolian type. In dissenting from positions so generally accepted on the high authority of Dr. Morton, I have the support of recent ethnological writers of the highest rank. Professor Retzius, a pioneer in exact craniometry, says: 'It is scarcely possible to find anywhere a more distinct distribution into dolichocephali and brachycephali than in America . . . From all, then, that I have been able to observe, I have arrived at the opinion that the dolichocephalic form prevails in the Carib Islands and in the whole eastern part of the American continent, from the extreme northern limits to Paraguay and Uruguay in the south; while the brachycephalic prevails in the Kurile (Aleutian?) Islands and on the Continent, from the latitude of Behring's Strait, through Oregon, Mexico, Ecuador, Peru, Bolivia, Chili, the Argentine Republic, Patagonia to Terra del Fuego.' . . . 'The brachycephalic tribes of America are found, for the most part, on

---

[27]Reference to the white man in the Stone Age throughout this work means the white man as a primitive and uncivilized man in the Rough Stone Age.

that side of the continent which looks toward Asia and the islands of the Pacific, and they seem to be related to the Mongol races. Dr. Daniel Wilson has advanced very similar views, and has supplied tables of measurements from 289 skulls by which the question is placed beyond all possible controversy."[28]

"It remains to note that the Pacific-slope type of skull pervaded not only the regions found by the Spaniards in possession of the civilized nations, but the entire continent, as far at least as the relics of the Mound-builders are distributed. The Mound-builders were certainly of the cranial type of the ancient Mexicans and Peruvians, and thus of the cranial type of all the natives of the Pacific slope, at least as far as Sitka. After the personal comparison of Peruvian skulls, with authentic Mound-builders' skulls from Michigan and Indiana, and others from dolmens and mounds in central Tennessee, I feel confident that the identity of the race of Mound-builders with the race of Anahuac and Peru will become generally recognized. So far as skulls from the mounds were known to science during Dr. Morton's lifetime, he recognized their close affinity with the ancient Peruvian and Mexican; but Dr. Wilson has insisted upon this affinity with a more considerable array of measurements to sustain the position; and has shown that numerous existing tribes of the south and southwest are similarly brachycephalic. The Abbé Brasseur de Bourbourg, after the ablest and most extensive researches, declares that the preaztec Mexicans or Toltecs were a people identical with the Mound-builders. The Mexican records indicate that they migrated from a country lying to the northeast, known as old Tlapalan, and that they were expelled by the hostility of the Chichimecs or barbarous tribes. The Toltecs or Nahuas displaced a still older and somewhat civilized people, the Colhuas. It was the relics of Toltecan civilization, according to Stephens, which the Spanish conquerors found in Central America; and there is little hazard in inferring the same identity in the sources of Peruvian and Mexican civilization as we find in the racial characteristics of the ancient inhabitants of those countries.[29]

"Colonel J. W. Foster, after much personal study of this subject, concluded that the Mound-builders possessed a conforma-

---

[28]"*Preadamites*," pp. 338-9.
[29]Winchell's "*Preadamites*," pp. 339-40,

tion of skull 'which was subsequently represented in the people who developed the ancient civilization of Mexico and Central America,' and that 'this people were expelled from the Mississippi valley by a fierce and barbarous race, and that they found refuge in the more genial climate of Central America.' "[30]

"I have included the Pueblo Indians of North American under the type of Asiatic Americans (p. 333). There is little room for doubt that they are the descendants of the builders of the cliff-dwellings, which have been so happily described and illustrated by Jackson and Holmes, in connection with Dr. Hayden's survey of the territories. Dr. E. Bessels says: 'There is not much room left to doubt that the present Pueblo Indians are the direct descendants of the ancient inhabitants of southern Colorado and New Mexico.' What is more important in the present connection is his decided identification of the cranial type of the mesa ruins, or ancient cliff-dwellings, with that of the Peruvians and that of mounds in Tennessee. 'Skull No. 1179,' he says,' might very well be taken for that of an ancient Peruvian' (p. 55). 'To show the resemblance between the skulls from southern Colorado and New Mexico . . . and those of the ancient Peruvians,' a diagram is given by Dr. Bessels, in which several profiles are superposed showing marked coincidences."[31]

Further on Professor Winchell says: "I recognize, therefore, among American aborigines, two general stocks of Mongoloids; one is Asiatic, and connects itself, structurally and geographically, with the nations of northern Asia; the other is Polynesian."[32] He maintains that the Hunting Tribes, crossing the South Pacific at a time when the connecting exposed land areas were far more extensive than now, landed on the west coast of South America, pushed across the mountains to the plains that are drained into the Atlantic; that they were gradually dispersed toward the north coast of South America, crossed the Caribbean Sea from island to island, and finally reached Florida from which point they were dispersed through North America. The remaining tribes, including the ancestors of the civilized nations, came, in accordance with him, from Asia by way of northwestern America. He concludes that the cranial index "is only one of the characters on

---

[30] Winchell's *"Preadamites,"* p. 340.
[31] Ibid., pp. 340-1.
[32] Ibid., pp. 343-4.

which a natural ethnic classification must be based; that it presents a considerable range among people whom a comprehensive judgment would pronounce identical, and that its indications may sometimes be entirely overborne by the weight of evidence drawn from the totality of characters."[33]

"It only remains, in discussing the genealogy of the Mongoloids, to remind the reader that this type included the prehistoric inhabitants of Europe. It is impossible, however, to indicate at present any particular family of Mongoloids to which these people may be certainly affiliated. It is likely, nevertheless, that their closest genetic relations are with certain Mongoloids now occupying northwestern Asia, and the Arctic shores of Europe.[34]

Thus we see that the Mound-builders and the prehistoric ancestors of the people who were found in an advanced stage of civilization in Mexico, Central America and Peru, as well as the Hunting Tribes found upon the discovery of America, are all declared to belong to the Mongoloid race. In consequence of this, or even conceding there was an indigenous American type not directly related to the Asiatic Mongoloid, it appears impossible that the White race could have had its original seat in the Americas or have found a home there during any period of its evolution, divarication, or divergence as a race; for, otherwise, some prehistoric evidence of them should have been found.

There have been discovered in North America numerous remains of prehistoric man and his primitive works. These have been found in various parts of the United States and in association with the remains of extinct animals in such manner as to indicate they lived contemporaneously. Where the degree of fosilization is the same and the surrounding circumstances indicate that the association of the remains where found could have resulted only upon the assumption of contemporaneous existence in life, the inference as to age should be irrefutable if that of either is known. Yet it seems that because the human remains thus found differ but slightly, if at all, from what is conceived to be the Indian type, their antiquity is denied by the ethnologist.[35]

The only possible proof of the antiquity of any type is, it seems, that skeletal remains of the type should be found in association with surroundings of a definitely known period free from cir-

---

[33]Winchell's *"Preadamites,"* p. 345.
[34]Ibid., p. 345.
[35]Prof. Lull's *"The Ways of Life,"* pp. 270-1.

cumstances that might show this association to have been due to accident. It appears, therefore, that the ethnologist refuses to admit the conclusiveness of the evidence as to the antiquity of the Indian type simply because of preconceived notions in the matter, and that further unquestionable evidence, cumulative in character, will be required before he will admit it.

When we consider what scientific research tells us about prehistoric man in Europe, we are confronted with the same conditions as were found to exist in America. We are informed that every tide of immigration into Europe of which we have any information encountered an indigenous population, who were ignorant of the cultivation of the soil, the metals, weaving or navigation. They lived in caves and had herds of sheep and goats. The ancient Greek writers refer to them as Cyclopes.

"Rawlinson says the Kelts 'found the central and western countries of Europe either without inhabitants, or else very thinly peopled by a Tartar race. This race, where it existed, everywhere yielded to them, and was gradually absorbed, or else driven toward the north, where it is found, at the present day, in the persons of the Finns, Esths and Lapps.' He adds: 'It is now generally believed that there is a large Tartar admixture in most Keltic races, in consequence of this absorption.' The Tartar indigenes, he says, may also have been, in part, driven westward. 'The mysterious Cynetians who dwelt west of the Kelts, may have been a remnant of the primitive Tartar occupants. So, too, may have been the Iberians of the Spanish peninsula.[36]

"Now, it is generally held that the Basques are a remnant of the ancient Iberes. They number about half a million. They speak a language known as Euscara, and dwell in the northeast provinces of Spain, and a small district in the southwest of France. 'The old geographers,' says Peschel, 'called them Iberians; they then peopled the whole of Spain and the southwest of France, but were early driven toward the west and south by the Kelts, and intermixing with them, in the district of the present Catalonian dialect, constituted the Keltiberians........According to Paul Broca, their language stands quite alone, or has more analogies with the American type . . . Of all Europeans, we must provisionally hold the Basques to be *the oldest inhabitants of our quarter of the world*.[37]

---

[36]Winchell's *"Preadamites,"* pp. 148-9.
[37]Ibid., p. 149.

"It appears, therefore, to be generally agreed that the Basques are a remnant of the ancient Iberians, and that they possess no ethnic affinities with the Noachites traced from their Asiatic center; but do indicate physical and linguistic relations with the type of Mongoloids. History, tradition, linguistics and ethnology conspire to fortify the conclusion that in prehistoric times all Europe was overspread by the Mongoloid race, of which remnants have survived to our times, in the persons of the Basques, Finns, Esths, Lapps, and some smaller tribes."[38]

"Some confirmation of this conclusion comes from the study of human skulls of the prehistoric period. The skulls from the cavern of Frontal, in Belgium, are markedly brachycephalic, and by the flattening of the occiput remind one vividly of the Mongoloid skulls from American 'mounds.' 'It is impossible to confound them,' says Pruner Bey, 'with the skulls of the Aryan race, where the contours are all oval. The angular contours of the crania found at Furfooz (Frontal), and the lozenge-shaped figure of the face, *class them clearly among the Turanian or Mongol races*, a conclusion confirmed by the learned curator of the Anthropological Society (of London), Mr. Carter Blake. The eminent president of the Anthropological Society of France, seeking to ascertain to what branch of the great Turanian race the ancient people of Furfooz might be referred, assigns them to the Ligurian or Iberian type, which still exists in the north of Italy and in the Pyrenees, and which history seems to indicate as the most ancient inhabitants of the countries of which it has preserved the memory. The analogy between the crania of Furfooz and those of this people is such that it seems impossible to contest the conclusion which M. Pruner Bey has so brilliantly established.' The skulls found at Solutré have also been studied by Pruner Bey, and decided to belong to a race which he designates a 'primitive mongloid race,' which is still represented by the Iberians, or so-called Ligurians, of the Gulf of Genoa, in the Pyrenees, and in arctic America."[39]

It thus seems that the earliest historical records indicate that the aborigines found in Europe upon the advent of the white man were Mongoloid; and science not only confirms history in this respect, but further declares that the most ancient relics of man

---

[38]Winchell's *"Preadamites,"* p. 150.
[39]Ibid., p. 151.

found in Europe must be classed as belonging to the Mongoloid type. The white man, therefore, is barred from Europe as a place in which he might have developed from a primitive man as well as from the Americas.

When we turn to Asia we are informed that the Dravidian and peoples Negroid in type occupied India as primitive inhabitants, and that the white man first appeared there as the conquering Aryan. India is, therefore, closed to the whites as a primitive fatherland. It seems to be universally conceded that Asia, outside of India and to the east of Persia, is and has been for ages Mongoloid in character; and science points out to us the Miao-tse, living in the mountains of southern China, as a remnant of the primitive Mongoloids who anciently occupied the whole country. The monogenetic evolutionist places the primitive home of the White race to the east of the Mediterranean in some indefinite place in southwest Asia in or about the Euphrates valley or the Persian plains. But even here we are advised that there was a more ancient, primitive Mongoloid people who were subdued by the whites. It is maintained that the Scriptures show that the Hamite and Abrahamite settlers expelled an earlier, primitive population, and that "Tidal, king of nations," was a Mongoloid ruling over Mongoloids, Tidal or Thargal, being a Turanian word signifying "great chief."

Professor Winchell says: "We find traces of an antediluvian, Tartar or Turanian population throughout Asia. It is not long since historians and ethnologists first noted the monumental and linguistic evidences of an older Hamitic stratum underlying the recognized Semitic civilizations of Babylonia and Assyria, and even of Canaan and Phoenicia. Now they inform us that unmistakable traces remain of a widespread Turanian stratum of people, still older than the first Hamitic settlements. Prichard says: 'The Allophyllian[40] nations appear to have been spread, in the earliest times, through all the most remote regions of the old continent—to the northward, eastward and westward of the Indo-European tribes, whom they seem everywhere to have preceded; so that they appear, in comparison with these Indo-European colonies, in the light of aboriginal or native inhabitants, vanquished, and often banished into remote and inaccessible tracts by more powerful invading tribes.'[41]

---

[40]Turanian.
[41]*"Preadamites,"* p. 137.

"A prehamitic population is recognized by Mr. C. L. Brace, an author of acumen and erudition, who after stating that we recognize, in primitive times, four families of languages, the Turanian, the Semitic, the Aryan and the Hamitic, says: 'The most ancient of these great families is the Turanian . . . The Turanians were probably the first who figured in the ante-historical period. Their emigrations began *long before* the wanderings of the Aryans and Semites, who, wherever they went, always discovered a previous population, apparently Turanian in origin, which they either expelled or subdued.' The first or 'Medean' dynasty (so called), in the annals of Babylonia, is regarded by Mr. Brace as a Turanian empire. 'Its Turanian character is derived from the inscriptions, which are in Turanian grammar, though with Hamitic vocabulary, indicating a great mixture with Hamitic population.' Simultaneously the Chinese empire rose into existence."[42]

"François Lenormant, an eminent original authority, affirms the existence of a pronounced Turanian element in the earliest populations and languages of the Mesopotamian regions. 'To the earliest date that the monuments carry us back, we can distinguish, in this very mixed population of Babylonia and Chaldaea, two principal elements, two great nations, the Shumir and the Accad, who lived to the north and to the south of the country.' The Shumir were Turanian, and had their capital at Sumere. The Accad were Cushite, and had their capital southward from the others, at Accad. The Sumerites spoke a dialect of the Uralo-Finnish family."[43]

It is a fundamental of all evolutionist theories that there is progress from a lower to a higher plane. The progress need not be continuous at all times; for all recognize that progress may be halted, or there may be an actual retrogression due to stress of particular surroundings, but in the end the test of evolution is progress. History and science bear out the fact of progress for the Mongoloid stock. History indicates that as a primitive people they occupied both Americas, Europe, and all of Asia outside of India; and that they have made progress in the development of civilization. Science, in its investigations of prehistoric man, pronounces him Mongoloid and his habitat the Americas, Europe,

---

[42] Winchell's *"Preadamites,"* pp. 139-40.
[43] Ibid., p. 140.

and Asia outside of India. The brown and the black man may
be dismissed in this connection with the statement that the primitive brown man was located in India and that he has made
progress; that the black man is and has been for ages in Africa;
and that scarcely any one will contend Africa was the primitive
home of the White race.

If the white man branched from a Dravidian or predravidian
stem, is it to be assumed that he was civilized when this differentiation occurred? If so, then must we likewise conclude the
parent stock was also civilized. This, scarcely any one will admit.
Did the whites become civilized in the act of differentiation from
the parent stock or immediately upon its consummation? This
appears absurd. It would seem that the process of differentiation by which a new type is brought about differing in many respects from its parent stock is one requiring a long period of
time and isolation from other races. We do not seem to have
a scintilla of tangible evidence that the White race passed
through any such period in southwest Asia. Is there any evidence of the white man appearing in southwest Asia as a primitive Stone-Age man? We find evidence of the Mongoloid of the
Stone Age in the prehistoric remains collected from the Americas,
Europe, and Asia, but we do not find any such remains of the
White race. Is it not, therefore, absurd to maintain that the
White race branched from a parent brown stem in southwestern
Asia and spent its infancy in that section, which was anteced-
ently occupied by a primitive Mongoloid type of which remains
are found, and in which we find no prehistoric (Stone-Age) re-
mains of a primitive white people?

It appears to be a fact that every bit of information we have
in regard to the early condition of the members of the White
race comes from the written records of this race, monuments
erected by it, or traditions in the possession of some of its
peoples. The early picture we have of them unfolds them to
us as an aggressive people conquering, subduing, exterminating,
or driving out the indigenous inhabitants of a new country; setting up governments and carrying on commerce in a manner to
be expected from a people far advanced in the stages of civilization. If this be true, whence came they? Where is located the
land in which these people, in a state of isolation, passed through
the gradient stages of progress essential to lift them from a primitive state to that in which they found themselves when they

came in contact with the primitive Mongoloid in southwest Asia or in Egypt? Surely, it was not Lemuria? No Monogenist evolutionist will advance such a theory. They all hold that none but black or brown men emerged from this buried land. That this land existed and that it was the home of a brown or black people of a primitive type, may be conceded readily upon some of the grounds urged for its reality; but that the blood of all mankind, in the face of facts as unfolded, should be required to look to Lemuria, of which no tradition exists in the human family, for its fatherland, and no attention paid to Atlantis, to which tradition and historical facts point as a reality, is utterly incomprehensible. The only explanation seems to be this: When evolution was advanced as a theory, the human mind had so accustomed itself to the belief in the descent of man from a common ancestor, because of mediaeval religious interpretation, that the same idea was carried into the new doctrine. Some new advocates of the theory pushed the doctrine of the fish-ape man, and referred all existing life to a single primordial life germ or colony of germs and fastened the monogenetic theory more firmly on all evolutionists. Trying to fix the primitive white man in a home place in southwestern Asia is a poor effort, as it seems from facts now known, to fit him into the monogenetic theory of evolution or creation. It seems so utterly foreign to all of our experience, that we should be justified in declaring him a madman who would maintain that this earth labored for ages in order to bring itself to the point where it might give birth to a few life germs at some particular point. It is conceivable that the primordial life element finding itself on the shore line between land and water might receive the natal impulses that would send it on the evolutionary path of one of the amphibians, depending upon surrounding conditions. On the other hand, it is a miracle, and seemingly an unnecessary one, that the life element which had responded to the natal impulses appropriate to a fish and accommodating itself to these impulses had become a fish, should at some time in its career approach the shore line and become something other than a fish. It does not appear at all unreasonable that organic life may be gradually changed, or even rapidly at times, under changed conditions not inconsistent with its adaptability; but it is utterly inconceivable how a fish in its natural element of water could by any minute gradations, or otherwise, become an amphibian or anything other than a fish.

Nor is it understood how any change in the surrounding conditions might result in a reflex action that would tend to turn a fish into an amphibian. There is nothing in the actual facts supporting the theory of evolution that requires us to accept the fish-ape man other than the dogma of him who advances it. Nor, on the other hand, is there anything in the facts supporting evolution that would prevent the different human species from tracing their origin to different sources. Certainly, if this is not true, the facts presented must have a peculiar appeal to the scientific mind which carries with it a conviction beyond the ability of the layman to grasp. That the origin of the human races in different sources would necessarily have resulted in a greater divergence than any with which we are acquainted, can be entertained only by one who believes in the fish-ape-man theory. On the other hand, the divergence in contemplation in this last is so vast in its proportions, it would seem that the types of men produced by it could have but little in common. The quality of differentiation must have been blessed in its early stages with a great precosity to have overcome the obstacles between the fish and the mammal, particularly in view of the fact that we cannot find there has been any divergence in human types during the last 6000 years. There has been mixture of races—amalgamation; there has been great evolutionary improvement—enlargement of knowledge; but there has been no divergence of type during the historical period. But let us pause here and, after investigation of conditions in ancient America, make inquiry of Atlantis with a view to learning if we may not there find a home for the White race, one more consistent with actual facts in our possession and with all more congenial.

The consulsion of the scientist that what are regarded as the two American types, in accordance with classification by cephalic index, conform most closely to the Mongoloid type, certainly justifies the conclusion that the Americas cannot be regarded as the home land of the White race in accordance with the accepted standards applicable to that race. However, the fact that the American type is regarded as conforming most closely to the Mongoloid, does not preclude there having been developed an independent aboriginal type in America, nor prohibit the presence among them, at a very remote period, of a large white element arriving from outside sources, as will be urged in the following chapter.

CHAPTER III.

AMERICA.

The popular conception, so far as relates to the inhabitants found in America upon the discoveries of Columbus and those who came after him, is that these people, from the extreme north to the extreme south, were one large, closely related family, designated as Indians. Included in this family were the savage tribes, the civilized or semi-civilized peoples, and the Eskimos as well, although these last are regarded as rather a distinctive variation from type approximating more closely to the Asiatic type of Mongoloid from which all Indians are supposed to have been derived.

When we try to probe that period of man's past that lies in obscurity beyond the dim mists of tradition, it is essential that we marshal all available facts most carefully before attempting to draw any conclusions. Furthermore, in applying these facts to establish premises from which probable conclusions may be drawn, there must be consistency between existing facts, facts deducible from history, what may be probable facts sifted from traditions, and facts given to us by those branches of science that have any bearing on the matter. We cannot expect this consistency to be perfect; and, where conclusions or theories conflict, those only should be accepted which contain most elements in their justification.

It furthermore seems to be in accord with our general knowledge that the following should be accepted as applicable to primitive man, whether his origin be referred to evolution or to a special creation, and should, therefore, not be lost sight of in probing into his prehistoric past:—

1. That in his lowest savage state large bodies of water presented an absolute barrier to the migration of man.

2. That in this state his movements on the land were confined, at first, to those areas or sections that presented the least natural obstacles to his progress without artificial aids which were developed later and brought into use as he made progress.

3. That such a condition of affairs divided ancient man into groups which were confined to comparatively small areas, and tended to fix the type with respect to the surrounding conditions in which they were placed.

4. That the first progress of the race, beyond the acquisition of fire and rude stone weapons, must have related to means of transportation and improved weapons and tools and methods of agriculture.

5. Improved means of transportation and weapons and tools enlarged the areas of operations of the people possessing them, and the adoption of agricultural methods made possible the support of greater numbers. Thus we can readily see that the more advanced and progressive people were soon venturing beyond their original habitat and coming in contact with their neighbors. It may be reasonably assumed that the earliest means of transportation had to do with the development of the canoe or small craft for transportation by water; and thus the rivers, small bays, and arms of water became the first arteries of communication for ancient man and extended the areas of occupation by the first progressive people. In this manner comparatively large areas between impassable mountains or other natural obstructions were occupied along river valleys or the shores of the seas and the foundations laid for the development of a distinctive type of man in these areas. Inter-continental communication, where great areas of land were separated by enormous stretches of sea, was left to that people, who, making the greatest strides in civilization, were able to develop vessels that could make the voyage across large bodies of turbulent waters.

There is no reason whatever why there should not have been great continental areas in the southern hemisphere during the time man has been on earth; and there is much reason for believing that extensive land areas formerly connected Australia, Asia, and Africa and some of the islands of the Pacific, and also formerly existed in the Atlantic. However, conceding even this, there is yet a preponderance of evidence to the effect that the great land areas of the world have been in the northern hemisphere during man's time on earth.

If it be conceded that man, or the immediate ancestor of man, was on earth at the time of the last great glacial period, it must be assumed he was an inhabitant of the extreme northern portions of Europe, Asia, and America during the warm period that gave

place to the glacial epoch. The only way in which this conclusion can be avoided, if the evolutionary process be accepted,
is by adopting the theory that the earth laid but one egg and
that all life came from this. But if we conclude that these areas
were generally in the occupancy of man or his ancestor, he must
have been in that stage of progress where he was confined in
his migratory movements to short and slow stages by the natural
means with which he was endowed by the Creator. Under such
circumstances he could but retreat southward in front of the glacial blasts in the continental spaces in which he found himself.
"Prof. Grote," says John T. Short, "thinks the first migration may
have taken place in the Tertiary period in Pliocene time, and that
the subsequent advent of the ice period cutting off all communication with the old world until recent times, produced a modifi-
cation in the race, and that man retired with the glacier on its
return to the north, where we see his descendants in the Eskimo.
If Prof. Croll's theory of climatic change resulting from the maximum excentricity of the earth's orbit be true, or even if the ordinary time at which the American glacial period is supposed to
have occurred be taken into consideration, we hardly think the
evidences of man's pre-glacial residence on this continent are sufficient on which to base a safe hypothesis. Of course Prof. Grote
would assign a comparatively recent migration to the civilized
nations."[44]
Applying the principles outlined above, let us see what should
have been the conditions found to exist in America upon the discoveries by Columbus. Any former land areas that may have
existed in the southern or mid Pacific must have had stretches
of sea between them and America that were impassable for primitive man of that day; and furthermore any northern connection
with Asia must have been blocked with ice early in the glacial
period. Under these conditions the inhabitants of America were
gradually driven south and kept in isolation from the peoples of
the other continents until the receding northern glacier opened
up a possible passageway to and from Asia by the Aleutian group.
In view of the fact that neither Egypt, Phoenicia, Greece, Rome,
nor modern Europe established communication with America
across the Atlantic prior to Columbus, we can safely assume that
the isolation of these people was not disturbed by any civilized

---

[44]"*North Americans of Antiquity.*" p. 512.

people situated from them across the Atlantic or Pacific as we know them now, further than might result from an occasional and accidental contact which could not affect these people in their blood as a race, whatever new culture might be thus accidentally introduced in a minor degree.

The conditions outlined were ideal for the production of an American type, dependent largely upon the ancestral type in America when the glacier began to grow. This period of isolation extended from the formation of the glacier to A. D. 1492, unless America was visited in the mean time by some civilized people situated closer to its shores than are now Europe, Asia, and Africa, which contingency we are not at present considering. In this vast period of time we should expect the development of a fixed type of some kind. It might have varied in one locality from that in another, but it would seem that there should have been a strong family tie evident in all. Any autochthonous civilization developed among them should not have been accompanied by any marked physical characteristics setting apart these civilized people from the great body of the indigenous inhabitants; and their traditions should have been local, relating to America, and pointing north or south in the direction of the natural migratory movements on the two continents. Furthermore this civilization should have been almost continuously progressive and without great breaks in the chain of progress if it arose among a people with racial unity. Naturally there might be some among such people who would prefer the open spaces and the life of a hunter to that of the settled community; and, in time, the latter becoming softened or enervated through the easy life of the civilized community might be overrun by the former more hardy members of the race. Under such circumstances, however, we should not expect a destruction of civilization and reversion to barbarism, but rather a temporary halt during the confusion of readjustment after conquest followed by a period of progress with renewed vigor.

What were the conditions found to exist in America? Instead of finding a fixed type of man speaking a common tongue, we found a people as diverse in complexion, color of eyes, and color and quality of hair, as may be found on other continents, and speaking as great or a greater variety of languages than may be found among any other people. The civilizations found in Mexico, Central America, and Peru have been pronounced indigenous

—resulting from development of the American Indian—by many writers upon this interesting subject; but that such should have been the case is absolutely inconsistent with what we know of the savage Indian. In spite of the wide range in physical characteristics that may exist among the savage tribes north of Mexico, they do enjoy in common certain mental and ethnic characteristics which place the origin of the American civilizations utterly beyond them. It is an incontrovertible fact that the Polished Stone Age and a Mental Age (certainly Copper Age if not Bronze or both) preceded the Rough Stone Age in the Mississippi Valley. The former was the result of the culture of the Mound-builders who preceded the Indian, the representative of the latter. It certainly, therefore, looks unreasonable to attribute the civilizations in America to the savage hunting tribes who were in the Stone Age and had apparently displaced a people of superior culture long before Columbus made his discoveries.

The antiquity of man in America is indicated by skeletal remains found, by the domestication of the llama and the dog, by the cultivation of certain absolutely American flora from such remote period that the original wild species has been lost; and the antiquity of civilized man in America is indicated by the Mound-builder remains and the ruins found in Peru, Central America and Mexico.

The fact that there is a disposition on the part of the scientist to give less weight to evidence indicating antiquity of skeletal remains found in America than would be given to the same facts elsewhere in the world, has been pointed out in a previous chapter. This is, of course, not scientific and can be defended on no valid grounds.

John T. Short says in respect to the antiquity of man in America: "In considering the question as to how long man has inhabited this continent, his influence upon nature cannot be overlooked. In the animal kingdom, certain animals were domesticated by the aborigines from so remote a period that scarcely any of their species, as is the case of the llama of Peru, were to be found in a state of unrestrained freedom at the advent of the Spaniards. In the vegetable kingdom more abundant testimony of the same nature is presented. A plant must be subjected to the transforming influences of cultivation for a long time before it becomes so changed as no longer to be identified with the wild species, and infinitely longer before it becomes entirely dependent upon cultivation for propagation. Yet we find that both of these facts have been accomplished with reference to the maize, tobacco, cotton, quiona and mandico plants; and the only species of palm cultivated by the South American Indians, that known as the *Gulielma speciosa,* has lost through that culture its original nut-like seed, and is dependent upon the hands of its cultivators for its life. Alluding to the above-named plants, Dr. Brinton remarks: 'Several are sure to perish unless fostered by human care. What numberless ages does this suggest? How many centuries elapsed ere man thought of cultivating Indian corn? How many more ere it had spread over nearly a hundred degrees of latitude and lost all resemblance to its original form?' Certainly this class of evidence, though furnishing no chronometric scale, points us to an antiquity for man on this continent more venerable than that suggested either by tumuli or architectural remains. The peculiar value of this argument rests in the fact that with the exception of cotton, none of the plants indicated has ever been cultivated by any other people than the aborigines of America, and could not have matured their characteristics of dependence in the old world, and been brought hither through the channel of immigration."[45]

Had the cultivation of Indian corn, tobacco, the quiona and mandico plants originated in the old world and been transplanted thence in the new world, it is inconceivable that their cultivation should not have been continued in the old world from the time of its origin until the discovery of America. Furthermore, it is inconceivable that any domestic plants of the old world could have been introduced into America by peoples separated from it by broad oceans and ignorant of its existence. We are therefore, dirven to the conclusion that these plants were domesticated either by the Americans themselves within America or were first cultivated by some civilized people situated closer to American shores than are the old world continents.

The Mound-builders occupied extensive areas within the present boundries of the United States, the principal of which were in the valleys of the Mississippi and Ohio Rivers. With reference to the civilization of these people, Short says: "However much writers may differ, we think the following conclusions may be safely accepted: That they came into the country in compara-

---

[45]*"North Americans of Antiquity,"* pp. 110-12.

tively small numbers at first (If they were not Autochthones, and there is no substantial proof that the Mound-builders were such), and during their residence in the territory occupied by the United States they became extremely populous. Their settlements were widespread, as the extent of their remains indicate. The magnitude of their works, some of which approximate the proportions of Egyptian pyramids, testify to the architectural talent of the people and the fact that they had developed a system of government which controlled the labor of multitudes, whether of subjects or slaves. They were an agricultural people, as the extensive ancient garden-beds found in Wisconsin and Missouri indicate. Their manufactures afford proof that they had attained a respectable degree of advancement, and show that they understood the advantages of the division of labor. Their domestic utensils, the cloth of which they made their clothing, and the artistic vessels met with everywhere in the mounds, point to the development of home culture and domestic industry. There is no reason for believing that the people who wrought stone and clay into perfect effigies of animals have not left us sculptures of their own faces in the images exhumed from the mounds."

"They mined copper, which they wrought into implements of war, into ornaments and articles for domestic use. They quarried mica for mirrors and other purposes. They furthermore worked flint and salt mines. They probably possessed some astronomical knowledge, though to what extent is unkonwn."

"Their trade, as Dr. Rau has shown, was widespread, extending probably from Lake Superior to the Gulf, and possibly to Mexico. They constructed canals by which lake systems were united, a fact which Mr. Conant has recently shown to be well established in Missouri. Their defences were numerous and constructed with reference to strategic principles, while their system of signals placed on lofty summits, visible from their settlements and communicating with the great water-courses at immense distances, rival the signal systems in use at the beginning of the present century."[46]

The sculpture of the Mound-builders, both of animals and men, has been pronounced in many cases to bear a striking resemblance to that of the Mexicans and is considered remarkably

---

[46]*"North Americans of Antiquity,"* pp. 96-100. This work was published in 1880.

lifelike. There is every indication that these people had commercial intercourse with the civilizations to the south in Mexico and Central America and furnished them with copper from the Lake Superior mines. Mexican obsidian has been found in the mounds of the Ohio Valley. It has been estimated that the metal removed from the copper mines would equal veins of varying thickness one hundred and fifty miles in length.

Why these people of a superior culture should have disappeared and given place to the savage Indian with his Rough Stone Age implements will probably never be known; that this did happen is unquestionably a fact. The traditions of the Nahuas, whose civilization was in the ascendency in Mexico at the time of the Conquest, make Hue hue Tlapalan their home land and state they came into Mexico from the north or north and west, or, as stated by some authorities, from the northeast. Short places Hue hue Tlapalan in the valley of the Mississippi and connects the Nahuas with the Mound-builders. In addition to the universal tradition as to northern origin among the Nahuas, he points out "other evidences of racial identity common to Mound-builders and Mexicans, such as pottery, sculptured portraitures of the facial type, etc." [47]

When the Mound-builders left their homes in the river valleys, we do not know. The Indians who succeeded them in the occupancy of this territory have no knowledge of, or any traditions relating to, their predecessors or their works, other than the fact that the latter were in existence when they first reached the territory. We have some information, however, as to the minimum possible time within which these works may have been abandoned. Trees of the forests that cover some of these works in the Ohio Valley, being continuous and unbroken with the surrounding forests, are found to be as much as six hundred years old, and in one instance as much as eight hundred years old when found, which last, if now living, would be about eight hundred and fifty years old. Referring to these forests, Short says: "Farther south, in the Mississippi Valley and near the Gulf, they are still younger than those at the north. So noticable is this that we are led to think the Gulf coast may have been occupied by the Mound-builders for a couple of centuries after they

---

[47]"North Americans of Antiquity," pp. 253-4.

were driven by their enemies from the country north of the mouths of the Missouri and Ohio Rivers." [48]

It is possible that, upon a critical study of the situation, Botany might inidicate the forests of the lower Mississippi Valley were younger by a century or two than those of the Ohio Valley, rather than the correctness of the conclusions apparently drawn by Mr. Short.

The fighting qualities of the Indian found in the boundries of the United States must be conceded by all; but, even admitting this, it does not look reasonable that a populous people of a superior culture should give ground before a savage uncultured people few in numbers. It is maintained by competent authority, and it seems on reasonable grounds, that the Nahuas, of whom the Aztecs were the latest arrivals in Mexico, represented the Mound-builders who migrated from their valley home. It seems inconsistent that a people, possessing sufficient energy and virile qualities to conquer a large part of the Maya domains and infuse new life into its administration, should surrender their old holdings under pressure from the Indian. It would seem more reasonable to attribute such movement to some calamitous natural, but now unknown, circumstances, such as a fatal contagious plague or some cataclysmic event in nature, or to an ambition for conquest in a more favorable clime where the people conquered had grown soft and effeminate under easy conditions of life.

Short concludes from certain Mexican dates, historically fixed, and the investigations of Prof. Valentini in connection with the symbols on the Mexican Calendar Stone, that the Nahuas arrived in Mexico from Hue hue Tlapalan about the year 231 A.D.

A people that seem to have been connected with the Mound-builders in remote times are the Cliff-dwellers. The ruins connected with these people are to be found in Utah, Arizona, New Mexico, and in west and southwest Colorado; and it is possible these people may have ascended the river valleys with the Mound-builders, crossed over the divide into the Oregon country, and eventually drifted south into the area in which found by the Europeans on entry into America.

"Innumerable fragments of pottery, superior to that now manufactured by the Mexicans," says Short, "are strewn everywhere in the neighborhood of the Casas Grandes." These ruins

---

[48]"*North Americans of Antiquity*," p. 105.

are considered by some authorities a station on the Aztec migration to Mexico; but, says Short, "certainly, no architectural analogies with the remains farther south justify this opinion."[49]

Short seems inclined to the belief that the first evidence of the Nahuas in America is to be found in the mounds in the Oregon country and that the greatest number of these people crossed the mountains and found their way into the Mississippi Valley. "The remainder of the Nahuas, we think," says he, "instead of crossing the Rocky Mountains, migrated southward into Utah, and established a civilization the remains of which are seen in the cliff-dwellings of the San Juan Valley and such extensive ruins as exist at Aztec Springs. It must be conceded that this hypothesis rests on linguistic and traditional evidence, as no affinity between the architecture of the Cliff-dwellers and either the Mexicans or Mound-builders is traceable."[50]

"We remarked," says he, "that this was a historic locality, as certainly it was if the legend obtained by Captain Moss from an old man among the Moquis is reliable. Mr. Ingersoll has rendered it in the *New York Tribune* for November 3d, 1874, as follows: 'Formerly, the aborigines inhabited all this country we had been over as far west as the head-waters of the San Juan, as far north as the Rio Dolores, west some distance into Utah, and south and south-west throughout Arizona and on down into Mexico. They had lived there from time immemorial-since the earth was a small island, which augmented as its inhabitants multiplied. They cultivated the valley, fashioned whatever utensils and tools they needed very neatly and handsomely out of clay and wood and stone, not knowing any of the useful metals; built their homes and kept their flocks and herds in the fertile river-bottoms, and worshipped the sun. They were an eminently peaceful and prosperous people, living by agriculture rather than by the chase. About a thousand years ago, however, they were visited by savage strangers from the North, whom they treated hospitably. Soon these visits became more frequent and annoying. Then their troublesome neighbors—ancestors of the present Utes—began to forage upon them, and, at last, to massacre them and devastate their farms; so, to save their lives at least, they built houses high upon the cliffs where they could store food and

---

[49]"*North Americans of Antiquity*," pp. 277-8.
[50]Ibid., p. 518.

hide away till the raiders left. But one summer the invaders did not go back to their mountains as the people expected, but brought their families with them and settled down. So, driven from their homes and lands, starving in their little niches on the high cliffs, they could only steal away during the night, and wander across the cheerless uplands. To one who has traveled these steppes, such a flight seems terrible, and the mind hesitates to picture the suffering of the sad fugitives. At the *Cristone* they halted and probably found friends, for the rocks and caves are full of the nests of these human wrens and swallows. Here they collected, erected stone fortifications and watch-towers, dug reservoirs in the rocks to hold a supply of water, which in all cases is precarious in this latitude, and once more stood at bay. Their foes came, and for one long month fought and were beaten back, and returned day after day to the attack as merciless and inevitable as the tide. Meanwhile, the families of the defenders were evacuating and moving south, and bravely did their protectors shield them till they were all safely a hundred miles away. The besiegers were beaten back and went away. But the narrative tells us that the hollows of the rocks were filled to the brim with the mingled blood of conquerors and conquered, and red veins of it ran down into the canon. It was such a victory as they could not afford to gain again, and they were glad, when the long fight was over, to follow their wives and little ones to the south. There, in the deserts of Arizona, on well-nigh unapproachable isolated bluffs, they built new towns, and their few descendants, the Moquis, live in them to this day, preserving more carefully and purely the history and veneration of their forefathers than their skill or wisdom. It was from one of their old men that this traditional sketch was obtained." [51]

The civilized Americans will be referred to later on, and we will now consider such evidence as we have in relation to the complexion, color of eyes, and color and texture of hair among the American Indians.

"Prichard, *Researches into the Physical Hist. of Mankind*, 4th ed., 1841, vol. 1, p. 269, after reviewing the question of the unity of the American race, remarks: 'It will be easy to prove that the American races, instead of displaying a uniformity of color in all climates, show nearly as great a variety in this res-

---

[51]"*North Americans of Antiquity*," pp. 302-4.

pect as the nations of the old continent; that there are among them white races with a florid complexion inhabiting temperate regions, and tribes black or of very dark hue in low and inter-tropical countries; that their stature, figure and countenances are almost equally diversified. Of these facts I shall collect sufficient evidence when I proceed to the ethnography of the American nations.' He fulfils this promise ably enough in vol. v, pp. 289, 374, 542, and other places. We respectfully refer the reader to the facts there accumulated." [52]

"The Menominees, sometimes called the 'White Indians,' formerly occupied the region bordering on Lake Michigan, around Green Bay. The whiteness of these Indians, which is compared to that of white mulattoes, early attracted the attention of the Jesuit missionaries, and has often been commented upon by travellers. While it is true that hibridy has done much to lighten the color of many of the tribes, still the peculiarity of the complexion of this people has been marked from the first time a European encountered them. Almost every shade, from the ash color of the Menominees, through the cinnamon red, copper and bronze tints, may be found among the tribes formerly occupy-ing the territory east of the Mississippi—the remnants of some of which are now in the Indian Territory and others in the North-west—until we reach the dark-skinned Kaws of Kansas, who are nearly as black as the Negro. The Indians in Mexico are known as the 'black people,' an appellation designed to be descriptive of their color. Viollet le Duc is of the opinion that the builders of the great remains in Southern Mexico and Yucatan belong to two different branches of the human family, a light-skinned and dark-skinned race respectively. The variety of com-plexion is as great in South America as among the tribes of the northern portion of the continent." [53]

Winchell says: "Further southward, along the northwest coast of America, dwell numerous other tribes which, according to the accounts, must be widely distinguished from the Hunting Indians of the interior. The Tlinket or Koloshian family, consisting of several tribes, are represented as lighter colored than any other North American aborigines. They have, indeed, been described as 'having as fair a complexion, when their skins are washed, as

---

[52]"North Americans of Antiquity," p. 189, Note 2.
[53]"Ibid., pp. 189-90.

the inhabitants of Europe; and this distinction, accompanied sometimes with auburn hair, has been considered as indicating an origin different from that of the copper-colored tribes." [54]

"The polite and friendly Mandans." Catlin says: "There is certainly great justice in the remark; and so forcibly have I been struck with the peculiar ease and elegance of these people, together with the diversity of complexions, the various colours of their hair and eyes; the singularity of their language, and their peculiar and unaccountable customs, that I am fully convinced that they have sprung from some other origin than that of the other North American tribes, or that they are an amalgam of natives with some civilized race." . . .

"A stranger in the Mandan village is first struck with the different shades of complexion, and various colours of hair which he sees in a crowd about him; and is at once almost disposed to exclaim that 'these are not Indians.' "

"There are a great many of these people whose complexions appear as light as half breeds; and amongst the women particularly, there are many whose skins are almost white, with the most pleasing symmetry and proportion of features; with hazel, with grey, and with blue eyes,—with mildness and sweetness of expression, and excessive modesty of demeanour, which render them exceedingly pleasing and beautiful."

"Why this diversity of complexion I cannot tell, nor can they themselves account for it. Their traditions, so far as I have yet learned them, afford us no information of their having had any knowledge of white men before the visit of Lewis and Clarke, made to their village thirty-three years ago. (This letter, it seems, was written in 1833.) Since that time there have been but very few visits from white men to this place, and surely not enough to have changed the complexions and the customs of a nation. And I recollect perfectly well that Governor Clarke told me, before I started for this place, that I would find the Mandans a strange people and half white."

"The diversity in the colour of hair is also equally as great as that in the complexion; for in a numerous 'group of these people (and more particularly amongst the females, who never take pains to change its natural colour, as the men often do), there may be

---

[54]*"Preadamites,"* p. 326. Winchell refers to Encyclopaedia Britannica and also to Peschel's *"Races of Man,"* p. 398.

seen every shade and colour of hair that can be seen in our country, with the exception of red or auburn, which is not to be found."

" . . . There are very many, of both sexes, and of every age, from infancy to manhood and old age, with hair of a bright silvery grey; and in some instances almost perfectly white."

"This singular and eccentric appearance is much oftener seen among the women than it is with the men; for many of the latter who have it, seem ashamed of it, and artfully conceal it, by filling their hair with glue and black and red earth. The women, on the other hand, seem proud of it, and display it often in an almost incredible profusion, which spreads over their shoulders and falls as low as the knee. I have ascertained, on careful enquiry, that about one in ten or twelve of the whole tribe are what the French call 'cheveux gris,' or greyhairs; and that this strange and unaccountable phenomenon is not the result of disease or habit; but that it is unquestionably a hereditary character which runs in families, and indicates no inequality in disposition or intellect. And by passing this hair through my hands, as I often have, I have found it uniformly to be as coarse and harsh as horse's mane; differing materially from the hair of other colours, which amongst the Mandans, is generally as fine and soft as silk." . . .

"The stature of the Mandans is rather below the ordinary size of man, with beautiful symmetry of form and proportion, and wonderful suppleness and elasticity; they are pleasingly erect and graceful, both in their walk and their attitudes. . . ." [55]

"In foot-note of p. 107 of vol. iii. of 'U. S. Explorations for a Railroad Route to the Pacific Ocean,' we are told,

"Many of the Indians of Zuni (New Mexico) are white. They have a fair skin, blue eyes, chestnut or auburn hair, and are quite good-looking. They claim to be full-blooded Zunians, and have no tradition of intermarriage with any foreign race. The circumstance creates no surprise among this people, for from time immemorial a similar class of people has existed among the tribe.' " [56]

"The nearest aproach to the natural condition and characteristic physiognomy of the pre-historic inhabitants of this continent, is observable in the Peruvian mummies collected in latitude 18° 30′ S., on the shore of the Bay of Chacota, near Arica, by Mr. Blake, and transferred by him to Boston. Many others have since been

---

[55] Catlin's *"North American Indians,"* Vol. I, pp. 93-5.
[56] Ignatius Donnelly's *"Atlantis: the Antediluvian World,"* p. 184, Harper & Brothers.

exhumed, and though embalmed and buried in a climate which preserves the brightest colors of the garments with which they were enshrouded, still the shrivelled condition of the corpses furnishes us the assurance that their type of features can never be truly recovered from nature. Dr. Morton has figured the head of one of these mummies in Plate I of the *Crania Americana,* from which the physiognomy may be partially restored by the aid of a vivid imagination. Notwithstanding the temptation which presents itself, and one which has been sufficiently indulged already, it would certainly be idle to speculate as to what that type might have been. However, one feature of the Peruvian mummies has been preserved true to life, and is of the greatest value in determining ethnic relations. The siliceous sand and marl of the plain southward of Arica, where the most remarkable cemeteries are situated, is slightly impregnated with common salt as well as nitrate and sulphate of soda. These conditions, together with the dry atmosphere rivalling that of Egypt, and in which fleshy matter dries without putrefaction, the human hair has been perfectly preserved, and comes to us as one of the best evidences of the diversity of the American races yet produced. In general it is a lightish brown, and of a fineness of texture which equals that of the Anglo-Saxon race. Straight, coarse, black hair is universally characteristic of the Red Indians, and is known to be one of the last marks of race to disappear in intermarriage with Europeans. The ancient Peruvians appear, from numerous examples of hair found in their tombs, to have been an auburn-haired race. Garcilasso, who had an opportunity of seeing the body of the king Viracocha, describes the hair of that monarch as snow-white. Haywood has described the discovery at the beginning of this century of three mummies in a cave on the south side of the Cumberland River, near the dividing line of Smith and Wilson Counties in Tennessee. They were buried in baskets, as Humbolt has described some of the Peruvians to bury, and the color of their skin was said to be fair and white, and their hair auburn and of a fine texture. The same author refers to several instances of the discovery of mummies in the limestone and saltpetre caves of Tennessee with light yellowish hair. Prof. Jones supposes that the light color of these so-called mummies of Tennessee and Kentucky was due to the action of lime and saltpetre." [57]

---

[57] Short's *"North Americans of Antiquity,"* pp. 186-7.

Referring to Central American ruins, Short says: "In all these reliefs the flattened cranial type is present, and no doubt represents the ideal of beauty among those ancient people. The stuccoes appear to have been moulded upon the undercoating of cement after it had become hard. The brush of the painter was then employed in its final embellishment. Adjacent to the eastern stairway leading downward into the main court of the palace are great stone slabs, forming a surface on each side of the steps fifty feet long by eleven feet high. Waldeck, Stephens and Bancroft furnish views of gigantic human figures sculptured in low relief upon these surfaces. Both the attitudes and expressions portrayed indicate that the groups represented are either captives or possibly victims for sacrifice. On the opposite side of the court, and on the stone face of the balustrade of a stairway, two figures, male and female, are sculptured, which, according to Waldeck, are of the Caucasian type. . . . ." [58]

"Dr. LePlongeon says of the columns at Chichen, 'the base is formed by the head of Cukulcan, the shaft by the body of the serpent, with its feathers beautifully carved to the very chapter. On the chapters of the columns that support the portico, at the entrance of the castle in Chichen-Itza, may be seen the carved figures of long-bearded men, with upraised hands, in the act of worshipping sacred trees. They forcibly recall to mind the same worship in Assyria.' " [59]

"Besides the sculptures of long-bearded men seen by the explorer at Chichen-Itza mentioned on a preceding page, were tall figures of people with small heads, thick lips, and curly short hair or wool, regarded as Negroes. 'We always see them as standard or parasol bearers, but never engaged in actual warfare.' He pronounces the features of the long-bearded men pictured on the walls of the queen's chambers to be Assyrian in their type." [60]

Referring to the Peruvians, Donnelly says: "The Quichuas—this invading people—were originally a fair-skinned race, with blue eyes and light and even auburn hair; they had regular features, large heads, and large bodies. Their descendants are to this

[58]Short's "North American's of Antiquity," p. 386.
[59]Ibid., p. 397.
[60]Ibid., pp. 401-3.

day an olive-skinned people, much lighter in color than the Indian tribes subjugated by them." [61]

"Very ancient ruins," says he, "showing remains of large and remarkable edifices, were found near Huamanga, and described by Cieca de Leon. The native traditions said this city was built 'by *bearded white men*, who came there long before the time of the Incas, and established a settlement.' " [62]

The same author, referring to the civilized peoples to the north, says: "That the population of Central America (and in this term I include Mexico) was at one time very dense, and had attained to a high degree of civilization, higher even than that of Europe in the time of Columbus, there can be no question; and it is also probable, as I have shown, that they originally belonged to the white race. Dêsirè Charnay, who is now exploring the ruins of Central America, says (*North American Review*, Jan., 1881, p. 48), 'The Toltecs were *fair, robust, and bearded.* I have often seen Indians of pure blood with blue eyes.' Quetzalcoatl was represented as large, 'with a big head and a heavy beard.' The same author speaks (page 44) of 'the ocean of ruins all around, not inferior in size to those of Egypt'." [63]

Some writers have attributed the Mexican civilization to Japan; but, most decidedly, such information as we have in regard to Japan and the Japanese negatives all such assumptions. Legendary Japan begins in 660 B.C. with Jimmu Tenno, who, from the south, landed on the principal island of the group in that year; but Japan had no written records till the sixth century of our era. "How long the Mound-builders occupied the country north of the Gulf of Mexico," says Short, "it is impossible in the present state of science to determine. Some authors conjecture that they were here two thousand years; that we think would be time enough, though after all it is but conjecture. It seems to us, however, that the time of the abandonment of their works may be more closely approximated. A thousand or two years may have elapsed since they vacated the Ohio Valley, and a period embracing seven or eight centuries may have passed since they retired from the Gulf Coast." [64].

[61]"*Atlantis: the Antediluvian World*," p. 391, Harper & Brothers.

[62]Ibid., p. 393.

[63]Ibid., p. 349.

[64]"*North Americans of Antiquity*," pp. 104-6.

When we consider this estimate together with the circumstance that these mounds were found to be covered with forests, it would seem reasonably certain the Mound-builders were flourishing in the Ohio Valley centuries, if not for thousands of years, before the legendary history of Japan began in 660 B.C.; and there is here being allowed the extreme claims as to antiquity by the Japanese. Furthermore, the structural works of note in Japan, indicating the archicultural tendency of its people, are represented only in feudal castles and bridge building, and these are not similar in design or character to the works found in America. Any Japanese contact with America must have been accidental in character and of negligible consequence.

Most writers who insist upon an Asiastic influence in the American civilizations seem to seek justification in alleged similarities in the respective mythologies or religious ceremonials or in the use of the serpent in decorative design or structural works; but in such instances the connection is found to be with the Hindu or with some people in southwestern Asia and not with the Mongoloid. That such influence should have found its way across the Pacific is even less likely than it should have crossed the Atlantic.

The answer to the suggestion that Egypt was responsible for the American civilizations seems to be this: Had such an event ocurred during the historic period, it would, in all probability, have been recorded on some of its monuments as a most distinguished triumph of one of its rulers. Furthermore, it seems scarcely possible that this might have been done in their infancy and before the historic period, when the sole great feat of navigation of which they make any record was the circumnavigation of Africa by Phoenician sailors in Egyptian ships about 611 B.C.

We must look elsewhere for the source or fountain-head of American civilization; but let us carry our investigation a little further and see what we can find in the way of enlightenment, if anything, by investigations that have been made into the languages of the people found in America.

"Probably one of the most incontrovertible arguments against American ethnic unity is that which rests upon the unparalleled diversity of language which meets the philologist everywhere. The monosyllable and the most remarkable polysyllables known to the linguist; synthetic and analytic families of speech, simplicity and complexity of expression, all seem to have sprung up and developed into permanent and in some cases beautiful and grammatical systems side by side with each other until the Babel of the Pentateuch is realized in the indescribable confusion of tongues. . ." [65]

"The Mexican scholar, Señor Melgar, is convinced that he sees resemblances between the names employed by the Chiapenecs in their calendar, and the Hebrew, and furnishes comparative lists to sustain," as Short says, "his hopeless theory."

Hebrew	Chiapenec	English
Ben	Been	Son.
Bath	Batz	Daughter.
Abba	Abagh	Father.
Chimah	Chimax	Star of Zodiac? the creator of rain.
Maloc	Molo	King.
Abah	Abagh	Name applied to Adam.
Chanan	Chanam	Afflicted.
Elab	Elab	God.
Tischiri	Tsiquin	September.
Chi	Chic	More.
Chabic	Chabin	Rich.
Enos	Enot	Son of Seth.
Votan	Votan	To give.
Lambotus	Lambat	River of Arica.[66]

Donnelly says, as to this: "And even after the lapse of so many thousand years most remarkable resemblances have been found to exist between the Chiapenec language and the Hebrew, the living representative of the Phoenician tongue." After giving the above list, he further states: "Thus, while we find such extraordinary resemblances between the Maya alphabet (He had shown this previously in his text, and it will be referred to later) and the Phoenician alphabet, we find equally surprising coincidences between the Chiapenec tongue, a branch of the Mayas, and the Hebrew, a branch of the Phoenician." [67].

This list may mean nothing to some ethnologists and philol-

---

[65]"*North Americans of Antiquity*," p. 190.
[66]Ibid., p. 475 and note.
[67]"*Atlantis: the Antediluvian World*," p. 234, Harper & Brothers.

ogists of repute, but it would be very trying to the credulity of
the average layman to be called upon to accept the likenesses
indicated as the result of accidental coincidence.

"Comparisons of the Indian languages with those of the old
world have often been made, most frequently in a haphazard
manner and to little purpose. Recently, however, Herr Forch-
hammer of Leipzig published a truly scientific comparison of the
grammatical structure of the Choctaw, Chickasaw, Muskogee and
Seminole languages, with the Ural-Altaic tongues, in which he
has developed many interesting points of resemblance. Prof.
Valentini has called attention to the fact that Ptolemy (Geography, Asia Minor, Chapter X, Armenia Major) gives in his list
of cities belonging to the Roman province in his time (A.D. 140),
the names of five cities situated in the region of the historic
Ararat, which have nearly their counterpart in five proper names
applied to localities in Mexico by its ancient colonists."

The names are:

Armenian.	Mexican.
Chol	Cholula.
Colua	Coluacan.
Zuivana	Zuivan.
Cholima	Colima.
Zalissa	Xalisco.

"Generally we have been disposed to pronounce all such coincidences accidental," says Short, " as most of them certainly are.
In this case we leave the decision to the reader. In this chapter
we have noticed two prominent families of languages, (1) the
Maya-Quiché, having such transatlantic affinities as to furnish
presumptive evidence that if it did not originate from, it was at
least influenced by the West European or African languages
(This does not refer to the Negro but to the peoples of North
Africa). (2) The great Nahua family, which linguistic researches,
together with the circumstantial evidence furnished by architectural remains, commercial intercourse and the testimony of early
writers, assign to at least a temporary occupancy of the Colum-
bian region on the North-west coast. Concede this fact, and you
must look elsewhere, possibly to the opposite continent, for the
early beginnings of a language so ancient and polished."

"While proof is not conclusive, yet we think it is presumptive that both of these families, as well as some other American languages, are of old world origin." [68]

"Why is it," asks Donnelly, referring to the above given list of geographical names, "that we find in Ptolemy's 'Geography of Asia Minor,' in a list of cities in Armenia Major in A.D. 140, the names of five cities which have their counterparts in the names of localities in Central America?" [69]

"The characteristics of the Maya-Quiché languages are; flexibility, expressiveness, vigor, approximating harshness, yet on the contrary rich and musical in sound. The Maya itself has more than once been compared to the Greek, and even said to be derived from it. Dr. LePlongeon, who for four years has been exploring the ruins of Yucatan and especially of Chichen-Itza, writes thus in connection with the discovery of a well-sculptured bear's head at Uxmal: 'When did bears inhabit the peninsula? Strange to say, the Maya does not furnish the name for bear. Yet one-third of this tongue is pure Greek. Who brought the dialect of Homer to America? Or who took to Greece that of the Mayas? Greek is the offspring of Sanscrit. Is Maya? Or are they coeval? A clue for ethnologists to follow the migrations of the human family on this old continent. Did the bearded men whose portraits are carved on the massive pillars of the fortress at Chichen-Itza, belong to the Mayan nations? The Maya is not devoid of words from the Assyrian." [70]

Donnelly's quotation of Andrew Lang's summary in regard to the views of Señor Vincente Lopez as to the Peruvian tongue is in part as follows: "Señor Lopez's view, that the Peruvians were Aryans who left the parent stock long before the Teutonic or Hellenic races entered Europe, is supported by arguments drawn from language, from the traces of institutions, from religious beliefs, from legendary records, and artistic remains. The evidence from language is treated scientifically, and not as a kind of ingenious guessing. Señor Lopez first combats the idea that the living dialect of Peru is barbarous and fluctuating. It is not one of the casual and shifting forms of speech produced by nomad races. To which of the stages of language does this belong—the agglutinative, in which one root is fastened on to another, and a word is

---

[68]"*North Americans of Antiquity*," pp. 496-7.
[69]"*Atlantis: the Antediluvian World*," p. 178, Harper & Brothers.
[70]"*North Americans of Antiquity*," p. 474.

formed in which the constitutive elements are obviously distinct, or the inflexional, where the auxiliary roots get worn down and are only distinguishable by the philologist? As all known Aryan tongues are inflexional, Señor Lopez may appear to contradict himself when he says that Quichua is an *agglutinative Aryan language*. But he quotes Mr. Max Müller's opinion that there must have been a time when the germs of Aryan tongues had not yet reached the inflexional stage, and shows that while the form of Quichua is agglutinative, as in Turanian, the *roots of words* are Aryan. If this be so, Quichua may be a linguistic missing link."[71]

"There is a Sanscrit root, *kr*, to act, to do: this root is found in more than three hundred names of peoples and places in Southern America." [72]

"Very recently Dr. Rudolf Falb has announced (*Neue Freie Presse*, of Vienna) that he has discovered that the relation of the Quichua and Aimara languages to the Aryan and Semitic tongues is very close; that, in fact, they 'exhibit the most astounding affinities with the Semitic tongue, and particularly the Arabic, in which tongue Dr. Falb has been skilled from his boyhood. Following up the lines of this discovery, Dr. Falb has found (1) a connecting link with the Aryan roots, and (2) has ultimately arrived face to face with the surprising revelation that 'the Semitic roots are universally Aryan.' The common stems of all the variants are found in their purest condition in Quichua and Aimara, from which fact Dr. Falb derives the conclusion that the high plains of Peru and Bolivia must be regarded as the point of exit of the present human race." [73]

"Language in aboriginal America," says Short, "may be pronounced a mystery of mysteries and a Babel of Babels." . . . "The geographical division and intermixture of languages, for instance, in California, is without a parallel elsewhere in the world. . . . . Supposing the continent to have received its population from several different quarters, the natural expectation would be that in the course of time this process of general intermixture would result in developing in each language much that was common to the others—hence the foundation for the hypothesis of their unity of origin. In the study of American languages

[71]"*Atlantis: the Antediluvian World*," pp. 400-1, Harper & Brothers.
[72]Ibid., pp. 401-2.
[73]Ibid., p. 402.

it has often been a matter of surprise that their structure and expressiveness indicates a degree of perfection far in advance of the civilization out of which they had sprung. This superiority, we think, can be accounted for on the principle, first, that the evolution of languages on this continent has been more active and constant here than elsewhere, though unfortunately not always operating under favorable conditions; and second, that in the frequent catastrophes which have resulted from inter-tribal warfare, even in language, the law of the survival of the fittest is apparent, in the preservation of those etymological forms and principles of structure which are most useful. . . . An examination of the poems of Nezahualcoyotl, king of Tezcuco, recorded by Ixtlilxochitl, will afford sufficient proof of the expressiveness and richness of the Aztec language." [74]

It looks but reasonable that a language rich in vocabulary and appropriate to all shades and degrees of nicety in expression of thought, thought and expression being the complements one of the other, could not continue in existence under the law of "survival of the fittest" except that a superior people, to whose mentality such expression of thought was appropriate, also survived. If, therefore, a people be found in the enjoyment of a method of thought-expression, speech, apparently advanced beyond the cultural station of the people themselves, but two conclusions can be drawn: Either these people are a decadent people who formerly enjoyed a more enlightened civilization; or they received their civilization and language from a more cultured people who have in time disappeared. In either case it is but natural to look forward to the eventual corruption and debasement of the language itself. Had the civilization in America been autochthonous, we should have been justified in looking for consistency between advance in culture and development in language; and under such conditions in America a civilization so arising should have been continuously progressive within reason. In the absence of this we must conclude the civilization was imported.

The archaeologists, ethnologists and philologists have occupied opposing and necessarily conflicting positions as to the origin and affinity in race and language of the American Indian (people found in America on discovery) with peoples of the old world. These views include the special creation of an Indian Adam and

[74]"*North Americans of Antiquity*," pp. 469-71.

Eve in America, and the development of the Indian type in the process of evolution from an aboriginal American ancestor; but the most popular view peoples America from elsewhere in keeping with the monogenetic theory of evolution.

The attempts to classify the peoples found in America and their languages by standards found applicable to Europeans and the people of western Asia has resulted in a hopeless confusion; and it seems to be generally held at this time that, while there is no directly evident connection, either in race or language, with the peoples of the old world, we should nevertheless regard the Indians as of Asiatic origin. The fact that American tongues do not show kinship to the European or Asiatic tongues in accordance with the tests applied by the philologists at this time, does not justify us in ignoring concrete examples of kinship in blood and tongue that may be brought to our notice. In the sciences relating to the origin and distribution of mankind, fashions of thought are set up from time to time as the pendulum swings from the old to the new view, and he who would question the approved opinion of the time has no standing in court. Unless absolutely irreconcilable, there is probably error and truth in both the old and new view, and doubtless with each swing of the pendulum new information is gathered that tends to a clearer conception of the ultimate truth.

Neither recorded history nor the traditions of any people, it seems, give us any record of any place on the inhabitable globe in which there was not found an aboriginal people with the exception of some isolated islands of the ocean and New Zealand. The Maoris, it appears, were the first inhabitants of New Zealand, which they occupied about 1400 A. D.

There can be little question that never before during his sojourn on the earth has man enjoyed such complete dominion over it as now. News agencies communicating by the telegraph, the submarine cable, and the wireless, condense and distribute the important events of each day through various instrumentalities to peoples in the remotest corners of the earth; and transportation by steam, electricity and air-service has brought in contact the most far distant and diverse peoples. Furthermore, Man's control over the forces of nature and his improvement in agriculture and industry and the control of disease have resulted in a greater population than was ever before upon the earth. China, though backward in many respects from the western point of view, should not be regarded as an example of a populous primitive people; for the Chinese are not a primitive people and have for ages been in the enjoyment of their land almost unmolested by turmoil of war with alien peoples.

In the present age, doubtless for the first time, man possesses a knowledge of the whole earth and its peoples. The world of the greatest civilizations that preceded our times, that of Egypt, Chaldea, Babylon, Greece and Rome, was confined to a small part of the habitable globe; and none of these great powers dared face the perils of the ocean to learn what lay beyond. Yet every movement of any of these peoples found, in accordance with their history or traditions, some other people had preceded them; and when the enlightenment of discovery revealed the modern world all continents were found to be inhabited.

How came the world to be so populated? In some mysterious way the monogenist has an original evoluted pair or small number of the ancestral type populate the whole globe. If the world was then as it is now, this necessarily imputes to primitive man an ability to undertake journeys and carry on sea voyages utterly beyond anything undertaken by the civilized Egyptians, Chaldeans, Greeks, Romans, or even the Phoenicians who were the most able of the ancient navigators.

Even if the physical conditions of the earth when man first appeared on it were different from what they are now, as was doubtless the case, it is inconceivable that enormous expanses of sea did not exist during all this period. These seas presented, where encountered, an impassable barrier to primitive man, who must have been feeble in resources as compared with any man known within the historic period, in any view of the theory of evolution. That a pair of such primitive people, or a few of them, produced by evolution in some isolated quarter of the globe, should populate the earth in all its parts and evolve the present types of mankind, which we know to have been fixed for over 6000 years, seems impossible of accomplishment within the span of time allowed man on earth. This population of the earth would appear possible only on the assumption that the earth was more prodigal in her gifts of the human life element, and that in obedience to the mandate of Nature man arose from the different soils of the earth.

The existence of flora and fauna of a like species in isolated spots on the opposite shores of an ocean lends credit to the belief that at one time there existed a land connection between the two upon which the species in question probably arose and flourished; but there is nothing in such situation to justify the contention that all life arose in this sunken area or that there may not have been an evolution of numerous independent species in the continental areas once connected.

The abundance of life upon the earth and the checks known to exist and operate against the multiplication of the most prolific forms of life in the constant warfare between species, point to the innumerable and inconceivably great difficulties in the path of any theory that requires the population of the earth from an original pair or small number of an original species, if it does not refute it altogether.

Primitive man, like his more advanced successor, doubtless followed the line of least resistance in his physical progress over the earth, and, more or less so, in his cultural advancement. Thus, the more advanced and capable pushed the less capable into undesirable localities where the conditions of life were harder and the people affected could survive only in limited numbers in a nomadic state or reduced to the family unit of organization. Since the recession of the northern glacier the parts of Asia adjacent to the Bering Strait and the Aleutian Islands, and the adjacent American shores to a less degree, have formed a country that presented a dreary, unattractive aspect and in which the conditions of life were hard. This part of Asia is sparsely filled with an unprogressive, nomadic type or family units of the Eskimo type. There is absolutely no justification whatever for the belief that any race movements of consequence occurred in this section other than the assumption that America was largely peopled from this source. That there was a dribble of humanity from this source into America may well be conceded, but that these Asiatic people should be largely responsible for the population of America seems impossible. We have no records, either historical or legendary, of any people of culture migrating to or moving through this no-man's land of Asia.

Let us now examine what has gone before in this chapter and try to find what it means within itself and what explanation of these facts, if any, can be offered. What thus appears is the result of a diligent and earnest effort to secure facts in so far as they could be had from limited available sources of information. It does not purport to be exhaustive; but, if these be conceded to be facts, the conclusion irresistibly follows that racial unity does not exist in America, and that at some remote period of time a large quantity of white blood from some outside source was infused into that of the aborigines.

An examination of the skeletal remains of the Mound-builders, of the ancient Peruvians, and of the people found in America on its discovery, discloses the fact that these people, with reference to the arbitrary division of the human species into *dolichocephalic* (long skulls), *brachycephalic* (round skulls), and *mesocephalic* (intermediate), are found to belong to two classes. In accordance with the skull measurements given by Winchell the people of America fall into the round-skull and long-skull divisions, the former including the Mound-builders, Mexicans, and Peruvians and generally the peoples of the mountainous regions on and near the Pacific coast in both continents. These skulls are thin while those in the long-skull division, which includes the Hunting Indians of the Atlantic seaboard generally, have a thick, heavy bone-structure. The same measurements, in accordance with a later change in the limits of the respective classes as used by Madison Grant in the classification of Europeans, would place these people in the intermediate and long-skull divisions. This arbitrary division in accordance with cephalic index indicates nothing in regard to race other than that the long and thick skulls could not have belonged to members of the white race in view of the fact that a thin skull is characteristic of that people. As a matter of fact, cranial type, with reference to the arbitrary division of the human species by cephalic index, is certainly of little value in America in determining racial character; and it is doubtful if this index alone is of great value in any case without reference to many other skull characters, such as facial angle, capacity, transverse and longitudinal sections, bone structure, etc., and other physical characters as well.

The coarse, straight, black hair of the Mongoloid is that usually found in the American aborigine, generally accepted as typical, and is said to be one of the last characteristics to disappear in amalgamation with other races. It is likewise a matter of common knowledge that red and flaxen hair, and brown or black, all either straight or wavy and of fine texture, are characteristic of the white races; and when these are found present on the remains of the ancient inhabitants of America, particularly red, flaxen or auburn, even irrespective of texture in these instances, it is strong presumptive proof that these people were either white or a cross of whites with other people. Similarly, blue or grey eyes are characteristic of a branch of the white family alone, and the presence of these eyes anywhere indicates white blood pure or adulterated. The presence of white blood among the Americans in ancient times is also indicated by the light complexion in numerous of its peoples which cannot be accounted for by infusion of blood since the discovery of America or attributed to the occasional and accidental, rather than deliberate, contacts of the Norse or others prior to such discovery. The sculptures of the Mound-builders and the carved figures and the mural decorations of the Central American ruins point to the presence of an outside people not indigenous to the soil; and the figures represented with beards and the physical features of the Caucasian are beyond question representations of some members of the white race in America.

Had these circumstances been found present in North Africa they would have been accepted as establishing beyond cavil, that at some remote period a considerable number of white people had found their way into this region and had been lost as a distinctive race in the process of amalgamation. Why should the same conclusions from the facts stated be considered as erroneous when applied to America, and be greeted with a smile of derision by that school of scientists which attributes greater feats to primitive man in populating the world from his original nidus than would have been the colonization of America from Europe by members of the white race at some remote period, even though we should not regard this last probable from our knowledge of the civilizations of antiquity in this region?

The striking likeness in some instances between the American tongues, particularly the Mayan and Peruvian, and some of the old world languages, pointed out by respectable authorities, cannot be ignored, and must be accepted as cumulative evidence pointing in the same direction as that which has gone before.

Another and most important fact that irresistably compels us to disregard any theory that American civilizations were the result of Indian development, is that previously pointed out that a people typical of the Stone Age Indian occupied the Ohio Valley after it had been vacated by a people of culture who were in the use of the metals. This to me seems conclusive as to all assertions in regard to the Indian origin of civilizations.

Respectable authorities in advocacy of the foreign origin of

American civilizations are not wanting, and as to this Short says: "The want of evidence for the theories which designate particular nations as the first colonizers of the Western Continent, long ago produced a feeling of distrust, which led some to repudiate all claims for the foreign origin of the first inhabitants of this continent. This theory, which claims for the most ancient inhabitants an autochthonic origin, has had from time to time among its advocates some of the most respectable ethnologists. The character of their attainments, and in many cases their arguments in behalf of this most remarkable hypothesis, command the respect of all who are interested in this fascinating field of speculation."[75]

"Lord Kingsborough," says Short, "is no doubt warranted in holding that the Nahuas were of old world origin at a very remote period prior to their having developed any special tribal characteristics, because of their singular and we think certain knowledge of the Mosaic deluge; but he is not justified in claiming for them any particular relationship to the Jewish or any Shemitic people."[76]

Abbé Brasseur de Bourbourg maintains, apparently from the traditions of the people themselves, that the ancestors of the tribes Quiché-Cakchiquel and Zutohil crossed the seas from the northeast "in darkness, mist, cold and snow;" that by evidence of language they must have come from Denmark and Norway "in small numbers, and lost their white blood by their mixture with the Indians whom they found."[77]

"The traditional history of both Mayas and Nahuas," says Short, "seems to indicate an old world origin. The former people clearly claim an origin which, if their traditions are worth anything, must be assigned to some Mediterranean country. While, on the contrary, the Nahuas persistently state that they came from the north or north-west. It is certain that many of their cosmological traditions closely resemble those of Central and Western Asiatic peoples. Why should the traditions of the ancient Americans be less reliable than those of the most ancient Egyptians, Greeks, or Hindoos?"[78]

Short maintains the colonization of America from Europe did

[75]*"North Americans of Antiquity,"* p. 155.
[76]Ibid., p. 460.
[77]Ibid., p. 476 (note).
[78]Ibid., p. 517.

not depend upon a land connection between the two, but might have been accomplished through favorable trade winds and the course and strength of the current of the Gulf Stream.

Brief reference will be made to some of the American traditions when we come to consider "Atlantis" further on; and, in the mean time, a tentative outline of the movements of prehistoric man in America will be given, which, it is hoped, will be less inconsistent with known facts than are some of the theories advanced.

It is first assumed that man, or his ancestor, was in America at the close of the warm period that gave place to the last glacial epoch in North America, and it is also assumed that this primitive creature was present in both continents. In the Northern continent these primitive peoples retreated before the glacier and at its greatest extension were confined to the southern part of the United States and the territory to the southward toward the Isthmus and Northern South America; whereas, under the more favorable conditions of the Southern Hemisphere, the aborigines to the south of the equator were inclined to gather in the southern part of the continent.

These primitive peoples were doubtless of the same general type with such divergence from this type as might be induced by the surroundings in which the numerous small bands found themselves. The migratory movements, although as slowly made as the compulsion of necessity would permit, must have resulted in mixture, combat, and confusion; then came readjustment in families or tribes to be disarranged again upon further tribal movements.

Upon the recession of the glacier the peoples of the Northern Continent began their reflex migratory movements toward the north, in which movement the Eskimos were doubtless the most northern people. The others gradually accommodated themselves to the changed conditions until finally the present limits of the United States were again occupied by human beings, but not so densely in all probability as the territory of Mexico and Central America.

During all this period it would seem that the people in the Southern Continent were in the enjoyment of more favorable climatic conditions and were, therefore, more favorably situated for development.

At some remote period, the date of which is not now known,

there appeared a foreign people of superior culture in the valley of the Mississippi and in the Central American region. These people must have possessed vessels that would enable them to navigate bodies of water of reasonable size with safety, at least under fair conditions of weather. To them the broad Mississippi Valley must have appeared as a treeless expanse of limitless extent. Up this valley and the main branches of its river they went. We discover them finally established in force in the Ohio Valley and that of the Mississippi. Some of them, as evidenced by remains of works of a primitive character and much less pretentious than those of the Ohio Valley, crossed the divide into the Columbia country, and, at a later period, moved south into the region in which were found the Pueblos and the Cliff-dwellers. That these latter people gave evidence of an infusion of white blood in the remote past is shown from our knowledge of the Zuni Indians, who, with the other Cliff-dwellers, may be assumed to be descendants of the original Mound-builder people and the aboriginal inhabitants. If credit be given to the Moqui legend, as it appears in the preceding part of this chapter and in which mention was made of the conflicts between these people and the savage tribes that drove them from the valleys they cultivated to the cliffs, we may here have evidence of the white man with stone implements; for it was stated that they "fashioned whatever utensils and tools they needed very neatly and handsomely out of clay and wood and stone, not knowing any of the useful metals."[79] Had the original Mound-builder ancestors of these people possessed a knowledge of the metals, it is assumed that it would have been preserved in their descendants, even though they were in small numbers originally, separated from their fellow tribesmen in the valleys across the Rocky Mountains, and early mixed in blood with the aborigines.

The Mound-builders moved up the Mississippi River and its tributaries and in time established populous settlements in these valleys, a small number, as stated above, crossing the divide into the Columbia or Oregon country and later moving south into the Utah country as the Cliff-dwellers. They undoubtedly met with aboriginal inhabitants in these regions, and civilized them and utilized their services. These aboriginal inhabitants were the pre-glacial people in North America who had migrated from

---

[79]"*North Americans of Antiquity*," p. 303.

the south into these valleys upon the recession of the glacier; and, in their northerly migration they probably went in two streams, one up the Mississippi Valley, the other entered the present boundries of the United States between the Rocky Mountains and the Sierra Nevadas and sparsely peopled this section.

It is abundantly shown that the Mound-builders in the valley regions soon displayed an advanced culture and mined copper in enormous quantities from the Lake Superior mines, which they worked in the open season, the workmen apparently withdrawing to the settlements to the south during the winter. They worked copper into all sorts of implements and ornaments, mined mica, manufactured cloth and pottery, engaged in agriculture, and demonstrated their proficiency in the art of sculpture, in which latter work there are doubtless preserved true representations of the then living peoples. They also built enormous earthworks in connection with their religious ceremonies, the burial of their dead, and the defense of their settlements; and, in accordance with some authorities, they even built canals.

These people seem with reasonable certainty to be properly classed as members of the Nahua family, which family was so prominent in the later stages of Mexican civilization through the successive dominance of groups or tribes of this family, the Aztecs being the last of the family to arrive in Mexico. Short fixes upon 231 A. D. as the probable date of arrival of the Nahuas in Mexico; but Winchell says this family, represented in the Toltecs, were in Mexico before the Christian Era, and he dates the movement of the Aztecs from Aztlan (Hue-hue-Tlapalan—all containing a suggestion of Atlan-tis) in 1090. Winchell also states the records and traditions of these people indicate the northeast as the direction of the home-land from which they came, and not the northwest as does Short.

At or about the time the immigrant Mound-builders appeared in the Mississippi Valley another body of these white immigrants settled in the Central American region and became the founders of the Mayan civilization, the oldest on the North American continent. It will be urged in the following chapter that these white immigrants came from the island of Atlantis and that they were in communication with the home-land until the great catastrophe that sank it in the ocean depths.

When these immigrants appeared in North America, a fact which alone shows them to have been a people of superior culture in this remote period, they may have still been in the Polished Stone Age, but from this they soon emerged on discovering and working the copper deposits in the Lake Superior region. That these immigrants from their first contact with the aborigines began to amalgamate with them may be safely assumed from the uniformly consistent testimony of history as to what always occurs under similar conditions; and this infusion of blood must have continued with acceleration after the submergence of the mother-country and the cessation of supply of new white blood.

While all this was going on in the Northern Continent, the peoples of the Southern Continent, who had enjoyed more favorable climatic conditions during the continuance of the northern glacier, had become more populous and had made progress from the point of view of the savage. When Peru had been occupied by another colony from Atlantis, the Indian tribes to the east of the Andes Mountains began their northerly migrations that brought them to the Caribbean Sea, through the West Indies, and eventually to Florida. These Hunting Tribes drifted up the Atlantic seaboard and reached the Great Lakes and the upper stretches of the Mississippi Valley after passing through parts of the States of Pennsylvania and New York on their way. Any scattering vanguard that may have drifted toward the mouth of the Mississippi in this migratory movement probably found it so well occupied by the Mound-builders that they were shunted off to the line of least resistance along the Atlantic seaboard. They had probably reached the Great Lakes before they had sufficiently populated New England to that point of menace that the Eskimo should have to retreat further north from this section. We do know that the Eskimo at one time occupied territory within the limits of the United States; that he invariably retreated toward the North on contact with the Indian; and most authorities, if not all, seem to agree that the Hunting Tribes appeared in the United States from the Southeast-Florida. The Icelandic records describe the natives met on the New England coast 1000 A. D. as *dwarfish,* a description entirely inappropriate to the Indian found in this region upon settlement by Europeans, but fully in keeping with the characteristics of the Eskimo.

It seems that about 1000 A. D. was an important date in connection with the movements of the Hunting Tribes. The Eskimo, as stated, were in New England about this date and must have given ground to the Indian soon thereafter; the movement of the

Aztecs southward into Mexico began about this date; and, if any credit is to be given to the Moqui legend, their ancestors were driven from their homes by savage tribes that came from the north about the same time. These savage tribes continuing westward from the Great Lakes and following some of the rivers to their sources in the Rocky Mountains entered the Oregon country in much the same manner as did the ancestors of the Cliffdwellers.

The aboriginal population being probably far denser in Mexico and Central America than in the Mississippi Valley, the process of amalgamation was carried on far more rapidly in the former territories after Atlantis was sunk than was the case in the latter area. This, with the easier life of the civilized South, probably soon showed itself in a retrogression of the people and their civilization. The more hardy and more nearly pure-blooded white Mound-builders, who were in commercial intercourse with the southern civilizations, if they did not enjoy a closer relationship, must have observed this retrogression; and the prospects of an easy victory over these retrograding people, the promise of booty and political power and an easier life, may have been a greater incentive for them to move into Mexico than any threat from incursions of savage tribes from the North, which probably did not arise prior to 1000 A. D. Be that as it may, they did move into the south; and even when the Aztecs came there must have remained to these people a certain amount of pure-blooded white leadership of genius; for their calendar, on the discovery of America, was found to be more accurate than that in use among the ·Europeans at that time.

That the civilizations of the Mound-builders, the Mexicans, and the Central Americans could have arisen as the work of a small number of white men accidentally cast upon American shores, does not conform to the facts we are able to sift from the dim and misty past of our continent. To plan and lead and carry on the great works accomplished by these civilizations required a numerous and intelligent body of leaders; and the fact that these white Atlanteans were at first numerous but later lost in amalgamation with the natives is borne out by the hair, eyes, features, and complexions of the peoples found in America on its discovery, as well as by the character of the civilizations found and the traditions in relation to them.

This suggestion as to the origin of the American aborigines

does not preclude all communication with Asia by way of Bering
Strait and the Aleutian Islands, but reduces immigration from
this source to small numbers and confines it to comparatively recent times.

Many other facts bearing upon this important matter point
to the same conclusions as those here drawn, among them the
traditions of the American peoples and many others. Some of
these will be referred to in the following chapter on "Atlantis."
That American traditions should receive the same fair consideration as is given those of European and Asiatic peoples, should
appeal to every fair-minded person. Short says: "The dim uncertainty which envelopes the most ancient period of American
antiquity, like that which obscures the beginnings of Egyptian,
Assyrian and Trojan history, to say nothing of the origin of the
venerable Asiatic civilizations, renders much of the effort in this
field unsatisfactory. Still the results are of surprising interest.
A new cosmogony, mythology and traditional history full of
weird poetic inspiration, an inspiration such as is begotten in
contemplating the struggles of nature's children after a higher
development, is added to the fund of human knowledge. The
poetry of the Quiché-cosmogony must some day find expression
in verse of Miltonic grandeur. The fall of Xibalba will no doubt
afford the materials for a heroic poem which will stand in the
same relation to America that the Iliad does to Greece. The
doctrines of the benign and saintly Quetzalcoatl or Cukulcan
must be classed among the great faiths of mankind, and their
author, alone of all the great teachers of morals except Christ
himself, inculcating a *positive* morality, must be granted a precedence of most of the great teachers of Chinese and Hindoo antiquity. It is the custom of many Europeans to regard America
as having no heroic or legendary period, no heroes like Achilles,
Aeneas, Sigfried, Boewolf, Arthur and the Cid; but who will review the romance of American antiquity and longer entertain this
view? A few years ago, writers dated North American history
from the discoveries made by Columbus and his immediate successors. Now they go back to the Northmen for a starting-point.
May not the beginning be pushed even farther back, and the
ancient history of America receive the attention of the historio-
grapher."[80]

---

[80]*"North Americans of Antiquity,"* p. 515.

CHAPTER IV.

ATLANTIS

Ignatius Donnelly, in his remarkable work, "Atlantis, the Antediluvian World," brings into review a host of facts which, directly or indirectly through the deductive or inductive process, point with irresistible force to the past existence of Atlantis as a verity. Not only must we come to this conclusion as to the existence of a physical Atlantis in the remote past, but we must also accept, as probable, the further conclusion that it was the land in which the ancestors of the White race spent the probationary period of their infancy and in which they developed a great civilization with far-flung colonies long before the land was engulfed in that great cataclysm which comes to us as the Deluge of the Bible.

The facts pointing to the existence of Atlantis are many. To begin, Solon, the great law-giver of Athens, visited in Egypt 600 years before the Christian Era, and, while there, learned many things from its wise men about the history of his own Greece and its relations with Atlantis in ancient times. A part of what was learned by Solon comes to us from Plato, who lived 400 B. C. Among other things, "The records inform us of the destruction by Athens of a singularly powerful army, an army which came from the Atlantic Ocean and which had the effrontery to invade Europe and Asia; for this sea was then navigable, and beyond the strait which you call the Pillars of Hercules there was an island larger than Libya and even Asia. (Asia Minor and North Africa correspond with Asia and Libya in ancient nomenclature.) From this island one could easily pass to other islands, and from them to the entire continent which surrounds the interior sea. What there is on this side of the strait of which we are speaking resembles a vast gateway, the entrance of which might be narrow, but it is actually a sea, and the land which surrounds it is a real continent. In the Island Atlantis reigned kings of amazing power. They had under their dominion the entire island, as well as several other islands and some parts of the continent. Besides, on the hither side of the strait, they were still reigning over Libya as far as Egypt and over Europe as far as the Tyrrhenian. All this power was once upon a time united in order by a single blow to subjugate our country, your own, and all the peoples living on the hither side of the strait. It was then that the strength and courage of Athens blazed forth. By the valor of her soldiers and their superiority in the military art, Athens was supreme among the Hellenes; but, the latter having been forced to abandon her, alone she braved the frightful danger, stopped the invasion, piled victory upon victory, preserved from slavery nations still free, and restored to complete independence all those who, like ourselves, live on this side of the Pillars of Hercules. Later, with great earthquakes and inundations, in a single day and one fatal night, all who had been warriors against you were swallowed up. The Island of Atlantis disappeared beneath the sea. Since that time the sea in these quarters has become unnavigable; vessels cannot pass there because of the sands which extend over the site of the buried isle."[80½]

The statements contained in this quotation are of a very startling character; and, unless founded upon facts within the knowledge of the Egyptians, it seems impossible that they could have conformed in so many respects to actual facts that came within the knowledge of Europeans only after the rediscovery of America by Columbus 2000 years later. How could an Egyptian priest, 600 years before the Christian Era, speak of the great sea (Atlantic) beyond the Pillars of Hercules (Strait of Gibraltar) of the Continent (North American and South America) that formed the true boundary of the sea, of the colonies of Atlantis (Mexico and Peru) in the continent beyond—how could one so do unless he spoke with the assurance that comes from historical records that accurately preserved past achievements of the race? At the time when Solon received this information no people of the then-known world were a seafaring people who could have imparted any of this information of their own knowledge. The Egyptians were never a seafaring people; and it was not until the reign of Pharaoh Necho, or Neku, II., who succeeded to the throne in 611 B. C., that Egyptian vessels, manned by Phoenician sailors, starting from the Red Sea circumnavigated Africa and re-

[80½]Report of Smithsonian Institution, 1915, pp. 220-1; Atlantis, Pierre Termier. Works of Plato, translated (into French) by V. Cousin, vol. 12, pp. 109-113, Paris, pub. Rey and Gravier.

turned to Egypt by way of the Mediterranean during the third year of the voyage. The most active navigators among the ancients were the Phoenicians, and the circumnavigation of Africa is probably their greatest achievement. Had they ever reached America we should have had some information to this effect. "Certain accounts," says Marion McMurrough Mulhall, "which have been handed down by the early Carthagenian navigators confirm the story told by the priest of Sais, of the submerged land which lay outside the Straits of Gades. Avienus, who was well acquainted with the Carthagenian records, writes of it in his own 'Ora Maritima'."[81]

We are inevitably driven to the conclusion that no man of Solon's time, or subsequent to him for a period of two thousand years prior to the discoveries of Columbus and those who came immediately after, had any information as to the size of the Atlantic, the continents beyond, and the civilizations in Mexico and Peru. No human being, however fertile his imagination, could produce a fable so pregnant with descriptive geographical facts that have no place in a fable, but which were found to have been descriptively true after a lapse of 2000 years. Egypt could only have known of the Atlantic and of the continents beyond with the colonies in Mexico and Peru from its association with a highly civilized people who kept records, who engaged in seaborne commerce, and through the sway of their empire linked together Europe and America. The priests of Egypt called this land Atlantis.

In the summer of 1898 a French cable was being laid between Brest and Cape Cod, and when the ship was about 500 miles north of the Azores the cable broke and it was necessary to drag the bottom with grappling irons for several days before the end of the cable was secured. The bottom of the sea was found to present the characteristics of a mountainous country with its high peaks, slopes and valleys. The summits of the peaks were found to be rocky and in the deep valleys were found oozes. There was brought to the surface by the grappling irons a number of small slivers of rock embedded between the teeth of the irons; and some of these are now preserved in the Musée de l'Ecole des Mines at Paris.

---

[81]"*Beginnings or Glimpses of Vanished Civilizations*," p. 21, Longmans, Green and Co., London.

Pierre Termier, Member of the Academy of Sciences, made these finds in their bearing on Atlantis the subject of a lecture delivered by him on November 30, 1912, before the Institut Océanographique of Paris; and, among other things, he said:

"The unanimous opinion of the engineers who were present at the dredging was that the chips in question had been detached from a bare rock, an actual outcropping, sharp-edged and angular. The region whence the chips came was furthermore precisely that where the soundings had revealed the highest submarine summits and the almost complete absence of oozes. The fragments, thus torn from the rocky outcrops of the bottom of the Atlantic, are of a vitreous lava, having the chemical composition of the basalts and called *tachylyte* by the petrographers."

"The matter was described in 1899 to the Académie des Sciences. Few geologists then comprehended its very great import. Such a lava, entirely vitreous, comparable to certain basaltic stones of the volcanoes in the Hawaiian Islands, could solidify into this condition only under atmospheric pressure. Under several atmospheres, and more especially under 3,000 meters of water, it might have crystallized. It would appear to us as formed of confused crystals, instead of being composed solely of colloidal matter. The most recent studies on this subject leave no doubt, and I will content myself with recalling the observation of M. Lacroix on the lavas of Mount Pelee of Martinique: Vitreous, when they congealed in the open air, these lavas become filled with crystals as soon as they were cooled under a cover, even not very thick, of previously solidified rocks. The surface which to-day constitutes the bottom of the Atlantic, 900 kilometers (562.5 miles) north of the Azores, was therefore covered with lava flows while it was still emerged. Consequently, it has been buried, descending 3,000 meters; and since the surface of the rocks has there preserved its distorted aspect, its rugged roughness, the sharp edges of the very recent lava flows, it must be that the caving in followed very close upon the emission of the lavas, and that this collapse was sudden. Otherwise atmospheric erosion and marine abrasion would have leveled the inequalities and planed down the entire surface."[82]

"Such are the data of geology. The extreme mobility of the

<hr />

[82]Report of the Smithsonian Institution, 1915, pp. 226-7, Termier's *Atlantis*,

Atlantic region, especially in conjunction with the mediterranean depression and the great volcanic zone, 3,000 kilometers (1,875 miles) broad, which extends from north to south, in the eastern half of the present ocean; the certainty of the occurrence of immense depressions when islands and even continents have disappeared; the certainty that some of these depressions date as from yesterday, are of Quaternary age, and that consequently they might have been seen by man; the certainty that some of them have been sudden, or at least very rapid. See how much there is to encourage those who still hold out for Plato's narrative. Geologically speaking, the Platonian history of Atlantis is highly probable."[83]

"In view of these facts, so familiar to any student of geology," says Short, "it is not difficult to conceive of the former existence of Atlantis where the *Dolphin* and *Challenger* locate the mid-Atlantic ridge, described as 1000 miles in width in the latitude of the Azores. Supposing the existence of an Atlantic continent in the Tertiary period conceded, we have no means at present of determining the approximate time of its subsidence, unless we associate it with the dim and uncertain legends of the Egyptian priests and the ancient Americans. Whether the Atlantidae who threatened to overthrow the earliest Greek and Egyptian states, but who were swallowed up by the seas in the engulfment of their island continent, were the inhabitants of the *Dolphin* and *Challenger* ridges and the colonists of Eastern America, must for the present at least remain in doubt, though strong probabilities point to the conclusion that they were."[84]

"Montesino tells us that at some time near the date of the Deluge, in other words, in the highest antiquity, America was invaded by a people with four leaders, named Ayar-mancotopa, Ayar-chaki, Ayar-aucca, and Ayar-uyssu. 'Ayar,' says Señor Lopez, 'is the Sanscrit *Ajar*, or *aje*, and means primitive chief; and *manco*, *chaki*, *aucca*, and *uyssu*, mean believers, wanderers, soldiers, husbandmen. We have here a tradition of castes like that preserved in the four tribal names of Athens.' The laboring class (naturally enough in a new colony) obtained the supremacy, and its leader was named Pirhua-manco, revealer of *Pir*, light ($\pi\tilde{\upsilon}\rho$, Umbrian *pir*). Do the laws which control the changes

---

[83]Report of Smithsonian Institution, 1915, p. 231, Termier's *Atlantis*.
[84]"*North Americans of Antiquity*," p. 505.

of language, by which a labial succeeds a labial, indicate that
the Mero or Merou of Theopompus, the name of Atlantis, was
carried by the colonists of Atlantis to South America (as the
name of old York was transplanted in a later age to New York),
and became in time Pérou or Peru? Was not the Nubian 'Island
of Merou,' with its pyramids built by 'red men,' a similar trans-
plantation? And when the Hindoo priest points to his sacred
emblem with five projecting points upon it, and tells us that
they typify 'Mero and the four quarters of the world,' does he
not refer to Atlantis and its ancient universal empire?"[85]

"All the traditions of Central America and Mexico," says Donnelly, "point to some country in the East, and beyond the sea,
as the source of their first civilized people; and this region, known
among them as 'Aztlan,' lived in the memory of the people as a
beautiful and happy land, where their ancestors had dwelt in
peace for many generations."[86]

"The tradition of Votan, the founder of the Maya culture,
though somewhat warped, probably by having passed through
priestly hands, is nevertheless one of the most valuable pieces
of information which we have concerning the ancient Americans.
Without it our knowledge of the origin of the Mayas would
be a hopeless blank, and the ruins of Palenque would be more
a mystery than ever. According to this tradition, Votan came
from the East, from Valum Chivim, by the way of Valum Votan,
from across the sea, by divine command, to apportion the land
of the new continent to seven families which he brought with
him. It appears that he had been preceded in America by two
others named Igh and Imox, if the researches of the Abbé Brasseur de Bourbourg can be relied upon. In the Tzendal calendar,
Votan's name appears as that of the third day, while Igh and
Imox are the first and second respectively. If, as is supposed,
the names represent the true succession of the Maya chiefs, there
is some ground for the Abbé's view. The doubtful portions of the
tradition which may be interpolations are the ambiguous assertions that he saw the Tower of Babel, and was present at the

---

[85]Ignatius Donnelly's "*Atlantis: the Antediluvian World*," p.
391, Harper & Brothers.
[86]Ibid., p. 348.

building of Solomon's temple. Probably the remains only of the former structure may be referred to."[87]

"While some of the details of the Votanic tradition are not worthy of a moment's consideration, it is quite certain that in the general facts we have a key to the origin of what all Americanists agree in pronouncing the oldest civilization on this continent, one which was gray and already declining when the Toltecs entered Mexico."[88]

The culture hero known among the Mexicans as Quetzalcoatl, the "plumed serpent," was named Gucumatz among the Quichés and Cukulcan among the Mayas; and to him was attributed the introduction of agriculture, the arts, etc. "From the distant East, from the fabulous Hue hue Tlapalan, this mysterious personage came to Tulla, and became the patron god and high-priest of the ancestors of the Toltecs. He is described as having been a white man, with a strong formation of body, broad forehead, large eyes, and flowing beard" . . He "was skilled in many arts, having invented gem-cutting and metal-casting. He furthermore originated letters and invented the Mexican calendar."[89]

"The hypothesis that the Nahua religion may have received some of its characteristics from India is altogether plausible and not without support in resemblances. The cosmological conception of the egg and serpent is found, as previously stated, on Brush Creek, in Adams County, Ohio. It certainly comes to us from Asiatic India. Serpent worship, not only among the people of the mounds but especially in Mexico, is the most patent fact revealed to us in ancient American sculpture. 'Humbolt thinks he sees in the snake cut in pieces, the famous serpent Kaliya or Kalinaga, conquered by Vishnu, when he took the form of Krishna, and in the Mexican Touatiuh, the Hindu Krushna, sung of in the Bhagavata-Purana.' Count Stolberg and Tschudi have both made arguments in favor of this view. Humbolt characterizes Quetzalcoatl as the Buddha of the Mexicans, the founder of the monastic establishments resembling those of Thibet and Western Asia. He further considers the flood of which they speak, identical with that of which traditions are preserved by the Hindoos, the Chinese, and the Shemitic peoples."[90]

---

[87]"*North Americans of Antiquity*," pp. 204-5.
[88]Ibid., p. 210.
[89]Ibid., pp. 267-8.
[90]Ibid., pp. 465-6.

The legends of the Mexicans and Central Americans in connection with the Deluge are declared by those who have investi-
gated to bear a much closer resemblance to the Deluge of the
Bible and that of the Chaldeans than is the case with the other
Old World traditions, and this, even though the Mongoloid Asiatics or peoples of Siberia, with whom the Americans are classed,
possess no traditions in regard to the matter.

"The most important among the American traditions," says
Alfred Maury, "are the Mexican, for they appear to have been
definitively fixed by symbolic and mnemonic paintings before any
contact with Europeans. According to these documents, the Noah
of the Mexican cataclysm was Coxcox, called by certain peoples
Teocipactli or Tezpi. He had saved himself, together with his
wife Xochiquetzal, in a bark, or, according to other traditions,
on a raft made of cypress-wood (*Cupressus disticha*). Paintings
retracing the deluge of Coxcox have been discovered among the
Aztecs, Miztecs, Zapotecs, Tlascaltecs, and Mechoacaneses."[91]

These traditions are not all the same. In one, a man and his
wife only are saved; in another, a man, his wife, and several
animals are saved and birds are sent out from the bark, which
is finally left on the mountain of Colhuacan. The story of the
Deluge from the "Popul Vuh," the Sacred Book of the Central
Americans, not only refers to a flood by water, but plainly includes
in the great cataclysmic event a seismic disturbance with the
accompanying fires of volcanic eruptions. Even among the uncivilized tribes the legend of the Deluge persists, and in the case
of the Mandan Indians there is preserved an image or representation of a vessel called by them the "Big Canoe" (the ark of
the ancient Jews) around which are centered certain religious
services in remembrance of the Flood. These legends are numerous, and, even among the uncivilized tribes in many instances,
point to an island in the East, or toward the sunrise as the
place of their origin.

"One of the most ancient races of Central America is the Chiapenec, a branch of the Mayas. They claim to be the first settlers
of the country. They came, their legends tell us, from the East,
from beyond the sea."[92]

---

[91]Ignatius Donnelly's "*Atlantis: the Antediluvian World*," p.
99, Harper & Brothers.
[92]Ibid., p. 234.

Bishop Landa, the first bishop of Yucatan, burnt many of the
Maya books "because they contained nothing in which were not
superstitions and falsities of the devil;" but he wrote a history
of the Mayas which contained a description and explanation of
their alphabet. This manuscript was preserved in the Royal
Academy of History, Madrid, where it was found by a French
priest, Brasseur de Bourbourg, who was enabled by it to decipher
some of the writings of the Mayas.

Donnelly takes a number of hieroglyphic characters representing the Maya alphabet and considers how a less complicated
alphabet might be derived from these by a natural process of
simplification, giving due regard to some marked, central characteristic of each hieroglyph and the manner in which it might
be modified in rapid writing from right to left by a commercial
people, as was the case with the Phoenicians and others. In this
way he traces eighteen of the Maya letters and shows them to
correspond with, in some cases to be identical with, the same
letters in Phoenician, Hebrew, Greek or Egyptian, one or more
of them.

"It would appear," says Donnelly, "as if both the Phoenicians
and Egyptians drew their alphabet from a common source, of
which the Maya is a survival, but did not borrow from one another. They followed out different characteristics in the same
original hieroglyph, as, for instance, in the letter *b*. And yet
I have shown that the closest resemblances exist between the
Maya alphabet and the Egyptian signs—in the *c, h, t, i, k, l, m,
n, o, q,* and *s*—eleven letters in all; in some cases, as in the *n*
and *k*, the signs are identical; the *k*, in both alphabets, is not
only a serpent, but a serpent with a protuberance or convolution
in the middle! If we add to the above the *b* and *u*, referred to
in the 'Proceedings of the American Philosophical Society,' we
have thirteen letters out of sixteen in the Maya and Egyptian
related to each other. Can any theory of accidental coincidences
account for all this? And it must be remembered that these
resemblances are found between *the only two phonetic systems
of alphabet in the world.*"[93]

"Juarros, in speaking of Palenque art, says: 'The hieroglyphics,
symbols and emblems which have been discovered in the temples,

---

[93]Ignatius Donnelly's *"Atlantis: the Antediluvian World,"* p.
232, Harper & Brothers.

bear so strong a resemblance to those of the Egyptians, as to encourage the supposition that a colony of that nation may have
founded the city of Palenque or Culhuacan.' Giordan found, as
he thought, the most striking analogies between the Central
American remains, as well as those of Mexico, and those of the
Egyptians. The idols and monuments he considers of the same
form in both countries, while the hieroglyphics of Palenque do
not differ from those of ancient Thebes. Señor Melgar, in a communication to the Mexican Geographical Society, has called attention to the frequent occurrence of the (T) *tau* at Palenque,
and has more studiously advocated the early relationship of the
Palenqueans to Egypt than any other reliable writer.''[94]

Marion McMurrough Mulhall says: "The following account
of the sinking of Atlantis is taken from Plongeon's translation of
the famous Troano MS., which may be seen in the British Mu-
seum. The Troano MS. appears to have been written about 3500
years ago, among the Mayas of Yucatan, and the following is its
description of the catastrophe that submerged the island of Posei-
donis or Atlantis. 'In the year 6 Kan, on the 11th Mulac in
the month Zac, there occurred terrible earthquakes, which continued without interruption until the 13th Chuen. The country
of the hills of Mud, the land of Mu, was sacrificed; being twice
upheaved it suddenly disappeared during one night, the basin
being continually shaken by volcanic forces. Being confined,
these caused the land to sink and to rise several times and in
various places. At last the surface gave way and ten countries
were torn asunder and scattered; unable to stand the force of
the convulsions, they sank with their 64,000,000 inhabitants'.''[95]

It seems that research, carried on subsequent to the time when
Donnelly wrote, discloses the fact that Bishop Landa's alphabet
did not furnish a complete key for the satisfactory translation
of the few Mayan manuscripts or codices that escaped destruction or for the translation of the carved glyphs upon public edifices and monuments. Lewis Spence says; "Landa's 'alphabet'
was at once hailed by Americanists as the key which would un-
lock the secrets of the Maya writing, the 'Rosetta Stone' of
America. But it was soon found that all attempts to decipher
the glyphs by its agency were only partially successful, and it

---

[94]*"North Americans of Antiquity,"* pp. 415-6.
[95]*"Beginnings or Glimpses of Vanished Civilizations,"* pp. 27-8,
Longmans, Green and Co., London.

has been conjectured that the Indian scribes, who looked upon the bishop as the ruthless destroyer of their ancient records, purposely misled him. At the same time most of the names and symbols for the days and months as furnished by him are known to be correct, as is found by a comparison of them with the glyphs appearing in certain native books known as the Books of Chilan Balam, where they are shown with their phonetic equivalents in European letters."[96]

This, of course, detracts from the full force and effect that might be given otherwise to Le Plongeon's translations; and it may do so somewhat in the case of Donnelly's deductions from Landa's alphabet in his comparisons with certain phonetic characters in the Egyptian and other alphabets, but it does not destroy the probative effect of his alphabetic deductions.

Spence not only ably supports the former existence of Atlantis as a physical fact, but, by many cumulative facts and logical deductions, urges that it was the source from which came the civilizations of Europe and America. He maintains, however, that the American civilizations could not have begun, as a result of Atlantean immigration, at an earlier date than the 1st century before the Christian Era, and, seemingly, without good and sufficient reasons. It seems to be reasonably well established that the Nahuas, or Mound-builders, entered Mexico about this time from the Mississippi Valley; and, assuming them to have been of Atlantean origin, Spence apparently overlooks their long occupancy of the valley prior to this migratory movement, and he also overlooks the undoubtedly older Mayan civilization. In support of his statement he suggests that during the gradual disintegration of Atlantis there was a period during which the former continental area was represented by two major islands; one, Atlantis, in the eastern part of the Atlantic in the vicinity of the Azores; the other, Antilia, in the western part of the ocean in the general location of the Antilles which are the remnants of this latter island. He further advances the suggestion that Atlantis was sunk by a cataclysm of nature far anterior to the engulfing of Antilia.

The civilization of ancient Egypt is so strikingly similar to that found in Central America and Peru that it seems inconsist-

---

[96]"*The Problem of Atlantis*," p. 127, by Lewis Spence, published by Rider & Co., London.

ent and highly improbable, if they came from a common source, that one should have arisen thousands of years before the Christian Era and the other but one century before, at which latter time the former civilization had long since been in decay. It seems but reasonable to assume the Egyptian and American civilizations began at or near the same period of time, and that the latter, upon isolation resulting from submergence of the homeland, was spent in amalgamation with the surrounding tribes. It is worthy of note that an elevation in the ocean beds of no great magnitude, when we consider cataclysmic disturbances that have visited the earth, would not only resurrect Atlantis, but make a land connection between Easter Island, on the one hand, and northern Peru and Central America, on the other.

Spence also assumes that the Cro-Magnons and the Azilian-Tardenoisian stock which he seems to regard as synonymous with Iberians were all members of the white race and Atlanteans.

In so far as I have been able to learn the Cro-Magnons are regarded by the authorities as distinctly Asiatic—that is Mongoloid or Turanian. If we are to look for present day descendants of the Cro-Magnon, it would seem that physically he survives in the Manchus and culturally in the Esquimaux. Madison Grant says, referring to the Cro-Magnon, "It has been suggested that, following the fading ice edge north and eastward through Asia into North America, they became the ancestors of the Esquimaux but certain anatomical objections are fatal to this interesting theory. No one, however, who is familiar with the culture of the Esquimaux and especially with their wonderful skill in bone and ivory carving, can fail to be struck with the similarity of their technique to that of the Cro-Magnons."[97]

One authority considers the Iberians as belonging to the Mongoloid family and that they are represented this day by the Basques and some other remnants, another regards them as belonging to the Mediterranean family of the white race in accordance with the classification adopted by many recent writers. Thus we may accept either until further research, if ever, reduces the matter to a reasonable certainty. A number of investigators have hesitated to include certain Turanian peoples, who closely approximate the white family, among the Mongoloids.

---

[97]"*The Passing of the Great Race*," p. 112, Charles Scribner's Sons.

If it be conceded that Atlantis was the home of the white race, there should be nothing remarkable in finding a mixture of Mongoloid and white surviving in the Canary Islands, nor any justification in concluding this mixture represented an Atlantean type. The principal physical connection of the Canary Islands with other land during the period since man existed must have been with the adjacent shores of Africa long prior to the time when the Negro had reached this region from the eastern part of the continent or Lemuria. It would be natural, therefore, to look for a type in the Canaries that resulted from a mixture of the white Atlantean and the Mongoloid or Turanian of northwest Africa.

Some of the matters mentioned in the preceding chapter and some of the authorities there quoted, bear directly or indirectly on the former existence of Atlantis as a civilized empire with extensive domains. The history of Peru, the traditions of its people, and philology, all point to the fact that its civilization was due to an invading, colonizing people, who conquered the country; and there are many indications that this period reached much further back into antiquity than any incident of which we have any knowledge in connection with ancient Egypt. Referring to the roads of Peru, Donnelly says: "These roads were ancient in the time of the Incas. They were the work of the white, auburn-haired, bearded men from Atlantis, thousands of years before the time of the Incas. When Huayna Capac marched his army over the main road to invade Quito, it was so old and decayed 'that he found great difficulties in the passage,' and he immediately ordered the necessary reconstructions."[98]

When the Spaniards conquered Peru they found a people far advanced in civilization. There was an organized government with its administration of justice; a priesthood in control of religious matters; public works administered by public authority; an extensive development of posts operated over an elaborate system of highways that rivalled in construction and extent any ever built by man, if it did not excell all. But on every hand was found abundant evidence of a former, greater, grander civilization that had long since been in process of decay. Such were the ruins found at Tiahuanaca,, at Gran-Chimu, the capital of the Chimus of Northern Peru, around Lake Titicaca, at Cuelap,

---

[98]"*Atlantis: the Antediluvian World*," p. 394, Harper & Brothers.

in Northern Peru, and at or near Huamanga. Vast structures of hewn stone in the form of temples, palaces, walls, and other works, were found in an advanced stage of decay and ruin; and they were of such character that they could have been neither initiated by nor carried to successful completion by the civilization then found in Peru. The roads were from 1500 to 2000 miles long, from twenty to twenty-five feet wide, and were paved with a mixture of lime, pulverized stone and bituminous cement. They were cut through solid rock in many places; ravines that were crossed were filled with masonry; and suspension bridges were in use ages before their introduction in Europe. At intervals along the roads were taverns, and a system of posts was maintained for the rapid transmission of despatches in the same manner as was done by the Persians and Romans. Aqueducts of hewn stone were constructed, one, 450 miles in length, across mountain ranges and rivers. These stupendous works were beyond the abilities of the Incas found in Peru by the Spaniards, or the Spaniards themselves. Thus, it appears conclusive that, however advanced the civilization of the Incas may have been, it was but the decadent display in reflection of a former, greater, creative age that had long since passed.

When we attempt to analyze the events indicated by facts that have been stated, and particularly those given in the preceding chapter in relation to the Quichua and Aimara languages, we find something like this: There appears upon the scene somewhere in the highlands of Peru a people at a time so remote that the language they speak is the most primitive form of Aryan speech known to man. This indicates the remotest period of antiquity to which any incident fact connected with the White race has been traced; and that it relates to the white man is supported by native traditions which point to a white, bearded race as the founders of this civilization and builders of its great works, and by the mummified remains found of these ancient builders. It is manifest that the later-day successors of the ancient white founders of this civilization—the Incas—were not only unable to initiate and carry through undertakings of the character wrought by the founders of the civilization, but they were likewise unable to prevent the decay of the civilization to which they had fallen heir.

If we concede the Atlantis of Plato was not apochryphal but represented an Atlantic country in which the progenitors of our race developed a great and powerful civilization with colonies in Europe, North Africa and the two Americas before it was finally overwhelmed by the Atlantic, the conditions with which we are confronted in Peru yield more readily to explanation. The following is ventured as a fuller visualization of events leading to the Peru of the Spanish Conquest:

At a very remote period in their movements from their island home, the Atlanteans found themselves, either by way of the Amazon or the north coast of South America, possibly both, in the table-lands of Peru. Here they began their work of building and of subduing the uncivilized people with whom they came in contact, keeping in communication with the home government and the colonies in Mexico through commerce and because of the influence of social and governmental ties. When they had arrived in sufficient numbers to enable them to get well started along the lines of progressive improvement, they found themselves more fortunately situated with respect to progress and ease of defense than the European colonies of Atlantis or even Mexico. In Europe the colonies of Atlantis were more or less always on the defensive from the continuous migrations and incursions of a constantly moving alien population or from other colonies, whereas the Peruvian colonies enjoyed comparative safety in the fastness of their table-lands from any incursions by the unorganized, uncivilized tribes that may have surrounded them. Furthermore, any prehistoric movements across the South Pacific that may have been responsible in any degree for the population of South America (the efficacy of which for this purpose, I seriously doubt) had long since ceased, in all probability, and the condition of the natives surrounding the Peruvian empire had been for ages much as they were found to be by the Spaniards. In this condition the advance made by the Peruvian colony was undoubtedly rapid. The colonists conquered, civilized, and utilized the natives in all their undertakings public and private. Unquestionably an admixture of blood began at once and continued to grow with the passage of time. This probably did not greatly affect the dominating, ruling element as long as communication with the home government of Atlantis was maintained.

The peaceful rapid progress of these colonists in their specially favored new home was, however, rudely dislocated and forever put an end to by the fearful cataclysm that wiped out the mother

country in one day, or some cataclysm of great magnitude that
resulted in the isolation of Peru from the mother country and
the sinking of a former land area in the Pacific extending as far
as Easter Island long prior to the final catastrophe. This must
have occurred at an early date because of the stage of the development of the language as found by Dr. Falb and Señor Lopez.
Upon the happening of either of these events, the incident demoralization and the resultant paralysis of all initiative could not
have been otherwise than of such magnitude that the people must
have been left for a long time in a helpless state of inactivity and
torpidity of mind. Fear of the future and interest in individual
safety must have been for long the dominating sentiments in all
minds. In this isolation, cut off from people of their own blood
and with all incentive to struggle onward and upward along the
path of progress gone forever, time witnessed the diffusion of
this white blood into that of the natives, the disappearance altogether of the pure white type, and the decay of the civilization
that held such magnificent promise in its early stages. The
natives found in Peru on discovery by the Spanish showed, by
comparison with other tribes on the continent, a large admixture
of white blood. The whites had left behind them to these natives a light complexion, a superior language, an enlightening,
civilizing influence, and a material civilization; but this was not
sufficient to enable the mixed-bloods to stem the tide of decay.
This is but another example of a superior people disappearing
from the face of the earth to the loss of mankind in general
through the process of miscegenation. How many instances of
this character does history record? The conditions in the table-
lands of Peru must have been favorable to the civilization that
sprung up and flourished for a time with the Aryan settlers in
this land. We know of no change in these conditions rendering
the surroundings prohibitive of its continuance. We should,
therefore, naturally look for the eventual recovery of these people from the shock of the great cataclysm and a resumption of
the march of progress by them. That this never occurred can
be explained only by the submergence of the white Atlanteans
in amalgamation with the surrounding peoples.

On examination into the ancient civilization of Mexico and
Central America, we are confronted with a situation very similar
to that found to exist in the case of Peru. When Cortez appeared upon the scene the Spaniards found that, while there

was in existence an advanced civilization, there was an abundance of ruins and records and traditions evidencing the existence of a former and much older civilization that had long since been in process of decay, although there was presented to the world a people far advanced in government and the useful and decorative arts usually found as the accompaniment of civilization. Among these people there was, however, a more markedly emphatic record of the fact that their civilized forbears were of a bearded white race that came from the East—from "Aztlan"—than was the case in Peru.

As stated above, the civilization found by Cortez in Mexico, while marked, was distinctly of a more recent origin than the Mayan civilization of Central America. Since that time there has been diffused into the body of the Mexican people a considerable quantity of white blood, but even with this leavening influence the present day people of Mexico are utterly incapable of undertaking such works as were carried through during the ancient civilization. This indicates, as was the case with Peru, that the white blood of the ancient civilization lost in a diffusion with that of the surrounding natives was a sacrifice which did not leave the resulting people in a condition that enabled them to carry on where the old left off.

The Mexicans seem to have gone further in the development of language than did the Peruvians; for, in accordance with Donnelly, "The Aztecs, like the Egyptians, had progressed through all the three different modes of writing—the picture-writing, the symbolical, and the phonetic. They recorded all their laws, their tribute-rolls specifying the various imposts, their mythology, astronomical calendars, and rituals, their political annals and their chronology. They wrote on cotton-cloth, on skins prepared like parchment, on a composition of silk and gum, and on a species of paper, soft and beautiful, made from the aloe. Their books were about the size and shape of our own, but the leaves were long strips folded together in many folds."[99]

"In addition to these stone and stucco records," says Short, "the Mayas had books, which Bishop Landa describes as written on a large leaf doubled in folds and enclosed between two boards which they ornamented; they wrote on both sides of the paper,

---

[99]"*Atlantis: the Antediluvian World*," p. 352, Harper & Brothers.

in columns accommodated to the folds; the paper they made from the roots of trees, and coated it with a white varinish on which one could write well. These books were called *Analtees,* a word which, according to Villagutierre, signifies the same as history. Bishop Landa confesses to having burned a great number of the Maya books because they contained nothing in which were not superstitions and falsities of the devil. Bancroft has quoted from Peter Martyr a description of these books, which conveys the additional information that they were written on many leaves joined together but folded so that when opened two pages are presented to view."[100]

It seems impossible that a people with the genius to build the great structures, the ruins of which cover twenty square miles at Gran-Chimu, Peru, and include "vast areas shut in by massive walls, each containing its water-tank, its shops, municipal edifices, and the dwellings of its inhabitants, and each a branch of a larger organization; prisons, furnaces for smelting metals, and almost every concomitant of civilization"[101]—it seems impossible that a people of this genius in the Empire of Peru should fail to keep in communication with a people endowed with a similar genius located on the table-lands of Central America and Mexico. Nevertheless it appears that when the Spaniard reached America neither of these people had any knowledge of the other. The fact is they were not the same people in either case as the original founders of the respective empires. Judging from the primitive form in which the Quichua and Aimara languages were found, and from the further fact that in Central America the evolutionary process in the development of language had proceeded to the point of phonetic writing, it would seem that the former colonists from Atlantis had come in lesser numbers than the latter and their isolation from the mother country and the rest of the world brought about at a much earlier period. The smaller number in Peru were in time absorbed by the indigenous peoples, and in their new found isolation these people, lacking in the genius of the founders of the civilization, not only failed to make evolutionary progress but gradually declined from a position of former splendor to the inferior civilized condition in which they were found on the rediscovery of America.

---

[100]*"North Americans of Antiquity,"* pp. 420-1.
[101]Ignatius Donnelly's *"Atlantis: the Antediluvian World,"* p. 393, Harper & Brothers.

As the American coast lines now stand, and under present climatic conditions, intimate intercourse between the Island Empire of Atlantis and the Central American coast would have been far more probable, with the best means that could be supposed available to Atlantean navigators, than would communication with Peru by way of the Amazon. However, the best considered scientific thought on the subject bears testimony to the existence in remote antiquity of a land connection between Atlantis and South America, there being now a ridge running from the supposed position of Atlantis toward the mouth of the Amazon.

It does not appear unreasonable, and it would account for the difference in development of language and other differences found to exist between Mexico and Peru, that a great convulsion which sank this connecting ridge with Atlantis, and possibly also severed Peru's connection with Easter Island, at a much earlier period than the greater convulsion which destroyed Atlantis itself, if it were greater, brought about the earlier isolation of Peru as compared with that of Mexico. The latter came with the sinking of Atlantis, and from that time on the gradual absorption of the white blood by the native element led to the inevitable, as it seems, decline of the civilization that had blossomed in Mexico. The earlier ravages of Atlantis by cataclysmal nature before its final disappearance probably hastened emigration to Mexico and its European colonists. This accounts for the advance made by Mexico, as compared with Peru whose means of communication were now limited to that with Mexico by way of Ecuador and Columbia, a difficult path of communication for a sorely stricken people unless there were urgent appeals arising from self interest or a community of interest. Under these conditions Peru to the south may well have been forgotten by a Mexico that made progress for centuries afterward.

Within the historic period the Americas have been isolated from the rest of the world—the Old World as it is called; and when rediscovered two outstanding civilizations were found to exist in them, one in Mexico and Central America, the other in Peru. These two civilizations had for ages been free from and unaffected by any race movements such as occurred in the Old World. The oceans formed an impassable barrier and limited any movement into these continents to that small trickle of humanity which might percolate through the Aleutian Islands or across Bering Strait; and we must conclude that any movement

of this kind could not, either in numbers or character of the
people involved, reach the magnitude of a menace to any civilized people established in Mexico or Peru. We must also believe
that the civilizations mentioned could not have been threatened
in any degree by the surrounding Hunting Tribes in the capacity
of an enemy at war. The civilizations mentioned were too far
advanced in the arts of war and too well organized to suffer from
any aggression on the part of the unorganized, surrounding tribes.
We should, therefore, be justified in our expectation that two
civilizations placed as were those of Mexico and Peru would
endure for ages, unless the people who founded them *voluntarily
effaced themselves through the process of amalgamation with the
surrounding indigenous people.* Otherwise the isolation enjoyed
by these people, who were freed from the aggressions of any other
warlike, civilized people, afforded them unlimited opportunities for
advancement in civilization and expansion.

In the meantime and throughout the same period, the civilized people who found themselves located on the shores of the
Mediterranean and in the southwest corner of Asia were in a
constant state of turmoil. This section resembled a human bee-
hive in which races and tribes, including the aggressive members
of the Turanian family, were constantly on the move, engaging
in wars of conquest, or fleeing from a conquering foe to avoid
the status of slavery. From time to time a semblance of law
and order was preserved through the supremacy of some particular people; but, on the whole, the opportunity for the development of a civilization under the ideal conditions of peace
and security in a chosen position, such as was enjoyed by the
American civilizations, did not exist in this region. The conditions in Egypt most closely approximated those in America in
this respect.

If we concede the Empire of Atlantis did exist; that in this
land our progenitors evolved a high civilization and became a
powerful people with colonies around the Mediterranean Sea and
in the Americas; and that this empire was swallowed up in a
great convulsion of nature—if we admit this, must we not, under
the circumstances given above, look to the colonies in America
which enjoyed isolation and peace, rather than to the tumultuous
colonies of the Mediterranean area, for light upon the ancient
peoples of Atlantis? This seems logical and its correctness is
certainly borne out partially by facts disclosed in America, as

would doubtless have been the case to a far greater degree had not the Atlantean founders of the American civilization permitted themselves, after severance from the fatherland, to be engulfed in the inferior blood of the surrounding natives. Certainly what evidence America gives pointing toward Atlantis should be allowed the greatest weight, if not deemed conclusive, as to the points covered.

Some of the outstanding points presented and requiring the existence of Atlantis for their harmonization with other facts are these:

The discovery of the most ancient or archaic form of Aryan speech in that of the Peruvians—the Quichua and Aimara languages—is a leading one. It seems impossible to accept the suggestion of Dr. Falb in respect to this, "that the high plains of Peru and Bolivia must be regarded as the point of exit of the present human race." It seems contrary to reason that the most virile, aggressive, and progressive members of the human race— the Aryan, or proto-Aryan, if you like,—could have had their origin or point of dispersion at this particular spot in the world and not have left a more lasting and durable evidence of this in numerous pure descendants upon the continent. The simple explanation that renders this otherwise abnormal circumstance, which is nevertheless a fact of the utmost importance, consistent with other known facts, is that formerly suggested: That the ancient Peruvians were white colonists from Atlantis; that they did not come in such numbers as enabeld them to dispense with the services of the indigenous population; that they imposed their language on this population, civilized them, and employed them in their works, either as slaves or laborers; that an early convulsion of nature cut them off from Atlantis and sunk a large part of the empire connecting Peru with Easter Island; and that before their language had developed beyond the primitive stage in which it was found into a higher form of complex speech, the blood of the ancient conquerors had become so diluted by native blood that this archaic language and a decaying civilization were passed on to the time when America was rediscovered.

The written and oral traditions and the monuments of the civilized Americans that bear upon the subject give evidence to the effect that the founders of these civilizations came from the East, over the sea; and all have legends of the flood in which one or more persons escaped the disaster, which legend, if it exists among the Asiatic Mongoloids, is an imported one. These legends pointing to the East as the place of the disaster, together with those of the Europeans in regard to the same matter, could have arisen only upon the occurrence of some such event as the engulfing of Atlantis.

The marked similarity, and in some cases identity, of words in languages on both sides of the Atlantic, and the sameness of the geographical names in Asia Minor and Central America, can be explained only by conceding it to be a fact that Atlantis existed as stated in the historical account given by Plato 400 B. C.; and what has been shown in regard to the alphabets in the eastern Mediterranean section and Central America can only be explained in the same way.

That whites were in America long before the historic period and were the originators of the ancient civilizations found therein cannot be seriously doubted; and the most reasonable explanation of their appearance, if not the only one, is that they originated in Atlantis. The connection of the Scandinavians and the Irish with America prior to the discovery by Columbus cannot assume a greater importance than would attach to an accidental contact or an occasional trading expedition. No one will seriously advance the opinion that the white blood found in America could be attributed to these sources. Among the civilized peoples the evidence of white blood was manifested in the ruling classes to the last; that among the Hunting Tribes seems evidently due to bands of whites becoming separated from the civilized people or those who escaped from Atlantis when it was swallowed up.

In spite of the fact that the Mediterranean area has been the scene of struggles by so many people, much evidence is here found, aside from that given by Plato, pointing to the existence of an Atlantis. In the mythology of the ancient peoples in this area there is an identity of many of their gods, and these are referred by Donnelly for their origin to the ancient rulers of Atlantis. His conclusions in this are ably supported by reference to the legends and myths of these people, all of which points to the West—to Atlantis. But no comment will be made in regard to evidence of the existence of Atlantis obtained from European or Old World sources other than a reference to India and to the Bronze Age.

The implements of the Bronze Age are, it seems, readily distinguishable from certain so-called bronze implements (Roman and others) which contain lead, the former being an alloy of tin and copper. These implements, indisputably of the Bronze Age, are found distributed in far greater numbers in the British Isles, Denmark, and the west coast of Europe generally, than in the Mediterranean in which the further east one goes the less the number found. This indicates that the west coast of Europe was nearer the source of supply which was necessarily, therefore, to the West. Naturally an Age of Copper should intervene between the Polished Stone Age and the Bronze Age. In and around Lake Superior were found copper mines that had been worked for ages when Columbus discovered America, and in America alone, it seems, is there found evidence of a Copper Age. From this the conclusion follows that Atlanteans worked the copper mines of Superior; that they first made implements of copper and subsequently developed bronze, which, as a commercial people, they carried to all the world.

"Although it is evident that many thousands of years must have passed since the men who wrote in Sanscrit, in Northwestern India, could have dwelt in Europe, yet to this day they preserve among their ancient books maps and descriptions of the western coast of Europe, and even of England and Ireland; and we find among them a fuller knowledge of the vexed question of the sources of the Nile than was possessed by any nation in the world twenty-five years ago."[102]

In India 2000 years before the Christian Era an Aryan people were in control; they possessed an alphabet, a language rich in expression and kept records. There is to be found among these records maps and descriptions of the west coast of Europe, including the British Isles, although these people have been heretofore almost universally conceded to have had their primitive home in the table-lands of Persia and were not a seafaring people. At the same time there was across the Atlantic, in the isolation of Peru, another people who had engaged in structural works of such magnitude that in some respects they excelled even those of Egypt, and these people were using a form of Aryan speech the most

---

[102]Ignatius Donnelly's "*Atlantis: the Antediluvian World*," p. 211, Harper & Brothers.

primitive known to man—all of which was shown by evidence brought to light 3500 years afterward.[103]

We find that the people in Egypt in remote antiquity used a pictorial form of writing — hieroglyphics, primitive writings of the character from which are derived phonetic alphabets. On the other side of the Atlantic we find in Central America, in remote antiquity, a people who engaged in structural works of the general character and magnitude of those peculiar to Egypt. We find one branch of these people using a tongue declared to be to a large extent that of the Greeks, another using a language closely akin to that employed by the Semitic peoples; and among these people is found an alphabet in a transitional form between the hieroglyph and a simple sign representing a sound, and from which can easily be derived a number of letters used by the races in the Mediterranean.

The monogenist argues that the human race must have arisen from a primitive type that was brought about by evolution at some one particular spot on the face of the earth; and, having studied the flora and fauna surrounding the Indian Ocean and having plotted its depths, he demands in the name of geology, biology, archaeology, philology, paleontology, etc., that the long-buried continent of Lemuria arise from the depths of the Indian Ocean. One black stem from this primitive home is pointed toward Upper India and from this stem is derived the Dravidians, a Brown people, and from this stem branches one that becomes the ancestor of all Mongoloids. Further along comes another branch from which the White race is derived. This detritus of whites is thrown off at some indefinite point in Southwest Asia. The unsatisfactory part of this seems to be that while prehistoric (by this is meant Stone Age) relics of Mongoloids are here found in abundance there are none found of the White race.

The plant life and animal life on both sides of the Atlantic, present and prehistoric, make the same demand upon the scientific mind for a land connection across the Atlantic, as is made for a connecting continent in the Indian Ocean. The difference between the two cases lies principally in this: The existence of Atlantis is not only demanded by scientific considerations, but is called for by the history and traditions of the White race, whereas

---

[103] If the Peruvians were Aryans speaking the primitive tongue, it cannot be conceived they entered Peru at a later date than their kindred were found to be in India.

there is not the slightest whisper of a tradition in any of the races that points to Lemuria. Of course it is realized fully that as we go back into antiquity we must reach some point, if evolution means anything, beyond which even tradition must cease. But why is Lemuria given such place of honor in the scientific mind and Atlantis persistently denied a hearing, when the speech and works of the White race had bridged the Atlantic for ages before the true historic period began?   One reason seems to be, that the admission of the existence of Atlantis might prove to be a severe blow to the monogenist. If Atlantis is conceded to be the home in which the White race developed its civilization, it would seem to go far toward fortifying the position of the polygenist as opposed to the monogenist; and certainly this concession would render simple of explanation many things that remain a mystery. The colonization of the Americas from this Island Empire would be a simple matter, as would also that of the eastern Mediterranean section. In this connection it does seem strange, however, that Spain should have been overlooked as a point for early settlement, but many reasons may have operated to bring this about. The Spanish peninsula with its gloomy and forbidding mountains may have been strongly occupied by a Mongoloid people, and, its coast lacking in harbors, the appeal of the eastern Mediterranean with its better climate and its multitude of harbors and its strategic, commercial position may have proved irresistible.[104]   A great catastrophe which wiped out the land connection of Atlantis with South America seems to be the only reasonable explanation of the early isolation of the Peruvian colony, and this may have resulted in considerable changes in the continent of Europe itself at the other end of the area considered.   As things now stand an elevation of the British Isles and the area immediately around to the extent of 600 feet would wipe out the Baltic Sea, the North Sea and the English Channel,

----

[104]Since writing the above there has appeared *"The Search for Atlantis"* by Edwin Bjorkman, published by Alfred A. Knopft. The author identifies Scheria, the farthest point reached by Ulysses in the Odyssey, with the Old Testament Tarshish and the later Greek Tartessos and with Atlantis, and locates this multi-named region in the vicinity of Cadiz, Spain, where have been found ancient ruins and where the racial characteristics of the people differ quite perceptibly from those of the Peninsula at large. It seems to me that, instead of identifying Atlantis, he has pointed out a colony of Atlantis in Spain,

and would result in a considerable projection of land into the Atlantic beyond Ireland to the westward.

Our scientists and those engaged in research work pertaining to man on earth should contribute toward a cyclopaedic work that would inculde all facts collected from time to time, together with critical well considered conclusions arrived at with reasons therefor, in order that the layman might appreciate, understand, and intelligently form opinions for himself. As it is, there is much duplication, uncertainty and contrariety in opinion, often based upon unlike premises, and altogether too much dogma. What is needed is not the dogmatic statement that this or that is a biological law, but the reasons for concluding that this or that opinion may be accepted as having the force of law in the light of all circumstances.

CHAPTER V.

THE MONOGENETIC THEORY OF CREATION.

Just as popular evolution, enigmatically, belittles race distinction and operates as a leveling influence where an elevating, ennobling influence is the crying need, so, in its turn, does the Christian religion in its practical effects often attain the same end. The proselyting Arab of Mohammedan faith readily makes converts among the blacks of Africa; for, when the black is received into his sect, he is accepted into the family as well and the daughter, if desired, is given in marriage. The Christian church seems now to accept fully the doctrine that the Bible teaches the descent of all mankind from Adam or Noah, and some of them are willing to go just as far as the Mohammedan Arab goes in Africa. However, the church in the South and, doubtless, most of them in the North, while extending the right hand of fellowship to the Negro, disclaim all intention of sympathy with any movement that has for its object social equality and eventual amalgamation of the races. But, whatever the intention may be on the part of the church, it unwittingly lends itself to the breaking down of the barriers, and the goal of the Negroes—social equality and amalgamation—moves on apace.

South Africa shows the pernicious effects of the missionary's teachings of social equality. It seems, when the slave trade began to wane and public sentiment succeeded in abolishing slavery throughout the regions under her influence, there arose in England a sort of self-induced, paranoiac, politico-religious sentiment, having for its object the dramatic presentation to the world of the uplift of the Negro by the Briton. It satisfied a mistaken religious zeal in the missionary element and, seemingly, it was good politics. The tendency was that the English should appear in the van of the Western nations in its enlightened treatment of the backward peoples and efforts toward their uplift. It was doubtless well received by these backward peoples, whatever may have been the view of the colonists who were in direct contact with the problems involved.

The "British missionaries," says Cox, "believing themselves to be the sole custodians of the Gospel, had arrived and begun to marry negroes. The missionaries were founding co-racial schools and forbidding the word 'color' to be used in these schools. Missionaries were parading white and black children upon the streets, causing them to carry banners with the inscription '*ex uno sanguine*' (of one blood). The colony itself fell under the influence of the missionaries. These strange custodians of the Gospel caused to be recalled colonial governors who would not accede to their program of equalizing the Caucasian with the negro. England was seething with 'philanthropy,' a philanthropy which was concerned almost wholly with the blacks, not the whites. In vain did the colonists still residing in Cape Colony call upon the mother country for redress. In vain did English settlers at Grahamstown, newly arrived from England, attempt to explain to the English at home that civilization itself was imperiled."[105]

This policy was responsible for the emigration of the Boers (descendents of Hollanders, Germans, and French Huguenots) from Cape Colony. They sought a new home to avoid race amalgamation and degrading competition with the blacks, and not to establish slavery anew. They did not represent the former slaveholding class in Cape Colony.

Referring to the period after the Boer War (1898-1902) Cox says: "How much the British missionary and Colonial Office have changed since the days of negrophilism! South African civilization lives in a new world of thought and hope. Missionaries have ceased teaching equality of races and have turned their efforts toward bettering the natives' morals and developing them as agriculturists and artisans. But what could be more ironical than the practical results of the teaching of the South African missionaries? The missionary undoubtedly intended to prove himself a benefit to the colony. He did not understand a race question—that it could not be settled as long as the races dwelt together."[106]

"Having seen the fallacy of teaching the negro that he was the equal of the Caucasion, the missionary turned to what he believed to be the real solution of the race problem—he expended

---

[105]"*White America*," p. 212.
[106]Ibid., pp. 219-20.

his energies in teaching the mixbreed and the negro to become efficient agriculturists and skilled artisans, with the result that the
native, with his low standard of living, is able to compete successfully with the white farmer and skilled laborer and drive
these latter lower and lower in the economic scale. Yet it is
upon the whites that civilization depends. Missionary teaching
will make the native more capable of competing with the whites
and forcing these from the country, but it will not and cannot
make the negro less or more than he is racially."[107]

"With the exception of the mongrel province of the Cape of
Good Hope (the province belies its name), the government is in
the hands of the Caucasian. Here negrophilism had done its
work; the future is dark. Cape Colony, the land of the 'tar
brush'; Cape Town the 'coffee-colored capital,' is to be considered
in separate class from Natal, the Free State, and the Transvaal.
The missionary taught the races that they were of one blood.
In Cape Colony it cannot be claimed that the teaching of the
missionary has been without practical result. 'The Gospel according to Exter Hall' has had its perfect work in and about
Cape Town. Surely the mixbreeds of the province of the Cape of
Good Hope are ample testimony to the influence of the ignorant,
negro-loving British missionary, whose chief effect upon the colony was to bring it to irretrievable disaster. When we behold
the results from miscegenation in Latin America and South Africa,
what white American is disturbed by the impotent rantings of
a neurotic negrophilist who condemns the American whites for
holding aloof from the American negro?"[108]

"The election of the Rev. A. C. Garner as Vice Moderator of
the New York State Congregational Conference and the election
of the Rev. H. H. Proctor, as Moderator of the Association of
Congregational Churches in Greater New York, are viewed," says
Mr. Lester A. Walton, "with accustomed complacency by white
members who say the elevation of the two Negro ministers squares
with the denomination's traditional stand on human rights."

"They tell you with pardonable pride that, since emancipation,
the Congregational Church, through the American Missionary
Association, has spent $30,000,000 on Negro education in the
South, which is said to be greater than the combined sum ex-

---

[107]"*White America*," p. 220.
[108]Ibid., pp. 221-2.

pended by all other religious bodies for the same purpose." * * * *
"The Rev. A. C. Garner, pastor of Grace Congregational
Church in Harlem, was put in nomination at Walton, N. Y., for
Vice Moderator by the Rev. Louis H. Johnston, pastor of the
Congregational Church at Patchogue, L. I., said to be a strong-
hold of the Ku Klux Klan." * *

"* * 'A strange cult of Nordicism is now coursing through
America. Its high priest is Lothrop Stoddard. It is significant
that this exaltation and laudation of the Nordic should have
resulted in making Stoddard's book one of the world's best sel-
lers. It is not armaments, but arrogance which threatens a
world war'."

" 'America is trying to lead the world into peace while we are
assuming here in our midst the same attitude of arrogance which
has always bred warriors and therefore war. Here in America
God had established a racial laboratory to try out the question
whether it is possible to bring together on the same streets men
of different colors, of different tongues, without their tearing at
each other's throats. Surely before we can hope to convince
the world that it should accept our leadership into the plains
of peace we must first have worked out a promising basis of
world peace here'."[109]

In so far as this particular church is concerned, no color line
exists. There could not be a more positive and practical demonstration of the fact that the Negro has attained equality, social
and otherwise, with these people. This did not occur just after
the Civil War, but only a few months ago.

Doubtless all churches in the South and most of those in the
North will indignantly deny that the slightest accretion to social
equality and amalgamation can be attributed to their teachings.
Nevertheless, the doctrine of the brotherhood of man is gnawing
at the race barriers and weakening race consciousness in the
whites. Religion appeals to the emotions, and when we accept the
doctrine of the brotherhood of man in the sense that we are descended from a common stock, are of the same blood, are con-

---

[109]Quoted from and article in the New York World for May 30,
1926, by Lester A. Walton and entitled *"Congregational Church
Mother of Negro Schools."* The fourth and fifth paragraphs
quoted from this article purport to express the sentiments of leading Congregationalists and appeared in the article under quotations.

sequently all equal, we emotionally establish a family relation
antagonistic to race distinction—one that will in the end obliterate all race lines. Every contact between the races in the coordination of religious matters dulls the rough edges of racial lines,
and each new occasion for contact, emotionally reinforced by a
false religious concept, wears further, until, in the course of
time, we shall have black Bishops, Moderators, Priests, and others
ministering alike to blacks and whites, if there be any whites
remaining.

"I allow myself," says Winchell, "to pause here briefly, for the
purpose of protesting against the policy of North American
miscegenesis, which has been recommended by high authorities
as an eligible expedient for obviating race-collisions. It is proposed to consolidate the conflicting elements by a systematic
promotion of interfusion of the white and black races. It is
proposed, in short, to cover the continent with a race of Griquas.
The policy is not more shocking to our higher sentiments, nor
more opposed to the native instincts of the human being, than it
is destructive to the welfare of the nation and of humanity. Wendell Phillips, who, if sex did not protect him, would be in danger
of acquiring the title of 'most eloquent platform virago,' has
sent down to posterity the following record: 'Remember this,
the youngest of you, that on the fourth day of July, 1868, you
heard a man say that, in the light of all history, in virtue of
every page he ever read, he was an amalgamationist to the utmost extent. I have no hope for the future, as this country has
no past, but in that sublime mingling of the races which is God's
own method of civilizing and elevating the world.'"[110]

This country has a past. It is as old as its people and reaches
back in remote antiquity to Adam or to the first primordial life
germs from which mankind was evolved. We are the richest in
traditions of any single political entity; and these traditions are
reinforced by historical facts showing that "God's own method
of civilizing and elevating the world," as represented by Wendell
Phillips, is a destructive disintegrant that will dissipate to the
winds any civilization inflicted with it.

"Bishop Gilbert Haven, whose charming personal qualities render it painful to attribute to him similar sentiments (referring to
Wendell Phillips), is recorded to have said: 'We shall live to

---

[110]"*Preadamites*," p. 81.

"see Helen's beauty in a brow of Egypt." We shall say, "What a rich complexion is that brown skin." . . . We shall be attracted to this hue because it is one of God's creations, and a beautiful one too; because it is the favorite hue of the human race; because, chiefly, we have most wickedly loathed and scorned it. . . . This law . . . is the grand undertone of all marriage. It is the Creator's mode of compelling the race to overleap the narrow boundaries of families and tribes, into which blood, so-called, invariably degenerates. . . . Amalgamation is God's word declaring the oneness of man, and ordaining its universal recognition."[111]

"And now Canon Rawlinson has added his name to this cluster of self-appointed conspicuities. 'It seems,' says he, 'that amalgamation is the true remedy (for the presence of Negroes in the United States), and ultimate absorption of the black race into the white, the end to be desired and aimed at.' The reader of Canon Rawlinson's article cannot but remark the inaptness of the examples cited of the harmless, or even beneficial, results of amalgamation. They are not examples of race-mixture, but only of different family stocks of the white race. The commergence of the white and black races in America might promote the advance of the black race, by annihilating it; but what of the interests of the white race, and the civilization which it alone has created? The policy would set back humanity, so far as America is concerned, to the position which it occupied before Adam—before the long struggle of contending forces had eliminated a race capable of science and philosophy, and evolved a civilization to which no other race ever aspired. It would be to hurl back the ethnic pearls selected with long-continued labor and risk, into the all-concealing ocean of humanity."[112]

An examination of the proper sources of information would doubtless disclose, as a fact, that the doctrine of the brotherhood of man, operating through organized religious bodies, has been, since the Negro first appeared in Ameirca, a disturbing, disorganizing influence pointing inevitably toward social equality and eventual amalgamation. The few examples referred to show that the evil results of this situation move on with swift acceleration; and the citing of any more instances would be but a further needless exposure of a discreditable condition.

111*"Preadamites,"* pp. 81-2.
112Ibid., p. 82.

The thought of a special creation by fiat of the Creator seems to be one that the evolutionist, who finds his origin in buried Lemuria, cannot entertain. He denies the Creator and puts the Laws of Nature in His place. To him matter and the laws governing it have existed without beginning and will continue to so exist without end. Often what is described as unthinkable would be more properly described as not understandable. Our limitations are such that matter and laws without beginning or end are as much beyond human conception as are the attributes of a Creator to whom the origin of such things, not understandable in themselves, may be referred. Instinctively we grope beyond the uttermost limits we may be able to reach; and consciously or unconsciously whether we accept the Scriptural account of creation or that of the evolutionist, we are confronted with some point of beginning. In the Scriptural account we are told that in the beginning God created certain things, and that at subsequent times He either created or fashioned certain other things; while, on the other hand, all evolutionists begin with a primordial form of germ life. The latter make no effort to explain the origin of this germ life, or, if they do, they refer it in general terms to the Laws of Nature. If we avoid that intangible, subtle process of deduction or induction by which the monogenist arrives at his theory, we must conclude that inevitably the evolutionist is confronted with a Creator in consonance with the summation of all human experience to the same extent as is he who accepts the Biblical account of creation.

Just as the evolutionist must make his theory conform to human experience and knowledge and in the end admit the Creator; so must he who accepts the Bible do so without reading into it dogmas and creeds that are inconsistent with known facts. Accepting it as a fact beyond question that the Old Testament and the New Testament are both inspired works; that they are based upon the writings of Moses and the Prophets, Christ and his Disciples; we are nevertheless confronted with the fact that the Bible, as we now use it, comes to us through the hands of many men and is a compromise between conflicting originals and translations from several sources. Under such circumstances, it is certainly incumbent on those of us who profess to accept the Bible to avoid man-made creed and dogma at variance with known facts, and confine ourselves to the observance of the great truths, teachings and precepts of undoubted authority that pervade the whole Book.

Man-made doctrines have often proved disastrous to the human race. The gradual perversion of the simple faith of the early Christians into a ritualistic, creed-inflicted organization for the aggrandizement of power, brought about the Reformation, filled the world with hate, and drenched it in Christian blood. The divisions grow, and peace is not yet.

All these hostile camps seem to have accepted the Middle Age conception as to the descent of all mankind from Adam—the bond of a blood brotherhood between all men—and the necessity of and inspiration for the salvation of the heathen. In the practical application of this doctrine of blood brotherhood and regard for the heathen, the Church often neglects the true welfare of our own people to whom alone the Bible was given, and promotes amalgamation and eventual race degeneracy—the destruction of the greatest work of God of which we have any knowledge, a superior civilized people.

In protest against this abominable doctrine of amalgamation under sanction of Christian religion, many devout Christians have been driven to extreme positions in refutation of the bond of brotherhood that destroys. A number of them have written on the subject of the brotherhood of man, as generally accepted by the churches, and claim that it is inconsistent with Adam being the first man, while others hold that the Adamic race was a special creation in which the other races were not included. Some of these put forth ideas and views which will never attain any degree of acceptance, but all of them agree that it is Biblically incorrect to regard Adam or Noah as the father of any but the white peoples of the earth.

One of the most remarkable of these works is that written by the Rev. B. H. Payne under the name "Ariel," entitled, "The Negro: What Is His Ethnological Status?" This was first published by the author in 1867; and a revised and enlarged edition, in which he purported to answer his critics, was published in 1872. Professor Alexander Winchell, LL. D., in his work, "Preadamites," pp. 189-90, refers, in a note, to the Rev. B. H. Payne's work in the following words:—"The opinion cited above (referring to statement in text, 'The opinion has been advanced that the Mongoloids are a mixed or mulatto race descended from Cain and a black wife.') may be found expressed on pp. 105,

107 and elsewhere. That the Canaanites also resulted from a
cross with the Negro is asserted on pp. 106, 113, 126. This is a
curious, even a phenomenal, production, containing much sug-
gestive matter almost inextricably mixed with a mass of mere
rubbish. The work is full of vain repetitions, and its style is exceedingly tedious. The author perpetually wanders from the
point to indulge in reflections mostly of an insulting character
toward those who disagree—especially if 'learned men.' It seems
to be the work of an ignorant, conceited, but strong-minded man,
dogmatic, pragmatic and captious to excess. The following are
some of the positions of the work: (1) That mulattoes run out at
the 'fifth crossing'—pp. 42, 94. (2) That the translation of the
Sacred Scriptures is excessively defective—pp. 97 *et passim*. (3)
That the Hebrew lexicons give meanings of Latin and Greek origin—p. 103. (4) That *'ish'* in the Bible means *negro, 'enosh'* a
mulatto, and *'anshey,'* one three-fourths white—pp. 104, 118, 134.
(5) That the Chinese and Japanese are a third cross with the
Negroes—pp. 105, 107. (6) That the Canaanites of Palestine
are a cross with the Negro—pp. 106, 113, 126. (7) That the
'land of Nod' means 'the land of vagabonds'—p. 109. ((8) That
Cain's son was Enosh and not Enoch—p. 111. . (9) That the
Negro can amalgamate with beasts—p. 127. (10) That the
tempter of Eve was a Negro—pp. 151, etc., 156-8. (11) That
the word Ham does not mean *black*—p. 55. To these not irrational assertions may be added the following indefensible opinions: (1) That God has a white complexion—pp. 95, 107, 138.
(2) That the world is but 6000 years old—p. 98. (3) That the
Deluge was universal—p. 99. (4) That the Negro is not a man—
pp. 100, 117 *et passim*. (5) That Adam was not intended to work
—pp. 69, 120, 121. (6) That it never rained until the Flood—
p. 121. (7) That the aboriginal inhabitants of all lands were
mulattoes—p. 126. (8) That fossil remains have been left by
Noah's Flood. This synopsis of *points* may be a sufficient introduction to a work which in its day produced a marked
sensation."

Professor Winchell was probably rather severe in his criticism
of the Rev. Mr. Payne; for, while Mr. Payne, in some instances,
shows a perverse disregard of facts that should have been within
the knowledge of any intelligent man who reads, and appeared
to take a delight in so doing, he, nevertheless, seemed to possess
an extended knowledge of the Hebrew tongue. Of course, I am

entirely lacking in any knowledge of the Hebrew tongue, but one would judge from the manner in which he handled his subject that the Rev. Mr. Payne was an accomplished Hebrew scholar. He calls attention to the various Hebrew texts, to their differences, to the circumstances under which the Bible was translated, the body of the men who did the work, to additions here and omissions there, and to incorrect translations in a few instances. He clarifies and renders understandable some texts that are otherwise unintelligible. He seems to show as conclusively as it is possible to show such thing that there is nothing in the Bible to justify, even remotely, the belief that the Negro is the descendent of Ham, or that any but whites are the descendents of Adam.

Other points advanced by the Rev. Mr. Payne, as indicated in the note of Professor Winchell, are: That the Negro was not a man, but at the head of animal creation, and that he was the tempter of Eve; that amalgamation with the blacks was the sin for which the world was destroyed by the Deluge; that the Israelites were directed to .destroy all Canaanites because the latter were a mixture of the whites with the blacks; and that the Lord at various times punished the Israelites for the same offense of amalgamation.

The Scriptures came to the White race, and at the time they were received the known world was that inhabited by the members of the White race alone.

It is not essential that we should, on the one hand, accept all the conclusions of the Rev. Mr. Payne; nor, on the other, is it essential that we should permit our mistaken Christian zeal for the uplift of the lowly to become a means to the end that the race receiving the Gospel shall be swallowed up in a degrading amalgamation.

Mr. Chas. Carroll in his book, "The Negro a Beast" or "In the Image of God," published by American Book and Bible House, St. Louis, Mo., 1900, claims the creation as revealed by the Scriptures to be as follows:—

"1. Matter, created 'in the beginning,' the basis of all formation—the material out of which all bodies are formed."

"2. Mind, a new element, which made its first appearance in the material universe on the 'fifth day,' in combination with matter as presented in the physical organism of the fish."

"3. Soul, a new element, which made its first appearance in the material universe on the 'sixth day,' in combination with matter and with mind as presented in the physical and mental organism of man." (p. 370).

He further says:

"That the elements of life—both plant and animal life—were parts of the original creation—matter and that they existed in matter prior to the formation of matter into the earth, is furher shown by the identity of language used by God in commanding the earth and the waters to bring forth plant and animal life, as follows:"

" 'And God said, Let the earth bring forth grass, the herb yielding seed, and the fruit tree yielding fruit after his kind, whose seed is in itself, upon the earth; and it was so.' "

" 'And God said, Let the waters bring forth abundantly the moving creatures that hath life.' "

" 'And God said, Let the earth bring forth the living creature after his kind; cattle, and creeping things, and beasts of the earth after his kind; and it was so.' " (p. 18).

" 'The breath of life' which God 'breathed into' man's 'nostrils' was spiritual, immortal life; life which, like God's life, never dies; 'and man became a living soul.' This spiritual, immortal life—this living soul—was a new element in the material universe. Hence, man, with whose physical and mental structure it was combined, is properly described as a creation." (p. 22).

"This spiritual, immortal life, this living soul, was a part of the substance of God. Hence its combination with matter and with mind, as presented in Adam, formed the connecting link, the link of kinship between the Creator and his creature. Thus, Adam became, literally and truly, as he is described in scripture, the son of God." (p. 23).

Mr. Carroll, accepting the Scripture as he finds it, concludes, as did Mr. Payne, that the Negro stands at the head of the beasts in creation; that there were but three creations, matter in the beginning, mind when animals were brought forth, and the soul when God breathed into the nostrils of Adam; that by creating the soul of Adam he and his descendents of pure blood became the sons of God, all other peoples remaining animals without souls.

Mr. Carroll seems, after a manner, to accept the evolutionary process subject to the special creations enumerated, and considers the views expressed by him as orthodox—conforming to the Scriptural text.

The author of "Anthropology for the People: A Refutation of the Theory of the Adamic Origin of All Races," who signs himself "Caucasian" (work published by Everett Waddey Co., Richmond, Va., 1891) repudiates in its entirety all theories of evolution, and claims the Scripture was intended for the Adamites alone; that the other races are Preadamites, as is, clearly and necessarily, to be inferred from the Bible itself; that these Preadamites were never in a covenant relation with God and are, therefore, not within the redemption of Jesus Christ.

He concludes his chapter on "Monogeny" in these words: "This theory is so offensive to our natural instincts, and is *prima facie* so absurd and preposterous, that it never could have been entertained by intelligent minds, but from the apprehension that belief in it was required by the Bible; and that is the only reason why it is now esteemed the orthodox faith of Christians. It is because of this prejudice, too, that Christians, who have been compelled to abandon the theory as utterly untenable, are afraid to encounter the prejudices that exist against the conclusions to which polygeny leads. Why close the eyes to palpable facts, and force the Bible to an issue with science and common sense?" (p. 26).

He concludes his chapter on "polygeny" in these words: "From this theory, that God made the yellow and the black races inferior, physically, mentally and morally, we infer that he designed them for a subordinate and dependent position; that to impose upon them the duties, obligations and civilization of the superior race and give them the same mental and moral training, is to do violence to their nature and must result in evil; that the Creator, having made different races, intended that the blood purity should be preserved, and for this purpose implanted the instinctive mutual and universal repulsiveness of races; that political and social equality is unnatural and repugnant to the best human instincts, and that miscegenation, or admixture of races, is not only an enormous sin against God, but a degrading bestiality which can result only in unmitigated evil and final destruction. Scientific thought must return to this theory, which is in unison with science, Scripture, reason, history, common sense and natural instincts. It will be found to have a unity and consistency in all its parts, which commend it as true." (p. 30).

"But if living creatures were brought into existence in this world only about six thousand or seven thousand years ago, how account for the various existing species of humanity? The answer is, that they were created on the sixth day, when God 'made the beast of the earth after his kind and the cattle after their kind,' and may properly be called pre-Adamites, as Adam and Eve were created after them." (p. 188.—Chapter on Chronology).

"It is the image of God, or the spiritual nature, that makes man a man, and man cannot, by his sinful act, make God's image in any other creature but the children of Adam. This spiritual nature is different from mind or intellect, and the difference is not of degree, but of kind. Adamites may be degraded to the level of beasts, but still they are men with high capacities and capabilities. No animal, and none of the human race not created in the image of God, can possibly become a man unless by a miracle. To repeat: it is the spiritual nature that differentiates man from beast, and the non-Adamites are as destitute of this nature as a dead man is of life. The spiritual and the non-spiritual can no more generate spirit than the living and the non-living can generate life." (p. 264,—end of Chapter on "Christianity and the Non-Adamite).

Whether or not we accept as orthodox the view that the Scriptures apply to the Adamites only and that included in the descendents of Adam are the White races alone, there is nothing in the Holy Writ requiring us to put in operation forces that will inevitably condemn future generations to a hopeless degradation through a process of amalgamation that will irrevocably place them among the lower orders of mankind and deprive them of all hope of future progress. It is assuredly possible that we may perform a Christian duty toward a people of a lower race in bringing about a humane solution of a situation that must of necessity bring about disaster by its continuance? Christianity surely does not require us to inflict a patent, irretrievable injury upon future generations, because of an unknown, possible, remote good, spiritually, that may be done to an alien people of low degree, who have never done the one slightest thing for the advancement of the human race or the furtherance of civilization? We can, as long as contact between the two races actually exists, be just and kindly helpful to them in every way; and solution by eventual permanent separation under the most favorable circumstances possible cannot be contrary to any sane view of modern Christianity.

Religion is a matter, the discussion of which with any active sectarian can be fruitful only of trouble and ill-will. The true function of religion seems to be the explanation of man's arrival on earth, what his future estate may be, and what are the fundamentals of conduct consistent with the scheme of creation and future reward after death. Generally speaking the religion of the ancient Egyptians may be considered to have been fundamentally orthodox; for we are told they believed in one God and a future existence depending upon merit shown in life—the immortality of the soul. This religion became a degraded, idolatrous religion of forms totally lacking in inspiration, as the people themselves became degenerate. The religion of the ancient Hindus seems also to have been of an exalted character. "In the hands of the Brahmans, this concept finally took the form of a godhead, composed of a triune person, or persons, called the Trimurti, the first of whom was Brahma, the creator; the second, Vishnu, the preserver; and the third, Siva, the destroyer of all things. This trinity was represented, not as a single person, as in the Christian theology but as three deities, in intimate union of relationship.[113] In the sixth century B. C. the religious order had become so corrupt and demoralized that Gautama, the Buddha, brought about a reformation. Allen in his "Evolution of Governments and Laws," says Gautama "was the son of the chief of the Sakyas, an Aryan clan dwelling about one hundred miles north from Benares, and was himself of the Cshatriya caste.[114] Cox, in his "White America," says Buddha was "an aristocratic mixbreed with yellow blood predominating, who stripped Hinduism (Brahmanism) of caste and sought a religious reformation that would level the races of India."[115] There is little need to worry over the blood of the reformer; for the ancient Aryan in his purity had doubtless almost entirely disappeared before this period. Buddhism never made any great progress in India where a debased religion was pleasing to a degraded, mongrel people who retained the caste system, the monumental relic of the failure of the Ayran whites to preserve their race in a sea of black humanity, for personal gratification and pompous display.

The Mohammedan does not appeal very much to us because of some features embodied in his faith. He, however, believes in the one and only God of whom Mohammed was the chief prophet.

---

[113]Ridpath's *"Library of Universal History,"* Vol. II, p. 663.
[114]P. 177. Published by Princeton University Press.
[115]P. 149.

He accepts much of our Bible and regards Christ as a prophet, but assigns him a place inferior to Mohammed.

The monotheistic theology of the Jews is based upon the Old Testament, which the different Christian sects accept in full except in so far as each sect deems it modified by the teachings of Christ as given in the New Testament.

These several religions referred to are of a character to appeal to the intellect and satisfy, in varying degrees, that ever present craving for an answer to the question, "Why are we here and what does it mean?" These are the only religions of which we know that can be dignified by name unless we include Confucianism, which is in no way on the high plane of any of those enumerated. The polytheism of the Greeks and the Romans is difficult to understand unless we accept the suggestion of Donnelly that, as young and sprightly colonists from Atlantis, they preserved the memories of the former rulers of Atlantis as their gods to which they added a new one in their pantheon from time to time. There is nothing startling in this; for efforts have been made even to canonize the late Charles Stuart, I., of England, and we all but deify our presidents at times as did the Romans at one time their emperors. But it seems of particular significance that these principal religions, all of which have so much in common, should have arisen from the White race, from the Semitic Arab and Jew and the Aryan Hindu.

The Old Testament is largely a history of the Jewish people; and we find throughout its pages an abundance of evidence that these people regarded themselves as superior to all races, and the specially chosen people of God from amongst the White races. They conceived that they were "selected out of all the multitudes of the earth, to perpetuate the great truth that there was but one God—an illimitable, omnipotent, paternal spirit, who rewarded the good and punished the wicked—in contradistinction from the multifarious, subordinate, animal and bestial demi-gods of the other nations of the earth."[116]

"And even skepticism must pause before the miracle of the continued existence of this strange people, wading through the ages, bearing on their shoulders the burden of their great trust, and pressing forward under the force of a perpetual and irresistible

---

[116]Ignatius Donnelly's "*Atlantis: the Antediluvian World*," p. 212, Harper & Brothers.

impulse. The speech that may be heard today in the synagogues of Chicago and Melbourne resounded two thousand years ago in the streets of Rome; and, at a still earlier period, it could be heard in the palaces of Babylon and the shops of Thebes—in Tyre, in Sidon, in Gades, in Palmyra, in Nineveh. How many nations have perished, how many languages have ceased to exist, how many splendid civilizations have crumbled into ruin, how many temples and towers and towns have gone down to dust since the sublime frenzy of monotheism first seized this extraordinary people! All their kindred nomadic tribes are gone; their land of promise is in the hands of strangers; but Judaism, with its offspring, Christianity, is taking possession of the habitable world; and the continuous life of one people—one poor, obscure, and wretched people—spans the tremendous gulf between 'Ptah-hotep' and this nineteenth century."[117]

Race pride or consciousness sustained these people during the centuries of countless race movements, wars and conquests, and carried them unscathed on to the Christian era through that turbulent period during which other civilizations crumbled in amalgamation with inferior peoples. What would have been the fate of the monotheism of the Jews had these people disappeared in amalgamation with other races not necessarily inferior races, but peoples of equal culture with whom they came in contact? Would the Christian faith have ever arisen under such circumstances? Can we believe a religion that comes to us in this manner through age-long preparation will justify or require in any degree a sacrifice of race pride in the superior capacities and potentialities with which the Creator has endowed us or the substance of these qualities themselves? A faith preserved to us by a favored people, through segregation, and requiring us to denounce and abhor as unchristian the very means employed by this people in order to transmit this faith to posterity, is an absurd proposition that carries its own refutation. For my own part I cannot subscribe to the doctrine that there can be divine inspiration in teachings that, in any of their ramifications, tend in the least to justify, sanction or bring about the destruction of the greatest work of God—a progressive civilized race. I maintain that the preservation in its integrity of a people who are the founders, builders and preservers of civilization—the preservation of the

---

[117]Ignatius Donnelly's *"Atlantis: the Antediluvian World,"* pp. 212-3, Harper & Brothers.

White race—is a work more divinely inspired than any other in which we are engaged. In doing this we insure civilization to the fullness of time; and thus confident in self security we can, in complete accord with the Christian spirit, aid all backward people by example and in every practical way consistent with the preservation of the race with its accompanying civilization and religious faith. If the Christian faith in its practical application to the affairs of man has for its object, or, irrespective of any intention in the matter, if it leads to the eradication of the race line between the White race and the Black race in furtherance of the Middle Age and uncritical interpretation of the Scripture in regard to the brotherhood of man, it is, indeed, time for another Reformation in America.

If a people become degenerate, however exalted their former station may have been, it is evidenced by a slump in their moral, mental, and physical characters—the true indices of worth; and, under such circumstances, it is simply childish to look forward to the survival of religion or any decent ethical principles. An exalted religion can exist only among a people of the highest type, and has never been found among any but such as possessed lofty ethical standards. A people lacking in these standards can not acquire them by lip service, or any other, in the profession of Faith.

"Christianity," says the Rev. A. H. Shannon, "should bring to the solution of these problems those sympathies so necessary to a full appreciation of all that enters into this race question. Science, on the other hand, should contribute to this solution a clear and complete intellectual perception of all that is involved. Christian sentiment should mitigate the harshness of science and, in turn, should become infinitely more helpful because of the direction of, and the chastening influence exerted by, scientific knowledge. On the part of those who have sought to assist the Negro there has been too much of undisciplined impulse, and this has found expression in many ways really hurtful to the race."[118]

" . . . . . . Religion should give a healthful moral atmosphere, as well as correct moral ideals. Otherwise, what is built with one hand is torn down by the other. Certainly religion should not vie with political parties for the first place as patron, if not

---

[118]"*Racial Integrity*," p. 19.

promoter, of social impurity. Here, as elsewhere, patronage must be considered as a practical indorsement."[119]

We have not yet reached the point where we can avoid the spectacle of a white congregation here assembled petitioning the God of battles for victory over another people of the same blood, from the same mold, representing the same civilization, enjoying in common the same moral, social and political aspirations and ideals, who are, elsewhere, sending up counter petitions of like tenor to the same God. Each justifies, on some ground or another, the preaching of the Gospel of Hate against the other. There may be some possible but obscure way in which this Gospel of Hate amongst peoples of the same race can be made to appear consistent with the doctrine of brotherly love that corrodes civilization and destroys a mighty people. Let some one justify, if it can be done!

---

[119]"*Racial Integrity,*" p. 63.

CHAPTER VI.

THE ECONOMIC ELEMENT IN THE RACE PROBLEM.

Efforts to solve our race problem not only meet with opposition in the teachings of some of our monogenetic evolutionists and from some who follow the monogenetic orthodoxy of the Christian Faith, but are opposed by the money-grubbing, professional, exploiting economist. The last is probably the greatest foe to any movement that looks toward a solution; for the international trust dollar, to a greater extent than ever before, now controls the instruments for shaping and guiding public opinion, and neither the Church nor the scientist is entirely free from subserviency to its powerful influence.

Commerce, trade, industry—to express it tritely, Big Business, —have ever had a controlling inffuence on the presence here and the continuance in our midst of the Negro.

When the discovery of America stimulated to activity the mind of the European, which had to a great degree been in a state of lethargy for centuries, these people were prompted to activities along different lines. Some were incited to religious endeavor along divergent paths resulting from different views, all tending eventually to a greater religious freedom; some received the urge for a greater political freedom. These together resulted eventually in the colonization of the newly discovered lands. In the colonization movement there also entered the consideration of material advancement or personal gain, and this was dominant in the adventurers who flocked to the sea in search of fortune. There was incessant war between the principal European powers while the colonization of America was being carried on, and during this period Big Business was confined to the corsairs. Of course there was in existence a manufacturing industry and a legitimate peaceful commerce in articles of trade, all of which were gradually growing, but the Big Business that produced large returns from quick turnovers was that of the corsair, who, in later times, developed into the slave trader. During this long period of unrest and war every merchant ship that left port was armed in some manner in order to insure a successful voyage. The larger of these armed vessels were commissioned by the sovereign to wage war against the enemy. The commissions issued by England were used largely against Spain with her richly ladened vessels from Central and South America. The reward in booty upon capture of these vessels was great; and, upon the cessation of war, many of these corsairs became pirates pure and simple, continuing to wage war against Spain and against all others found at sea who could not resist them. Safety of waterborne traffic in times of peace and a gradually improved public sentiment, led to the suppression of piracy; but the slave trade was left as a legitimate means of accumulating large fortunes and the slave remained an article of commerce. Spain, Portugal, France, Holland and England engaged in the slave trade: and England did not busy herself to make the slave trade illegal until the period was nearing when her largest slave market would be closed. The market in the United States was closed by limitation in the Constitution, to all intents and purposes, not later than 1808.

The colonists were practically forced to receive slaves at the hands of the English; and in New England, though slavery as an institution was not economically sound, the ship owner and the skipper gladly took advantage of the slave trade as a means to secure a fortune.

"The transactions of one slaver may be cited as illustrative of those of many others. The cargo of the *Caesar*, out-bound, was: 82 barrels, 6 hogsheads, and 6 tierces of New England rum; 33 barrels of best Jamaica spirits; 33 barrels of Barbadoes rum; 25 pairs of pistols; 2 casks of musket-balls; 1 chest of hand-arms; 25 cutlasses. The return cargo was 'In the hold on board of the scow *Caesar*, 153 adult slaves and 2 children.' Brook's History of Medford, pp. 436, 437. The books of another give a more detailed account:

Dr. The Natives of Annamboe.		Gals.	Per Contra.		Cr. Gals.
1770 April			1770 April		
22.	To 1 hogshead of rum....	110	22.	By 1 woman slave....	110
May 1	" rum	130	May 1	" 1 prime woman slave	130

2	" 1 hogshead rum....		105	2	" 1 boy slave 4 ft. 1 in.	105
7	" "		108	7	" 1 boy slave 4 ft. 3 in.	108
5	" cash in gold	5 oz. 2		5	" 1 prime man slave	5 oz. 2
5	" " 2 oz.					
5	" 2 doz.	3 oz. 0		5	" 1 old man for a Lingister	3 oz. 0
	of snuff 1 oz.					

History of Medford, pp. 436, 437."[120]

The economic unsoundness of slavery was the deciding cause of its disappearance in New England and the North. Of course there were some in these sections, and the same held true in the South, who were, on principle and because of their religious scruples, opposed to slavery. It remained, however, for a later generation, untainted by the actual existence of slavery amongst them, to pride themselves on an alleged moral superiority and view with abhorrence the continuance of this institution amongst a people whom they regarded as an enemy to free institutions and as political opponents who were to be crushed. In the meantime there had been a development in the production of cotton, owing to the invention and use of the cotton gin, which made an abundance of cheap labor a necessity. Cotton production became Big Business in the South and slavery, as a means to the end that this business be carried on successfully, was deemed a necessity. Thus, probably, a gradual, peaceable wiping out of slavery was foredoomed by the appearance of the cotton gin; for there was, beyond all question, a strong sentiment in the South against slavery.

Soon the country was arrayed in two hostile camps. The North, free from the contamination of slavery, which had ceased to exist with it because it was economically unsound, and forgetting that it had reaped large rewards from the slave trade, placed itself upon a superior moral plane from which it looked down with ill-concealed loathing upon the social and political institutions in the South. The South, on the other hand, found itself in a desperate situation. It was confronted with a condition in which it found a very large part of its population (in some localities a great major-

[120]McMaster's "History of the People of the United States," vol. ii., p. 16.

ity) to consist of a people, the most backward, degraded, non-progressive, savages of which history or tradition gives any information—a people furthest removed from the White race of any of the human family in all the potentialities of civilization and progress. With these people present, the State, social and political, had to be maintained in the face of hostile political action and moral condemnation by the North; and history furnished no parallel situation for guidance of the South in the circumstances. It was an original situation without precedent. The North soon came to the point where it was interested only in expressing its deep resentment with the situation and its determination eventually to end slavery as an institution. Even though many in the South were not favorably disposed toward slavery, they could not, in the face of the hostile North, do other than make common cause in defense of the institutions existing in the South as the only possible *modus vivendi*. Inevitably the criminal Civil War was brought about in which a people descended from a common stock and who had, consciously or unconsciously, the same eventual religious, moral, social, political and material aspirations, were at each other's throats and spilling each other's blood. The preservation of the Union was the one desirable consummation of the conflict; and even this is of doubtful value, if we are to continue in our blind course and eventually cease to be a white people. It might have been better to have left the South to itself, if by this a part of the Union would have been saved to the whites. This is certain, the race question is no nearer solution than when the blacks were held in slavery.

History is supposed to give us facts in regard to the human race; and the following statement, while it may not anywhere be given as an historical fact, is such a necessary conclusion from such known facts that it may be stated as one: It is, that the Negro could not possibly have been introduced amongst us in such numbers as he was and law and order maintained unless he had been held as a ward or slave of the State, or of the individual under the control of the State; and, furthermore, if the Negro, who has never anywhere or at any time acquired a civilization of any character, should acquire any degree of civilization, it will be due to the restraints imposed on him during slavery and since by the superior civilized whites.

But let us return to the subject matter of this chapter: that Big Business injects itself into every attempted solution of the race question. The Hawaiian Territory is one of the most beautiful and blessed spots on the face of the earth. Its climate and soil are such as to make it one of the desirable garden spots of the world. These islands were acquired by the United States only after a long and persistent fight by the late Senator Morgan from Alabama and others interested in this matter. They are of the utmost importance to us strategically, and in order fully to realize this strategic value it was absolutely essential that immigration to these islands, having due regard to the rights of the natives, should have been limited to Americans (whites). At the time of annexation the natives seemed doomed to extinction and that this assumption was correct is borne out by subsequent events.

Under these circumstances, the simplest sort of regard for the future welfare should have impelled us to have seen that these islands became the abode of Americans (white). What has been done? Big Business in the islands had to do with the production of sugar. The owners of the sugar plantations required an abundance of cheap labor in order to secure high profits, or possibly any profit at all. They were not interested in the character of the population of the islands; they were interested in profits; and, therefore, Japanese labor was introduced in large numbers. These Japanese seem now to demand higher wages than formerly. They may have organized among themselves, or they may be engaged in more profitable pursuits than formerly—probably both. Stoddard says, in regard to this: "These Asiatics arrived as agricultural laborers to work on the plantations. But they did not stay there. Saving their wages, they pushed vigorously into all the middle walks of life. The Hawaiian fisherman and the American artisan or shopkeeper were alike ousted by ruthless undercutting. To-day the American mechanic, the American storekeeper, the American farmer, even the American contractor, is a rare bird indeed, while Japanese corporations are buying up the finest plantations and growing the finest pineapples and sugar. Fully half the population of the islands is Japanese, while the Americans are being literally encysted as a small and dwindling aristocracy. In 1917 the births of the two races were: American, 295; Japanese, 5,000! Comment is superfluous."[121] Whatever the situ-

---

[121]"*The Rising Tide of Color,*" pp. 279-280, Charles Scribner's Sons.

ation may be, Associated Press despatches gave us the news a
few months ago that the sugar planters were experiencing difficulty in getting sufficient cheap labor; and the solution of their
needs, as suggested by themselves, was reported to be an additional immigration from Japan.

It is unfortunate that, after all the waste of white blood during
the last internecine struggle, war still remains as a possibility,
if not a probability. The Hawaiian Islands are of paramount
strategic value to us in case of war with some Asiatic power. The
only Asiatic power with which we could become involved in the
near future seems to be Japan. Let us hope that such a war
will not arise, but it is foolish to attempt to hide from ourselves
existing facts. Has not Big Business, in the guise of sugar
planters, irrevocably injured these islands as an asset in case of
war by making them a colony of the prospective enemy? The
only solution of this situation seems to be a drastic one that would
limit immigration into the islands to Americans (white); that
would forbid the alienation of the land to any but Americans
(white); that would, if it were found necessary so to do, purchase
all holdings not in American (white) hands and hold them for
sale to actual settlers from America (white), subject to the afore-
mentioned alienation law. *Something should be done.*

We have no quarrel with either China or Japan. The exclusion of any people whom we choose from these United States
is a right that has existed from time immemorial and is embedded
in original principles in which International Law had its inception. In its application to the exclusion of Chinese and Japanese,
the question of race superiority or inferiority does not enter in
the remotest degree, though some of the Japanese and Chinese
insist, contrary to the facts and without the slightest justifica-
'tion, that it does. The question is an economic one pure and
simple. The American cannot compete with either the Jap or
the Chinaman and because of this the admission of either without restraint simply means the disappearance of the American
within the span of a few decades. Therefore, the question is
one of self-perservation; and we are, of course, interested in
the preservation of our own type in which we, most naturally,
take a pride. The elements brought to bear and deemed fundamental in considering the relations between the whites and the
blacks, do not exist in a comparison between the Mongoloids,
as represented by the Chinese and the Japanese, and our own

race. If we are to compare the past, present and potential achivements of the Chinese and Japanese with that of the White race, the process savors of that where a comparison is made between the different branches of the Whate race and the results differ in degree, depending upon the investigator. We may admit that the finest type of prehistoric man yet found (some insist the finest type that ever existed)—the Cro-Magnon race—is deemed to be Asiatic or Mongoloid; but that does not excuse lack of pride in our own type or condoning its destruction through a needless competition with another type whatever its real worth may be. We cannot, however, shut our eyes to the fact that a powerful minority in Japan waxes wroth over exclusion on the fictitious ground of alleged inferiority implied in this, and preaches war for the purpose of opening up both continents of America to Asiatic colonization and control.

California would have been flooded with Chinese and the Pacific States now an Asiatic land, had not the discovery of gold taken to this section an enormous immigrant body of whites, who, in time, saw exclusion of Asiatics was essential to their own preservation; and yet some of our war-patriots, who were interested in the profits of contracts, or had become blind from frenzy, were willing to flood the country with Asiatics for the purpose of obtaining an abundant supply of cheap labor during the war period and suggested their importation for this purpose.

The economic side of the race problem has shown itself in the southern part of Africa where white colonists have gone to make homes for themselves and convert it into a white man's land. Here, the settlement of whites of the laboring class, skilled or unskilled (or, in fact, of any whites who were not capitalists), was discouraged by enforced competition with imported Asiatics. Because of this, a new country in the temperate zone, which held promise of becoming a white man's land if the native black population only was to be dealt with, was rapidly becoming the land of the brown man from India. The planter, farmer, manufacturer, or other man engaged in business, who employed imported coolies, was so pleased with the condition of affairs that he bitterly resented the exclusion acts brought about in aid of European immigration.[122]

[122]Neame, L. E., *"Oriental Labor in South Africa,"* Annals of the American Academy of Political and Social Science, September, 1909, Vol. XXXIV, No. 2, p. 181. See also Stoddard's *"The Rising Tide of Color,"* pp. 277-8.

That Big Business is regarded by the Negro as his friend in indirectly advancing his social aspirations and aiding in eventual amalgamation, as the result of uplift-work to make the Negro contented and to hold him as a source of cheap labor, is recognized by the Negroes themselves. In one of the works of a Negro writer[123] consulted by the author of this work, the community of interest between the Negro laborer and the capitalists, both North and South, is stressed in a number of instances. He points out, as he conceives the situation to be, that the movement of the Negro into industrial centers protects the capitalist against the exhorbitant and unreasonable demands of organized white labor; that the employment of the Negro in industry is a boon to the Negro himself; that the capitalists and aristocrats in the South recognize it as a fact that Negro labor is essential to the South, and is the only protection of the capitalist and aristocrat against the poor whites, who would soon have things their own way in the absence of Negro labor; and that, because of this, the conditions surrounding the Negro in the South have been improved so far as relates to education, transportation, and general living conditions, and even political privileges are made possible by the situation.

The idea that the Negro is essential to the South—that there are certain sections and certain occupations in which he alone can furnish the requisite labor—is a fallacy entertained not only by the Negro, but by a vast majority of the whites in the South. This grievous error should be put to rest forever. If we wish it, we can secure a white man to take the place of every Negro in

---

[123]It is but fair, where the views of a writer are criticised, to place the words of the writer before the reader in order that the latter may form his own conclusions in regard to the correctness of the inferences drawn. The author of this work wrote to the author of the volume referred to above, asking permission to use certain quotations from his work. The reply to this request was characteristic. It contained briefly a statement as to the circumstances under which information contained in another work might be used, and under what circumstances quotations might be made. He wished to know if the work in preparation was a scientific one, or what its character might be, or just what was being attempted, before he answered the request to use the quotations from his work. He was informed the writer was not a scientist and the work in preparation could not, therefore, be described as a scientific work. He was, however, advised of the general character of the work.

the South who performs any useful labor; and if this were done the South would be better off, and America and the world as well. In experiments conducted on a cotton plantation in Arkansas with Italians from North Italy, it was found that a greater yield of cotton was produced per acre than was possible with the Negro, although the Italian had to be instructed in the whole process of production which was entirely new to him. Furthermore, the Italian tenants were thrifty, saving, contented and reliable; and, in spite of all that may be said, assimilable. A similar experience resulted upon the introduction of Italians on the cane fields of Louisiana. This change cannot be wrought in a day or a night, but selected immigrants to replace the Negro can be had whenever we are willing to seriously work out a plan and carry it through.

Referring to the migration of the Negro from the South to other parts of the Union Professor Jerome Dowd says: "Among the social causes we need to set down the lynchings, peonage, poor educational opportunities, injustice in the courts, chaingangs, segregation laws, resulting in discomfort in travel, the deprivation of library and public park facilities, the exploitation of the Negro tenants by the white landlords, the bad housing conditions, and the general feeling that it is the purpose of the whites 'to keep the Negro down.' Evidence that these considerations are important factors is found in the effort of the white people, in sections where labor had become scarce, to bring about better conditions as an inducement for the Negroes to remain at home."[124]

"So far as domestic service is concerned, the South would be better off without the Negro or other domestic class just as the West is better off without such a class. In the West every member of a family is habituated to domestic work and, by means of up-to-date kitchen and other household equipment, the people live on a high standard and save millions of dollars which the Southern people throw away on servants. The departure of the Negro would raise the wages of all labor, and give the South a laboring class living on high standards and forming an assimilable element of citizenship. If the Negroes were out of the way, the South would have the same chance to get white labor as any other section of the country. A Southern man, or Northern man for

---

[124] *The Negro in American Life,* p. 252, The Century Co.

that matter, can hardly be found who would not admit that the South, or any other section, would be better off with a population all white. But while the Southern people realize this fact, they are not anxious to see the change come about. They are adjusted to the state of things which exists, and, upon the whole, they like the Negro."[125]

The Negroes "should be able to hold and enlarge the field, in which they have gained entrance as both skilled and unskilled workers, in the world of mining and manufacturing. Any kind of work which by custom has come to belong to a group of Negroes will be easy to retain as compared to kinds of work in which the Negro has only an individual and precarious foothold."[126]

"Among the lines of activity offering the prospect of immediate advancement to the Negroes, I would suggest the training of larger numbers of them for the skilled trades. A great drawback to the Negroes at present is that they furnish an oversupply of raw labor which is everywhere the most irregular in demand or the poorest paid. The best service which could be rendered the Negro would be to provide for him more and better-equipped industrial schools with the view to relieving the pressure in the unskilled trades, and enabling him to earn better wages, and secure more regular employment. There is a large field for the Negro in the skilled trades in serving his own race. And in a great many kinds of skilled trades, now occupied by the whites, the Negro could find entrance, if he had an efficiency equal to that of the whites. The vast resources yet undeveloped in this country will insure a great demand for labor for many years to come, and the Negro should qualify himself to share in supplying that demand."[127]

"In the line of professional careers there are extensive opportunities still available for the Negro, both within his own race and in open competition with the whites. In the profession of teacher in the common schools and in colleges, in the ministry, in medicine, dentistry, law, literature, and art, there is a growing demand, made necessary by the increasing Negro population. In most of the professions the services of the Negro are limited almost entirely to his own race, but in some of the professions of the highest

[125]"*The Negro in American Life,*" p. 259, The Century Co.
[126]Ibid., p. 577.
[127]Ibid., pp., 577-8.

rank, such as authorship, music, painting, and sculpture, the Negro can count on a liberal support from the white public."[128]

"All primary schools for Negroes, it seems to me, should be equipped for instruction in the industrial arts, especially domestic economy, and, in the rural districts, agriculture. And, with our development of a rich and philanthropic class, we should make liberal gifts to such special schools as Hampton and Tuskegee, and not leave them entirely to Northern generosity for their expansion.[129]

Professor Dowd, in the first of the foregoing paragraphs quoted from his work, mentions a number of "social causes," as he terms them, in explanation of the migration of the Negro from the South. Human society seems naturally to resolve itself into different strata even among a homogenous people. A common interest in business pursuits, in the professions, in the arts, the sciences, amusements, religion, and other matters, brings together, in more or less intimate association, various and sundry people within the body politic; but, as has always been the case, the greatest contrast exists between the very rich and the poor. If we can but for a moment lose sight of race consciousness, we shall find that very largely the causes enumerated in explanation of Negro migration are commonly matters of complaint in organized society and have nothing whatever to do with race. It is a matter of common knowledge that the rich man stands a better chance in the courts than does the poor one. This does not mean the courts are venal or entertain any bias. The fact that the rich man can and does present his case in all of its best aspects through the employment of ablest counsel, whereas the side of the poor man may be inadequately presented through counsel, or without any counsel, sufficiently explains the results of litigation in this respect in most instances. Segregation and exploitation by the landlord are facts confronting the poor in every city, town, and village in America, and it does not depend upon race, color, or previous condition of servitude.

It thus appears quite conclusively that the Negro and many of his friends who are fanatically interested in his uplift, attribute the ordinary social ailments to race prejudice when the Negro is affected by them. That race prejudice does exist is an indis-

---

[128]*"The Negro in American Life,"* p. 578, The Century Co.
[129]Ibid., p. 580.

putable fact—one that makes easy the explanation of all ills of the Negro by attributing them to it; but thinking persons should be able to discriminate between facts and propaganda due to prejudice or self-interest.

There is one view of the transportation question that may relieve it of some of the stigma due to alleged discrimination, but this should not operate to prevent the alleviation of conditions where required by existing hardships which can be remedied within reasonable limits. The transportation companies are not expected or required to furnish a more comfortable means of transportation than the ordinary day coach unless traffic justifies such additional comforts. The fact that such facilities are provided for one community does not justify its requirement for another where the operation would be at a loss. If, therefore, transportation companies furnish additional facilities for each race as justified by the increase in demand for accommodation from the two races respectively, it should be relieved of any charge of discrimination.

Although Professor Dowd enumerates the causes above mentioned as influencing the Negro in his migratory movement, he states further along in his work that the Negro was influenced "primarily by economic considerations, and no other theory is consistent with the facts."[130]

There is nothing astonishing in the fact that the Negro should make progress as the result of the tremendous expenditures made and the enormous amount of work done in behalf of his uplift; or that he should, within reasonable limits, take advantage of the industrial situation in his own interest; or that in individual cases he should make such progress as he has in Durham, North Carolina, where "there is a textile mill which manufactures hosiery, the product being sold by white salesmen in North Carolina, South Carolina, Georgia, Alabama, and New York."[131]

On the other hand, it is rather astonishing that one should admit the inferiority of the Negro; that one should admit we are weaker industrially and as a military power because of the presence of the Negro—that one should do all this, and yet regard the preparation of the Negro for competition with the white man as the first step in the solution of a problem he regards as insolu-

---

[130]*The Negro in American Life,*" p. 258, The Century Co.
[131]Ibid., p. 94.

ble, which seems to be the position of Professor Dowd if one should try to fix it with relation to the several conclusions at which he arrives throughout his work.

We are confronted with a situation in which organized capital, controlling the vital industries of the country, seeks an abundance of labor the cheapest to be had compatible with production. These corporate bodies have become dehumanized, impersonal, soulless. They have set up a code of economics that seems to have been accorded a place of more sanctity in the body politic than the Decalogue itself. The primal, basal law of this code—one to which the fate of the empire itself is of secondary consideration— is the supply of an abundance of cheap labor. The Negro is utilized to the extent it is possible to do so, then resort is had to immigration to fill the needs. In one instance the native American is compelled to compete with the Negro, in the other, with cheap European labor in the person of the immigrant. The native American laborer can compete with neither the Negro nor the cheap European laborer; his standard of life is lowered to the point where he cannot thrive, produce and rear a family; and he, therefore, becomes degraded, reduced in numbers, and will eventually disappear. If the immigrant becomes Americanized, he and his children take their place in the vicious circle to disappear in the end as did the original American laborer. No sacrifice can be too great to keep the wheels of industry moving. The greatest claim that can be made to stewardship of national affairs by either party is that it keeps the wheels of industry turning, or it knows how to speed them up when the other party through mismanagement has let them slow down. In the mean time, we have race wars, amalgamation with its consequent degradation, anarchy, communism, socialism, pacifism, and other so-called ills. The remedy for the "Red" is to catch him and hang, electrocute or imprison him. That for socialism and communism is to send the subjects so afflicted to an Americanization school, where they can learn the stereotyped views as to the Constitution, politics and economics. If this, with a reasonable amount of ridicule and general lecturing as to the evil course pursued, does not cure, then some cause for imprisoning the culprit may be easily found. The remedy, in so far as discontent of the Negro is concerned, is to give him additional educational facilities, greater social and other privileges and hasten him along the road of amalgamation and social equality. Even prohibition, the Constitutional moraliza-

tion of the people, meets with approval of the makers of the corporate code of economics, and to them in the final analysis is due
in all probability the incorporation of this Amendment. Prohibition was to make for sobriety in the industrial worker and docil-
ity in the Negro, thus increasing the industrial output. The industrialist, who would regard an examination of his books of records
and accounts as a communistic invasion of all rights of the individual and contrary to the fundamentals of organized society
and the Constitution under which we live, looks with complacency
upon the invasion of the home and the indignity of search without
warrant in order to prevent the use of a beverage that does not
lubricate the wheels of industry.

Industrialism as it now exists with us makes the offspring of
a decent American who is interested in the future welfare of his
children a heavy liability difficult to meet, whereas, in the case of
the low-grade immigrant and the Negro, the more numerous the
progeny the greater the earning capacity of the family and the
more desirable the situation from the point of view of the head
of the family. Pride as to decent conditions of life and the preparation of the child for the future part it must play by education
and wholesome surroundings, does not serve in anywise to check
the number of the family; and, when for any cause this *economic
unit in the field of labor* is unable to provide for itself, either private philanthropy or state agencies dole out the necessities sufficient to keep this unit going until they can be provided by themselves. Thus, entirely aside from any loss of good race stock
through amalgamation, the inevitable tendency of the present industrial situation is to cause a dwindling of this stock, a dwindling that increases as time passes.

If we confine our observations to the average individual (excluding the mentally afflicted and the criminal) it is safe to conclude that every individual conceives himself entitled to the
fruits of his labors, acquired without invasion of the rights of
others; and that no individual is so much of a pacifist that he will
not fight for the protection of what he has so acquired—fight
either as an individual or as a citizen of the State that protects
him in these rights. When man refuses to fight, unless it is the
case of an exceptional religious zealot, it is because he does not
think the cause in which he is sought to be enlisted a just one.
Likewise, we may safely conclude that communism, the extreme
doctrines of socialism, and many other organized movements in

the body politic, are not within themselves objective evils to be eradicated by harsh measures, but rather evidence of an unhealthy condition in the industrial body.

Industry, a most potent instrument for advancement, including progress in its broadest ethical sense, should not be permitted to become a fetish destructive of the higher qualities of the race and of the race itself. Corporate bodies (the modern corporations) were brought into existence to meet the requirements of modern business. When business became so large that the necessary investment could be had only through the association of numerous individuals in the enterprise, the corporate body with a perpetual succession, the quality of never dying, came into existence; and it acted through its corporate officers instead of through the discordant voice of its numerous holders. Recognizing the impracticability of personal supervision by each corporator or holder of shares, the body, as stated, acted through its officers and the individuals were relieved from the strict and harsh common law liability of the individual who was engaged in business, and their actual liability limited to the subscription of the individuals or some amount proportional thereto. It was not to be supposed that a man would subscribe to an enterprise and assume the common law liabilities in regard to such undertaking, when, by the very nature of the organization, he could not direct its operation; and, therefore, this provision for a limited liability was a wise and just one. It could not, however, have ever been contemplated that corporate bodies should become dehumanized; should be freed from all restraints and incur none of the liabilities of the individual. Corporate bodies (Big Business) must be humanized, then racialized; they must be brought to a realization that Big Business is not the end of human endeavor, but a means—an instrument—to be used in the evolutionary progress of the race and humanity; that future generations are of more consequence than exploitation for the present accumulation of swollen fortunes; that a reasonable prosperity for all in a homogeneous community of sturdy forward-looking members of a civilized, progressive people, is of far more consequence than the most spectacular display of a decadent civilization borne upon the backs of a decaying people suffering from many social evils and threatened with extermination in amalgamation with inferior peoples. We have not gone so far that adjustments cannot be made to bring religion, science and industry into cooperation in the furtherance of racial integrity, the betterment of the American type, and, eventually to bring about concerted action amongst all members of the White race for their own progress and the advancement of the human race. This is not utopian but is well within the range of practical accomplishment without disturbance or dislocation of any of the processes now in operation in the civic body; but it can be so accomplished only by a people steadfast in purpose, with a clear vision of the end sought before them, and worthy of the lofty spiritual sentiment essential to its realization.

PART II

PART TWO.

CHAPTER I.

IS THE NEGRO A BLACK WHITE MAN?

Is the Negro a black white man? In other words, with the same opportunities, will he respond progressively to his environment to the same extent as the white, or even approximate it?

Professor Dorsey asks himself the question, "In other words, are there *higher* and *lower* races?" He responds, "Common sense says 'yes'. Common sense also said: There are ghosts. Witches turn milk blue. Any idiot can see that the earth is flat!"[132]

But Professor Winchell says: "The old question of the zoölogical value of the intervals separating races has been vacated of all importance. The differences existing are patent to all observation. There they are, beyond all question; call them what you will, that will not alter their value, their significance or their force. Call them varietal, racial, specific or generic in value; that does not affect in the least the nature and the reality of the thing which we contemplate, and its implication as a phenomenon in the course of Nature's processes. Undoubtedly, racial distinctions are as wide as those which we regard of specific value among Quadrumana and other Mammals."[133]

"To sum up: The theory of race equality, in a certain limited sense," says Dowd, "may be rationally defended, that is, we have reason to believe that all races of men have the same mental faculties, and that in general ability to learn they differ in no important degree. But, due to many centuries of natural selection, the races of men have not now equal capacity to adapt themselves to the same environmental conditions, nor to attain to the same accomplishments."

"Race equality means that, whereas differences in hereditary value exist among all varieties of plants and animals, the races

---

[132]*"Why We Behave Like Human Beings,"* p. 40, Harper & Brothers.
[133]*"Preadamites,"* pp. 86-7.

of men form an exception to the rule and through all the vicissitudes of climate and social revolution have remained undifferentiated. It means that the biological principle of natural selection does not apply to human beings, that no matter what climatic differences men may have been subjected to, the average value of each group remains the same. It means that sexual selection is inoperative among men, that no matter what principle may govern the choice of human beings in mating, each generation in every group remains endowed with equally desirable inheritance. It means that there is no such thing as social selection, that in the long history of warfare among men, it has made no difference what type of men have been killed, the average quality of each racial group remains the same. It means that all history is nonsense which speaks of the decadence of peoples, that race values always remain the same for each race throughout its history. It means that the science of eugenics is 'bunk,' that, no matter how races or individuals may intermix, the resulting progeny always yields to each group the same proportion of physically and intellectually efficient individuals. This is, indeed, a complacent philosophy, which no man of the first order of ability has ever believed in."

"For the most part our modern apostles of race equality and amalgamation represent a reaction against a class of racial philosophers who have gone to the opposite extreme of attributing all progress to the enrichment of racial inheritance. The equalitarians and amalgamationists sneer at such writers as Madison Grant, who holds a brief for the Nordic race, and who overlooks the influence of all environmental factors in social progress. They speak of him and his followers as neo-Gobineaus, and they find in the evident fallacy of the one-sided view of Grant and Gobineau a proof that all progress has been due entirely to environment.................... .... The neo-amalgamationists say that there is no evidence satisfactory to their minds that races are unequal. And their conclusion is perfectly sound from their point of view, for they rule out, as unsatisfactory or as no evidence, all the facts of history and biological data which do not lend color to their obsession."[134]

"While I do not believe in the equality of the human races, any more than in the equality of dogs or of tobacco, I would not

[134]"*The Negro in American Life*," pp. 394-5, The Century Co.

wish to be understood as having the slightest sympathy with the idea that the Nordic race is the paramount race of the world. The Nordic race is the greatest race only in the sense that it is better adapted than any other race to the Nordic region. Other races are equally well adapted to their environments and have made contributions to culture equal to those of the Nordics."[135]

The above summary of Professor Dowd in regard to the subject of racial equality, in so far as given, appears to be a temperate statement of the inferences necessarily drawn from a critical, judicial examination of all facts within our knowledge, whether obtained through scientific research or gathered from the pages of history; and the general acceptance of these should firmly fix us in our determination to find a solution for the race question in America. However, I cannot refrain from stating my conviction that, if ever there was a time when the mental faculties and general ability to learn were the same for all races, which I seriously doubt, such time must have been so remote that it requires tens of thousands of years to span it, not a few centuries. The broad chasm that exists between the whites and the blacks has been the same throughout the sixty centuries of the historic period.

"There exists to-day," says Madison Grant, "a wide-spread and fatuous belief in the power of environment, as well as of education and opportunity to alter heredity, which arises from the dogma of the brotherhood of man, derived in its turn from the loose thinkers of the French Revolution and their American mimics. Such beliefs have done much damage in the past and if allowed to go uncontradicted, may do even more serious damage in the future. Thus the view that the Negro slave was an unfortunate cousin of the white man, deeply tanned by the tropic sun and denied the blessings of Christianity and civilization, played no small part with the sentimentalists of the Civil War period and it has taken us fifty years to learn that speaking English, wearing good clothes and going to school and to church do not transform a Negro into a white man . . ."[136]

It does not seem to me that Madison Grant necessarily denies that environment may have its effect upon the human race, but rather that he affirms adaptability to environment for age-long

---

[135]"*The Negro in American Life*," pp. 395-6, The Century Co.
[136]"*The Passing of the Great Race*," p. 16, Charles Scribner's Sons.

periods in the remote past has fixed in each race certain definite traits that persist, are inherent in the blood and pass to future generations, are hereditary. He undoubtedly denies that environment and educational facilities, produced through evolutionary process by one people, can, through mere enjoyment by another who never contributed materially to the improvement of either environment or education, supply the latter with the productive hereditary traits of the former, particularly if under the influence of these advantages for but a comparatively short time. No one is so bold as to proclaim that they find hereditary traits induced by our existing environment. The answer to this lies in the dim-distant future.

"Walk the streets of Washington for a single day," remarks William Archer, an English author, "and you will realize that the colour-problem is not, as some English and North American writers assume, a chimera sprung from nothing but the inhuman prejudice of the Southern white. It is not a simple matter which a little patience and good-temper will presently arrange. It is a real, a terrible difficulty, not to be overcome by happy-go-lucky humanitarianism."[137]

"It may be a great pity," says the same writer, "that Nature implanted race-instincts deep in our breasts—Nature has done so many thoughtless things in her day. But there they are, not to be ignored or sentimentalized away. They are part of the stuff of human character, out of which the future must be shaped. The wise statesman will no more disregard them than the wise carpenter will disregard the grain of a piece of timber—or the knots in it."[138]

Archer says: "Hearing a great deal of loose, illogical, inconclusive talk on the colour question, and having himself taken a 'mighty liking' to these 'gentle, human, dark-skinned people' as he saw them in a Chicago music-hall and elsewhere, Mr. Wells formed the opinion that there was no reason at all in the Southern frame of mind. His conclusion is that 'these emotions are a cult;' and by a cult he evidently means a contagious, fanatical folly."

"Now, Mr. Wells is a man for whose essential wisdom I have a very high respect. If I were bound to acknowledge myself

137Taken by permission from William Archer's "Through Afro-America," p. 9, copyright by E. P. Dutton & Co., Inc.
138Ibid., pp. 9-10.

the disciple of any living thinker, I should have small hesitation in selecting him as my guide and philosopher. But his chapter on 'The Tragedy of Colour' in 'The Future in America' is tinged with what I cannot but take to be a dogmatic impatience of all distinctions and difficulties of race. Before writing it, he might, I think, have asked himself whether the theory of sheer race-monomania was not, perhaps, a rather too simple way of accounting for 'emotions' felt with absolute unanimity (in a greater or less degree) by some twenty million Southern white people. The arguments he heard might be weak, ill-informed, inconclusive; the conduct in which the emotions expressed themselves might often be indefensible and abhorrent; and yet there might lie at the root of the emotions something very different from sheer unreason. I think Mr. Wells should have been chary of 'indicting a nation' without more careful reflection and a closer scrutiny of evidence."[139]

"I have very real diffidence," says Archer, "in contesting the deliberate judgment of a man like Sir Sydney Oliver on a question which he has deeply studied; but I cannot believe with him that the problem is simply one of Southern unwisdom. On the contrary, I believe that, however unwise in much of her talk and her action, the South is in the main animated by a just and far-feeling, if not far-seeing, instinct. That there has been an infinitude of tragic unwisdom in the matter, not in the South alone, no one nowadays denies. But I believe that the problem, far from being unreal, is so real and so dishearteningly difficult that nothing but an almost superhuman wisdom, energy, and courage will ever effectually deal with it."[140]

Mr. Archer, as I understand him, points out in other parts of his text, in explanation of the attitude of Sir Sydney Oliver, that the view point of the latter is that of a British administrator in the West Indies. The islands administered were essentially the black man's land, and thoughts of home of the white man there residing, however permanent or temporary such residence might be, reverted to other islands, the British Isles, the land of the white man. Furthermore, Jamaica was converted into a crown colony in order to avoid drifting into the same sort of political chaos with which the South has been confronted since

---

[139]Taken by permission from William Archer's "*Through Afro-America*," pp. 199-200, copyright by E. P. Dutton & Co., Inc.
[140]Ibid., p. 201.

the War Amendments. The white man rules in Jamaica and the Negro or man of color is rewarded, as deemed deserving by the white man, by a petty office here or there. Thus there is no political competition as there is with us, and there is peace in this black man's land ruled by the white. But it is a black man's land. The Englishman so situated evidently looks upon the South in the same light as he does upon the West Indies; but we in the South regard the Southern States as the land of the white man. The question is, *How long will this be true?*

Referring to the tone of the Negro press and that of the declarations of the mulatto leaders, Professor John Moffatt Mecklin remarks: "Their language implies that the negro is only an Anglo-Saxon who is so unfortunate as to have a black skin. Such a race philosophy only works injustice to the negro himself and it is high time to discard it."[141]

Even those equalitarians who are engaged in uplift work fail to apply the same code of morals and general conduct to the Negro as is applied to the whites; and in thus overlooking lapses in them that are condemned and punished in the whites they silently affirm facts of race differences that they are at particular pains to vociferously deny. These differences cannot be explained by lack of opportunities and advantages on the part of the Negro; for he has, to a greater or less degree, continuously had before him for 6000 years the example of adjacent or near by civilizations. His traits persist under all circumstances.

"These differences," says Mecklin, "are found only at the lower level of instinct, impulse, and temperament, and do not, therefore, admit of clear definition because they are overlaid in the case of every individual with a mental superstructure gotten from the social heritage which may vary widely in the case of members of the same race. That they do persist, however, is evidenced in the case of the negroes subjected to the very different types of civilisation in Haiti, San Domingo, the United States, and Jamaica. In each of these cases a complete break has been made with the social traditions of Africa and different civilisations have been substituted, and yet in temperament and character the negro in all these countries is essentially the same. The so-called 'reversion to type' often pointed out in the negro is in reality but the recrudescence of fundamental unchanged race

---

[141]*"Democracy and Race Friction,"* p. 46, Macmillan Company.

traits upon the partial breakdown of the social heritage or the negro's failure successfully to appropriate it."[142]

The individual American upon his birth becomes heir to the moral, religious, social, political, and civic institutions of his time together with the manners, customs, and habits through which expression is given to the ethnic forces underlying these institutions. Training during childhood and youth results in an adult who has assimilated this social heritage or civilization. The results attained pre-suppose a social heritage arrived at through evolutionary process—the work, so to speak, of untold preceding generations; and also there is pre-supposed the production of hereditary traits in keeping with the social heritage. One is the complement of the other, each in delicate adjustment with the other; and, therefore, it can be readily seen that people who are strangers to this social heritage, and consequently possessed of inherited social traits incompatible with it, cannot be introduced in numbers in this community on terms of civic equality without a disruption of the social heritage of which the moral, religious, social, and civic institutions are its elements, and of the manners, customs, and habits through which they are made manifest.

"It is certain, then," says Mecklin, "that there is much inarticulate wisdom in the race antipathy which the uncritical humanitarian would class with the fear of mice and rats. To be sure, it often seems stubbornly irrational and even flagrantly undemocratic . ."[143]

After all, the difference between the black man and the white is the difference between the culture found in Africa and that found in Europe or America.

Anthropology has time and time again given us the measurements of the Negro's limbs, body and organs; his cranial capacity and physical characteristics, in comparison with like measurements and characteristics of the whites. Differences exist. Those shown may be striking in a way, but they do not, in themselves, carry a necessary conviction of superiority on the one hand or inferiority on the other. There is much variation within our own race, and we know that a large brain does not necessarily imply a high degree of intelligence.

---

[142]"*Democracy and Race Friction*," p. 74, Macmillan Company.
[143]Ibid., pp. 146-7.

No one who has ever seen a member of the Negro race will have any difficulty in recognizing one afterward. The kinky wool, the flat nose, the thick lips and the black or yellowish or bluish black skin of the Negro marks him out from every one else. But, even here, there is nothing tangible from color alone to argue superiority or inferiority; or from kinky wool or thick lips.

We do know this, that the characteristics indicated are those of the Negro and mark him as one of the distinct branches of the human family. In passing judgment upon the worth, ability or potential capacity of the Negro, neither color, kinky wool, flat nose, nor thick lips count for anything; but when judgment is finally passed these distinguishing characteristics will still remain. He should be judged by the standards that find a place in history; and these are impartial and not concerned with the color or other physical characteristics of the people of whom it treats. History is the record of human events from the time when records began. It records the struggle of the human race from a lowly position in the oblivian of the past to the superior position it now occupies. It records the conduct of the numerous peoples mentioned in the record; it tells what they did, good or bad, helpful or hurtful in the progress of man; all is laid bare for the comment, criticism or judgment of the people living to-day, just as the record we make will be spread across its pages for the edification or shame of those who come after us.

Is there any other method of determining the worth of the Negro than by referring it to history and considering the deductions thus arrived at together with existing facts, before coming to any final conclusion? If there is any other method of reaching the matter that carries with it that confidence which necessarily follows a conclusion based on correct premises, such method has not been disclosed to us by the Creator.

Let us see what a cursory examination of history discloses. Donnelly, in his work "Atlantis," goes far, if he does not do so beyond a reasonable doubt, toward establishing it as a fact that a great empire antedating the Egyptian civilization existed in the Atlantic under the name Atlantis; and that its people had reached an advanced stage of civilization. That the people of Atlantis included both the large ruddy type and the brunette type of whites, and that the empire held sway from the middle

Mediterranean to Mexico and Peru, inclusive, seem to be as conclusive as the existence of Atlantis itself.

"Besides the sculptures of long-bearded men seen by the explorer at Chichen Itza mentioned on a preceding page," says Short, "were tall figures of people with small heads, thick lips, and curly short hair or wool, regarded as negroes. 'We always see them as standard or parasol bearers, but never engaged in actual warfare'."[144]

Thus it appears that the Negro, in an inferior capacity as is usual with him, was associated with the civilization of Atlantis which ante-dated that of Egypt.

The civilization of Egypt was that of the white man, and the Negro was associated with the Egyptians at an early period in their history.

The Chaldean and Babylonian civilizations represented the work of white men, and the Negro was even brought into contact with these civilizations through the slave marts of the ancient East.

The civilization of India, founded by a virile, upstanding branch of the Aryan race, came directly in contact with a numerous Negroid people in the peninsula.

The subsequent civilizations of Assyria, Persia, Asia Minor and the Mediterranean—all white—were so situated that their trade, commercial enterprises, and other operations brought the Negro within the influence of these respective civilizations.

The above-given summary takes into consideration the more prominent white civilizations up to the breaking up of the Roman Empire; and these, together with that of China and the Americas, include all important civilizations to that time. There is much direct evidence that the civilizations of Mexico, Central America and Peru were the work of the whites of Atlantis; and there is some evidence that white culture may have influenced the Chinese civilization. This last statement is not intended as in any way giving credence to that unsupported and ridiculous contention by some writers that the Mongoloid type is the result of a cross between blacks and whites; for there is as much evidence in support of the development of the distinct Mongoloid type as that of any other type of man.

The record as a whole, portrays the slow, difficult, onward and

---

[144]"*North Americans of Antiquity*," pp. 401-3.

upward march of human events, in which the torch of progress, laid aside by one people, perhaps temporarily at times, is passed to another. There is progress in the end.

Throughout these centuries of unremitting toil and labor, hope and despair, joy and suffering, plenty and want, peace and war, victory and defeat—in fact, throughout all this period that tested to the full the endurance and capacities of a people, the only actors upon the stage were members of the White race.

What, in the mean time, had the Negro been doing? During all this time we cannot find that the Negro ever undertook individually anything of greater magnitude than the supply of his simple wants by hunting with the crude implements of a savage and gathering from a pelntiful natural supply fruits for food and leaves or limbs of trees for shelter. His only concerted activities were confined to savage, tribal warfare. Numerous members of the race were within the influence of the civilizations that flourished from Atlantis and Egypt to the breaking up of the Roman Empire; and, even though this contact had resulted alone from the fact that the Negro was a slave among these respective peoples, he, had he possessed any of the potentialities of a civilized, progressive people, should have carried or sent to his people in Africa some of the uncalculable blessings of a civilized people. But this contact did not result solely from slavery; for, in Egypt, when the Egyptians extended their power up the Nile to the south, the borders of civilization were brought to the Negro's door. This was also the case in the East-African Region of the Straits of Bab el Mandeb and the Gulf of Aden, where he was face to face with the Hamitic and Semitic civilization of Arabia,[145] the Ethiopia of the Bible. In India the Negroid (strongly so in the south and in the Island of Ceylon) peoples lived side by side with the conquering Aryans.

Such glimpses as we can get of Negro life must convince us beyond shadow of doubt that the Negro in the African jungles, first disclosed to the modern European by the Portuguese navigators, was the same shiftless, non-progressive, unmoral, non-

---

[145]The Hamites and the Semites, both at a period that must have been very remote, crossed into this section from Arabia. Ethiopia, now commonly considered to have always meant a land of Negroes, at one time referred to Arabia proper and doubtless also included Arabian colonists on the adjacent shores of Africa. To the latter it has become more or less permanently attached.

self-helpful savage that roamed the wilds of Africa at history's dawn. He had learned no lesson that he could apply from either Atlantis, Egypt, Chaldea, Babylonia, Assyria, Persia, Greece, Rome or any other people. He has proved himself incapable of profiting by any of these examples and lifting himself from his initial slothful savagery. During these centuries, the only Negro that made any progress whatsoever, in accordance with the standards of civilization established by the white man, was he who, under duress of slavery, was compelled to deport himself reasonably in conformity with the standards of his master. The Greek slave to a Roman master carried to the latter the arts, literature and many branches of learning to the great profit of the Roman; the Negro slave, on the other hand, has, throughout history, reverted to barbarism on removal of the restraining authority of the superior race.

This casual survey compels us to the conclusion that the influence of powerful civilizations extending through several thousand years has been unable to change or alter the Negro, or kindle within him any aspirations for the better, fuller life of civilization.

If the Negro has not been affected in any way by these civilizations, has he, in turn, left any lasting impression upon these civilizations?

The Negro appeared in small numbers and only as a slave among the peoples representative of most of these civilizations; and, while there must have been a small infusion of his blood, as is always the case where two races live together, his effect upon these peoples was negligible. In the cases of India, Egypt, North Africa and western and southwestern Arabia, however, the result of the presence of the Negro has been marked and fatal.

The Aryans who conquered India were, of course, members of the White race. They were adventurous, brave, virile, possessed of a high civilization and a rich literature. They were proficient in the arts and built great public works. They found themselves in the midst of a numerous indigenous population strongly Negroid in character; and, in order to perpetuate the dominance and purity of the conquerors, an elaborate caste system interwoven minutely with their religion was instituted.

". . . The Sanskrit word for caste," says Westermarck, "is 'varna,' i. e., colour, which shows how the distinction of high and low caste arose in India. That country was inhabited by dark races before the fairer Aryans took possession of it; and the bitter contempt of the Aryans for foreign tribes, their domineering spirit, and their strong antipathies of race and of religion, found vent in the pride of class and caste distinctions. Even to this day a careful observer can distinguish the descendants of conquerors and conquered. 'No sojourner in India,' says Dr. Stevenson, 'can have paid any attention to the physiognomy of the higher and lower orders of natives without being struck with the remarkable difference that exists in the shape of the head, the build of the body, and the colour of the skin between the higher and the lower castes into which the Hindu population is divided.' This explanation of the origin of Indian castes is supported by the fact that it is in some of the latest Vedic hymns that we find the earliest references to those four classes—the Brahmans, the Kshatriyas, the Vaisyas, and the Sudras—to which all the later castes have been traced back. The Incas of Peru were known as a conquering race; and the ancient Mexicans represented the culture-heroes of the Toltecs as white . ."[146] What has become of these fair conquerors who so boldly pushed into this new land? They no longer exist—search where you will. If there are any whites in India to-day, aside from the newly arrived Europeans, they are restricted to a handful of wanderers in the hills of northern India; and the statement is made by some that there are now no other whites in this country. This difference in opinion must arise from difference in view as to what constitutes a white, but is of little importance because it relates to such an insignificant number of people. Once they were there in numbers and formed a powerful, civilized empire, as is attested by the language, literature and material ruins of a former civilization. What has become of them? It is bosh to talk of climatic conditions making these white conquerors into men with black skins within the period of occupancy by them. There is not one iota of data upon which to base any such conclusion, but there is, on the other hand, much to contradict any such theory. They have disappeared in the process of amalgamation with the surrounding Negroid races. In their place we find a people weak in purpose, weak in execution, vacillating and unreliable, but, with all, discontented and forever striving for something indefinite and intangible beyond their reach or understanding. They are incapable

---

[146]*"The History of Human Marriage,"* pp. 368-9.

of preserving peace amongst themselves or defending themselves against a foreign enemy; and there is no evidence of potential capacities in them that would put them in the ranks of the civilized hosts ever battling for the uplift of mankind. This final result has been reached through the sacrifice of the white blood of the original conquerors which has been lost for all time. The fact that the highest caste may still possess considerable white blood and the resultant population generally may be much superior to the indigenous peoples found by the invading Aryans does not compensate for the loss of white blood in a world in which we find a growing sentiment for union among all non-white peoples, and these very people in hostile array against us. Of their own accord they class themselves with the colored races as against the whites.

Let us see what we may learn from an examination of the early Egyptian situation. Donnelly, beforementioned, advances with much reason the probability of the colonization of Egypt from Atlantis. Certain it is, that the first settlements were made near the mouth of the Nile at a period so remote that the delta of the river has been much added to by slow accretion since that time. It is further known the early Egyptians were members of the White race, and that gradually they pushed up the Nile toward Negro territory. The movement toward contact between the races was by the Egyptians, not the Negro. The latter then, as now, was inflicted with that incapacity of inertia which rendered him incapable of intitiating and carrying through anything not connected with his simple savage wants, and was incapable of aggression against the Egyptians. Contact between the Egyptian and the Negro resulted in the importation of the latter as a laborer or slave. Big Business here was the production of luxuries and the erection of great public works and monuments. Because of an overwhelming desire for self-glorification, ease, pleasure, and the gratification of pompous wealth in the ruling classes, the means introduced into the body politic with this end in view, resulted in eventual race suicide. Amalgamation, slow and frowned upon in the beginning, moved along with swift acceleration as time passed and the number of Negroes increased, sweeping with it into the abyss of degradation all former race pride and self-respect. The final result is a people far removed from the lofty position occupied by their ancient forbears, and who, in the awakening world-wide movement against white dominance, place themselves in the ranks of the non-white world. This state of degradation and imbecility is the direct result of amalgamation, and a positive loss to the white world. The Sanskrit Hindu settled in the midst of those carrying the potential germ of future Hindu destruction, while the Egyptian, just as we have done in America, imported what proved to be the cause of his future elimination from the peoples of the world that count.

Professor G. Elliot Smith, University of Manchester, England, is of that school which maintains that civilization was invented by one people, and that it was spread through the world by contact, association and admixture with other peoples. "At the beginning of the fourth millenium B. C., Egypt," says he, "was occupied by a population almost entirely free from the two chief alien elements which began to appear a few centuries (five or six) later, and throughout the whole of her subsequent history exerted such a profound influence upon Egyptian culture."

"The proto-Egyptians were a branch of that swarthy, narrow-headed, black-haired people of small stature that I have called the 'Brown Race,' which probably assumed its distinctive traits somewhere in North Africa—probably at its eastern end—and from its original home spread until it occupied the whole littoral of the Mediterranean, north and south, and Western Europe, the eastern shores of Africa as far as Somaliland, and the southern coastlands of Asia, at least as far as India."[147]

"In the course of time this race became to some extent differentiated into two branches, Mediterranean and Ethiopian, occupying respectively the milder and the hotter parts of this extensive domain. But the attempts which have been made by Professor Giuffrida-Ruggeri and others so to emphasize this distinction as to separate the two branches into independent races is opposed to all the facts of the case."[148]

A branch of the Alpine race that had specialized in seafaring, and whom he designated Armenoids, made its way into Egypt at the beginning of the historic period and was responsible for the stimulation of civilization in northern Egypt in accordance with Professor Smith. "At about the same time as the Armenoid and Mediterranean influence began to exert itself in the north,"

---

[147]"*The Influence of Racial Admixture in Egypt*," Eugenics Review, Vol. 7, p. 169.
[148]Ibid., p. 170.

says he, "the southern extremity of the Egyptian population began to mingle with an alien race of a very different character. For just before the time of the first dynasty small negroes, in some respects akin to pygmies, began to appear in Lower Nubia; and from this time onwards this influence, and that of a variety of other negro tribes, became more and more potent."

"If the alien influence that was brought to bear on Egypt from the north exerted a stimulating effect upon the development of her culture, it is equally certain that the negro infiltration from the south was a drag and a hindrance."

"That this is not mere surmise, but a conclusion based upon irrefutable facts, the evidence collected by the Archaeological Survey of Nubia clearly demonstrates."

"The development of civilisation in Nubia presents a remarkable contrast to that of Egypt, especially when it is considered that the one territory adjoins the other and that both form parts of the same narrow ribbon of habitable land on the banks of the Nile. Nubia was not only almost entirely uninfluenced by the momentous developments that followed from the contact of peoples in Egypt, and especially Lower Egypt, but in addition her culture was definitely degraded as the influence of the dark races of the south made itself more and more felt."

"This contrast between Nubia and Egypt is particularly instructive from the emphasis it affords to those factors to which I have called attention in the foregoing remarks; for it demonstrates in the most striking way the reality of the far-reaching effects of admixture respectively with a stimulating, virile, white race and a retarding and sensuous black race, to both of which, in varying degrees, Egypt was subjected throughout the whole of her history from the time of the First Dynasty onwards."[149]

"The operation of similar factors did not cease with the downfall of the Ancient Egyptian Empire, for ever since then Egypt has continued to be subjected to these two conflicting racial influences; even at the present day intermingling with the negroid populations of the south is still going on, and from the north a continuous stream of Syrians, Armenians, Greeks and other people from the Mediterranean littoral continue to pour in. But there is this difference—while Egyptian blood is constantly being adul-

---

[149]"*The Influence of Racial Admixture in Egypt,*" Eugenics Review, Vol. 7, pp. 181-2.

terated with negro, there is little intermixture with the more virile northern peoples."

"Whatever the explanation, however, the fact is indubitable that the population of Egypt as a whole has now to a large extent reverted to the type of the proto-dynastic period, but with the difference that it is permeated through and through with negro admixture in varying degrees."[150]

It seems that skeletal remains of prehistoric man have been found in Africa only in three instances, though indications of his presence are otherwise found in his works of art on the walls of caves, and these mural decorations are of a character similar to the Moustrian art of Europe.[151] The latter is associated with the Neanderthal man, who was, in all probability, extinct as a type, through disappearance or absorption, long before the white Alpines came to Egypt from their home in Atlantis or elsewhere. In view of the fact that the Abrahamite settlers appear to have expelled a primitive Mongoloid people, and of the fact that prehistoric peoples in general occupancy of Europe subsequent to the Neanderthal man have been pronounced Turanian or Mongoloid, it may not be far from the facts to assume that the ancient Egyptians, white Alpines, came in contact with such a people as the indigenes when they settled in the Delta.

Professor Smith says: "There is reason to believe that other members of the southern Armenoids made their way—perhaps by the Euphrates—to the Persian Gulf, and that the blending of these people with the representatives of the Brown Race population already established there may explain the distinctive features and aptitudes of the Sumerians."

"If the story of Herodotus is to be believed, it is interesting to note that it may have been the descendants of these people, after an intensive cultivation of the art of navigation for several centuries in the Persian Gulf, who, as Phoenicians, migrated to the Levant, and after contact with their own distant relatives, and aided by the knowledge the latter had independently acquired in the Mediterranean, undertook the first really great maritime enterprises the world ever witnessed."[152]

---

[150]"*The Influence of Racial Admixture in Egypt,*" Eugenics Review, Vol. 7, p. 182.

[151]Prof. R. S. Lull's "*The Ways of Life,*" p. 272.

[152]"*The Influence of Racial Admixture in Egypt,*" Eugenics Review, Vol. 7, p. 176.

The speech of Sumir seems to be generally conceded to have been agglutinative and the people Turanian or related to the Mongoloid family.[153] If the Sumerians are admitted to be Turanian (related to the Mongoloid stock), and if Professor Smith's suggestion that they resulted from an amalgam of one branch (the Ethiopian) of what he calls the Brown Race and the maritime branch of the Alpines (he divides the Brown race, as he calls it, into two branches—not distinct races—the Mediterranean and Ethiopian), it must be concluded that what he designates as the Brown Race are in fact a Turanian people. Attention was called in the chapter on Atlantis (see p. 97, Chap. IV.) to the conflicting views as to the classification of the Iberians or Basques as Turanian or Mediterranean; and it would seem that it might not be improper to regard that indefinitely described ancient Hamitic people, spread over northern and northeastern Africa and in southwestern Asia and described by Professor Smith as a Brown Race, as a Turanian people. If there is any merit in this, the Mediterranean race, accepted as one of the divisions of the white race, should be regarded as an amalgam of this ancient Turanian people in various degrees with the other two branches of the White race.

White North Africa (white when Egypt was white and down to Roman times) has been dealt with a little more kindly by the mutations of passing time. The desert on the south and to the east toward Egypt formed a barrier between it and the home of the Negro. The Negro, brought in slowly by the way of the oases and from Egypt, affected slowly and in small degree at first the dominant white blood; and it is fortunate that there yet remain some people of North Africa who are of pure white stock—the Berbers. It may be that most of the Negro blood in North Africa came through the Arab who had himself been contaminated.

There are still Arabs of pure stock and it is to be hoped that race pride may be awakened among them so that this valuable remnant may be saved to the White race. From the glimpses that may be had of the early Arab, it seems that this Semitic people were possessed of characteristics quite different from those of the Hebrew. The early Arab in the peninsula of Arabia (Ethi-

[153]Madison Grant's *"The Passing of the Great Race,"* p. 239, Charles Scribner's Sons, and Winchell's *"Preadamites,"* p. 140.

opia of the Bible) seems to have been a virile, restless, aggressive, pioneering character. His early operations remind one of those incident to the dispersion of the Norsemen, Anglo-Saxons or Nordics at a much later date. In remotely ancient times they crossed to the African shore as aggressors against the natives, and it is possible, if not probable, that they were the purveyors of the African slave to the earliest historical civilizations. They have been engaged in the slave trade for thousands of years and have left unmistakable evidence of their blood in the natives of East Africa and some of the tribes in the interior and to the southward. It is among these we find the most progressive and advanced Negroes in Africa. The result of this age-long process has been the infusion of a considerable amount of Negro blood in the Arab of southwest Arabia. This aggressive and progressive people pushed into the Euphrates valley, Syria and Asia Minor. We find them besieging Constantinople from 668 to 675 A. D.; and, in 710 A. D., they had crossed the strait and landed at Gibraltar after having overrun all of North Africa. A few years later they had conquered the Spanish peninsula and ruled from Cordova to Bagdad. Swinton in his "Outlines of the World's History," says: "In the intellectual history of the Middle Ages the Saracens played a remarkable part. When Europe was sunk in the grossest ignorance, this clever people were actively engaged in the cultivation of scince, learning, and the arts. The schools of Cordova vied with those of Bagdad in the collection of books and the encouragement of science, and from them proceeded nearly all that was original in the medicine, physics, and metaphisics of Europe during the Middle Ages."[154]

This view of the early civilizations down to the breaking up of the Roman Empire, in so far as race has any bearing upon civilization, compels us to the conclusion that, whether or not a black skin, kinky wool, flat nose and thick lips have anything to do with civilization, the Negro, to whom these characteristics belong, is an inferior, non-progressive man, who, during the historic period, has been utterly incapable of attaining any degree of civilization except under duress form a superior white people, and whose presence in the body politic is a menace to racial integrity which, if continued, results in early degradation and

---

[154]Pp. 231-2.

eventual disappearance of the superior race to the irremediable loss of posterity.

A consistent record of incapacity to lift itself from an initial slothful, primitive state extending through thousands of years, during all of which time enlightening influences were present and surrounding physical conditions conducive to, if not ideal for, advancement, irresistibly compels us to the conclusion that such a people are totally lacking in the characters and elements requisite to produce or sustain a civilization. This record cannot be rebutted by evidence of a veneer imposed by a superior people and cast aside as an outworn garment upon removal of restraint.

Nothing can add to the conclusiveness of this record or detract from its force.

CHAPTER II.

HAS THE NEGRO ACQUIRED CIVILIZATION SINCE
THE DISCOVERY OF AMERICA?

A period of about a thousand years elapsed between the crumbling of the Roman Empire under pressure from the Teutons and the discovery of America. During this period there was going on that process of blending of language, thought, customs, laws, industry and the various activities that enter into the life of a people between the opposite extremes of the Roman and Romanized Provincial with a corrupt civilization, on the one hand, and the Teuton with his rather rough, primitive standard of civilization, on the other. The Roman civilization had utterly failed in the end. The Romans in position of authority had become effeminate, licentious, corrupt and incompetent for leadership in small affairs, not to mention the concerns of an extensive domain; the people, likewise, had become corrupted and enervated through the extravagances and incompetencies of the State and because of their own indulgences and profligacies and strifes due to the great divergencies between the peoples themselves. To add to the anarchy and chaos of this situation the people seem to have been afflicted with an atrophy of mind and of incentive to do and act as reasonable men should. There was indecision and inaction. Amongst these people burst the virile and energetic Nordic from parts of Europe beyond the former domains of the Empire. Accustomed to deal with his immediate surroundings and not with far distant situations, the Nordic cut up the Empire into small holdings, and, ruling by military force, gave rise to what was afterward known as the feudal system of tenure. All the people were thrown into one heterogeneous mass governed by military rule, which in the end gave an impulse to individualism, leadership being largely the result of individual prowess and shrewdness, and the situation tended toward fixing individualism as an idea in the body politic, in contradistinction to the apparently prevailing idea in preceding civilizations that all should be left to a ruling caste in which the priesthood was usually dominant. From this long, dark, formative period, during which at times it looked as though civilization might be lost to Europe, there eventually emerged modern Europe; and it is in those States whose people have become homogeneous that the power and leadership of Europe lies.

When America was discovered the Europeans who controlled their own destinies were confined to that small territory between middle Europe and the Atlantic. The other members of the White race were mostly under the yoke of the Mongoloids as represented by the Turanian Turk. The Turk had taken Constantinople and had securely established himself in Europe to a point not far distant from Vienna, and the Saracen had but a few months before been driven from his last stronghold in Spain. The European was thus all-but driven into the Atlantic by impact of the successive invasions that came from the direction of Asia; and the discovery of America acted as a stimulant and came in time to give the European an outlet in a westerly direction over the sea for his reawakened energies. During this long period of European inactivity in the world's affairs, the honor of the White race to leadership in civilization was being maintained by the Arab.

From the time of the fall of the Roman Empire until the discovery of America the principal contact of the Negro with the outside world, if not the sole one, was through the Semitic Arab; and this arose principally from the slave trade in which the Arabs were engaged, supplying the demand for slaves in the eastern Mediterranean area, North Africa and the Euphrates valley. This had but little effect on any of the parties other than injury to the Arabs themselves through the absorption of Negro blood and the elevation of the Negro in the African slave centers by the infusion of Arab blood. Thus our hasty review of contact between Negroes and whites is brought down to the discovery of America, after which an enormous traffic in slaves sprung up in the West and great numbers of blacks were taken to both Americas and the West Indies.

In consequence of the introduction of the Negro as a slave in the Americas and the West Indies, we find that there are to-day over 12,000,000 Negroes in the United States; that the island of Haiti is occupied entirely by a Negro population; that Cuba has but a comparatively small pure white population which is being gradually submerged in the numerous black or colored population of the island; that the remaining islands of the West Indies are populated almost entirely by Negroes, or colored people, the few whites there found being such as are compelled to remain for economic reasons or held there because of trade or commercial connections; that Brazil from Rio north contains an enormous mongrel population in which the Negro blood forms a large element, there being throughout this region mixtures in various degrees of Negro, Indian and Portuguese blood; that throughout the remainder of so-called Latin America (Spanish Argentine and Chile, which are white, should be designated as white Spanish America and not Latin America) there exists a mongrel population consisting mostly of a mixture of Spanish and Indian blood, though sometimes with a small amount of Negro blood.

What has the Negro done for himself in any of these territories? Cuba, now free for about twenty-eight years, is gradually drifting into the control of the mongrel population of the island; and, when control by the whites is ended, as apparently it will be in time, the United States must intervene as it was compelled to do in Haiti. In the latter island the Negroes have been free for about a century and a quarter. They have enjoyed this freedom under conditions most favorable for a progressive forward movement on the part of the Negro, if he possessed innate capacity for progress or improvement. These favorable conditions include natural ones such as favored geographical position, an ideal climate that rendered possible the growth of a great variety of products, both necessities and luxuries, an extremely rich soil that came to the aid of climate in the production of an abundance of everything grown. The location of the island also made the position of the Negro favorable to progress because of the political situation brought about internationally. The European powers, hesitating to act directly in the acquisition of the island on account of the Monroe Doctrine, were yet prompted to secure the good will of the islanders, hoping, probably, that in some future contingency acquisition might become a possible fact; and, in this effort to secure the good will, those seeking to extend the trade and commerce of the respective countries ably seconded the efforts of the home governments. Likewise America was ever ready to lend a helping hand, and do anything within reason to extend or cement friendly relations with the islanders. Under these conditions as favorable for progress as could be imagined almost, the island being situated in the direct lines of a considerable sea-borne trade, the Negro degenerated even from the position of advantage over his former savage state that he had acquired while in slavery; and such a condition of degenerate, savage barbarism was brought about that the United States was compelled to occupy the Island on July 28, 1915, in the interest of peace and to abate an international nuisance.[154½]

Liberia has not been mentioned above. This country was set up under the protection of America as a refuge for the Negro in his native land, one in which he could, with aid and under protection from the outside, freely progress along his lines of natural development. A considerable number were colonized from America. The condition of these people may be judged from the following quotation:

"A late 'Minister to Liberia' from the United States, who left that country in disgust in the fall of 1887, himself a Negro, and, of course, not prejudiced against his race, published, in the year 1888, some of his experiences and observations on that land, which has a climate well adapted to the Negro and fertile soil, producing the most vluable crops, fruits and minerals in the world, and requiring nothing but industry and enterprise to make it an exceedingly rich and prosperous country. After giving a most deplorable account of the government, of the material condition of the people, and of the administration of the law, he proceeds to say:

'There are one hundred nude persons to every one wearing clothes. They have no statute against indecent exposure. Every great man in Liberia has his harem. Divorces are easily obtained. Pay the court ten dollars, and he frees you from the bond of wedlock. On account of licentious and incestuous practices, you will find on your arrival in Liberia fully forty per cent. of the civilized population covered from head to foot with running sores and ulcers. They refuse to attempt to heal them, stating that they would die should they do so. Every man is a born politician, being governed by the Liberian adage, "One Negro capable of holding office, all Negroes capable of holding office." The govern-

---

[154½] The comment about Cuba's racial condition may appear rash in view of the fact that two-thirds of her population is supposed to be white. However, miscegenation does not seem to be frowned upon there to the same extent as it is with us, and indisputably the race problem in Cuba is a serious one.

ment maintains no public schools of any kind. The missionary schools teach the native children exclusively. Charitable people in this country and in England have expended in Liberia for education and improvement nearly seven million dollars. If everything in Liberia was sold, except the individuals, not more than one million dollars could be realized. The colonization Society claims to have aided twenty-two thousand civilized Negroes to go to Liberia since they first went there in 1822. To-day, in the whole of Liberia, in a population, native and civilized, of fully one million, only about twelve thousand can be said to be civilized'."[155]

What has happened to the Negro in the United States of America? Since freedom, particularly during recent years, he has received the solicitous attention of members of our own race both North and South, these attentions running the gamut from those societies interested in the welfare of fallen colored women to those interested in higher education for the Negro. These solicitous attentions are not, by any means, confined to the North; for some few of the most enthusiastic in dissipating their energies along these lines are native amongst us in the South. The directing forces in the government of our respective Southern States seem to have been possessed in recent years of a frenzy to do something for the education of the Negro; and the moving cause is to be found in Big Business, engineered through our chambers of commerce and in other numerous ways at its command. The Negro is regarded as an asset in the industrial situation, and, in order to placate him and quiet the agitation of the leading Negroes, his demands as to education and in other ways are being heeded without any regard to the character of education, how it is being given, and to what it leads. If this education of the Negro had in view the eventual solution of the race problem we have with us, no one would go further than would I; but I protest against a policy blindly adopted for temporary economic gains and that will in the end make conditions worse. That the system, as it is, leads inevitably to more trouble is the necessary conclusion from the observation of events through which we daily elbow our way, and from an examination of the writings of the leading Negroes themselves; and we must conclude that no one knows better the aims of the Negro than he himself.

---

[155]*"Anthropology for the People,"* "Caucasian," pp. 314-5.

The same author to whom reference was made on page 137 of this work protests strenuously against the policy of segregation in domicil; and, while he recognizes that white opposition to indiscriminate mixing is based upon the fear of miscegenation, he does not regard miscegenation as an evil, and points with apparent exultation to the fact that the laws brought into question in the Louisville segregation case were declared to be unconstitutional by the Supreme Court of the United States.

Why should the Negro object so strenuously to segregation, when, in its absence, there would be constant provocations to breaches of the peace and riots—in fact, incessant race war? Why should we be deprived of this palpably plain method of preserving the peace between the races? Is this a mere gesture on the part of the Negro—a mere theoretical contention? No, there is an ulterior purpose. It is merely one of the steps in the fight for social equality, another step toward the consummation of that "so-called evil"—miscegenation. Necessity and reason require that segregation laws be construed as coming within the Police Powers reserved to the States.

The same author seems to regard the restoration of white rule in the South and the ousting of the Negro from office as something just short of a national calamity, and he attempts to draw a picture of the condition of these Negro ex-office-holders that will appeal to the reader's sympathy.

What about the scene in the South when the whites had been disfranchised and the governments of the States were in the control and administration of the Negro? Reconstruction! A nightmare of debauchery and corruption in which with a sickly, sentimental humanism as director there was enacted in the Southland the most tragical human drama of all times—one in which the Gospel of Fraternity and Equality was to be enshrined even though all civilization were destroyed and the land converted into a jungle of barbarism and degraded humanity. Those who lived through it wish to forget it; those of us who have been told about it, wish never to hear of it again; those of us who have read of it, will never open the book again, but we shall gladly lend it to our friends who did not suffer by it and know nothing about it. To bemoan the fate of any of the characters swept away in the ending of Reconstruction, whether black or white, is to display a childlike ignorance of all fundamentals that enter into the progress of the human race and a total misconception of what is meant by "civilization," or is essential to the production of a God-serving, Christian community.

The only thing that could possibly satisfy the educated Negro, it seems, is that the whites should abdicate all governmental and social functions to the Negroes and should be governed in all they do by the counsel of "The Talented Tenth." All that appears in the work referred to is based upon the assumption that the whites are a savage, cruel people who, assuming falsely a superiority, have unjustly held in subjugation the Negro, degraded him by slavery from some imaginary, superior position he held before, and that they continue to withhold from him his birthright, included in which is a complete recognition of social equality. If his premises were true, his conclusions would be deserving of high commendation. But, in view of the fact that civilization is the result of white achievement, and has been always in keeping of the white man, and further of the fact that the Negro has always been a savage and the only progress he has ever made has been under duress of white control and direction—in view of all this, the effusions of the educated Negro are all a menace to the peaceful relations of the races, tend to confuse the situation and render more difficult the eventual solution.

Not less disheartening to those of us who wish to solve the race question in the only possible way that would be just to all concerned, were statements made at a recent session of the Senate of the United States by certain Senators from the South to the effect that we in the South had solved the Negro question. The occasion was one in which the enforcement of the 18th Amendment was under discussion. Certain other Senators had twitted the Senators from the South in regard to other Amendments that were not being enforced (referring to the 14th and 15th Amendments); and they were answered by several Senators from the South to the effect that these Amendments were enforced in all respects and that the Negro question had been solved. The Negro question had been solved! ! ! Solved! When all we have done has been to establish an educational qualification, and then hasten to educate the Negro so that he may easily overcome the only legal obstacle to his control in many parts of the South! Solved, indeed! The near future will give us a taste of this solution.

Stone says: "It is difficult to read with patience some of the utterances of Southern men, who have not the excuse of ignorance, on the subject of the political supremacy of the white man. In

entire disregard of the elementary facts and history of the operation of Negro suffrage in the South, they tell how this or that
state is now rid of all danger from the Negro in political life. It
is doubtful if there is a state in the South which would not be
largely controlled by Negro voters if the white people in it were
to divide among themselves. It has not been eight years since
the country was horrified at the racial political outbreak in
North Carolina. The preceding census (1890) showed but 561,-
018 Negroes in the state, as against 1,055,382 whites. The Negroes were thus but 34.7 per cent. of the total population. Out
of ninety-seven counties in the state there were only sixteen in
which the Negro formed as much as 50 per cent. of the total population. Yet as a result of a division among the white people, and
a combination of Populists, Republicans, and Negros, the latter
gained partial control of the state, and a period of corruption and
riot ensued which became as intolerable as anything during Reconstruction days. The culmination was a bloody conflict along
racial lines, with the usual inevitable result. The decent people
of the state gained control, and another amended constitution
was added to the honor roll of Southern efforts to insure white
supremacy without resort to violence or fraud."[156]

The same spokesman for the Negro race in America, to whom
reference has been made before, complains that rampant lawlessness forbids freedom of speech on the part of the professional
Negro, and that the leaders of the Negro schools have to be very
circumspect in their behavior in the South.

For quite a number of years the Hampton Normal Institute
has, under white management, taught social equality in a most
effectual way though it may not appear as a subject in the curric-
ulum of the school. We have no means of knowing what goes
on in the other schools entirely given over to Negro control, but
it would be far better to have such teaching done in the Hampton
school by members of their own race than by whites.

The same apostle of Negro rights, as he sees them, deplores the
fact that the educated Negro, the "Talented Tenth," has gone
North where his audience is limited; and the Negro in the South,
deprived of the guidance of these leaders, is left to make the best
terms he can.

When we are dealing with mathematics the reasoning employed

---

[156]"*Studies in the American Race Problem,*" pp. 364-5.

must hew close to the line in order to arrive at the solution that will prove correct under all checks; but when we enter into consideration of human affairs we are confronted with a different situation. No two of us react to identical surroundings in the same manner throughout. Surrounding conditions affecting our senses do not appear identical to any two of us, and do not, therefore, produce the same responses from us—the identical responses. In consequence of this any judgment formed by a white man in regard to the reaction of the Negro to his surroundings is subject to the limitations with which we are hedged about, nevertheless it would appear that the reaction of the Negro to what he claims to be his true surroundings does not correspond to that which should be expected from a mature character representative of a people who possesses, potentially or actually, possibilities of an advanced civilization.

If the Negro race is a race potentially capable of great progress; if it has been degraded and brutalized by slavery at the hands of the white man; if the latter still continues to oppress him and deprive him of his just rights—if all this be true—what should be the reaction in the case of an educated Negro who has the good of his race at heart and is anxious to do all he can for the elevation of his people? Would such a man make an issue of the exclusion of the Negro from white districts, or would he content himself among his own people working for their spiritual and material uplift? Would such man concern himself with the fact that in our public conveyances separate accommodations are provided for the two races, or would he attempt to show his people what transportation meant and how it was carried on? Would such man attempt to thrust himself into the society of his oppressors, or would he build up a social system among his own people based upon lofty conceptions of duty and justice? Would such man attempt to force his people into a position of governmental authority over a numerous body of his former oppressors, or would he interest himself in civics and attempt to instruct his people as to what government means in order that they might eventually greatly benefit themselves in some place free from the overlordship of their former oppressors? To such person there might be visualized a migratory movement of his people to their fatherland in Africa, and a united, highly civilized, progressive and powerful Africa as the culmination of his labors. The actual aims of the Negro, as gathered from the declarations of their leaders, can

not be construed as forming a constructive program for the betterment of the race.   They are merely the ill-directed babblings of
an immature race—one that in process of development has reached
and been halted at that stage of maturity corresponding to youth
in the individual life of the civilized white. While it is possible
the Negro may be in the youth of his development, yet all indications are that he presents a case of permanent arrest of development.

The Negro is a great imitator; and, in selecting those whom
they shall imitate and what they shall imitate, they invariably in-
cline to the spectacular. He is often found with a great degree
of native eloquence, even in his uneducated savage state. These
characteristics alone are sufficient to mislead the general public,
who are personally ignorant of the Negro or have not informed
themselves as to the position of the Negro in history, when they
come to judge the capacities of the race by reference to the Negro
individual who is educated. We have Negro physicians, surgeons,
lawyers, educators, and other types of educated Negroes. Some
of them have done creditable work along the lines of their particular endeavor, and it may be that some deserve high commendation for the position they have reached; but it must be remembered that this was accomplished in a country where all control
and direction of affairs, however bungled at times, was in the
hands of the superior whites, and where there has been a considerable infusion of white blood into that of the Negro under
consideration. What has education done for the Negro either in
Liberia or Haiti?[157]

Comment as to what the Negro may have accomplished since
the discovery of America will be concluded by some comparisons
with Latin America; and by Latin America is here meant Central and South America outside of Argentine and Chile, and there
should be included with these Costa Rica as well, it seems. Argentine and Chile are white and in much less danger of ever becoming otherwise than are the United States of America. We will also
leave out of consideration Brazil in which there is a large element of Negro blood, and thus confine ourselves to those coun-

---

[157]Throughout the West Indies the population seems to be divided into three classes: the Negro, the Colored and the White.
With us the classification is White and Negro. Included in the
latter are all colored persons or mulattoes, and it is the exception
and not the rule to find an educated pure black.

tries in which the Negro element is insignificant but in which the pure white, the Spaniard, forms a continuously dwindling small number. The great and overwhelming bulk of the people in these countries is composed of the native Indian or a mixture of Indian and Spanish blood. The latter largely control and direct the affairs of the respective States. We have long since regarded the efforts of these people toward government with derision, and unfortunately most of us have come to consider them Spanish. They are no more Spanish than a mulatto is white. Nobody who has studied history and the races of mankind will hesitate to declare that the Mongoloid race is far superior to the Negro race. The high, ancient and long-continued civilization of the Chinese bears irrefutable evidence of their capacities. Upon whatever peoples the foundations of the Central American and Peruvian civilizations may have rested in the far distant past, the fact is that the American indigenes, who were similar to the Mongoloid peoples, and who were found in these empires upon discovery of America, were maintaining a civilization far advanced along the path of progress; and the class controlling the destinies of these countries now are the descendents of the former ruling classes with an admixture of Spanish blood. Every fact in history, and every fact in anthropology or biology or any other science that has to do with the races, would justify us in the conclusion that the descendents of these two civilized peoples would possess abilities and capacities enabling them to move continuously along civilized lines to a far greater degree than might be possessed by the mulatto, the offspring of the white and the degraded Negro who had never known civilization except in the capacity of a slave. The Mexicans have, indeed, maintained a continuous, unbroken civilization from the times of the Spanish conquest. They have their orators, patriots, physicians, surgeons, artist, musicians, scientists, and other learned men. Who would dream of comparing what the Mexicans have done and are doing to anything the Negro has done or might possibly do in a state of complete independence? But however far advanced the Mexican may be by comparison with Liberia or Haiti, he does not measure up to the requirements of modern white civilization. He shows incapacity for government as evidenced by the occurrence of revolution after revolution. The patriot instead of going to the meat of things as they are and trying to find some substantial ground upon which to build lastingly for progress, indulges in bombast and theatrical display, and imagines that in the delivery of a high sounding oration he has performed a useful act in the interest of the State. Like the Hindu, he is most of the time in a turmoil, social, religious, political or industrial, striving for something intangible beyond his reach or comprehension. In his rebellions and wars of repression, he displays a savage cruelty and enjoyment of excesses not in keeping with the progress of modern civilization. Can we imagine the utter savagery, degeneracy and turbulence of a State to the south of us peopled with Negroes instead of Mexicans as at present.

"It seems very probable that education and contact with the Caucasians will have a tendency to modify the Negro's traits, and I am certain," says Professor Dowd, "that in the United States natural selection is working towards the elimination of certain traits which stand in the way of the Negro's survival. However, judging from what we know of the persistence of the characteristics of races, even when subjected to new and varying environments, as for example in the cases of the Indian and the Jew, I do not believe that the characteristics of the Negro will undergo any marked change for many generations."[157½]

It seems to me that these conclusions of Professor Dowd are absolutely inconsistent with the summary arrived at by him in the matter of racial equality; and that he permits his sympathies for the Negro to delude him into a belief in his future progress without any historical or scientific basis for it, and contrary to a correct interpretation of existing facts. The Negro has been under the discipline of the white races for 6,000 years, and the only result of this association has been amalgamation—the degradation and loss of the whites and the replacement of the blacks by a possibly superior mongrel.

Such progress as the Negro has made consists in the acquirement of the outward superficial evidences of education and culture. There has been no evidence of the development in him of traits indicative of moral forces or constructive ability of the character required to build and maintain civilizations. On the contrary, the doctrines preached by the educated mulattoes and the objects for which their organizations strive are direct menaces to the peace and safety of the country. This mischievous situation is the result of educating the mulatto into a discontent with his sur-

---

[157½]"*The Negro in American Life*," pp. 408-9, The Century Co.

roundings—a discontent in which he venomously assails the white man for withholding from him civic and political privileges that came to the white as the result of an age-long development, and in which he does nothing for the moral or material uplift of his own race. There has, however, to some extent been brought into existence among the Negroes a desire for national expression; and the American Negro, beyond question, possesses qualifications superior to any ever enjoyed by his race for the realization of this legitimate aspiration in which may be found the long-needed encouragement of inspiration.

CHAPTER III.

IS THE NEGRO IN AMERICA A MENACE TO

CIVILIZATION?

Whatever the aims of the Negro may be, they are, as stated before, to be inferred, in a large measure in any event, from the declarations of his leaders.

"The Negro in Literature and Art" is a work by a Negro author, Mr. Benjamin Brawley; and the following quotations from this work disclose to some extent the Negro's ambitions and, at the same time, display some of his characteristics:

"Every one must have observed a striking characteristic of the homes of Negroes of the peasant class in the South. The instinct for beauty insists upon an outlet, and if one can find no better picture he will paste a circus poster or a flaring advertisement on the walls."[158]

"In some of our communities Negroes are frequently known to 'get happy' in church. Now a sermon on the rule of faith or the plan of salvation is never known to awaken such ecstasy."[159]

"That preacher who will ultimately be the most successful with a Negro congregation will be the one who to scholarship and culture can best join brilliant imagination and fervid rhetorical expression. When all of these qualities are brought together in their finest proportion the effect is irresistible."[160]

"Gathering up the threads of our discussion so far, we find that there is constant striving on the part of the Negro for beautiful or striking effect, that those things which are most picturesque make the readiest appeal to his nature, and that in the sphere of religion he receives with most appreciation those discourses which are most imaginative in quality. In short, so far as the last point is concerned, it is not too much to assert

---

[158]P. 4.
[159]P. 5.
[160]P. 6.

that the Negro is thrilled not so much by the moral as by the artistic and pictorial elements in religion."[161]

"There is something very elemental about the heart of the race, something that finds its origin in the African forest, in the sighing of the nightwind, and in the falling of the stars. There is something grim and stern about it all, too, something that speaks of the lash, of the child torn from its mother's bosom, of the dead body riddled with bullets and swinging all night from a limb by the roadside."[162]

"It is the call of patriotism, however, that America should realize that the Negro has peculiar gifts which need all possible cultivation and which will some day add to the glory of the country. Already his music is recognized as the most distinctive that the United States has yet produced. The possibilities of the race in literature and oratory, in sculpture and painting, are illimitable."[163]

We learn from what has been quoted above, some of us doubtless having heard it for the first time, that there are castes among the Negroes, and that one of them is the "peasant class." It does not appear what are the others. It is assumed, however, that one, the highest doubtless, consists of the "Talented Tenth," a term in general use among Negro writers, and intended, apparently, to include the educated Negro—the doctor, lawyer, preacher, artist and writer. There is here, also, an admission that nothing appeals to the Negro so much as that which is spectacular and theatrical; and this characteristic of the race is so much one of the youth of the higher races that it should have the serious attention of scientists in order to determine whether this means the race is in the infancy of its development or that it is a case of permanently arrested development, as it seems to be from the best information available. We are advised that the heart of the race is elemental, grim and firm, cherishes a memory of the African forests, slavery and lynchings, and asks that this be changed through a realization of what true patriotism means.

The same author quotes with approval some of the rhapsodies of Dr. W. E. Burghardt DuBois: One, a poetic personification of our race problem, which ends with the declaration that this

[161]Pp. 6-7.
[162]Pp. 7-8.
[163]Pp. 8-9.

problem, or rather the "color line," is the problem of the twen-
ieth century;[164] another, in which he soliloquizes apropos the
lowly in this life, and awakes to a realization that he is riding on
a "Jim Crow" car;[165] and a third, in which the Muses translate
him into that psychological bliss marked by erasure of the color-
line, and in which he finds himself the intimate of Shakespeare,
Balzac, Dumas, Aristotle, Aurelius and whom he wills, and from
this lofty height he clearly visions the "Promised Land" in which
there is no color line.[166]

What lies behind the plaint in all this? The author from
whom this was taken seems to have no lamentation as to the
material, educational or spiritual welfare of his race, but is concerned in the social organization of the land and its governmental
administration from which he is excluded. He is not interested
in the advancement of his race, but in the political and social
privileges withheld by the white oppressor. He wishes to impress
the reader with the dizzy intellectual heights to which he has
climbed; with the fact that he is the familiar of the great English
bard; that he has an intimate knowledge of the French literary
world, though he mentions but two, Balzac, the vulgar, and
Dumas in whose veins there flowed some Negro blood; that there
is no color line drawn in his association with any of these, or
with the philosophers of Greece or Romans of note; and that
despite all these accomplishments which place him preeminently
above the herd of his white oppressors, he is denied his rightful
position of distinction socially and politically. No one has any
desire to hinder any member of his race from attaining the highest intellectual eminence of which he is capable; for such person,
if his energies were directed along the proper lines, would be of
the greatest help to his race. He states frankly that "the problem
of the Twentieth Century is the problem of the color-line." It
is, and so far as the Negro is concerned its solution means the
wiping out of the color line.

The author of "The Negro in Literature and Art" recognizes
the fact that the Negro possesses a native eloquence in a large
degree, and says, as to this:

"The Negro is peculiarly gifted as an orator. To magnificent
gifts of voice he adds a fervor of sentiment and appreciation of

[164]"The Souls of Black Folk," p. 40.
[165]Ibid., pp. 73-74.
[166]Ibid., p. 109.

the possibilities of a great occasion that are indispensable in the work of one who excels in this field. Greater than any of these things, however, is the romantic quality that finds an outlet in vast reaches of imagery and a singularly figurative power of expression. Only this innate gift of rhetorical expression has accounted for the tremendous effects sometimes realized even by untutored members of the race. Its possibilities under the influences of culture and education are illimitable."[167]

On page 87 of this work he makes Reverdy C. Ransom of the A. M. E. Church say, on the occasion of the one hundredth anniversary of Garrison, in Faneuil Hall, Boston, December 11, 1905:

"What kind of Negroes do the American people want? That they must have the Negro in some relation is no longer a question of serious debate What kind of Negroes do the American people want? Do they want a voteless Negro in a republic founded upon universal suffrage? Do they want a Negro who shall not be permitted to participate in the government which he must support with his treasure and defend with his blood? Do they want a Negro who shall consent to be set aside as forming a distinct industrial class, permitted to rise no higher than the level of serfs or peasants? Do they want a Negro who shall accept an inferior social position, not as a degradation, but as the just operation of the laws of caste based on color? Do they want a Negro who will avoid friction between the races by consenting to occupy the place to which white men may choose to assign him? What kind of a Negro do the American people want? * * Taught by the Declaration of Independence, sustained by the Constitution of the United States, enlightened by the education of our schools, this nation can no more resist the advancing tread of the hosts of the oncoming blacks than it can bind the stars or halt the resistless motion of the tide."

This last is a demand, in words that cannot be misunderstood, for a complete and full acceptance of the Negro socially, politically and industrially in the body politic of America with all that will necessarily follow from it, and a prophecy that it must inevitably come. In other words, the Negro's solution of the race question is a complete obliteration of the color line; and

---

[167]P. 83.

the National Association for the Advancement of Colored People stands squarely for this.

Referring to Booker T. Washington, on page 93, he says: "His Atlanta speech is famous for the *so-called* compromise with the white South: 'In all things that are purely social we can be as separate as the fingers, yet one as the hand in all things essential to mutual progress'." The italics are here inserted to emphasize what appears to indicate the views of the author of "The Negro in Literature and Art" as to the sincerity of Booker T. Washington in this speech; for he goes on to say: "On receiving his degree at Harvard in 1896, he made a speech in which he emphasized the fact that the welfare of the richest and most cultured person in New England was bound up with that of the humblest man in Alabama, and that each man was his brother's keeper."[168]

On page 95 Booker T. Washington is quoted as saying in a speech at Harvard: "If through me, an humble representative, seven millions of my people in the South might be permitted to send a message to Harvard—Harvard that offered up on death's altar young Shaw, and Russell, and Lowell, and scores of others, that we might have a free and united country—that message would be, Tell them that the sacrifice was not in vain. Tell them that by habits of thrift and economy, by way of the industrial school and college, we are coming up. We are crawling up, working up, yea, bursting up—often through oppression, unjust discrimination and prejudice, but through them all we are coming up, and with proper habits, intelligence, and property, there is no power on earth that can permanently stay our progress."

That the work of Booker T. Washington was of much value to the American Negro from the point of view of progress in material welfare and education, will hardly be denied; but that in this he was building for future friendly coordination and peace between the races, will scarcely be maintained by any informed person. The situation in this respect is very ably presented by Mr. William Archer, an English writer.

Referring to Tuskegee, he says: "My second reflection took the form of a query. I did not doubt for a moment that Mr. Washington's work was wise and salutary; but I wondered whether the material and moral uplifting of the negro was going

---

[168]Pp. 93-4.

to bring peace—or a sword. In other words, do the essential and fundamental difficulties of the situation really lie in the defects of the negro race? May not the development of its qualities merely create a new form of friction? And far beneath the qualities and defects of either race, may there not lie deep-rooted instincts which no 'Atlanta Compromise' will bring into harmony?"[169]

"Tuskegee marks an inevitable stage of the conflict; but is it the beginning of the end? I wonder?"[170]

" . . . But supposing that, by the exercise of infinite patience for fifty or a hundred years, a condition something like that indicated in the Atlanta formula were ultimately attained, would it be desirable? And could it be permanent?"[171]

"The assumed improvement of conditions would, of course, imply a steady increase in the numbers of the black race; so that, even with the aid of immigration, the white race would probably not greatly add to its numerical superiority. Let us suppose that at the end of fifty years the coloured people were not as one in three, but as one in four, and that this ratio remained pretty constant. Here, then, we should have a nation within a nation, unassimilated and (by hypothesis) unassimilable, occupying one-fourth of the whole field of existence, and performing no function that could not, in their absence, be at least as well performed by assimilable people, whose presence would be a strength to the community. The black nation would be a hampering, extraneous element in the body politic, like a bullet encysted in the human frame. It may lie there for years without setting up inflammation or gangrene, and causing no more than occasional twinges of pain; but it certainly cannot contribute to the health, efficiency, or comfort of the organism. Is it wonderful that the Atlanta Compromise, supposing it realized in all conceivable perfection, should excite little enthusiasm in the white South?"[172]

"But to imagine it realized in perfection is to imagine an impossibility—almost a contradiction in terms. We are, on the one hand, to suppose the negro ambitious, progressive, prosperous, and, on the other hand, to imagine him humbly acquiescent in his

---

[169]Taken by permission from William Archer's *"Through Afro-America,"* pp. 112-3, copyright by E. P. Dutton & Co., Inc.
[170]Ibid., p. 113.
[171]Ibid., p. 210.
[172]Ibid., pp. 211-2.

status as a social pariah. The thing is out of the question; such saintlike humility has long ceased to form any part of the moral equipment of the American negro. The bullet could never be thoroughly encysted; it would always irritate, rankle, fester. Mr. Washington's formula in renouncing social equality is judiciously vague as to political rights. But one thing is certain—neither Mr. Washington nor any other negro leader really contemplates their surrender.[173] It is quite inconceivable that the nation within a nation should acquiesce in disfranchisement; and the question of the negro vote will always be a disturbing factor in Southern political life. Either he must be jockeyed out of it by devices abhorrent to democratic principle and more or less subversive of political morality; or, if he be honestly suffered to cast his ballot, he will block the healthy divergence of political opinion in the South, since, in any party conflict, he would hold the balance between the two sides, and thus become the dominant power in the State. This will always be a danger so long as the unassimilated negro is forced, by his separateness, to think and act first as a negro and only in the second place as an American. Even if the Atlanta Compromise were otherwise realizeable, the friction at this point would always continue acute."[174]

"I venture to say that no one—not even Mr. Washington himself—really believes in the Atlanta Compromise as a stable solution of the problem. The negroes who accept it as an interim ideal (so to speak), never doubt that it is but a stepping-stone to freedom of racial intermixture. They see that so long as constant physical propinquity endures, the colour barrier between the sexes is factitious, and in great measure unreal, and they believe that at last the race-pride of the white man will be worn down, and he will accept the inevitable amalgamation. The ultimate forces at war in the South are the instinctive, half-conscious desire of the black race to engraft itself on the white stock, and the no less instinctive horror of the white stock at such a surrender of its racial integrity. This horror is all the more acute—all the more morbid, if you will—because the white race is conscious of its own frailty, and knows that it is, in some sense, fighting a battle against perfidious nature. It is a hard thing to say, but I have little doubt it is true, that much of the injustice and cruelty to

---

[173]See quotation from Mr. Stone, p. 243 of this work.
[174]Taken by permission from William Archer's *Through Afro-America,*" pp. 212-3, copyright by E. P. Dutton & Co., Inc.

which the negro is subjected in the South is a revenge, not so much for sexual crime on the negro's part, as for an uneasy conscience or consciousness on the part of the whites. It is because the black race inevitably appeals to one order of low instincts in the white, that it suffers from the sympathetic stimulation of another order of low instincts."[175]

Referring to the Negro on the stage, the author of "The Negro in Literature and Art" states: "If we pass over Othello as professedly a Moor rather than a Negro, we find that the Negro, as he has been presented on the English or American stage, is best represented by such a character as Mungo in the comic opera, 'The Padlock,' on the boards at Drury Lane in 1768."[176]

Othello is, of course, claimed as a Negro with its implication of social prominence at the time when the incidents portrayed are supposed to have taken place.

The same author states on page 99 of his work that "The Birth of a Nation" is "a deliberate and malicious libel on the race," referring to the Negro race, and goes on to say: "In different ones of the Negro colleges, however, and elsewhere, are there those who have dreamed of a true Negro drama—a drama that should get away from the minstrelsy and the burlesque and honestly present Negro characters face to face with all the problems that test the race in the crucible of American civilization."

After commenting on the presentation of several plays at some of the schools, he states: "Another experiment was 'Children,' by Guy Bolton and Tom Carlton, presented by the Washington Square Players in March, 1916, a little play in which a mother shoots her son rather than give him up to a lynching party."[177]

Lynching is a very much to be regretted species of lawlessness and should be fought to the point where it will disappear. Such thing is regretable for the reason that an innocent person may suffer, and further because of the fact that condoning in any way such procedure tends to bring about a general disregard of and contempt for the law. However, in so far as the punishment for rape by lynching is concerned, the greatest evil seems to be the possible taking of an innocent life, which is, of course, sufficient to condemn it in unmeasured terms. But, in view of the fact that

---

[175]Taken by permission from William Archer's, "Through Afro-America," pp. 215-7, copyright by E. P. Dutton & Co., Inc.
[176]P. 97.
[177]P. 100.

such a lynching merely hastens the inevitable penalty of law in
case of guilt, its demoralizing effect in bringing the law into contempt is not comparable with that resulting from the continuous
but futile attempts to enforce the 18th Amendment or evade the
evil consequences of enforcing the 14th and 15th Amendments.
The Negro in his protests against lynching overlooks entirely the
crime that usually induces a lynching and will go to any length,
in most instances at least, to protect the rapist-brute not only
from the mob, but from the penalty of the law itself.

In an appendix to the work to which reference has been made,
there appears a final chapter, entitled "The Negro in American
Fiction." In the course of this chapter, the author says:

" . . . And no theme has suffered so much from the coarse-
ness of the mob-spirit in literature as that of the Negro."

"As a matter of fact, the Negro in his problems and strivings
offers to American writers the greatest opportunity that could
possibly be given to them to-day. It is commonly agreed that
only one other large question, that of the relations of capital and
labor, is of as much interest to the American public; and even
this great issue fails to possess quite the appeal offered by the
Negro from the social standpoint. One can only imagine what a
Victor Hugo, detached and philosophical, would have done with
such a theme in a novel. When we see what actually has been
done—how often in the guise of fiction a writer has preached a
sermon or shouted a political creed, or vented his spleen—we are
not exactly proud of the art of novel-writing as it has been developed in the United States of America. Here was opportunity for
tragedy, for comedy, for the subtle portrayal of all the relations
of man with his fellow man, for faith and hope and love and
sorrow. And yet, with the Civil War fifty years in the distance,
not one novel or one short story of the first rank has found its
inspiration in this great theme. Instead of such work we have
consistently had traditional tales, political tracts, and lurid melo-
dramas."[178]

"Just there is the point. That the Negro is ever to be taken
seriously is incomprehensible to some people. It is the story of
'The Man that Laughs' over again. The more Gwynplaine protests, the more outlandish he becomes to the House of Lords."

"We are simply asking that those writers of fiction who deal

---

[178]Pp. 145-6.

with the Negro shall be thoroughly honest with themselves, and
not remain forever content to embalm old types and work over
outworn ideas. Rather should they sift the present and forecast
the future. But of course the editors must be considered. The
editors must give their readers what the readers want; and when
we consider the populace, of course we have to reckon with the
mob. And the mob does not find anything very attractive about
a Negro who is intelligent, cultured, manly, and who does not
smile. It will be observed that in no one of the ten stories above
mentioned, not even in one of the five remarked most favorably,
is there a Negro of this type. Yet he is obliged to come. America
has yet to reckon with him. The day of Uncle Remus as well
as of Uncle Tom is over."[179]

"Some day we shall work out the problems of our great
country. Some day we shall not have a state government set at
defiance, and the massacre of Ludlow. Some day our little children will not slave in mines and mills, but will have some chance
at the glory of God's creation; and some day the Negro will
cease to be a problem and become a human being. Then, in
truth, we shall have the Promised Land. But until that day
comes let those who mold our ideals and set the standards of
our art in fiction at least be honest with themselves and independent. Ignorance we may for a time forgive; but a man has
only himself to blame if he insists on not seeing the sunrise in
the new day."[180]

Let us see if we can skeletonize the great American (?) novel
that would appeal to and satisfy the members of the "Talented
Tenth" caste. Of course, such theme would be beyond the comprehension of the "Peasant" caste.

A very much educated member of the "Talented Tenth" becomes enamored with a beautiful white maiden. She reciprocates
his passion, but obstructions exist to the happy consummation of
the union in the form of laws against miscegenation and opposition from the parents of the would-be bride. They flee to a
distant and inaccessible part of the State. Race passion runs
high. The Negroes and whites are in hostile array, both parties
being armed and ready to precipitate a bloody battle. In this
situation a great Negro orator and educator, a super-member of

---

[179] Pp. 157-8.
[180] Pp. 158-9.

the "Talented Tenth," seeks out the Governor of the State and convinces him, through the eloquent manner in which he presents the case, that the time has arrived when miscegenation laws should be wiped from the statutes. The Governor, being a man of keen perception and a great humanitarian filled with brotherly love for all mankind, readily agrees with the great "Talented Tenth" orator to jointly address the two armed forces facing each other in hostile array. These joint addresses are made; and, largely through the eloquence of the Negro orator, both sides agree to lay down their arms and depart in peace, with the understanding that a special session of the Legislature is to be called to repeal the laws against miscegenation and pass such further remedial laws as will insure absolute equality in all respects for the Negro. The Legislature meets, the repeals and enactments desired are carried through, and the happy couple are joined in holy matrimony. In consequence of these events America becomes great and assumes her proper place among the peoples of the earth. The recalcitrant whites are eventually sent to fill the mills and the mines with laborers; for a few of the discontented were still left. Soon the color of the people becomes yellow, or brown, the color that Bishop Gilbert Haven so much admired. Most remarkable of all, these brown or yellow people maintain their superiority over all peoples of the earth, particularly the few remaining whites in Europe.

This novel would undoubtedly appeal to and satisfy the "Talented Tenth;" for it truly represents the "Promised Land" they constantly hold before themselves. When a novel of this character can be written and accepted by the American people, the color line will long since have ceased to exist; and the former sturdy qualities, that made it possible to subdue a new world peopled with warlike savages and set up within it a government that promised so much directly and indirectly to the members of the White race and indirectly by example to all others, will have been lost forever to the great injury of mankind. A novel or a play of the character desired by the "Talented Tenth," necessarily contemplates the erasure of the lines of demarcation between a highly civilized people, who were its initiators in the remote past and the keepers of civilization from then till now, and a people whose whole history is summed up in the expression, "a pliable, plastic savage, who, under duress, is capable of some but no great progress." All of his aspirations and all his antics in behalf of social equality and political control savor of the un-developed child, but are none the less dangerous and will prove fatal in the end unless abated. Truly does the author quoted state that "the day of Uncle Remus as well as of Uncle Tom is over;" and that it is a waste of time "to embalm old types and work over outworn ideas."

The following from "The Old World in the New," by Professor Edward Alsworth Ross, University of Wisconsin, is deemed very appropriate here:

"I am not of those who consider humanity and forget the na-tion, who pity the living but not the unborn. To me, those who are to come after us stretch forth beseeching hands as well as the masses on the other side of the globe. Nor do I regard America as something to be spent quickly and cheerfully for the benefit of pent-up millions in the backward lands. What if we become crowded without their ceasing to be so? I regard it as a nation whose future may be of unspeakable value to the rest of mankind, provided that the easier conditions of life here be made permanent by high standards of living, institutions and ideals, which finally may be appropriated by all men. We could have helped the Chinese a little by letting their surplus millions swarm in upon us a generation ago; but we have helped them infinitely more by protecting our standards and having something worth their copying when the time came."[181]

How much will the Negro contribute to the realization of this lofty conception of America's true mission? Nothing! On the contrary, his continued presence in our midst will in the end de-prive us not only of all hope to leadership, but of any right to consideration among the progressive forward-looking peoples of the world. W. Laird Clowes, an English writer, aptly says: "Only when the negro shall have departed will the name of the United States truly represent anything more than a magnificent as-piration.[182]

The same authority on Negro needs that was first referred to on page 137 cannot resist the temptation to bring to the atten-tion of the reader examples of intermarriage between whites and blacks; and, while he seems to cite these instances with approval, he condemns illicit cohabitation between the races and would have

---

[181]Preface, p. 2, The Century Co.
[182]"Black America," p. 214, Cassell & Company, London.

us believe that the offspring of these illicit unions are looked upon with contempt by members of the Negro race.

It seems to be difficult for the educated Negro to get away from the overwhelming desire to intermarry with the whites. He may frown upon illicit cohabitation between the races, but he is forever reaching out for that equality that will sanction intermarriage.

This same authority maintains that the Negro was bestialized by the development of the cotton industry, and that as a result of slavery he lost his pioneering spirit. When introduced in this country as a slave, the Negro with the Australian constituted the most degraded and savage portion of the human race. He was inevitably benefited by slavery and, so far as relates to a pioneering spirit, he never possessed one.

"The years, both of slavery and of freedom, passed by the Negro on this continent," says Stone, "constitute but an insignificant span in the life of that people; yet if we blot out the achievements of the American Negro who has passed through slavery, what has the race left to boast of? And if we but go one step farther, and from the achievements of the 'American Negro' obliterate all that the American mulatto has accomplished, what ground indeed would be left to those whose sentiment and sympathy have apparently rendered them so forgetful of scientific truth?"[183]

" . . . . . It is the voice of the mulatto, or that of the white politician, that is heard. If the statutes of those states which have been charged with discriminating against the Negro were not in any wise enforceable against the mulatto, I strongly suspect that America's race problem would speedily resolve itself into infinitely simpler proportions."[184]

The utterances of the educated Negro point with such unanimity to the one goal for which they are all striving—social equality—that it is useless merely to add cumulative evidence. However, as indicative of the spirit of the members of the "Talented Tenth," the following is given:

"What, then, is this dark world thinking?" asks Dr. W. E. B. DuBois, and he answers: "It is thinking that as wild and awful as this shameful war (referring to the World War) was, *it is*

---

[183]*Studies in the American Race Problem,* p. 429.
[184]Ibid., p. 433.

nothing to compare with that fight for freedom which black and brown and yellow men must and will make unless their oppression and humiliation and insult at the hands of the White World cease. The Dark World is going to submit to its present treatment just as long as it must and not one moment longer."[185]

This "Talented Tenth" exponent of Negro rights in America has enlisted on the side of the colored world and evidently looks forward with considerable pleasure to the day of reckoning.

The National Association for the Advancement of Colored People, at one of its annual gatherings in New York a few years ago, came to the conclusion that the time had come when they should make a concerted movement in the strife for social equality. They selected Virginia as the field in which an intensive campaign should be carried on with this end in view. When news of this character is broadcasted through the country by the Associated Press, it must be taken at its face value. It must be accepted, of course, as representing the aims and purposes of this organization, the most powerful in the ranks of the Negroes.

It seems that the field in Virginia was well chosen, if one of the states of the South was to be selected. The Hampton Normal Institute has been for years one of the prominent institutions of learning for the Negro, and is among the few that very properly lay great stress upon manual or industrial training. We may concede that in its inception the controlling motives leading to the establishment of this school were evidenced in a desire to fit the newly made freedmen into the industrial life of the body politic. Previously the efforts of the Negro had been directed by the will of the master; and, although he had been greatly benefited by the restraints under which he was held during slavery and by the example and instruction of the superior race with whom he was constantly thrown, he had not been taught to rely upon himself, and any effort to fit him into the position of independence thrust upon him was highly commendable. For many years this school was conducted with reasonable conformity to surrounding public opinion in regard to the relations between the races. Gradually, almost imperceptibly, the virus of social equality began to undermine racial barriers in the school and the effect of this was manifested in the surrounding community. The school grew more powerful with the passing of time, and

---

[185]*"Darkwater,"* p. 49, Harcourt, Brace and Howe.

a very potent factor in this growth, the dominating one, was donations that came in from time to time from influential and wealthy sympathizers in the North. Prominent and influential men in the North were placed on the Board of Trustees together with some members from the South whose association with the school might be of benefit to it locally. In time the institution became richly endowed, and, with the increased student body, came a corresponding increase in the faculty drawn from amongst educators who were interested in this sort of work. Thus there was gathered together in time an influential body of people who were, generally speaking, in sympathy with the aspirations of the Negro, and whose social activities were centered in a large degree around the school. Hampton is not a large town. It has not the facilities for accommodation and does not, therefore, get any of the large theatrical productions, musicals, operas, noted lecturers, etc. The Normal School has the facilities for their accommodation and frequently secures noted lecturers, musicians, singers, players, etc., for the entertainment and instruction of the student body and friends from Hampton and vicinity. Thus there has grown up a sort of clientele in the neighborhood largely dependent upon this institution for entertainment and consequently inclined to be sympathetic toward the institution. These ties are strengthened in other ways. The institution employs men in the professions, and expends large sums of money in the community. In the expenditure of these sums, it can easily be seen that it would most naturally go to those who, if not in active sympathy with the school, would not oppose it in any of its measures. In other words, the school has come to be regarded in the light of a big industry in the community; and it employs the usual instruments of and is given the usual position of primacy demanded by Big Business and received by it. Through the insidious operation of the forces outlined, the position of the school became so powerful that its present administration was enabled with impunity to abandon a custom, uniformly adhered to by former administrations, of separate seating arrangements for whites and blacks at school entertainments. They introduced the innovation of indiscriminately seating members of both races at these entertainments. In fact, by the methods of instruction employed and the relations existing between the members of the two races at the school, racial distinctions are discarded, and the student body is led to believe that the sole difference between the races lies in the matter of coloring.

The situation became so acute that there was, through the instrumentality of the Anglo-Saxon Club of Hampton and others interested, introduced in the General Assembly of Virginia a race segregation bill applicable to places of public amusement where a charge is made for admission. This was done before the politicians realized what it meant, and the bill soon reached that stage where it could not be quietly killed but had to be either supported or opposed. The politicians were smoked out and compelled to take sides, a procedure very distasteful to them. *They will support no proposed movement to solve the race problem, or that in any way disturbs the present trend of affairs, nor will they take the initiative themselves.* This bill met with opposition at hearings before the General Assembly from the chambers of commerce, the missionary element and some politicians. The bill became a law; but Big Business, the brotherhood-of-man disciples, and the politicians who dared not oppose the measure openly—these united forces have seen to it that the Anglo-Saxon Clubs have been the recipients of a sedative that has apparently proved lethal. At a hearing before the Senate Committee of the General Assembly, the two local members of the Board of Trustees stated that they were as much opposed to social equality as any one present, and that, if the bill were postponed for two years, they believed the matters complained of would be so corrected that the contemplated legislation would not be needed for that purpose. These gentlemen are still members of the board; traditions as to race relations are still openly flaunted in the face of the community; and the segregation law is violated in spirit, if not in letter, by subterfuge or evasion. It is to be regretted that a school noted for industrial training of the Negro should have fallen to such an unwise administration.

"In the city of Chicago there is an organization known as the 'Manasseh Society.' Membership in this society requires that each man shall have a negro wife and that each woman shall have a negro husband. Three or four years ago, according to The Chicago Blade, this society had a membership of 480."[186]

"Dr. Frederick L. Hoffman, in Eugenics in Race and State, Volume II, 1923, quotes Professor A. E. Jenks, of the University

---

[186]"*The Negro a Beast or In the Image of God,*" by Chas. Carroll, p. 280, 1900.

of Minnesota, who with an assistant made a study of the racial intermixture by marriage in St. Paul-Minneapolis. Professor Jenks, describing a club, says: 'This club is known as the "Manassas Club" and has about 200 members in the twin cities, its only rule for eligibility being that the negro seeking admission have a white wife'."

"The only objection raised to this horrible situation, says Professor Jenks, 'is raised by the black women, whose chief objection is that such marriages deprive a black girl of the opportunity of marrying a worthy black man." ("Eugenics in relation to the New Family and the law on Racial Integrity," p. 7.—Pamphlet issued by the Bureau of Vital Statistics, State Board of Health, Richmond, Va., 1924.)

"There are about 12,000,000 negroes of various degrees of admixture in the Union to-day. Of the population of Virginia, nearly one-third is classed as negro, but many of these people are negroid, some being near-white, some having actually succeeded in getting across into the white class."

"The mixed negroes are nearly all the result of illegitimate intercourse. The well known moral laxity, resulting from close contact of a civilized with a primitive race, makes illegitimate intermixture an easy matter. This is illustrated by the fact that the illegitimate birth-rate of Virginia negroes is thirty-two times that of Rhode Island, while the District of Columbia rate is thirty-seven times, and that of Maryland is forty-six times the Rhode Island rate."

"In the days when slavery was still a blight upon our State, it was quite a common occurrence for young white men or bachelor slave owners to father children born to the negro servants."

"The history as related to me of at least one colony of people known as 'Issue' or 'Free Issue,' which have now spread over several counties is that they originated in part in that manner."

"It was considered undesirable to retain these mulattoes on the place, bearing the family name, and a number from one county were given their freedom and colonized in a distant county. These intermarried amongst themselves and with some people of Indian-negro-white descent, and received an additional infusion of white blood, either illegitimately or by actual marriage with low-grade whites."

"At present these people are claiming to be white, or Indian, and under the former law, when a person with one-sixteenth negro blood could be declared white, they were able in some instances to establish their claim legally."

"These mixed breeds are not classed as white by the people of the community, and will not associate with the genuine negroes. Five hundred or more in number, they thus constitute a class of their own, and a serious problem in that county and others to which they migrate."

"If refused classification as white, they claim to be Indian, and as such, have been accepted in the birth reports to avoid listing them as white."

"In a recent test case, the court, upon evidence submitted from our birth records reaching back to 1853, and from the testimony of old residents, decided that these people under the new 'Racial Integrity' law, cannot be permitted to intermarry with whites."

"Another large colony which extends over into North Carolina probably has a similar origin. We have also compromised with these, and accept certificates as Indians, which indicates to us that they are not white."

"In another county are about forty descendants of an illegitimate mating of a negro man and white woman, four generations back. All of these have been succeeding in being classed as white, though under the new law our office has supplied clerks who issue marriage licenses, school authorities, Commonwealth's attorneys, physicians and local registrars with a complete family tree, with the injunction to class them as colored in the future."

"Similar conditions exist in other localities, though not yet so far advanced. A case was recently discovered where a white man married a mulatto woman (probably in another State), and now has nine children, four of them being reported to our office as white. Investigation revealed the fact that two other women bearing the same family name had mated with white men and were raising large families of children."

"Another man whose birth was reported in 1878, both parents being registered as colored, had the court declare him a white man under the one-sixteenth law, married a white woman, and has four children reported as white by physicians * * *."

"These examples illustrate the fact that even in Virginia, where the question of race and birth receive as much attention as anywhere in the country, the process of amalgamation is nevertheless going on, and in some localities is well advanced. Complete ruin can probably be held off for several centuries longer, but we have no reason to hope that we shall prove the one and only example in the history of the world, of two races living together without amalgamation.[187]

"In reference to nearly everything which concerns the welfare of their race," says Professor Dowd, "the Negroes of our country are divided into two opposing camps. One group seeks the interest of their race through law enforcement, and the enactment of more legislation designed to protect the Negroes against unfair discriminations, and its general attitude towards the whites, especially the Southern whites, is one of antagonism. The other seeks the interest of their race through the elevation of its economic, educational, and moral status, with the view of preparing it for the exercise of whatever rights and privileges belong to free men. And this latter group, in all of its policies, seeks a better understanding and cooperation between the races."[188]

"The question they (referring to the Negro leaders in the North) are more interested in than any other is that of social equality, and their main efforts are directed to the abolition of all laws or arrangements which would prevent the free intermixture of the whites and blacks in schools, vehicles of transportation, hotels, restaurants, theaters, parks, etcetera, and to build up a public sentiment which would do away with every form of discrimination on account of color. They assume that the Negro is equal to the white man, and that whatever interferes with the free intermingling of the two races is merely the result of narrow prejudice. They look with disfavor on any author who makes a plea for any kind of racial integrity. A recent reviewer in the *Journal of Negro History* refers to 'the idea of racial integrity' as 'the fundamental cause of race hate'."[189]

"The organization of the N. A. A. C. P. definitely divided the Negroes of the United States into two opposing schools of thought. The one, composed mostly of Northern mulattoes, emphasized political action, and, because of its general indictment of the whites (the Southern whites in particular), and its violent and braggadocio spirit, was called the militant school. The pro-

[187]From a paper entitled, *"Virginia's Attempt to Adjust the Color Problem,"* read by Dr. W. A. Plecker, State Registrar of Vital Statistics, Richmond, Va., before the American Public Health Association, at Detroit, October 23, 1924.
[188]*"The Negro in American Life,"* p. 502, The Century Co.
[189]Ibid., p. 503.

gram of the N. A. A. C. P. for 1921 relates entirely to political lines of action, and is as follows:"

"1. Anti-Lynching legislation by Congress.

"2. Abolition of Segregation in the Departments at Washington.

"3. Enfranchisement of the Negro or reduction of southern representation, if necessary.

"4. Restoration of Haitian independence and reparation, as far as possible. for wrongs committed there by the American administration, through Congressional investigation of both military and civil acts of the American Occupation.

"5. Presentation to the new President of a mammoth petition of say, 100,000 *bona fide* signers, collected by the various branches, requesting the pardon of the soldiers of the 24th Infantry imprisoned at Leavenworth on the charge of rioting at Houston, Texas.

"6. The abolition of jim-crow cars in interstate traffic.

"7. Treatment of colored men in the Navy; where once many ratings as non-commissioned officers were held by Negroes, now colored men can enlist only as mess boys, in other words, as servants.

"8. Appointment of a National Inter-Racial Commission to make an earnest study of race conditions and race relations in the United States.

"9. Appointment of colored assistant secretaries in the Labor and Agricultural Departments which would give the Negro official representation in the two phases of national life where he needs most and suffers most.

"10. Continuance of the fight in the Arkansas cases."[190]

Professor Dowd seems to view the situation with calm contentment. He has no fear of amalgamation although he points it out as a fact that, everywhere among the Negroes, the light colored complexion is preferred, and that the mulattoes "form a sort of *aristocratie de couleur,* and stand aloof from the blacks."[191] One of his grounds for justification in this conclusion is what he conceives to be a number of pertinent instances in which widely different races have occupied the same territory in segregation without this evil effect. He says: "Instances of

---

[190]*"The Negro in American Life,"* p. 515, The Century Co.
[191]Ibid., p. 97.

territorial segregation of races in the same country are the Japanese and Ainu of Japan, the Malays and Negritos of the Philippine Islands, the Europeans and the aborigines of South Africa, the Yankees and Sandwich Islanders in Hawaii, and the Americans and Amerindians of Porto Rico. The most striking instance of race stratification is in India."[192]

It would seem that none of the examples cited by him supports his contention when subjected to critical examination. Beyond question primitive peoples are markedly impressed with consciousness of kind, and, when they extend their activities beyond the provision of simple necessities for self and family, their collective action is due to primitive race consciousness and not to the common interest of the tribe or some part of it in an undertaking for the betterment of the tribe or the individual. In other words, it is simply gregarious in character. This primitive race consciousness persists until an advanced culture brings about a desire for national expression and eventually civilization with stratification of society as a result of diversification or differentiation in the mental attitude, moral forces, intellectual pursuits, and in commercial and industrial activities. Specialization may proceed so far that race consciousness among a civilized people will manifest itself only in the case of a direct and positive external danger.

The Aïnos were isolated in the extreme northern island of the Japanese Main Group; neither race has lost its primitive race consciousness; and they have not been engaged in any joint undertakings. Under such circumstances it is not surprising that the Aïnos should have survived. The same identical conditions have operated and are still in operation to preserve the integrity of the Malays and Negritos in the Philippine Islands. The conditions in South Africa seem to be quite different from what Professor Dowd imagines them to be; for, in accordance with all reliable authority, Cape Colony indisputably has on her hand a very serious race problem, entirely aside from that of the blacks, in connection with the mixed bloods resulting from the crossing of blacks and whites.

The natives of the Sandwich Islands are estimated to have numbered about 300,000 when Cook discovered the Islands in 1779, and in 1872 there were 51,531. This enormous decrease "has been attributed by most writers to the profligacy of the

---

[192]"*The Negro in American Life*," p. 471, The Century Co.

women, to former bloody wars, and to the severe labour imposed
on conquered tribes and to newly introduced diseases, which have
been on several occasions extremely destructive. No doubt these
and other such causes have been highly efficient, and may account
for the extraordinary rate of decrease between the years 1832 and
1836; but the most potent of all the causes seems to be lessened
fertility."[193] Only a small remnant of these people remain; and
it is but reasonable to assume that there survives as large percent
of mixture between native and Yankee as could be looked for
under such adverse conditions. In 1898 there were about 37,000
pure-blooded Hawaiians and about 10,000 mixed-bloods.

If Professor Dowd, in referring to the Amerindians of Porto
Rico, has in mind the descendents of the aborigines, they must be
Amerindians in a sense similar to that in which certain people are
admitted to registration as Indians under the new Racial Integrity Law in Virginia. These latter people, a mixture in various
degrees of black and white blood, are classed as non-whites and
permitted to register as Indians on claim of Indian blood. The
occupation of Porto Rico by Americans has been of short duration and the conditions not favorable for amalgamation between
them and the so-called Amerindians.

In accordance with the Encyclopedia Britannica, Eleventh Edition, the total population of Porto Rico was 583,308 in 1860,
798,565 in 1887, 953,243, or 277.5 per square mile, in 1899; and
in this last mentioned year 589,426, or 61.8%, were classed as
white, 304,352 as mixed bloods, 59,390 as Negroes, and 75 as
Chinese.

"By 1520 philanthropic churchmen directed their attention to
the miserable conditions of the natives; but remedial legislation
was largely nullified by the rapacity of subordinate officials, and
before the end of the 16th century the natives disappeared as a
distinct race." (The Encyclopedia Britannica, Eleventh Edition.)

"Some Carib Indians survive in Dominica, and traces of another Indian tribe, the gentle Arawaks, whose women were re-
puted the handsomest in the world, can still be detected in the
interior of Porto Rico. There are Hindus in Trinidad and Martinique, Syrian traders on most of the islands, and Chinese everywhere. But these are merely flavorings in the West Indian pepper-

---

[193]Darwin's *"The Descent of Man,"* p. 186.

pot—the substance of the dish is everywhere Negroes, Negroes, Negroes."[194]

The conditions of contact between us and the Negro are entirely different from those of the peoples cited above. Through specialization in almost every conceivable way our race consciousness has become so dulled it does not manifest itself unless we are nationally threatened by a recognized and imminent danger from without or within, or some specialized body of great power within the body politic conceives its interest to be threatened and appeals to race pride in its search for support.

This primitive race consciousness manifests itself in every public act and utterance of the Negro; but, however rigid segregation may be in domicile or in the enjoyment of public utilities, the intimate association in jointly carrying out the innumerable undertakings of every day life tends to smother race consciousness in the individual and eliminate race repugnance in the furtherance of amalgamation.

The preservation, in a great measure at least, of the racial integrity of two primitive peoples who live in segregation, the one from the other, though adjoining, is the logical consequence of primitive race consciousness; but that racial integrity can be preserved where a highly civilized people uses in intimate association a backward, inferior people in carrying on its numerous specialized operations, seems impossible.

No comment need be made in regard to that "most striking instance of race stratification" in India.

It may well be that the Negro leaders are divided into two distinct camps as regards the Negro's *immediate* aims and there may actually be ill feeling between the two; but that does not mean that the results achieved in the end may be different.

That the aims of the Negro of the North and the N. A. A. C. P. are to be taken seriously should be apparent to any one who has taken an interest in the race problem. Anti-Lynching legislation was seriously threatened during the 1st Session of the 68th Congress; and the favorable report by the majority of the Committee on the Judiciary in the House was apparently based on the "Lynching record for 1923," furnished by the National Association for the Advancement of Colored People upon the telegraphic re-

---

[194]"*An Ethnological Potpourri*," Arnold Hollriegel's "*The West Indian Pepper-Pot*," from Berliner Tageblatt, Liberal Daily, November 14, published in "*The Living Age*" for January 1, 1927.

quest of Hon. L. C. Dyer, a member of the Committee. The Committee proceeded on the assumption that a lynching is a denial, by the State within which it occurs, to the person lynched of that "equal protection of the laws" guaranteed by the 14th Amendment. To hold that "equal protection of the laws" can extend further than the nullification of discriminatory laws that in effect fail to protect, is simply to annihilate the last vestige of independent authority in the States. The whole thing is nothing more or less than an effort to extend illegally the criminal jurisdiction of the United States, and it seems impossible to find authority for such procedure in the Constitution. There is nothing approaching a direct grant of criminal jurisdiction outside of that relating to the punishment of treason, the government of the land and naval forces, and territories of the United States. It can arise in no other cases except as a necessary incident to the execution of granted powers in the prevention of unlawful obstruction; and the extension of criminal jurisdiction by implication, even if the Negro does wish it, is a dangerous doctrine that should find no support amongst us.

Haiti was occupied under a Democratic Administration, and its continued occupancy is now being opposed by a Democratic Senator. There is no intention here to intimate that the Senator is not acting entirely on his own responsibility and in response to his own convictions and sympathies; or that he has the least sympathy with the N. A. A. C. P. It can be safely assumed, however, that this organization knows what is going on and is backing the Resolution of Senator King to its utmost.

The matter of the enfranchisement of the Negro, or reduction of representation from the South, is agitated at almost every session of Congress, and it is reasonable to attribute the largest part of this, if not all, to the efforts of the Negro.

Everywhere the Negro in his own race seems to prefer the lighter color; and his race consciousness uniformly asserts itself in protest against any discrimination that seemingly places him in contrast with the whites. In conflict with the tendency of primitive race consciousness to produce segregation and contentment in association with his own race, is another manifestation of race consciousness in the aggressive assertion of an equality, if not superiority, not possessed, when in contact with a superior race. The Negro knows that he is really inferior to the white man, and he attempts to bury the actualities in an aggressive campaign for equality, which merely adds to his unreasoning frenzy. There can be no acknowledgment of the equality of the Negro that carries conviction unless all discriminations are removed and he is accepted fully into the American family.

William Archer, an English student of our race problem, says as to race equality: "Our theorists are, on the whole, too much inclined to confound instinct with prejudice. It is absurd to class as pure prejudice the white man's preference for the colour and facial contour of his race. This is no place for an analysis of our sense of beauty; but to maintain offhand that it is an unmeaning product of sheer habit, with no biological justification, is simply to shirk the problem and postpone analysis to dogma. Does any one really believe that the genius of Caesar and Napoleon, of Milton and Goethe, had nothing to do with their facial angle, and could have found an equally convenient habitation behind thick lips and under wooly skulls? The negro himself (as distinct from the mulatto rhetorician) takes his stand on no such paradox. Whoever may doubt the superiority of the white race, it is not he; and it is a racial, not merely a social or economic superiority to which he does instinctive homage. It does not enter his head to champion his own racial ideal, to set up an African Venus in rivalry to the Hellenic, and claim a new Judgment of Paris between them. If wishing could change the Ethiopian's skin there would be never a negro in America. The black race, out of its poverty, spends thousands of dollars annually on 'anti-kink' lotions, vainly supposed to straighten the African wool. The brown belle tones her complexion with pearl powder; and many a black mother takes pride in the brown skin of her offspring, though it proclaims their illegitimacy. There can be no reasonable doubt that amalgamation, in the negro's eyes, means an enormous gain to his race. It means ennoblement, transfiguration. It is quite natural that he should not too curiously inquire whether the gain to him would involve a corresponding loss to the white man. That is the white man's business, not his. The one thing his instinct tells him is that, if he can break down the white man's resistance and make the Southern States a brown or yellow man's land, he will have achieved a splendid racial triumph."[195]

The leaders of the Negroes in the South are differently situated

---

[195]Taken by permission from William Archer's "*Through Afro-America*," pp. 223-225, copyright by E. P. Dutton & Co., Inc.

from those in the North; and it is but natural that they should seek a *modus vivendi* under which the practical operations would be those fitted to their surroundings. If the leaders in the South are preparing by present uplift work for future demands of the same character as those now made by the Northern leaders, then the difference in the end is a disagreement as to the time when demands for erasure of the color line shall be made.

Not even a single insignificant fact can be found in all history, as I see it, that lends credit to any belief or hope that there may be a parallel development of the two races along their respective lines of genius free from the menace of amalgamation.

"The general opinion of the world, as we know," remarks J. B. Crozier, an English writer, "is that these mixtures may be safely permitted, provided always that the Government in power will see to it that strict *justice* is done alike to all the races and creeds concerned, without fear or favour . . ."[196] But, he adds: "I venture to affirm on the contrary . . . that of all the political curses which can befall a nation, this mixing of inherently antagonistic races, colours, creeds, and codes of morality, is the one which, when once it has been allowed (it matters not for what reason), is of all political complications the most irremediable by any and every known instrument for the uplifting of mankind— whether by the exhortations of the Pulpit or Press, by Legislation, by the Good Will of all concerned, or even (if the races are any way evenly matched) by Physical Force itself, short of a war of extermination—as, indeed, the Negro problem in America, the Jewish problem on the Continent, the mixture of races and creeds in Austria-Hungary, in the Balkans, in Ireland, and in India, bear only too eloquent and despairing witness."[197]

"And the reason," says he, "is as simple as it is deep and universal, and may be put in nutshell—namely, that the pure white of Justice, which is believed to be the remedy for all political evils, will be strained and degraded by the impure colours of the mixtures into which it has to plunge and dye its hand, long *before* these mixtures will admit of justice being applied to them; and, further, that the higher moral code of nations, instead of being raised by the attempt to apply it, will, during the progress of the

---

[196]*"Sociology Applied to Practical Politics,"* p. 120, Longmans, Green and Co., London.
[197]Ibid., p. 121.

experiment, become more and more deranged, until it descends, with its lynchings and homicides in its train, to the level of barbarism again. My contention, in other words, is that the application of pure justice to these mixtures can never get a foothold at all, but will be blocked at every turn from the start; and that to imagine or expect otherwise is of all delusions and utopias the most hopeless—besides being fraught with the most terrible consequences to the posterity of any and every nation that embarks on it."[198]

Dr. Crozier further remarks:— "A Government might just as well say, 'Go to! we must try and rectify the injustice and inequality of Nature whereby a single bull in a herd of a particular breed is permitted to drive out all its poorer and weaker rivals of other breeds equally good, by allowing to each and all of them indifferently within the *same* enclosed field an equal number of cows,' as to attempt to realize a civic and social justice and equality among a motley admixture of human races of different colours, traditions, and codes of morality, on the same area of soil. It can only be done by keeping these races *apart* in their respective countries; precisely as justice, or equality, to all bulls can only be done by keeping them with their equal contingent of cows in separate fields. Otherwise, what will be the result? Why this (and it is the pathos of the whole situation), that the very end for which all good men are striving, namely, to do justice and mercy to all poor human souls of whatever race, or colour, or creed, will be damned by the very *means* which are being taken to effect it. For, as the mixture of negroes and whites in America bears witness, instead of getting that high ideal of justice which is the flower of civilization, you will get—what? Lynching, or a return to that lowest form of justice which is proper to barbarism; and so the work of the ages will all have to be done over again from the bottom upwards. The mere presence of alien races and colours in sufficient numbers on the same area is enough to work its damning effects even without intermarriage, the vote, or social promiscuity. For just as the pigeon-fanciers tell us that you can spoil a particular strain by keeping other breeds alongside of it, even when there is no intermixture in the mating; so all we should have to do in England, for example, would be, as I said in another article, to admit a sufficient number of Kaffirs into the coun-

---

[198]"*Sociology Applied to Practical Politics*," pp. 121-2, Longmans, Green and Co., London.

try to do menial or unskilled labour, and a sufficient number of Chinese or Japanese to do the more refined and skilled forms, when it could safely be predicted that, within a generation, hardly a self-respecting Englishman, short of starvation, would be found to do a stroke of menial labor for love or money—as was seen in the Southern States of America before the war, and as we see, in a way, in the South Africa of to-day. And if respect for honest labour is recognised by all as an indispensable preliminary to social justice and equality, and to the best well-being of States, would not this be a fine stultification of our end by the very means with which we are seeking to effect it?"

"The root-fallacy of it all lies, as I have had so often to repeat, in not perceiving that Justice is not an unlimited bank credit which can be brought down from Heaven and drawn on like divine grace to its full amount at any time, but is in each and every age of the world, and as a matter of actual concrete fact, strictly limited by the material and social *conditions* of the time; as on a chess-board, where the prospects of the game are determined at each point by the relative positions of the pieces on the board, and not by the mere goodwill of the players; so that if you have whites, negroes, Chinese, Mahomedans, and Hindoos confronting one another in the street, and spitting in each other's faces as they pass, the amount of social justice that either gods or men can get out of such relationship will quickly be discovered to differ *toto coelo* from what can be got without effort or strife from the simple relations of fellow-citizens of the *same* blood, colour, religion, and code of social morality on the same area of political soil. And just as the properties of a chemical compound, whether of prussic acid or our ordinary food, will depend on how you arrange, by bringing together or keeping apart, the same chemical elements common to both; so the character and quality of the justice and the social morality you can get out of men will depend on whether you mix the different races, or keep them apart, on the same areas of soil."[199]

And, says he, "until the Millennium comes, there is no political complication which will more surely act as a direct incentive to murder, anarchy, and every form of moral degradation, than these unblest and thrice-accursed unions. The whole scheme of

---

[199]*"Sociology Applied to Practical Politics,"* pp. 124-6, Longmans, Green and Co., London.

Nature goes dead against them, and all history is strewn with the ruins of the nations that have either knowingly encouraged, or unwillingly have been forced to submit to them."[200]

---

[200]"*Sociology Applied to Practical Politics*," p. 123, Longmans, Green and Co., London.

Note—The reading of Dr. John Beattie Crozier's work "*Sociology Applied to Practical Politics*" is recommended to Americans who are interested in the preservation of our democratic institutions.

CHAPTER IV.

THE MENACE

THE EDUCATION GIVEN PRODUCES DISCONTENT.

There can be no doubt that the introduction of the Negro into America as a slave was the greatest crime perpetrated by the White race within the historic period. We, the whites, have been bitterly paying the penalty, both in peace and war, in a loss of moral stamina and a diminishing Christian zeal, in the substitution of uncertainty and chicanery for directness and open dealing, and uneasiness for contentment. We have suffered a loss of ideals and of confidence in ourselves, and we have not yet reached the limits of the penalty in which we are involved because of this crime. We have suffered, are suffering, and will continue to do so unless we are willing to make the final atonement that will cleanse us of the offense committed, unwittingly as I believe, by our forefathers.

Whatever doubts may honestly exist as to the absolute identification in all respects of some of the civilized peoples of antiquity, there can be no doubt as to the absolute identity of the Negro race throughout the ages, its antiquity, and its fixed characteristics from the remote past till now. Therefore, there can be no doubt that slavery in America, irrespective of the selfish motives or extravagant and distorted religious views that promoted its institution, was, from the point of view of Negro advancement, the much needed school in which he was prepared for any possible national aspirations that might be unfolded to him in the future; but the training he has received since Emancipation and the experiences through which he went during the Reconstruction Period, have more and more unfitted him to remain as a part of the body politic in America unless we are willing to sacrifice our aspirations and institutions in order that he may remain with us.[201] On

201 That this is a fact well understood by the Negro leaders and one that gives them courage in their aggressive campaign for the removal of all discriminations against them should be apparent

the other hand, his training as a whole has so equipped him that he may hope with some reason to give expression to his national aspirations if transported to Africa under favorable circumstances. His preparation would, however, have been better had he been instructed with this end in view from the time of Emancipation.

In the early days of slavery the position of master and servant was clearly understood. There was no competition between the two, the superiority of the one and the inferiority and dependence of the other were mutually recognized. The situation assumed something of a patriarchal society in which, most generally, there existed an esteem and consideration between master and slave and not infrequently an affection as well.

The agitation of the slavery question, its eventual abolition as one of the incidents of a bitter Civil War, and particularly what has been done since the Civil War, have completely obliterated former friendly relations and substituted therefor suspicion and dislike, and, on the part of the Negro, the development of ambitions incompatible with peaceful relations.

It was almost uniformly the testimony of disinterested European observers that, as a rule, the Negro slave was contented and happy. Beginning with Emancipation and ending with the close of Reconstruction, these childlike and naturally goodnatured people were led by war-maddened or unscrupulous persons to indulge in all sorts of extravagant ideas as to their capacity to govern and right to rule in the land that had witnessed their "base degradation in servitude."

When common sense began to assert itself in the North and the armed forces used in support of the Negro and his leaders were withdrawn, the corrupt, wicked, and beastly machine was destroyed. Though common sense asserted itself thus far, there was lack of courage to undo the evil that had been done in tinkering with the Constitution on the pretense, or even supposition as it honestly might have been in some cases, that human liberty was being advanced. The disappointment of this child-

---

from the words of Reverdy C. Ransom, a Negro preacher (quoted on p. 184), that: "Taught by the Declaration of Independence, sustained by the Constitution of the United States, enlightened by the education of our schools, this nation can no more resist the advancing tread of the hosts of the oncoming blacks than it can bind the stars or halt the resistless motion of the tide."

like good-natured people was great. Disappointment became a deep, sullen resentment that filled a vast reservoir within their being capable of being drawn upon at any time by the unscrupulous, and this condition is made more dangerous by education in that it broadens the activities prompted by resentment.

Without having formed any plans for the solution of the problem and in the expectation that the Negro would be with us forever, a large body of our people have become interested in many cooperative measures, religious, educational, and industrial in character, with the hope and expectation that, with education and a general amelioration of the conditions of life for the Negro, a better era would be brought about.

The Negro having had a taste of political power during Reconstruction, having had held before him the promise of social equality during that period and since by unscrupulous persons or mistaken zealots, and the War Amendments still holding out to him promise of both, it is simply preposterous to imagine that education of the Negro will make for peaceful relations between the races.

The sum total of all these efforts, it seems to me, has been the gradual wearing away of the race barriers so far as the whites are concerned, and an intensification of the ambition of the Negro to offensively assert his assumed equality even though it should result in wrecking the State itself.

Our energies directed toward the education of the Negro have not been niggardly given. At first (after emancipation) these efforts were entirely in the hands of Northern philanthropists and friends of the Negro, but recently there has been displayed as much enthusiasm for uplift work and education of the Negro among the people of the South as among those of the North; and in North Carolina there was spent more for the education of the Negro during Governor Morrison's administration from 1921 to 1925, than there was on the education of the whites during the period from 1900 to 1904.

The churches, chambers of commerce, and educators have united in various and sundry cooperative educational and uplift movements. These forces have established numerous schools, colleges, and universities throughout the land, most of them top-heavy, inappropriate, and filled with mulattoes—not Negroes. Endowments are bountifully distributed for educational purposes, included in which are studies and investigations bearing upon the relations of the races. One of these philanthropic donations seems to have been given for the purpose of benefiting the Negro through the study of racial relations. It operates through a corporate body which seems to have made provisions for the establishment of fellowships at the University of Virginia for the study of the Negro. The net effect of all these movements seems to be securing special privileges and consideration for the Negro at the expense of the whites by neglecting the latter in many instances and by wearing away the barriers between the races.

In this uplift and educational work, the missionary element has been prominent; and among the churches the Congregational Church takes the lead. This church has, since Emancipation, contributed over $30,000,000 to the education of the Negro in the South; and the organization of this church in the State of New York has a Negro minister for its Vice-Moderator, and the organization in New York City has one for its Moderator.

"My own impression," says W. Laird Clowes, an English writer on our race problem, "as derived from somewhat wide observation, is that, since the emancipation, the distance has really as well as apparently increased, and that it is still increasing. Whites and blacks have less in common than of yore; there is less chance than there ever was of their working together peacefully for good; and racial antagonism, nourished by both sides, grows daily. There are many signs, too, of this growing antagonism. On the side of the negro there is a desire to be what the white man is, and to do what the white man does—to elevate himself to the same level of privileges, with or without the pre-requisite education and fitness for the elevation. He argues blindly that the legal right confers the needful fitness. The law opens positions to him, and he is a voter. Why then should he not vote himself and his friends into the positions? And education by no means tends to decrease the friction, seeing that the white man is as prejudiced against an educated negro as against an ignorant one. On the contrary, it adds to it. When the uneducated black thinks himself the equal of the white, the educated black cannot be expected to submit resignedly to be regarded as the white's inferior. Yet he is obliged to affect the resignation which he cannot feel. He must suppress his real sentiments, or he must risk physical maltreatment."[202] Of course the Negro knows he is inferior, and he resents it as would be ex-

---

[202]"*Black America*," pp. 90-1, Cassell & Company, London.

pected in a people physically mature but with the development otherwise of the immature youth. The mulatto, superior in mental make up and attainments, just naturally resents being excluded from the ranks of the whites and included within that of the Negro.

"Unfortunately," says Clowes, "there are no symptoms whatever that the spread of education among the negroes is causing, or ever will cause, the diminution of white prejudice against the race."[203]

It gives added confidence to my conclusions as to the futility of education as a peace measure, to find they are in accord with those of the late Dr. Samuel Macon Smith, whom I was fortunate enough to have as the pastor of my church when I was a boy.

"And Dr. S. M. Smith, D. D., of Columbia, South Carolina, writing in the *Presbyterian Quarterly* for October, 1889, takes the same view. His conclusions are thus summed up by the Raleigh *State Chronicle:—*

'The patent panacea for all negro defects, education, does not mend matters in the least; an "educated" negro is just as much negro as before, just the same raw hide volume with the incongruous addition of a gilt edge; he is only a little more aggressively offensive than his less ornate brother. Social complications are not at all lessened by education, nor mitigated by "light complexions" either.' " [204]

Other English authors, Archer and Bryce, also take the view that education not only fails to make for harmony between the races, but rather makes the situation more hazardous and complicated.

"The very carelessness of the negroes," says Clowes, "on the subject of the white man's most cherished creeds and principles has more than once gone near to provoke a dreadful outbreak. The article already cited from the Selma *Independent* narrowly escaped doing so, although it contained only vulgar threats. More dangerous was an article that was printed in August, 1887, in another negro paper, the Montgomery *Herald.* 'Every day or so,' it said brutally, 'we read of the lynching of some negro for outraging some white woman. Why is it that white women attract negro men more than in former days? There was a time when

---

[203]"*Black America,*" p. 119, Cassell & Company, London.
[204]Ibid., p. 165.

such a thing was unheard of. There is a secret to this thing, and we greatly suspect it is the growing appreciation of the white Juliet for the coloured Romeo as he becomes more and more intelligent and refined. If something is not done to break up these lynchings it will be so that after a while they will lynch every coloured man that looks at a white woman with a twinkle in his eye.' "[205]

Such articles as these are the result of the so-called education of the Negro. Articles of a similar character, though not so bad as this unless under exceptional circumstances, are of daily occurrence in the Negro press throughout the country.

Of the total number of Negro children in the United States between the ages of 5 and 20 years, 9.2 per cent were going to school in 1870; 32.5 per cent, in 1880; 32 per cent, in 1890; 31.3 per cent, in 1900; 54.4 per cent, in 1910; and 54 per cent, in 1920. The corresponding percentages for the whites between the same ages were: 51.2, 58.2, 55.4, 54.5, 62.6, 67. Thus, in accordance with "Abstract of Fourteenth Census, 1920," the school attendance of Negro children of the ages given increased from 9.2 per cent to 54 per cent from 1870 to 1920, whereas that for the whites increased from 51.2 per cent to 67 per cent for the same period.

From the same source of information it appears that illiteracy among the whites of ten years of age and over decreased from 11.5 per cent in 1870 to 4 per cent in 1920, whereas that of the Negro for the same period decreased from 81.4 per cent to 22.9 per cent. The trend of the times is here sufficiently indicated; and this accomplishment, pointed to with pride by so many, has been brought about by whites whose legal control of the land depends upon the bar to the franchise of the Negro erected through the introduction of an educational qualification. This resolves itself into a game of ten pins in which the pins can be set up but once—a highly intellectual and exciting game.

The racial cooperative movements, entirely outside of any religious organizations, that have been put in operation by educators in schools and colleges, industrial concerns and chambers of commerce, are something appalling. They increase the appetite for a greater social contact; increase discontent with the existing order; and lead us further from solution.

---

[205]"*Black America*," pp.141-2, Cassell & Company, London.

There appeared in The Virginian-Pilot for January 24, 1927, under the caption "The Jim Crow Law," the following article quoted from The Charlottesville Progress: "Repeal of the Jim Crow law, enacted in 1904 to require transportation companies to provide separate places for white and colored passengers, was recommended yesterday by the Maryland Inter-racial Commission in its report to Governor Ritchie and the General Assembly."

"In its report the commission stated that any reason for the law which might have been in existence when it was enacted has been removed by the progress made by the Negro race in recent years."

"But the South is not yet ready for such a step. Inborn prejudices, made more poignant by smouldering memories of the reconstruction days, still remain. And as long as they remain there can be no repeal of the Jim Crow law without trouble resulting."

"There is no question that repeal of the law would mean a forward stride for the South. It would mean that the South recognizes the possibilities and worth of the Negro race to its civilization, and that it is willing to give the Negro the same privileges as the white race."

"There are many, however, who see another side of the question. And in order to effect such changes, time must be allowed for the healing of the old war wounds and the awakening of a newer and greater respect for the dark race of this country."

The Daily Press, Newport News, Va., June 29, 1926, carried the following news item: "Campaign to Raise a Million to Fight 'Jim Crow' Law Is Started at Chicago Meeting. Chicago, June 28.—A campaign to raise $1,000,000 to fight the segregation and disfranchisement of negroes and 'Jim Crow' laws was launched yesterday at a mass meeting of the National Association for the Advancement of Colored People in annual conference here. The movement was formally opened by James Weldon Johnson of New York, secretary of the association. The principal address of the meeting was delivered by Clarence Darrow."

"Characterizing the practices against which the campaign fund will be directed as constituting the 'last vestige of slavery,' Johnson declared that 'such a fund will be a demonstration of the mass power which the negro intends to use, and will serve notice upon the country of the negro's determination to secure and maintain every fundamental right with every other American citizen.' "

" 'The federal government,' Johnson said, 'will use a navy to prevent a man from taking a drink, but will not empower a deputy marshal to protect the negro's ballot.' "

"Darrow hailed the beginning of the end of race prejudice in America in his address."

" 'The new generation of white men,' he said, 'has no feeling of race hatred. This spirit is professed particularly by those of the younger generation, who are expressing themselves in public addresses as favoring the equality of races. They cannot fail to affect the mass of the people.' "

"The negroes of the United States are better educated than ever and are just beginning to help themselves, Darrow said."

The review here set forth presents anything but a pleasing aspect; and shows us that all these various, feverish activities, irrespective of the intent behind them, are working the destruction of race barriers and with it that of the people who are the responsible actors in all this. This can all be changed by adopting a fixed and definite policy as to solution, when education and uplift work as applied to the Negro will have some definite end in view, and will appeal to all whites for enthusiastic support. As things stand now, we forget many needs of our own people in our ill-directed and mischievous zeal for the Negro. Many white sections are still clamoring for adequate school facilities and an alleviation of social and other surrounding conditions; and surely the foreigner invited to our shores has some claim upon us; and, if not in his interest, we should see our way clear to doing something for him in our own interest in view of his assimilable character. These last two classes do not seem to hold any appeal for the Negrophile philanthropist.

It seems remarkable that we should be accused of entertaining hatred for the Negro simply because we refuse to accept equality of the races, or to grow enthusiastic over the political guarantees given the Negro under the Constitution; and that we should be the recipients of abuse because we withhold approval of aimless, experimental uplift-movements, which, disregarding science, history and common sense, are based upon the absolute sameness of the races. For myself, I entertain no ill will toward the Negro, but would, on the other hand, compensate him for what our forefathers did by making it possible for him to realize some of his nationalist or racial aspirations in the only field in which it is possible for them to be realized. I must admit, however, a deep-seated impatience with the members of our own race who, realizing the peril, remain mute and inactive, and with those who permit a silly sentimentalism to blind them as to the real situation, and neglect the opportunities presented for a truly great spiritual work.

If the Negro were so placed, through geographical segregation in a State of his own, that he had his destiny in his own hands, education would be relatively of the same value to him as to the white man; but it is simply folly to imagine that education will make for peace and a common understanding where they occupy the same area as distinct and separate peoples.

AMALGAMATION.

Amalgamation grows apace despite assertions to the contrary by casual observers and even by writers who have gone exhaustively into the subject of race relations but have failed to get the proper insight into this particular angle of the question. Absolutely accurate data on the subject cannot be had; for the best available general information, that coming from the census returns, is admittedly subject to considerable error. It can be readily understood that insuperable difficulties prevent absolute accuracy in the census returns as made in this respect. The lessons of history in regard to amalgamation will be ignored by the average American who imagines himself free from the penalties that followed in similar situations among other people. The only way in which he can be convinced is by absolutely accurate data, and the only way in which this can be obtained is through the operation of a race registration law in each State in the Union. Until this is done the most reliable information to be had is that collected by individuals who have devoted years to this study and availed themselves of every opportunity for investigation; and the conclusions arrived at by them are of the greatest value in forming any conception of the true situation. Dr. W. A. Plecker, Registrar of Vital Statistics, State of Virginia, the Rev. A. H. Shannon, formerly of Mississippi, now of Washington, D. C., Major E. S. Cox, author of "White America," and Mr. John Powell, both of Richmond, Va., are gentlemen who, among others, have devoted years to the study of amalgamation. They all conclude it is a menace to the country and that unless our race problem is solved within the near future, it is but a question of centuries when we shall be a people of the same general type and capacities as are the Hindus.

The mulatto, or near white, who lives in our neighborhood cannot marry into a white family, because he is known and such marriage is forbidden by law. He may move into a distant part of the State or to another State and pass for a white. This is done clandestinely, for it could not be otherwise done, and no record of such cases can be obtained. The mismating may show itself in a marked reversion to type of the lower order of ancestor in some future generation, and it most assuredly will manifest itself in a general type inferior to its white ancestor. The marked exception, which may occur at rare intervals, does not vitiate the rule.

Estabrook and McDougal in their work, "Mongrel Virginians," give the history and important characteristics of what they call the "Win Tribe," and refer to several other similar bodies throughout the State. These various bodies number about two thousand, dwell in more or less seclusion and intermarry amongst themselves, though there may be an occasional infusion of new blood from the outside, or a migration from the body of a member or members occasionally. They claim to be Indian, or at least class themselves as such, whereas they are as a matter of fact a conglomeration of Negro, Indian and white. They compose a body of people the State would be infinitely better off without. Similar bodies exist in other States. The work just mentioned does not take any account of the ordinary mulatto that lives and moves and has his being among us in our every day life.

No State in the Union exercises more care in the preservation of racial integrity than does Virginia, but all this will avail nothing unless a solution of the problem is soon found.

"Where civilization has met savagery," says Archer, "elsewhere than in Africa, the savage race has generally dwindled to a degraded and negligible remnant. The African races alone have shown considerable tenacity of life and considerable power of putting on at any rate a veneer of civilization. This is as much as to say that only between Europeans and Africans has the active competition arisen which is the essence of the race problem. In some part of Spanish America it has resulted in the practical fusion of the races; a solution which, as above noted, commends itself to some thinkers. But where fusion is resisted, the problem must one day become acute; and that day has arrived in the Southern States. There the two races are more nearly than anywhere else

on a footing of numerical equality; there, more than anywhere
else, is the ambition of the African race stimulated by political
theory and seconded by education, organization, and considerable
material resources. The Southern States, then, are, so to speak,
the great crucible in which this experiment in inter-racial chemistry is working itself out. There you can watch the elements simmering. To some hopeful eyes they may even seem to be clarifying and settling down. The following pages will show that I, personally, am not confident of any desirable solution, unless a new
element of far-sighted statesmanship can be thrown into the
brew."[206]

"We are here at the very heart of the problem," says he. "All
other relations are adjustable, at a certain sacrifice; but not this
one. If the two races are to live together without open and lawful intermingling, it must be at the cost of incessant demoralization to both. 'Miscegenation,' in the sense of permanent con-
cubinage and the rearing of hybrid families, may be held in check
by the strong social sentiment against it, but nothing can hold
in check the still more degrading casual commerce between the
white man (and youth) and the coloured woman. It is probably
this fact, quite as much as the hideous proclivities of the criminal negro male, that hardens the heart of the white woman
against the black race. Nor is the unwholesomeness of the condition measured by the actual amount of laxity to which it leads.
Temptation may in myriads of cases be resisted; but this order
of temptation ought not to be in the air. It cannot be good for
any race of men to be surrounded by strongly-accentuated Sex,
which, for ulterior reasons, whereof the mere animal nature takes
little account, is placed under tabu."[207]

The Rev. Mr. Shannon lays particular stress upon the indirect
approval or endorsement of amalgamation in political rewards
given the mulatto, and in privileges and rewards held open to
him in institutions of learning for Negroes.

"The late Rev. Hugh Price Hughes," says he, "city missionary
of the Wesleyans, and whose field of labor was in East London,
once visited a Southern city in which are located some of the

---

[206]Taken by permission from William Archer's *"Through Afro-
America,"* pp. xii, xiii, Introducton, copyright by E. P. Dutton &
Co., Inc.
[207]Ibid., pp. 214-5.

largest and wealthiest of the institutions of which we speak."[208]
"The work to which Mr. Hughes gave the best part of his
life brought him into close personal contact with all classes of
people and afforded rare opportunities for sociological study and
investigation. That he was eminently qualified for the responsible position to which his Church assigned him is fully shown by
the length of time he was, by the judgment of his brethren, retained in this class of work, and by the unusual success which
attended his efforts."[209]

"Dr. Hughes was not a man who could be indifferent to anything relating to the welfare of humanity. Before him, in his
work in cosmopolitan London, he had a miniature world. To a
man of his deep piety, tender sympathies, and buoyant type of
Christian faith, such work would necessarily lead to a broader
conception of the needs of humanity than usually comes to those
ministers of the gospel who are called to serve congregations
representing no great contrasts of race or of social stratification.
The consuming zeal for missions exhibited by him was no less
the product of his own field of labor than of his thorough con-
secration to the work of the ministry."[210]

"Mr. Hughes was not predisposed in favor of the South," says
Mr. Shannon.[211]

"He found gathered in the halls of these institutions, not the
negro—the African in whom he was so deeply interested—but
largely a mixed race representing the negro as modified by the
infusion of the blood of almost every other race. As 'college cir-
cles' he found more than one 'exclusive aristocracy' into which
few full-blooded negroes gained admission."[212]

"By reason of his acquaintance with social conditions elsewhere, and being free from that blinding effect produced by life-
long familiarity with a given situation, he comprehended at a
glance the meaning of conditions which, by reason of their familiarity, no longer impressed others. Later, he expressed the keen-
est disappointment at what he saw. His conception of mission
work was not to foster and dignify a social condition contrary to
the teachings of Scripture and subversive of good morals, but to

---

208"*Racial Integrity,*" p. 59.
209Ibid., pp. 59-60.
210Ibid., p. 60.
211Ibid., p. 61.
212Ibid., p. 61.

preserve the negro race intact and to assist it in reaching, intact, the highest plane of civilization and religious development of which it is capable. Not amalgamation, but independent development, should be the destiny of the negro, whether in America or in Africa. The highest interests of both races will be best conserved by the two races being kept separate and distinct. It was a report of this visit of Mr. Hughes which first led me to undertake a study of this feature of the negro problem."[213]

"At no time," says he, "has the menace of the 'mulatto problem' been so serious as it is to-day, yet this feature of the negro problem has settled into one of moral putrefaction while, by reason of its conscience-benumbing influences, its true import is not recognized. There is a close analogy between the effect of a narcotic benumbing the nerve system of the individual body and the vitiation of the moral and ethical standards of a race. The suspension of moral and ethical principles, in so far as the negro is concerned, by those who attempt to assist him, lies at the basis of the errors now being made in dealing with the negro, and constitutes, in its various manifestations, by far the most hurtful feature of the present situation and the most discouraging feature in reference to the future of both races. The interests of society, North and South, black and white, demand that the public awake, revise its classifications, and arouse to the wrong being done the negro, as well as our own race, by allowing a class neither white nor black to pose as negroes and to monopolize so much that is intended for the negro."[214]

"It is sufficient, at this point, to say that present conditions all encourage the negro to seek release from his racial limitations by ultimate escape from the race itself, instead of leading him to raise the standing of the race by honorable achievement. This truth is of the highest importance, and, with various modifications, is frequently reiterated in this volume."[215]

"However harsh it may seem to put the illegitimate child of either race under social ban when considered individually, yet both human and divine laws recognize the fact that he cannot be dealt with on his individual merits without endangering the most sacred interests of society. In this case, we should recognize the

---

[213]"*Racial Integrity,*" p. 62.
[214]Ibid., pp. 72-3.
[215]Ibid., pp. 78-9.

fact that the ideals and the ethical standards of a race are in peril."[216]

"The practical attitude of the government toward the moral phases of the negro problem is not so well understood. It is not quite consistent to deny political prerogatives to a man who publicly marries two or more women and acknowledges and supports them and their children, on the ground of protecting the morals of the people, yet throw the influence of government patronage— always implying indorsement—to men who cannot, perhaps, so much as name their fathers, and to whose support the father usually contributes only the price of a lustful debauch: to men whose origin, at a point more or less remote, defies all those restrictions which, in our dealings with our own and all other races except the African, we recognize as the bulwark of both personal and national character. Is it right that, by government patronage and indiscriminate religious benefactions an 'aristocracy of shame' should be built up? Is it right that the innate sensual tendencies of negro womankind, already stronger than those of the women of any other race, should be reenforced by the prospect of improving the condition of the offspring by ignoring virtue? The action of the United States government in dealing with Mormonism constitutes a sufficient precedent to warrant all necessary discrimination in the case of the mulatto."[217]

"Pathetic as may be the position of the mulatto, the American people cannot afford to allow this feature of the negro problem to be settled by blind forces. It cannot be left to the 'logic of events.' Each day sees the problem of the amalgamation of the races assume more serious proportions."[218]

"The negro problem is not, primarily, one in the realm of economics. It is essentially a moral problem. It is reduced to this: Which is better, a mongrel race whose origin is in sin, and which represents the worst of all the races; or a race, whatever its limitations, yet true to its own racial peculiarities and striving to attain, intact, the best and highest of which it is capable?"[219]

"Our studies and investigations lead us to the conclusion that the philanthropic activities of individuals and Churches and the patronage of the government are being so directed as to con-

[216]"*Racial Integrity,*" p. 80.
[217]Ibid., pp. 90-1.
[218]Ibid., p. 84.
[219]Ibid., p. 94.

stitute a menace to the virtue and to the home life of the negro. Not through lack of interest in, or deep concern for, the negro race, but largely through pity and through lack of discrimination, Politics, Philanthropy, and Religion, as now administered, are practically and effectively arrayed against the racial integrity of the negro."[220]

"Consideration for the negro race as a whole has had but little place in the efforts made in its behalf since the close of the Civil War. Practically everything has been done on the individualistic basis. Especially is this true of the work of the educational institutions founded in the years immediately following the Civil War. These had the advantage of entering a new field and the responsibility of establishing the ideals that were to prevail."[221]

"The opportunity that came to them then cannot return. Their policy is now settled, their constituency has been won, their future has been determined. That these institutions will continue to cherish the mulatto and continue to advance his interests is reasonably sure. That they will continue to send out mulatto teachers and preachers whose origin utterly unfits them to impress those lessons of virtue and chastity which the negro so desperately needs to learn, that they will continue to send into professional life those whose success will only still further strengthen the influences already at work for the destruction of laudable race pride and the home life of the negro and for the degradation of the white race, is equally certain. The negro race is poorly able to spare the least of social stimulation to right living and to a high moral standard, and the white race is poorly able to spare aught from its present relatively high standard of intellectuality."[222]

"The average negro, after spending a few years in such an institution, usually enters life yearning for what is unattainable, either educated out of sympathy with his race or into the temptation to promote racial antagonism in order to gain a livelihood."[223]

"The economic ideals of Hampton and Tuskegee are those which should have prevailed at the close of the Civil War. It was impossible, perhaps, that such could have been the case. An

[220]"*Racial Integrity*," pp. 94-5.
[221]Ibid., p. 272.
[222]Ibid., p. 272.
[223]Ibid., p. 274.

era of experiment was to have been expected. These institutions, however, are not upon higher moral ground as respects amalgamation than are those which neglect the economic and industrial training of their students."

"For at least two reasons, then, the institutions now under discussion are a positive menace to both the negro and the white race. If they did nothing more than to educate the negro out of sympathy with his own race and his necessary environment, or into the temptation to create racial antagonism, this would be tical administration, utterly fail to enforce fundamental moral principles, when they 'cause the bastard to thrive' to the detriment of the race they seek to help, when they practically suspend that part of the moral code which relates to social purity, we feel some sympathy for the man who characterizes their work as a 'forty-year-long crime'—a crime not merely against humanity at large, but particularly against the race they seek to assist."[224]

If the black and white blood in the country were mixed in the process of amalgamation, the final result, based upon the present numbers of the respective races, would be something slightly better than an octoroon, assuming the additional white blood to be an advantage to the mongrel product. However, if amalgamation is to come, the final outcome will not be so favorable provided immigration be stopped; for the tendency of modern industrialism, as pointed out before, is to reduce more and more the size of the native-born American family, and it may be said safely that many of these will resist amalgamation till in the end they disappear entirely. Thus the black blood will gradually assume a greater proportion in the final product than that contained in the octoroon unless the doors are thrown wide open to Europe and all classes and conditions of people freely invited to enter.

Are we carelessly and thoughtlessly, or with our eyes wide open and in cold blood, going to condemn future generations irrevocably to such a state of affairs?

Some who have given attention to the race problem seem to think they find evidence of the gradual dwindling in numbers of the Negro and his eventual disappearance by death of the race

---

[224]"*Racial Integrity,*" pp. 276-7.

in America (not amalgamation) in the study of modern conditions of life and statistics relating thereto. No such conclusion can be arrived at from a study of the census returns.

In 1790 there were 3,172,006 whites in the United States, and in 1920 there were 58,421,957 whites born of native parents. This represents an increase of 1841%. However, this increase is not due to the original number alone, but as well to all immigrants who came in subsequent to 1790 and to whom there was born a second or later generation in America. In 1790 there were 757,208 Negroes, and this number had increased to 10,463,131 in 1920, representing an increase of 1381%. The Negro immigrant coming into the United States may be regarded as negligible in considering the numbers given; and therefore, the difference in the increase of the two races would be less if there were any way of determining the actual increase due to the original number of whites in America free from subsequent immigration.

A consideration of the 50-year period from 1870 to 1920 brings the percentage of increase of the two races closer together. In increase of 60,483,623 over the number for 1870 which was 34,337,292; but, deducting 13,920,692 foreign born and 15,764,366 born of foreign parents, there remains an increase of 30,798,565 which includes 7,030,880 born of mixed (native and foreign born) parentage. The native-born white population in 1870 was 28,095,665, which included 4,167,098 born of foreign parents and 1,157,170 born of mixed parents. It can be readily seen that the increase indicated in 1920 and the numbers used as representing the original stock in 1870 are subject to indeterminate errors due to a continuous immigration movement into the country. However, accepting these two figures the increase for the 50-year period amounts to 109%.

There were 5,392,172 Negroes in America in 1870, and this number had grown to 10,463,131 in 1920, an increase of 5,070,959, or 94%.

The figures here given clearly show that the increase between the original native white element and that of the Negro would closely approximate the same figure provided we could eliminate entirely the numbers due to immigration.

The census for 1910 gave the number of mulattoes as 2,050,686, whereas that for 1920 recorded only 1,660,554. This is regarded by all who have given the matter careful study as grossly inaccurate.

MENACE IN FUTURE WARS.

Although no European nation has to contend with a domestic race problem of the character of our own, all Central America and South America, outside of Argentine and Chile, have almost the identical problem. The problem, even where acutely domestic, has its international aspects; for there is being brought about a world-wide unity in opposition to the White race. This opposition is one of growing intensity; it feeds upon hate resulting from wrongs, real or fancied; and is insidiously supported by ambitious schemers who withhold the dogs of war till the arrival of that propitious moment in which they may hope for success.

During the late war we were able to use and control the Negro. He was utilized to the extent of his abilities not only in agriculture, in industry, and in non-combatant positions, but—improperly so, I believe—he was equipped and used as a soldier. He has been much praised for what he did; and there has been passed in the House of Representatives and favorably reported in the U. S. Senate a bill to erect a special monument in commemoration of the services of three Negro regiments comprising the Ninety-third Division.

Even if we concede unstintedly every particle of praise to which the Negro may be entitled, is there any one so much his partisan as to maintain that America would not have been far more proficient in agriculture and industry and generally more efficient in the conduct of the war, could the magician's wand have converted the 12,000,000 American Negroes into the same number of native-born whites? The white went into the war as an individual representing the whole—as an integral part of the body politic with some conception and appreciation of the aims of the body politic; the Negro, on the other hand, performed what was required of him mechanically, merely because it was required of him, and without any conception of patriotism, what it was to be an American, or anything else involved in the situation. He was there without issues of any character in which he was interested, and his job was to get through with the situation as best he could. This is, of course, a lamentable condition of affairs from the point of view of national safety or efficiency, but it seems to have been the logical result of the situation as it existed. The conditions with which he was surrounded in Europe have been reflected since his return in many demands of a social and political nature.

The Negro behaved creditably during the World War where he was interspersed in small units among larger white units, and this is the method employed by the Europeans in the use of their colored troops. When we attempted to use an army of Negroes it proved a huge failure. General Bullard, who had commanded Negro troops before the World War and was an experienced and successful officer in handing such troops, was during the World War in command, among other troops, of the 92nd Division, composed entirely of Negroes. In his "Personalities and Reminiscences of the War" he attributes fifteen cases of rape to this division; he refers to their hopeless inefficiency and indifference; to the fact that they failed to do anything on the fighting line; and that the French, regarding them as a menace to the line, requested their withdrawal. Owing to the inefficiency of this division and the inability of the authorities to protect the French women from them, it was among the first, if not the first, division sent home; and one French woman reported she was ravished five times by men of this division while a part of it was awaiting transportation to the port of embarkation.

"No respectable military man," says Dowd, "would hesitate to say that our fighting force in the World War would have worked more smoothly and effectively if it had been all white."

"The race problem can no more be eliminated from military affairs than from civil affairs. From the drafting to the mustering out, the presence of the Negro in our army was a source of manifold and perpetual discord, dissipating the time and energies of the War Department and the commanding generals in efforts to preserve discipline among the soldiers."[225]

"Race prejudice is a hard fact, and military commanders, of whatever attitude towards the Negro problem, have to deal with the fact, which they find it difficult to harmonize with military efficiency. The 372nd Negro regiment was so wrought up over the question of social equality that it was next to useless as a

---

[225]"*The Negro in American Life,*" p. 231, The Century Co.

fighting unit until the crisis of the war was passed and the regimental officers were reorganized."[226]

That the Negro showed courage, even heroism in instances, should not cause any astonishment or prompt one to unusual comment except there were unusual circumstances; for courage is common to all races. Courage, if not heroism, is often displayed among gregarious animals by the male of the herd in protecting it from its enemies and by the female in protecting its young.

"Brehm states, on the authority of the well-known traveller Schimper, that in Abyssinia when the baboons belonging to one species (*C. gelada*) descend in troops from the mountains to plunder the fields, they sometimes encounter troops of another species (*C. hamadryas*), and then a fight ensues. The Geladas roll down great stones, which the Hamadryas try to avoid, and then both species, making a great uproar, rush furiously against each other. Brehm, when, accompanying the Duke of Coburg-Gotha, aided in an attack with fire-arms on a troop of baboons in the pass of Mensa in Abyssinia. The baboons in return rolled so many stones down the mountain, some as large as a man's head, that the attackers had to beat a hasty retreat; and the pass was actually closed for a time against the caravan."[227] It may be that these baboons had something corresponding to our Hall of Fame and the leaders in this fight were assigned an honorable place therein.

If some years from now we should be faced with a world-wide Anti-White War, does any one suppose we would then be able to control and use the Negro as we did in the last? He might well cause civil strife and so reduce our efficiency as to become eventually the deciding factor against us; and he doubtless would be prompted and encouraged in this by the lessons learned from the teachings of the mulatto organizations and what is being done in the various uplift movements.

In any war we may have *in the near future with a people of the White race*, and I believe this contingency remote, we may be able to handle the Negro element without insuperable difficulty; for in a struggle between whites they would be more or less indifferent, possibly favoring ourselves. In view of the fact, how-

[226]"*The Negro in American Life*," p. 232, The Century Co.
[227]Darwin's "*The Descent of Man*," pp. 81-2.

ever, that any possible war we may have in the near future will be with an Asiatic Power, possibly in conjunction with Mexico, it is almost certain that we shall have a Negro Civil War on our hands as well. Is it possible that this is not clearly apparent to all—to even those who do not see a danger in the threat of amalgamation? If so, they are blind to the menacing language constantly used in Negro writings and publications. The latest comes in the form of a protest against the exclusion of a Negro student of the Textile High School, New York City, from a citizens' military training camp provided for whites in that State and requiring him to apply to a camp in another State provided for Negroes. This protest to the President was written by one George W. Harris, editor of the New York News, and the matter was referred by the President to the War Department.

Among other things the protest said: "No more outrageous discrimination has ever been practiced against a colored citizen by any southern state than the United States Army is proclaiming as its practice in the matter of colored youths ambitious for military training."

"The blunt language of Col. Fleet's ban against them savors of the proscription of the Confederacy as expressed by Judge Taney in the Dred Scott decision rather than that of a commanding officer of the United States Army in the twentieth century. We need not go into the injustice and discrimination laid out in the relief so inhumanely offered by Col. Fleet."

"Bluntly he states: 'We are not permitted to accept colored men in the C. M. T. camp in this area.' He makes this insult to colored youths in saying: (quoting Col. Fleet's letter, in which it was suggested that the student apply to C. M. T. officer, 4th corps area, Atlanta, for admission to colored citizens' camp, etc.)"

"White youths must attend when accepted training in their own area. Their transportation is paid, as is their maintenance. For colored boys in the northern states to be forced to go for training to the south at their own expense and under racial conditions that obtain in Dixie, is to deny them training. This is insult added to injustice."

"For the United States Army to draw this color line against colored boys anywhere is not only a hideous outrage, but wantonly unjust. The nation is putting rancors in the vessels of its peace when it proclaims this monstrous policy against the coming colored generation. We can say to the nation very frankly that this they will not stand for. The white world is on the verge of war with the colored world. America has not a friend among any of the colored races in Africa, Asia, or America due to this very color line proscription and persecution."

"Surely the United States will not expect her own colored citizens to fight against those colored races in the event of war with China or Japan or Mexico or Nicaragua or Haiti—to set up the same color line in those foreign countries that it now officially sets up not only in her Army and Navy, but as well in its citizens' training camps. This is an issue, Mr. President, that will not down. We ask that you settle this question and that you settle it right."

"As the nation's commander-in-chief, we ask that you order this color line dropped before the exigencies of war make it necessary as a war measure. We speak advisedly when we say that such outrages as the exclusion of Burnell are sowing dragons' teeth which will later beset the nation's pathway."[228]

THE MENACE TO INDUSTRY.

Our regard and admiration for the forefathers who made America should be unbounded and unqualified, as it also should be for the instrument of government they produced. It was the most perfect code devised by man for the body politic and contained the greatest promise that had yet come into the possession of mankind for the future civic development of the race. But to regard the government then established as perfect, as fitted for all times and suitable to all characters of people, is simply absurd. Nor was it so regarded by the founders of America. However, with a sturdy homogeneous people, descendents of the colonial and revolutionary stock, the development of democratic principles and material progress from the foundations laid were immeasurable in possibilities. With such a people, whatever the stress of circumstances which might test to the limit its mental, moral and social traits, the extremes of all social disorders would have been avoided. As it is, greed, mistaken religious zeal, and stupid sentimentalism have resulted in bringing about a heterogeneous body instead of a homogeneous body of the original blood. This heterogeneous body displays a diversity of ideals,

---

[228]*"Army and Navy Register,"* April 9, 1927.

some of which are irreconcilable, and in some instances there are groups without any ideals but striving aimlessly for something indefinable to them and to which they cannot give intelligent expression.

Ever since the World War there has been discord and social unrest, and many of the forces operative in our heterogeneous mass have been emphasized as being in the interest of discord and anarchy. These hidden forces that manifest themselves in trying situations and, boiling to the surface, carry wreck and ruin, sometimes, it may be, even among a stable, homogenous people, inevitably hasten the destruction of a people when it is composed of discordant and antagonistic race elements.

The smug reactionary industrialist, who poses as a conservative, may think he is now safely entrenched and that he can proceed with the exploitation of the Negro and ignorant immigrant without danger to his vested interests. The pendulum never swings to one side and stops there. Italy, Poland, Greece, Turkey, and Spain are dominated by reactionary forces that justify their conduct on the ground that theirs was the only expedient to conserve the general welfare through the preservation of order and the avoidance of anarchy. Russia is attempting to give expression to some satisfactory method of government by the people, appropriate to the genius of her people and their present cultural condition; and she will eventually shake herself free from anarchy and emerge into the light of stable self government. The remaining portions of Europe are simmering more or less in a state of unrest.

Were we a homogeneous people of the old stock, we could look with sympathy upon this world-wide turmoil and possibly aid in the restoration of confidence and civic contentment; for we would, under such circumstances, be free from any fear of serious danger to ourselves. But when we contemplate the fact that our greatest city contains in native-born Americans only about 25 per cent of its population (if we went back to those who had been here two generations, it would be much less), and that the Negro composes about a ninth of our total population, it is simply folly to imagine that we are immune from the evils of radical discontent when the pendulum journeys in that direction.

The Negro leadership in the N. A. A. C. P., which we have professed to ignore as inconsequential, grows in power as time passes, and what is done under the leadership of such apostles as Dr. DuBois becomes each day a matter of graver concern to the American people. Their slogan, to express it concisely, is assimilation by amalgamation, and any means to this end meets with their approval.

Dr. DuBois teaches the Negro that the most glorious pages of Egyptian history were enacted under the leadership of a Negro queen and resulted from Negro culture;[229] that the cultured Negro gave to the world domestic animals, agriculture, the use of iron,[230] and was the first builder of cities (Speech at Elizabeth City, N. C., Normal College at commencement exercises in June, 1927); that the Negro earned his freedom largely by armed rebellion, poison and murder;[231] that the early free Negroes and mulattoes fought for assimilation by amalgamation, as did Frederick Douglass (he married a white woman), even in his old age;[232] and that race prejudice and slavery are responsible for the present degradation of the Negro. Furthermore, Dr. DuBois, recognizing some of the evils in modern industrialism, seems to advise the Negro to use "Socialism" as a club with which to fight his battle for assimilation.[233] It would seem that "Socialism" as a doctrine pure and simple would find few disciples among the Negroes; but, during periods of unrest and disorder, any catch word or phrase may serve as the rally cry for the discontented or those who are chronically in opposition. If the smug industrialist finds satisfaction in such a situation as this then he is, indeed, blind; for teachings of the character outlined are daily finding a greater response among the mulattoes and the numerous body of blacks and leading more and more to a chronic condition of anarchy or war. In the absence of a definite program for solution, all efforts in behalf of the Negro by the industrialist, the educator, and the churchman, are construed by him as an indirect endorsement at least of his eventual aim, directly striven for or unconsciously sought,—assimilation.

229"*Darkwater*," p. 74.
230Ibid., p. 166.
231Ibid., p. 136.
232"*The Souls of Black Folk*," pp. 48-9.
233"*Darkwater*," pp., 100-4.

CHAPTER V.

POLITICAL AND CIVIC ASPECTS.

My conception of an ideal democracy is a land occupied by a homogeneous people in the enjoyment of the best educational facilities, and in which each individual is free to pursue prosperity and happiness in accordance with his own bent, and without restraint except in so far as it is essential to the equal enjoyment of these same pursuits by all. Education and homogeneity are essential to the success of democratic institutions; for in the conception of democracy is involved the equality of the constituent elements of the body politic. This equality must not be a theoretical equality based upon the fiat of law in constitutional provision or legislative enactment, but that based upon essential facts which go to show an actual or proximate equality in all civic elements. This can be closest approximated in a body politic formed from a homogeneous people—a people with the same antecedents and with the same aspirations political, social, material and moral. Absolute equality does not exist between individuals; no two are identical in capacities; no two react in identically the same way to the same surrounding circumstances. These differences cannot be wiped out by mandate of law or any scheme devised by man for the purpose of bringing all members of the body politic to the same level. There is no truer statement than the one in Physics to the effect that water seeks its own level. We see this law in operation in a never ending stream from the elevated mountain slopes to the sea; but, as fast as one small particle starts on this journey to the sea, the operative forces of Nature are supplying another for the same journey. Just so it is with the levelling forces operating amongst a homogeneous people. Education narrows the chasm between the mentality of greatest capacity and that of the least, or at least renders it less glaring and makes cooperation more harmonious, but it can never make them the same; for, in the process of reproduction, growth and adolescence, the life cells of the human organism, within the limits imposed by heredity, are subject to countless and different combinations, surrounding circumstances, and stimuli, which result in a new human organism differing from its parents and its brothers and sisters. These differences that exist between the offspring of the same parents are still more marked in the larger family of race; and those between the races themselves, particularly between the extremes of the White and the Black races, are startlingly broad and should be recognized by all of us unless we choose to shut our eyes to glaring facts with which we are surrounded.

In this ideal democracy which we have supposed (not ideal in the utopian sense, but eminently practical), the situation is one that inevitably makes for progress, if material conditions of life are not too hard. Education can never free us from mistakes, but it will lessen them; for, in the process of education, we are acquiring the accumulated experience of others that, even in a superficial education, covers a vast field beyond the reach of the most intelligent and long-lived, if acquired through his own individual experiences. Thus education in a homogeneous body politic reduces political action to its simplest form and insures progress, peace and prosperity; for, however complicated the issues or however diverse opinions may be as to the remedy, the proper solution will eventually be had in pursuit of the policy, that *what is best for the community is best for me* and *vice versa.*

Let us suppose that into this ideal, democratic body-politic there is introduced a great number of inferior people—members of an inferior race without ideals of any kind and utterly incapable of initiating, carrying through, or maintaining any measures relating to progress or civilization—and that these people are given the franchise by an outside imperial power with the intention and expectation that they shall use it. What should we expect the result to be under such circumstances? If these newly enfranchised people obtained control of governmental affairs, we should look for an impractical, corrupt, debased and disgraceful imitation of what had gone before in previous administrations— a character of proceedings similar, except for the presence of the vicious element in it, to what might logically proceed from irresponsible boys playing government in their school buildings without the restraint of the teacher's presence—a conduct of affairs which, elevated to the plane of the practical administration of the government of a civilized people, would be a living disgrace. Such a situation would result in immediate action on the part of the homogeneous civilized portion of the community for the removal of this destructive weapon—the right of franchise—from the hands of this inferior people. If the accomplishment of this purpose were merely the simple matter of declaring the will of the civilized people in an orderly, legal manner, the damage wrought would be of little consequence; for the remedy, disfranchisement and eventual removal of these people, would be proceeded with, and, thence afterward, the orderly progress of affairs would be resumed. But should it be insisted by this controlling, outside, imperial power that the mandate of political equality be carried into effect in its fullness, what would be the result? Unhesitatingly, the only answer is, that the civilized body of the people would resort to fraud or force, or both, to evade the mandate of the fundamental law and try to preserve its civilization. Unless they had lost all the characteristics incident to a civilized people, they would resist to the last extremity the placing in the hands of an ignorant, degraded people the well being of themselves and their institutions—all the result of an age-long growth and development handed down through civilized progenitors. That everything should be thus surrendered, could result only from annihilation or intimidation at the point of the bayonet. But even if these people are left free to practice evasion or fraud or use force, what would be the result? The use of force and fraud for a long period as an essential to the preservation of their institutions would, in the end, result in general demoralization of the people resorting to such means. The sense of justice would be blunted; the standard of right and wrong would become variable and depend upon what was conceived to be self interest; familiarity with fraud and lawlessness in one direction would render the use of both in other public matters less repulsive to us than formerly, and in the end there would not be any hesitancy to employ any means that yielded the result desired. Civilization would gradually disappear, with slow, scarcely perceptible movement at first, but with increasing acceleration as time passed.

This condition would be much worse if the body politic, among whom these debased people were thrust as political equals, were, although homogeneous in accordance with our supposed case, not yet sufficiently educated to bring about the best results through the exercise of their franchise in a democratic State. The deporable conditions outlined in the ideal community as incident to the attempt to escape the penalty of legal enfranchisement of a mass of degraded and unfit people would be much enhanced by lack of education in the homogeneous body. This situation is one fruitful of opportunities for exploitation by organized, greedy plunderers whose only aim is a return upon the investment, irrespective of the cost to the State or the welfare of the body politic. The degraded people are encouraged to look forward to full participation in all governmental affairs and eventually to complete acceptance in the social organization; the uneducated portion of the superior people are forced into competition with the degraded inferior people and their condition lowered instead of bettered; the educational facilities afforded may even be so colored that they operate as a means to an end that the exploitation may be helped rather than hindered by a true insight into conditions as they actually are; and all means availble for shaping public opinion to an approval of the existing order of things may be employed without stint. Even a condition of real prosperity and security may be so simulated as to lull the public conscience and deceive the enlightened sentiment of the community.

"While democracy is fatal to progress when two races of unequal value live side by side," says Madison Grant, "an aristocracy may be equally injurious whenever, in order to purchase a few generations of ease and luxury, slaves or immigrants are imported to do the heavy work. It was a form of aristocracy that brought slaves to the American colonies and the West Indies and if there had been an aristocratic form of governmental control in California, Chinese coolies and Japanese laborers would now form the controlling element, so far as numbers are concerned, on the Pacific coast."[234]

"It was the upper classes who encouraged the introduction of immigrant labor to work American factories and mines and it is the native American gentleman who builds a palace on the country side and who introduces as servants all manner of foreigners into purely American districts. The farming and artisan classes of America did not take alarm until it was too late and they are now seriously threatened with extermination in many parts of the country. In Rome, also, it was the plebeian, who first went

---

[234]"*The Passing of the Great Race*," pp. 10-1, Charles Scribner's Sons.

under in the competition with slaves but the patrician followed in his turn a few generations later."[235]

"Democratic ideals among an homogeneous population of Nordic blood, as in England or America, is one thing, but it is quite another for the white man to share his blood with, or intrust his ideals to, brown, yellow, black, or red men."

"This is suicide pure and simple, and the first victim of this amazing folly will be the white man himself."[236]

Judge Thomas M. Cooley says: "Basis of Suffrage. During the last quarter of a century, while the agitation for an enlargement of civil rights has been violent, sentiment has had a great and extraordinary influence on public affairs in America. It has much affected the discussion of political privileges, and considerable numbers have insisted that suffrage was a natural right, corresponding to the right of life and liberty, and equally unlimited. Unless such a doctrine is susceptible of being given practical effect, it must be utterly without substance; and so the courts have pronounced it. In another place it has been shown that liberty itself must come from the law, and not in any institutional sense from nature; and still less can that come from nature in which all the people cannot possibly participate, and in respect to which, therefore, positive law becomes absolutely essential in order to prescribe qualifications, the possession of which shall be the test of right to enjoyment. A gift by nature must be absolute, and not contingent upon the State coming forward afterwards with uncertain and changeable enactments to name conditions, and point out the persons who may enjoy the bounty. But there is a further objection which is equally insurmountable: suffrage cannot be the natural right of the individual, because it does not exist for the benefit of the individual, but for the benefit of the State itself."

"Suffrage is participation in the government; in a representative country it is taking part in the choice of officers, or in the decision of public questions. The purpose is to keep up the continuity of government, and to preserve and perpetuate public order and the protection of individual rights. The purpose is therefore public and general, not private and individual. What-

---

[235]"*The Passing of the Great Race,*" p. 11, Charles Scribner's Sons.

[236]"*The Rising Tide of Color,*" Grant's Introduction to, p. xxxii, Charles Scribner's Sons.

ever suffrage is calculated to defeat the general purpose,—whatever, if permitted, would tend to break up government, to introduce anarchy, and to bring upon the people the innumerable mischiefs which would follow from the destruction of public order,— is not only inadmissible on reason, but is proved by the consequences which follow to be condemned by the great Author of government. To say that one whose participation in government would bring danger to the State, and probable disaster, has nevertheless a right to participate, is not only folly in itself, but it is to set the individual above the State, and above all the manifold interests which are represented by it and bound up in its destiny. Such doctrine is idle. Suffrage must come to the individual, not as a right, but as a regulation which the State establishes as a means of perpetuating its own existence, and of insuring to the people the blessings it was intended to secure."[237]

The general principle, as true and as universal as the law of gravitation, that Democracy, to whatever degree it may manifest itself among any peoples, is the result of an age-long process and arises only where there is homogeneity of blood and a high cultural standard pervading the body of the people, is necessarily involved, by inference, in the quotations given above, if not directly. Conversely, to proclaim Democracy based upon manhood suffrage appropriate to a community composed of civilized whites and even the most advanced Negroes, where the two are in somewhere near equal numbers, is to disregard flatly all history and all information we have in regard to the relations of widely different races living in the same community. No greater crime against Democracy could have been committed than the enfranchisement of the Negro in America. It worked untold injury to the cause of Democracy both in America and the world at large; for, when we were compelled in the preservation of civilization to repudiate by fraud and violence the constitutional mandate, improvidently imposed, as to the equality of all men irrespective of race, Democracy was brought into disrepute and held up to contumely and ridicule by its enemies throughout the world.

The condition of the South after the Civil War was comparable in every respect to that of the democracy outlined above into which there had been injected a large body of primitive, savage people, and whose homogeneous population had not been accus-

---

[237]"*Principles of Constitutional Law*," 2nd. edition, pp. 259-260.

tomed to the best educational advantages of the times. The
Negro is the alien race element amongst us, the provisions of the
14th and 15th Amendments, the outside imperial power imposed
upon us to our everlasting detriment. No good can come of
quickening the pulse beats by reference to the trying times when,
and the manner in which, our right to honest, white, American
government was taken from us and we were compelled to don,
in its stead, the habiliments of the hypocrite and make chicanery,
deceit, fraud and force the familiar, usual procedure in public
affairs. But good can come from the recognition of the patent,
open and glaring issues arising from this situation, and meeting
them by solution—a just solution that will weigh the equities
of all concerned.

Do not for an instant imagine that I am disparaging the
South! We have heard much recently about "down-trodden"
Belgium and France "bled white;" but the world does not give
us another example of a people who have displayed such re-
cuperative powers as have the people of the South.[238] The trans-
formation that has occurred, between the time when I first recalled my surroundings with any appreciation of what they meant
and now, is something marvelous, indeed—one beyond the comprehension of our fellow countryman of the North to whom the
ravages of the war, aside from a possible wound or loss of some
one dear to him, were made manifest only in a slight increase
in tax burdens and moderate fluctuations in industry due to after-
the-war adjustments. In the South, however, there was not only
loss of life and loss and destruction of property, but the social,
industrial and political organization of the people was torn up
by the very roots. My earliest recollection is that of a youngster
born in a land in which the hand of the oppressor lay heavily.
Everything appeared hopeless. The decision in the resort to
arms had been against us. Yet there persisted the determination to resist to the end, as and when we could, that undeserved
and unexpected indignity of debauchery by the blacks and their
associated white-plunderers. There was scarcely a hamlet, village or town along the coast that had not felt the ravages of war

---

[238]It seems that the per capita wealth of the South in '60 was
not again reached until 1904. The assessed values of Southern property decreased to the extent of $2,100,000,000 from 1860 to
1870; and from 1870 to 1880 there was a further depreciation of
$67,000,000.

in material destruction; and this condition was common to other sections, as well, unless remotely situated from even the minor operations of the war. We were miserably poor; those who were not land poor, were just plain poor; industry was at a standstill; crops were mortgaged before they were produced; the turnover of the merchant was small, his pay uncertain; the professional man, while probably the best situated economically, was often puzzled as to how he might collect his fee; public schools, as now known, did not exist, and private schools were found, almost without exception, only in the cities and towns; and yet our contribution in taxes to defray the expense of defeat and humiliation was exacted. Over all was ·the heavy hand of the conqueror determined, as a last resort, through military coercion if necessary, to place political control in the hands of the blacks in default of ready acquiescence on the part of the former master to his equal participation in government.

The hand of coercion has been withheld, though it may threaten at times, and for long the situation has held promise. The active participants in these stirring scenes have nearly all gone to their reward; even the youngsters whose first serious thoughts were absorbed in contemplation of this early, gloomy and unpromising situation, have mostly played their part in the body politic. Together they have compelled confidence in their real Americanism from their fellow countrymen from whom they were temporarily estranged. Mutual understanding and appreciation and greater friendship, result inevitably from closer association and better knowledge one of the other.

Former poverty, low production, and stagnation in industry, have given place to plenty, if not opulence, to improved methods, diversity and increase in agricultural products, to an intensive diversified industry; and confidence has taken the place of distrust. Not the least advance in all this has been the achievement in education.

The picture is roseate and has the heady ·effect of old wine. But let us not forget, in our intoxication induced by prosperity, that modern industrialism has its evils to be corrected in the interest of race preservation and uplift; and that the black shadow of the former slave era is still threatening.

The testimony of thoughtful persons—those whose opinions carry weight—is almost unanimously to the effect that the enfranchisement of the Negro was a colossal blunder, and that his presence in the body-politic is a grave menace to the future welfare, politically and in all matters that have any bearing upon our future estate. In fact, there may be said to be a uniformity of opinion among all who have informed themselves, if we exclude the fanatical and the demagogues.

Many writers, politicians and statesmen have borne testimony to the fact that Democracy is an evolutionary form of government naturally arising when, through an age-long process of development, there comes into being a people homogeneous in blood and culture. In so far as a homogeneous, savage people, living in tribal relation, may be said to have any government, it may be described as democratic; but, probably, a more appropriate description of the actual situation in such case would be, a community in which extreme individualism existed and in which it was curtailed only in emergencies requiring tribal concert. If in such community there arose individuals endowed with a genius enabling them to benefit the tribe greatly along some particular line of endeavor, such men, if their work were appreciated by the tribe, would be accorded a leadership and direction in such matters. Thus may have started that development in statecraft which led to the King, the Monarch, the Limited Monarchy and eventually to Democracy.

"When we pass to the sphere of politics more debatable questions emerge," says James Bryce, an English writer. "Equality of rights might seem to be here also that which is fairest and most likely to make for unity and peace. But the Backward race may be really unfit to exercise political power, whether from ignorance, or from an indifference that would dispose it to sell its votes, or from a propensity to sudden and unreasoning impulses. The familiar illustration of the boy put to drive a locomotive engine might in some communities be no extreme way of describing the risks a democracy runs when the suffrage is granted to a large mass of half-civilized men."[239]

The same author further on says: "The moral to be drawn from the case of the Southern States seems to be that you must not, however excellent your intentions and however admirable your sentiments, legislate in the teeth of facts. . . . ."[240]

[239]"The Relations of the Advanced and the Backward Races of Mankind," p. 38. Quoted by permission of publisher, Oxford University Press, London.
[240]Ibid., p. 89.

"Below the surface of the words of these two men," says Stone, "there lies the fundamental difference of the point of view of respective racial self-interest. To the mind of Dr. Washington this government will be 'a republic only in name' if a certain large mass of its population does not share equally in its control. To the mind of Senator Platt successful free government must be based upon a homogeneous population, possessed of a 'high degree of virtue and intelligence,' while without an understanding of 'the true principles of government' we have 'a republic only in name.' Mr. Washington sees some millions of Negro citizens 'governed without their consent,' if we may so interpret his words.[241] Mr. Platt is looking only at those qualities the possession of which must be a condition precedent to even 'the capacity to consent,' if the government is to endure. And to Senator Platt's utterances is added an additional significance. He was addressing himself immediately to the question of the possibility of maintaining a self-governing republic, in fact as well as in form, in a country wherein about one-third of the people were of the race for which Mr. Washington is the usually accredited American spokesman. The author of the 'Platt Amendment' was discussing the future of Cuba."[241½] Senator Platt emphasized the fact, in connection with the contemplated government of Cuba, that homogeneity was essential to the preservation of free government, and that it could be neither established nor maintained by a sentimental desire for liberty. If homogeneity is essential to the erection and preservation of democracy in Cuba, is there not the same demand for it in the United States of America?

Professor Walter F. Willcox, who contributed some of the papers in Stone's "Studies in the American Race Problem," appreciates the incongruities in the situation where attempts are made to apply a theoretical democracy to widely diverse people in the same territory. He says: "The greatest problem which modern democracy has to face is perhaps this: Can the democratic forms developed among a homogeneous people with unifying traditions, like the people of England, Old and New, be extended to people widely different in race, religion, and ethical and social code? Can English forms of government ultimately

---

241 See quotation from Mr. Archer, p. 187, of this work.
241½ "*Studies in the American Race Problem,*" p. 393.

apply to India and Egypt and South Africa? Can American forms be extended to the two races at the South or in the Philippines? Either the public opinion of one race must dominate, as that of the whites has done in India and the South, or the two races must cooperate so far as to develop a common public opinion. The latter is the only true democracy."[242]

Professor Nathaniel S. Shaler, late professor of geology, Harvard, says: "It is well to understand that the experiment of combining in a democratic society, in somewhere near equal numbers, two such widely separated races as the Aryans and Negroes, has never been essayed. Even under arbitrary governments the association of less discrepant folk has proved impracticable."[243] Of course this has been attempted under the provisions of the 14th and 15th Amendments, and Professor Shaler meant that it had not been attempted elsewhere.

Stone points out the fact that opposition to Negro suffrage does not have its inception in prejudice based upon a color scheme of classification, as is always insisted by the equalitarians; but is aimed at a lack of qualifications to exercise the privilege in the interests of the State or the presence of characteristics that would render its use a positive menace to democracy and the State. He remarks: "It is said that any discussion of Negro suffrage at this late day, is purely academic—that the principle is permanently fixed in our political system. We are not at all concerned with the accuracy or inaccuracy of this proposition. We are not interested in Negro suffrage *per se,* but rather in its elements—in certain facts which accompany it and characterize it and differentiate it from the concrete act and expression of self-governing capacity among other men. We have so long talked about the Negro that we have fixed him in our minds as the individual object upon which centres an opposition which in fact is really directed to the attributes and traits for which he stands. It would be humanly impossible to perpetuate and disseminate opposition to Negro suffrage, for example, if Negro suffrage did not stand for something more

---

[242]*"Studies in the American Race Problem,"* p. 475, Part Five, containing papers by Prof. Walter F. Willcox.

[243]Prof. N. S. Shaler's *"The Neighbor,"* p. 180, Houghton Mifflin Company.

definitely objectionable to the Caucasian mind than a more or less shadowed complexion."[244]

"The simple truth," says he, "is that Negro suffrage was the most artificial creation ever known to our history. The only natural thing about it was its death. It could not be kept alive by normal means. Just as the Reconstruction governments fell to pieces like card houses as soon as the artificial prop of Federal power was removed by Hayes, so Negro suffrage could not survive the first legal test imposed upon it by its opponents. We may force the ballot upon whom we please in this free country, but further than this we cannot go. We cannot insure its intelligent use by persons not intelligent; we cannot insure its honest use by persons without a sense of political morality; we cannot insure its retention by those to whom we have given it, if they were not ready to receive it, or if the grant was unwisely bestowed. Any state in the Union might give the ballot to children fifteen years of age, but no state could guarantee its proper use in childish hands."[245]

He also brings to our attention the fact that the Negro need not be in a majority to threaten the welfare of the State, and that he "is generally a thorn in the flesh of those who seek to break up corrupt municipal machines. Just as he is thus used by white and mulatto politicians in Northern cities, so has he been used time and again in Southern states. His pliability makes him specially valuable in controlling a balance of power, and his greatest potential harm to the Southern white man and himself by no means depends upon a Negro majority. To respectable people in the South the most offensive use of the ballot ever made by the Negro, as likewise the most vicious use ever made of the Negro by unscrupulous white men, has been in deciding issues between white men themselves. And to do this a majority is not necessary —only capable and unscrupulous leadership and a willing and irresponsible tool."[246]

He then goes on to show the evil results arising from a political division among the whites in North Carolina that brought about a situation approximating conditions during Reconstruction. (See ante pp. 174-5.) Referring to tests that may be required to de-

---

[244]*Studies in the American Race Problem,* p. 354.
[245]Ibid., pp. 358-9.
[246]Ibid., pp. 363-4.

termine qualifications for suffrage, he remarks: "In order to be of any real value such tests must presuppose the same general potential capacity and attributes among all to whom they are applied and whose degree of development they are assumed to indicate. Between the masses of the English-speaking white race and those of the American Negro, no artificial test can indicate the possession of the same measure of capacity for self-government. It is idle to talk about 'determining in exactly the same manner the qualifications' of two masses possessing such different racial histories and backgrounds, as well as such widely different developments, as those which characterize the white man and the Negro."[247]

The inevitable evil consequences that follow occupancy of the same territory by widely separated races is summarized by James Bryce as follows: "These troubles may be apprehended whatever the form of government, for they spring out of the nature of things. But others vex the political sphere. If one race enjoys privileges denied to the other, it is likely to abuse its power to the prejudice of the Backward people, placing them, it may be, under civil as well as political disabilities, or imposing heavier taxes upon them, or refusing them their fair share of benefits from the public revenue. If, on the other hand, both races are treated alike, granted the same suffrage, made eligible for the same offices, each will be disposed to organize itself separately for political purposes, so that a permanent separation of parties will be created, which, because irrespective of the issues that naturally arise from time to time, may prevent those issues from being dealt with on their merits, and may check the natural ebbs and flows of political life. The nation will, in fact, be rather two nations than one, may waste its force on internal dissensions, may lose its unity of action at moments of public danger. Evils of this order tend to be more acute the more democratic a government becomes. Two courses are open, but each will have elements of danger. If political privileges are refused to the Backward race, the contrast between principle and practice, between a theoretic recognition of the rights of man as man and the denial of them to a section of the population, will be palpable and indefensible. If that lower section be admitted to share in the government, an element

---

[247]"*Studies in the American Race Problem*," pp. 373-4.

will be admitted the larger part of which will be unfit for the
suffrage, being specially accessible to bribery and specially liable
to intimidation. So, too, though the evils described may exist
whatever be the condition of the lower race, they will become,
in one sense at least, more accentuated the more that race advances in intelligence and knowledge. Slaves or serfs who have
been bred up to look upon subjection as their natural lot bear
it as the dispensation of Nature. When they have attained a
measure of independence, when they speak the tongue and read
the books and begin to share the ideas of the dominant race, they
resent the inferiority, be it legal or social, to which they find
themselves condemned. Discontent appears and social friction
is intensified, not only because occasions for it grow more frequent, but because the temper of each race is more angry and
suspicious. These phenomena, present even where the races are
not very diverse in habits of life or level of culture, as is the
case with Greeks, Armenians, and Turks in various parts of the
East, or with Moors and Jews in Morocco, may become of graver
import as between races so far apart as whites and negroes in
the Gulf States of North America, or whites and Malays in the
Philippine Isles, or Europeans and native fellahin in Egypt."[248]
    W. Laird Clowes, an English writer, in his work "Black
America," in reply to the question, "Why not allow the majority
—no matter what may be its hue—to rule," says: "The answer
is that the experiment has been to some extent tried, and has
utterly failed. The history of the attempt and of the failure is
given in the following chapter. The outlines of that history
must be studied by every one who aspires to understand the
nature and the difficulties of the Southern problem as it exists
to-day. I do not, therefore, apologise for setting forth at some
length the gloomy narrative of one of the most extraordinary
episodes in the modern history of any civilized country. If I
needed further excuse, I might find it in the fact that my story,
though it deals with events of comparatively recent occurrence
and of a very terrible character, is unknown to the majority of
Englishmen. Even in the North it is now well-nigh forgotten;
and only in the long-suffering South are the hideous lessons of

---

[248]"The Relations of the Advanced and the Backward Races of
Mankind," pp. 30-2. Quoted by permission of publisher, Oxford
University Press, London.

it still fully remembered."[249]   He refers, of course, to Reconstruction.

"I do not believe," says Raymond Patterson, "any intelligent, fair-minded, and liberal Northern man can spend even a few months in an exclusive investigation of the race question without becoming convinced, as I have become convinced, that the granting of suffrage to the negroes, immediately after the war, was a horrible blunder. For while here and there one may find negroes who are eminently fitted to exercise the right of suffrage, the time has not yet come when it is safe to give the ballot to the illiterate negro millions. It is doubtless true that the methods adopted by the South to eliminate the negro from politics were at first generally cruel, and are now frequently unconstitutional, but an honest survey of the situation must prove that they adopted the only way to repair the serious breach in the social and commercial fabric of the South, and that the end justified the means."[250]

"It is a simple thing to stand in a Northern pulpit or to sit in a Northern office chair and from that safe vantage ground to speak or write about equal rights, the genius of the American Constitution, the beauty of a free ballot; but the political situation in the South is not a matter of theory, but of fact. If it happens to come in conflict with our American institutions, so much the worse for the institutions. Looked at from the standpoint of theory, the existing political situation in all the Southern States is a cruel outrage, a manifest violation of the basic principles of the Declaration of Independence; looked at in the light of social, commercial, and moral conditions, it is evident that to disturb present conditions rashly, in obedience to the voice of uninformed Northern demagogues, would be disastrous, first to the white man, but ultimately and most completely to the black man."[251]

"The Southern people may be trusted," says Professor Shaler, "to find the value of the Negro in his new condition as they did in the old. They recognize that in this vigorous, very human folk, they have a supply of labor which is absolutely necessary in fields

---

[249]"*Black America*," pp. 16-7, Cassell & Company, Limited, London.
[250]"*The Negro and His Needs*," p. 109, Fleming H. Revell Company.
[251]Ibid., pp. 112-3.

which do not tempt white people. They know, or must learn, that the value of this population can be had only by developing and suitably promoting those of the blacks who show themselves fit for advancement. There is no other way open to us except to trust the future of the Negro to the white people with whom he is in contact. All the expedients of the reconstruction period resulted in hindering the advance of the work it was intended to accomplish, for the reason that it set the races over against each other; it broke up the old friendly relation which had effaced the most serious of the tribal prejudices, and set these persons in flame. Any further effort to force an adjustment will be likely to result in something like race war. That we best trust, and may fairly trust, to the South to contrive safety and justice out of the situation has happily become evident to the whole people. By putting the burden on those who are best fitted to bear it we shall sooner and more surely bring them to deal with it in the manner in which men of our race are accustomed to deal with grave social problems—painstakingly and with justice."[252]

Professor Nathaniel S. Shaler came, it seems, from slaveholding stock and, though he was in sympathies against the South during the Civil War, he admired the Southern people and appreciated the magnitude of the problem left after the war. He, however, took a hopeful view of the future, the source of which seems, largely, to have been memories of the pleasant relations existing in the household as a child between himself and the domestic slaves. The old "Black Mammy" traditions may be of historical and other value, but few memories of this type come from the Reconstruction Period, and, all in all, writers influenced by these traditions may becloud the issues. This attitude of mind and lack of appreciation of the true conditions explains the following remarks when he says: "As for the miserable subterfuge commonly known as the 'grandfather clause,' by which this end was accomplished (admitting illiterate whites to vote but excluding Negroes), I am ashamed that it should have been invented by Americans.[252½] These remarks are in violent contrast to those of Mr. Stone given, ante p. 175. The relations between the races that count are those between the masses of the whites and the masses of the blacks; and these

252"The Neighbor," pp. 335-6, Houghton, Mifflin Co.
252½Ibid., p. 332.

cannot be determined by reference to *ante bellum* conditions or left to the direction of leaders in industry or the missionary element.

"The worst of the political aspects of the Negro problem," says Professor Dowd, "is the mischief done by white demagogues. The fact that the Negro vote ofen has a deciding influence in the nomination and election of candidates for office opens the way for the white demagogue to get in power by coddling the Negro and pandering to his prejudices. In the North, the white demagogue, in attempting to ride into office on the Negro's back, is prone to outdo the most radical Negro, in charging the Southern whites with every kind of injustice to the Negro population, and he chimes in with the radical Negro leaders in proclaiming the franchise laws in the South unconstitutional and outrages upon the natural rights of the citizens. At the same time, the white demagogue in the South is apt to curry favor with the lower type of his own race by a constant harping upon the Negro issue, or making a business of corralling the Negro vote in the hope of gaining some elective or appointive office for himself. The Northern white demagogue has a motive for stirring up in the Negro a bitterness against the Southern whites, and the Southern white demagogue has a motive for stirring up in the whites a bitterness against the Negro. Thus the presence of the Negro in our midst gives a special field for the flourishing of a type of white politician who otherwise would remain in obscurity. Since the Civil War the Negro voters have been only dice and trump-cards for white demagogues. They have introduced into our political life a new game of chance, played for a few white men's benefit, and to the detriment of the Negro."[253]

Referring particularly to the enfranchisement of the Negro by the Civil War Amendments, Professor Dowd says: "As a result of the Civil War and the radical domination of Congress following it, our Constitution was amended with a view to preventing the Southern states from disfranchising the Negro. It was decreed that there should be no limitation of suffrage on the basis of color. The enactment of these amendments made it necessary for the white people of the South to maintain their supremacy by resort to intimidation, ballot jugglery, and forcible exclusion of

---

[253]*"The Negro in American Life,"* p. 587, The Century Co.

the Negro from the polls. The use of such methods, however, was so humiliating to the Southern people, and so conducive to social disorder, that the wiser of their leaders sought to accomplish their object by enacting franchise laws with provisions which would exclude the great mass of Negroes on other grounds than color or race. Such franchise laws were enacted in nearly every Southern state, and were sustained by the Supreme Court of the United States; so that now white supremacy is maintained in the South by due process of law. It would be a monstrous solecism if, under our Constitution, white supremacy could be provided for in our colonies and not in our states."[254]

"The people of the South are thoroughly reconciled to the fact that the provisions of our Constitution, prohibiting any discrimination in civil rights on account of race or color, are there to stay. During the Reconstruction times, when these provisions were added to our Constitution and put in force, the Southern people bitterly opposed them because they could not foresee how such provisions could be carried out without rendering permanent the deplorable state of things which the Reconstruction era had brought about. The Southern people now know that the new provisions of the Constitution do not prohibit a state from excluding from the franchise those citizens who cannot make an intelligent use of it; and, because the repeal of the new provisions of our Constitution is impossible and unnecessary, the Southern people are firmly resolved to live under and obey the Constitution as it stands."[255]

"However, the South is in favor of protecting itself against a possible relapse into the Reconstruction horrors by enacting franchise laws which, while conforming to our Constitution, will exclude from the ballot the element of the population which is a menace to good government. These franchise laws are much criticised on the ground that they are not applied alike to the whites and blacks. For instance, it is claimed that illiterate Negroes are strictly excluded from voting while illiterate white men vote without molestation. Now, the facts of the matter are about as follows: First, in most of the Southern states Negroes who are legally qualified to vote are allowed to do so without hindrance. For instance, in Virginia and North Carolina

[254]"*The Negro in American Life,*" p. 496, The Century Co.
[255]Ibid., p. 584.

qualified Negroes are as unhampered in voting as qualified white people. Second, in some states where the Negro population is very great, the suffrage tests are applied more stringently to Negroes than to whites. The reason for this stricter scrutiny of the Negroes is because experience has shown that their votes have been a menace to good government, and the object of the new franchise laws is to remove this menace. Now, admitting that the laws are more strictly applied to the Negroes, it does not follow that the discriminations against them are solely on account of their race or color; for, even in South Carolina, one may see at many polling places Negroes, known to be good citizens, depositing their ballots without any objection whatever from the white people. The fundamental reason, therefore, for excluding the mass of Negroes from the ballot is their unfitness, and not merely their color."[256] Professor Dowd candidly admits, however, that the Negro will never be permitted to rule the white man, irrespective of the qualifications possessed by the former.

We seem to arrive at a remarkably mixed situation from the conclusions: that it was a mistake to enfranchise the Negro; that to avoid disaster the South resorted to force or used fraudulent methods; that later there was found to be no need of this since the Negroes could be excluded by legal methods; that the South has become "thoroughly reconciled to the fact that" the 14th and 15th Amendments are here to stay and "are firmly resolved to live under and obey the Constitution as it stands;" that at the same time the whites cannot and will not permit the Negro to vote where it would result in Negro control, and that we now discriminate against him in carrying out the restrictive franchise laws.

Professor Dowd strives laboriously to show we should be contented with the provisions of the 14th and 15th Amendments, or, at least, we could survive under them, and should not be alarmed at the general political aspect, so far as relates to the Negro; but, as a matter of fact, he makes out a good cause for dissatisfaction with the situation and repeal of these Amendments. Perhaps he was attempting to apologize for the situation.

It seems that we are developing a positive genius for the advocacy and support of Constitutional Amendments of a far

---

[256]"*The Negro in American Life,*" pp. 584-5, The Century Co.

reaching and dangerous character—such as tend toward lawlessness and the general demoralization of the people. To maintain that we "can always find rational and constitutional grounds for protecting" ourselves against the menace of the Negro vote, as Professor Dowd does on page 586 of his work, fails, it seems to me, so far as constitutional grounds are concerned, to take into consideration the 15th Amendment itself, what has been done under it, and all existing facts relating to the matter. Owing to the fact that the great body of the Negro population was uneducated and illiterate, an educational qualification was sufficient to bar them temporarily from the exercise of the franchise. All that we have done in the South to protect us from this menace, since we ejected him from authority by force, has been to establish an educational qualification, in some instances combined with a property qualification. If there is any other way to accomplish this, free from the discrimination of race, color, or previous condition of servitude, forbidden by the 15th Amendment, it has not yet been announced by the discoverer and has escaped the vigilance of many an earnest inquirer. It is a difficult problem to do a thing forbidden to be done in such a way that it is not done at all. The educational qualification serves temporarily as a bar to the exercise of suffrage by the Negro; but its effectiveness is even now rapidly diminishing under the stimulus to Negro education, and in a short time our sole legal remedy will be ineffective. Then we shall have to resort again to force and fraud. Even as it is now the law is not, as is admitted in the foregoing quotations, applied with even handed justice to the Negro and the white alike; and how any one can find cause for congratulation in law-enforcement of this character and contentment with a provision of the Constitution that makes such procedure essential, is incomprehensible to me.

From the time of the adoption of the Constitution until the Civil War suffrage qualifications and the civil rights of the individual were wholly within the discretion of the peoples of the respective States; and during this important period of our history no one dreamed of hampering the States by limiting their powers in these matters, nor had there arisen anything during all this time to indicate the slightest need of such change. The qualifications for suffrage were liberalized from time to time as demand was made and conditions justified, and the same may be said of legislation affecting civil rights generally. The 14th and 15th Amendments have retarded development, and if they were wiped out bodily a great impetus would be given to that natural development of civil and political rights consistent with the good of the State and justice to all. All property rights in the States were safe before these Amendments and they would now be safe without them.

"To take the ground that all the complicated phases of the modern problem of race relations are attributable to Reconstruction," says Stone, "or to any other one line of policy, anywhere or at any time, would be to assume a wholly untenable position. The simpler the form of relation between two different races the simpler will be the problems between the two; the more complex the relation the more complex its problems. The simplest relation that could exist between the white and Negro races, in the mass, was that of physical control of one by the other. The most complex relations that can exist between the two, or between any racial groups, are those predicated upon a condition of actual or technical equality. And the complications to which this relation gives rise will be difficult and severe in proportion to the degree of artificiality which characterizes the equality sought to be established. The greater the natural differences in the way, the more complicated and serious will be the problems incident to the artificially created relations. The mere grant of immediate freedom to a large mass of Negro slaves would inevitably have produced its own racial problems. Every step taken toward the removal of the further barriers between white and black multiplied such problems and created new ones. The only escape from a cataclysm lay in allowing sufficient time to elapse between the removal of one barrier after another for the races to adjust their relations to the change along normal lines. But this would not have been 'Reconstruction.' That was a process the logical dogma of which was the proposition that nature has erected no barrier to racial equality which legislation cannot remove."[257]

"Is is frequently declared," remarks Stone, "that nothing better than the present arrangement in this country has been suggested by its critics—that the system adopted in 1867-70 was the best that could have been devised. This is superficial. This

---

[257]*"Studies in the American Race Problem,"* pp. 252-3.

much only need be suggested in reply: Even a purely negative policy would have been better than the one adopted.   Under the former, with the political status of the Negro left with the States, each would have been free to evolve an adjustment which would have been satisfactory to both races.   Beyond question this would not have been the same in all the states.   The perniciousness of the present system is that it is ironclad.   It leaves no room for local and individual adjustment.   Under the political *status quo ante bellum* each state would have been at liberty to experiment along its own lines, and, above all, every state would have had the advantage of the practical operation of the efforts of every other.   And these several efforts of necessity would have been in the direction of devising means of admitting to the privileges of the body politic such members of the other race as might be qualified by education, property and character."[258 & 259]

Professor Dowd appeals to the leaders of the Negroes to alleviate the situation by recognizing it in its true light and urging their followers to refrain from qualifying *en masse*.   In other words, an appeal is made to the Negro leaders to curtail one of their rights in the prevention of an evil which we are unable to avoid either because of lack of vision or lack of courage.

"It seems to me," he says, "to be a settled fact, demonstrated over and over again, that neither the Negro, nor any other colored race will ever be allowed to exercise civil rights in the United States to the extent of controlling any part of our government.   And, therefore, I think it the part of wisdom for Negro leaders to recognize this fact, and not to make too much ado over the franchise in states where the Negroes constitute a menacing portion of the population.   They should, at least, limit their complaints to cases of unquestionably qualified Negroes who have been denied the ballot, and they should cease to hold up to the mass of their race the false idea that the franchise is a right, instead of a privilege depending upon fitness for good citizenship.   In states where the Negro population is not a men-

---

[258]*"Studies in the American Race Problem,"* pp. 380-1..

[259]Professor Mecklin, in his *"Democracy and Race Friction,"* p. 94, expresses very much the same views in regard to the rejection of the so-called "black codes" of the Southern States intended for the purpose of bridging the chasm between slavery and freedom, and the substitution therefor of Reconstruction.

ace, I think that the white people are willing to coöperate with the Negro leaders in seeing to it that all qualified Negroes are allowed to vote. In the matter of the Negro franchise in the South there is opportunity for Negro leaders to exercise a wisdom and discretion which will reflect credit on themselves, and, at the same time, pave the way for a larger number of Negroes to qualify for the suffrage and to profit by its privileges. They should appreciate the fact that the harmonious living together, in the same territory, of two races as unlike as the Negro and the Caucasian is one of the most difficult of problems, and that any straining of the Negro in the direction of political activities is apt to make the problem more difficult."[260]

"In the face of the greatest problem that confronts a democracy, and one which has nowhere been solved, it would seem to be the part of wisdom of Negro leaders to stress some other point of race relationship than that of political equality, which in other races has come about by a slow evolution, following the attainment of equality in other respects."[261]

If, as is conceded by the great majority of all thoughtful persons who have given the matter due consideration, the 14th and 15th Amendments were improvidently added in the heat of passions aroused during the Civil Strife, and particularly if this were illegally done, as appears to be a fact, and if clinging to these two provisions is provocative of political discord and confusion and promotes contempt of law, let us in God's name try to remove them.

Taking the right to vote from the Negro will not of itself solve the race problem, but it will be immensely beneficial in that it will bring about the following results:

(1) It will make for law and order in removing from the Constitution a provision the observance of which, in the sections for which it was primarily intended, would result in such evils that it would be resisted to the last extremity.

(2) It will avoid the evils that will shortly arise when the Negro, who is now being educated so as to meet the educational qualification (the only impediment that can be put in his way legally) for voters. invokes the provisions of the 15th Amendment in his own behalf.

---

[260]"*The Negro in American Life,*" p. 586, The Century Co.
[261]Ibid., p. 588.

(3) It will remove a purchasable, corrupt electorate in places where he does vote.

(4) It will enable the whites in the South to affiliate with that party whose policy confirms most closely to the beliefs of the individual; and will make possible a real progressive party where none now exists.

The combination of the above results, which must inevitably follow from wiping out the 15th Amendment, cannot be otherwise than reflected in an improved sentiment and practice in governmental affairs. Furthermore, when the Negro realizes that the existing hypocritical and dangerous situation is to be replaced by an absolute bar to participation in and control of governmental affairs by him, except in so far as the respective States may permit this, he will lend a more willing ear to proposals of solution by segregation. Particularly will this be true, if he conceives himself fit to control his own affairs. The anomalous position of hypocritically purporting to confer the franchise and withholding it in practical application, produces a situation of grave danger under any circumstances, but particularly so when made the football of party politics. The Democratic Party in the South purports to be the white man's party, interested in white supremacy, and the solution of the race problem. This is pretense—buncombe. The Republican Party purports to be the special friend of the Negro, and interested in the exercise by him of his political rights. This also is buncombe; for they know he is unfitted for this, and that, if he should exercise the franchise, it would be to the public injury. For political purposes the parties are interested in the preservation of the *status quo*. There are, of course, some exceptions to this in both parties.

When it was found that protection from hostile legislation against "privileges and immunities" of the 14th Amendment did not insure the franchise to the Negro, this was done in direct terms by the 15th Amendment. Though technically it does not give the franchise, it does so in effect by forbidding discrimination. In view of the fact that the right to vote and the right to hold office are not "privileges and immunities," and prescribing qualifications for officers by the State does not come within the inhibitions of either the 14th or the 15th Amendments, it would seem that the State may prescribe, by Constitutional provision or act of legislature where its Constitution permits, that its officers shall be white citizens.

The decisions of the Supreme Court all point to the validity of a qualification of this character for office holders. If this were done in the South, it would go far toward avoiding the evil effects of the 15th Amendment in an effective legal manner. The enactment of such provision would also do much toward reconciling the Negro to serious discussion of solution by segregation.

Much has been said in the last few years in regard to State Rights. These may be restored to what they were prior to the Civil War by abolition of the 14th and 15th Amendments. The 14th Amendment was intended to assure to the Negro his civil rights and was never intended to hamper the State in all legislation as it has done under construction by the Supreme Court. It was intended to confer on Congress the right to intervene by provision of law in behalf of the Negro, and not to give the Supreme Court the right to review all legislative enactments by the State.

"The congress shall have power to enforce by appropriate legislation the provisions of this article," and "The congress shall have power to enforce this article by appropriate legislation," are parts, respectively, of the 14th and 15th Amendments. That these added sections mean that the provisions of these Amendments are entirely and solely within the discretion of the Congress, and that the Supreme Court cannot rightfully act until the Congress has expressed its will in the matter and State enactments are found to conflict therewith, is proposed here as the true intent and correct interpretation. If this can be maintained, some of the harsh provisions of both Amendments may be legally avoided as a temporary paliative until active steps for solution are underway.

CHAPTER VI.

SUMMARY AS TO RACES.

From what has gone before, it should appear to the investigator who views the record of human events in an open frame of mind that the following conclusions must be arrived at as the irresistible, logical sequence of indisputable, outstanding facts:

(1) That the present advanced stage in human progress is due to the peculiar genius of the White race, which, from the remotest times we have been able to probe in any field of research till now, has been found in the van of progress—the originators, builders and preservers of civilization. All history points to this as a fact so glaringly evident that none should fail to recognize it as such, or hesitate to accept the necessary implications involved in this circumstance. There is but one civilization of the all of which we have any knowledge that may have arisen entirely uninfluenced by that of the white man— the Chinese: and this last has exerted no influence whatever upon the affairs of the human race outside of its own Asiatic habitant. There is even evidence that the Hamitic or Semitic populations in the Euphrates-Persian area may have given an impetus to or been responsible in some degree for this civilization; for these people and members of the Turanian family seem to have been associated together in the civilizations of Shumir and Accad.

(2) One of the necessary implications involved in the above is that the White race is in blood, mental and moral characteristics—in some vital principle that sets them apart—differentiated from all other races; and the chasm between it and the Negro race can be closed only by swamping all humanity in the cesspools of amalgamation and withdrawing civilization forever from the heights it has already attained. These differences exist. They are patent, selfevident, and cannot escape recognition by any one who will look or investigate. The differences are there irrespective of whether their production is referred to evolution or special creation. The consideration of evolution would be

entirely foreign to this work but for the fact that some of its adherents seem to regard it as a vehicle for the transmission of propaganda favorable to the obliteration of race lines. Such works do harm among those who do not think; but any careful consideration shows such advocacy false to the doctrine of evolution itself. Evolution, whether monogenetic or polygenetic, is based upon differentiation in conjunction with adaptability to changed conditions of existence. By this, and by this alone, is explained the arrival of the White race, the Mongoloid race, the Brown race and the Black race. I should like to be able to understand the workings of a mind that worries itself and the world in the advocacy of an alleged natural process that operates solely through bringing about changes which when produced are not changes or are immaterial and of no consequence. This is simply an absurdity. One of the most deplorable features of the whole situation, however, is that religion, which should be operative as an ennobling, elevating influence upon the race, lends itself to the destructive application of that conception of brotherly love which springs from the absurd belief in a common descent from Adam—a proposition as lacking in the elements of reason as that of certain evolutionists that differences are not dissimilarities but similarities.

(3) The existence of the white type and civilization in any center are synchronous, as are also the decay of civilization and the disappearance of the white type. No other explanation of this decay can be made in many instances.

(4) Just as forceful and just as necessary as any of the other conclusions, is the one, that the Negro and the white cannot occupy the same territory without amalgamation and the disappearance of the white type. It cannot be denied that Aryan Hindus, the White Egyptians, the white North African, and many of the Arabs have disappeared in this manner, the whites being lost to the world in their replacement by an inferior mixed race, and the distinctive civilizations they founded lost for all time. The Peruvian and Central American civilizations were likewise lost in amalgamation of the white Atlanteans with the inferior indigenous types surrounding them. History is replete with examples of replacement of one white civilization by another; but it does not give us a single example of the replacement of a white civilization by that of any other race, or of the permanent

loss of any white civilization except through the process of amalgamation with some other race.

There has been preserved to us from our first glimpse of the remotest past the distinctive types that belong to the Negro race, the Mongoloid race and the White race; and it seems there should be added to these a distinctive Brown race as typified in the Dravidians. There may have been in the remotest past a greater variety of types than those indicated above, certain of which have disappeared in process of amalgamation though it seems amalgamation is peculiarly the result of the association in common undertakings in a civilized State of an inferior, backward people and a superior civilized people. Others still may have altogether disappeared under stress of changed conditions to which they could not accommodate themselves. Certain it is, that the types indicated above were in full and complete development in the remotest historical period; and that these types have persisted in their purity ever since, except where affected by admixture between races, and have shown no evidence of further divergence. That there has been a great amount of mixture between the races cannot be doubted, and many of the shades between black and white, black and yellow, and yellow and white may be accounted for in this way. But, however numerous these mixtures may be, it does not in the least affect the fact of race types that exist, the principal of which are the Negro, Mongoloid and White.

Any intelligible consideration of that evolutionary theory which derives all mankind from a common ancestor must, of necessity, give to each distinctive type developed, a continental area and an age-long period of isolation in order to produce the type. Therefore, in one respect—at one stage in the progress of human evolution—the monogenist and the polygenist must be in agreement. In other words, there must be, in accordance with either, a time when the Negro, the Mongoloid and the White shall each appear in full development and in the occupancy of continental areas; and, therefore, although my reading has been confined to a small number of authorities, I, nevertheless, consider the following conclusions as the most consistent explanation of the early dispersion of the races, involving, as I believe it does, the least conflict and the greatest agreement of alleged facts put forth by these authorities:

(1) *The Black race.*—There is no insuperable difficulty in the

acceptance of Lemuria as a former land area in which the Black race may have had its primitive home. This former existence is called for by some authorities in botany, zoology, ethnology, philology, and biology in explanation of the plant and animal life found bordering on the Indian Ocean, and is demanded in support of the monogenetic theory of evolution. The former existence of Lemuria is not inconsistent with geology, and might well explain the presence of Negroid peoples in the Philippines, the Malay Peninsula, southern India and Australia, as well as in Africa; but this does not, as I believe, preclude Africa from being a part of the primitive home-land, if not the original, of the Black race, unless it can be shown that this land is of too recent origin and was not in existence when Lemuria was above the water, or was for some other reason unfitted for human abode. That the black man went into Africa from Lemuria, as is assumed by the monogenetic evolutionist, presupposes a concurrent existence at one time of both. The Black race was incapable of reaching any point not in land connection with their homeland, not being navigators, and they were by their incapacities prohibited from doing this in the face of opposition from a superior people. That Lemuria and Africa formed the primitive home of the Black race from which have come the Negro, the Australian, other Negroid peoples and the Dravidians, seems reasonable in that it conforms to known facts and may not be inconsistent with any. The greatest divergence among these is found in the Dravidian type, the most advanced of them all.

(2) *The Mongoloid race.*—The primitive home of the Mongoloids seems to cover the wide range of all Asia outside of the southern peninsulas, all Europe, and the two Americas. This is arrived at in conformity with the preponderance of opinion that the prehistoric (Stone Age) relics of man in these areas are Mongoloid in character. Lull, among the latest authorities, admits the magnificent Cro-Mangon race, with its so-called "disharmonic face," is Asiatic, in other words, as I take it, Mongoloid.[262] The White man in Europe, southwest Asia, North Africa and the Americas, is always found to be civilized in a greater or less degree, having knowledge of the cereals, domestic animals and the metals, and appears in the character of a colonist. Throughout this vast area assigned to the Mongoloids there appeared a num-

---

[262]*"The Ways of Life,"* p. 288.

ber of types, varying from the fixed and numerous type of the Chinese to other and darker types and to yet still other and lighter types that approximated the whites. These different types of Mongoloids, aside from the results arising from admixture with other races, are distinctly Mongoloid and yet as varient, if not more so, as the types found in the recognized divisions of the white race. There seems to be no valid reason why it should not be conceded that America contributed with its indigenous type which was later affected in some degree by contact with the Asiatic Mongoloids.

(3) *The Brown race.*—It may be stated that the generally accepted division of races by many authorities is into the White race, the Brown race, and the Black race, to which is added by some the American Indian as a fourth race. In this classification the Mongoloid is included in the Brown race.

Winchell, who assumes all mankind to have been evolved from a common ancestral type, says, referring to the origin of the Brown race: "In this view, we should contemplate the Australian and Papuan as two closely related Black races, from which have descended the two related Brown races—the Dravidian and the Mongoloid. In such case, of course, the common premongoloid and predravidian stock was never spread over the continent of Asia."[263]

It seems that practically all authorities concede the Dravidians to have been one of the primitive brown peoples derived by evolution from a predravidian stock; and most monogenists derive the Adamic stock from a Dravidian stem. The Mongoloid characteristics are so numerous and prominent that there is ample justification, it seems, for putting them in a class by themselves. If this be done, there remains but one typical derivative type of the Brown race—the Dravidian. The other peoples that go to swell the members of this race to formidable numbers in accordance with the usual classification, are, therefore, such as became brown through the process of amalgamation; and it may be safely stated that a great part of the existing brown peoples represent a mixture of white blood with that of the black or primitive brown man, and, possibly, in some instances with the Mongoloid.

Professor Dowd, on page 526 of his work,[264] "The Negro in

263"*Preadamites,*" p. 313.
264"*The Negro in American Life,*" The Century Co.

American Life," says: "The English ethnologist, Keane, agrees with Quatrefages that the Negro race once occupied vast domains in Asia, Oceania, and Africa, but has been steadily losing ground as a result of yellow and white immigration. A branch of the Negro race which at one time spread over a large part of India has entirely disappeared as a result of the encroachments of the white race, leaving, as evidence of its existence there, only the present dark-brown Dravidians, who represent an early mixture of the Negro and Aryan. In Africa, within the historic period, the Negro in the North has been yielding territory to the more aggressive Semites, Libyans, and Berbers; and in the South and West, to the races of Europe." (He refers to Keane, "Ethnology," Ch. XI. as authority for the first statement; to Quatrefages, "The Pygmies," p. 52, and Keane, "Ethnology," p. 254, as authority for the second statement; and makes the third statement as his own conclusion.)

This is a picture of his weakness that should lead us to be very hopeful of the Negro question in the United States. It clearly indicates that the Negro is incapable of competing with either the White or the Mongoloid, or, for some reason or another, in the presence of either he dwindles in numbers or fades away entirely except for a small insignificant number of mixed bloods. The Negro, we are told, once occupied vast domains in Asia, including a large part of India, and that in India he has entirely disappeared as a result of "encroachments of the white race"; that the only evidence of his having been there is found in the Dravidians; and that in North Africa, within the historic period, the Negro has been yielding territory to the whites.

The unfortunate thing about this picture is that it is largely fiction. Regarding the Mongoloid as a distinctive type, if there is any justification whatever for believing in a derivative Brown race as the result of evolution, the Dravidian is that type and is so considered by most authorities. It seems that any thought that the Dravidians resulted from a cross between Aryans and Blacks would place the Aryans in India at a period for more remote than any date agreed upon as the time of their arrival. But if we concede the Dravidians constitute the last remnant of the Negro in India surviving in a Dravidian-Aryan amalgamation, the question naturally arises as to where are the aggressive whites that brought about this situation. If they survive they have black or brown skins, and a survival of this type should not lull us into a sense of security.

Quatrefages held that the Negro originated in Southern Asia, and he divided mankind into the White, Yellow and Black races. He, therefore, did not concede any derivative Brown race in the evolutionary sense, and must have considered all brown peoples the result of amalgamation of blacks with other peoples. How he should have singled out the Dravidians as an example of amalgamation and the only one in India seems incomprehensible.

The best authorities lead us to believe that the Negro was never in North Africa or Egypt until he was brought there by the civilized whites; and it is folly to talk about the recession of the Negro in these regions where the ancient white colonists have been replaced by Blacks and Browns. We can boast of Negro recession in the presence of whites in India only by classing Blacks and Browns as white; and in Egypt and North Africa the recession is of whites before blacks, as it was in fact in India after the arrival of the whites in that section. Most of the peoples classed as Hamitic, Semitic, and even Aryan, in Abyssinia, Egypt, the Soudan, and North Africa, are, aside from the modern European, peoples of mixed blood in which the Negro predominates. In North Africa there are, it seems, some pure Berbers and probably some pure Jews and Arabs.

That Lemuria, a large expanse of land connecting South Asia, Africa, Australia and some of the islands, once existed and was the home of the Black race seems reasonable and apparently conforms to the best considered results obtained from research in all lines that have a bearing upon the matter.

That there should also have developed somewhere in this region a primitive Brown race of which the Dravidian is the type seems not improbable; but when we go beyond this we enter into uncertain grounds because of the fact that the shade of brown will include within its ranks so many people that are plainly the result of fusion between the White, the Mongoloid and the Black races.

(4) *The White race.*—The same scientific considerations that require the existence of Lemuria in explanation of the flora and fauna on opposite sides of the Indian Ocean, also demand the former existence of Atlantis in explanation of the flora and fauna on the opposite shores of the Atlantic. In addition to this, the traditions and history of the White race point to Atlantis as its

primitive home; and it is only by the admission of its existence that the presence of white colonists in Peru and Central America on one side of the Atlantic, and in Europe, on the other, with kinship between the two in language, alphabet, customs, religion and character of public works, can be explained.

The progenitors of the White race must have dwelled in Atlantis for ages before the three branches of the race emerged from its shores as civilized colonists to the Americas, Europe, North Africa and southwest Asia. Probably the earliest colonists, members of the Aryan branch, went into Peru from the Empire of Atlantis over the land connection that formerly existed in or about the region where now lies the mouth of the Amazon. The submergence of this land connection in a convulsion of nature isolated these Peruvian colonists, as before pointed out; and this must have resulted in stimulating emigration from the Empire to Central America and the Mediterranean area. Should there be discovered any evidence of a former civilization along the valley of the Amazon it would strongly fortify this assumption and indicate that this valley was formerly a much more highly elevated area that subsided when the land connection with Atlantis was submerged. But whatever views may be entertained as to these suggestions, it must be accepted as a fact that Atlantis existed; that it was in all probability the primitive home of the White race; and that its final submergence gave rise to all legends respecting the Deluge.

The story of Plato and the connection between the Maya alphabet of Central America and that of Phoenicia and of Egypt are sufficient, within themselves, to justify the conclusion that in Atlantis with its civilized Atlanteans lay the common source from which came the tongues and methods of writing on both sides of the Atlantic. Had this connection, the existence of which must be conceded and explained, been around the world in the other direction, some evidence of the route taken would be found. None exists, so far as we know. Many acceptable conclusions in human affairs are based upon less satisfactory premises.

It seems that the brunette Hamite must have been the first to venture in the eastern Mediterranean section and implant his civilization in Egypt and southwestern Asia. These must have been followed closely to the same general section by the Semitic tribes, while the Aryan populations went in two streams, the southerly one to the east through the Black Sea and hence to the plateau of Iran or Persia, the other to the northwestern section of Europe. The Aryans, as they appear in history, are engaged in two migratory movements; one, into the valley of the Indus and the peninsula of India, is a continuation of the former eastern migration; the other is a reflex movement that brings them from the east into Europe on the north coast of the Mediterranean.

The earlier Hamitic and Semitic populations that reached the north shore of the Mediterranean found a Mongoloid people with whom they amalgamated where they did not drive out or destroy them. Eventually the remnants of these Mongoloids, not absorbed in process of amalgamation, were driven, one, in the north of Europe where it still survives in the Finns and a few other kindred peoples around the Baltic; the other, into the south of France and into Spain where it survives in the Basques. By the absorption of this Mongoloid blood the brunette white of south Europe was made darker still; and it was these people with whom the Aryan Greeks and Romans came in contact in their reflex movement toward the west; and it was the descendents of these, in turn—all of them—who were overrun by the Teutons in the disintegration of the Roman Empire.

That the blood of an original Mongoloid type has darkened the complexion of the south European brunette, particularly in Spain, cannot, it seems, be doubted; and this holds true as to the populations in southwest Asia. On the other hand, the Turk, derived from an original light-colored Mongoloid type, is now essentially white through the absorption of white blood.

Considerable has been written recently in regard to race matters in which assertions are made as to a much wider diffusion of Negro (Black) blood than is justified by facts. The early dispersion of the Negro (Black), limited him on the north in Asia to the Malay Peninsula and India, and in Africa on the north to the Desert of Sahara. In India amalgamation with the indigenous population utterly destroyed its ancient civilization and the Aryan type. In Egypt amalgamation with the imported Negro resulted in the destruction of its civilization and the disappearance of the old Egyptian type. In North Africa the same mixture of blood, resulting from the importation of slaves, has made Négroid the great majority of the people of this section, and the west coast and southwest corner of Arabia has been largely afflicted with a Negroid population. All this is conceded as incontestably true and is surely sufficiently appalling without attribu-

ting the same contamination in instances without historical justification. That there is a large element of Negro blood in the
south of Europe, Asia Minor and southwest Asia, is, as it seems,
a statement without the slightest justification of historical fact
behind it. The Greeks, the Romans, and the white Asiatics outside of India and southwest Arabia, were not in contact with the
Negro at any time; they made slaves of captives in the wars they
waged, one with the other; and the only possible Negro blood
that could have been absorbed into that of these people arose
from Negro slaves imported from Africa. This number must
have been small compared with that in our own country, and
furthermore a very large number of the Negro male-slaves in the
East have been eunuchs for much over 1,000 years. The Greek
in Europe probably saw his first Negro when his people became
navigators and began trading with Egypt. Probably a slight addition of Negroid blood was infused into that of Spain during the
Saracen occupancy. This Saracen civilization was the work of
the Semitic Arab of the East, free from the Negroid contamination that was being brought about by amalgamation of the races
in northern Africa. After the expulsion of the Saracens a small
amount of Negro blood may have been introduced into Spain
during the later period when the slave trade was a profitable
branch of commerce, as was the case with Portugal to a greater
degree.[264½]   This was probably insignificant in comparison
with what we have already absorbed on the percentage basis. It
is insidiously progressing while we, in an imagined security, do
not know it is going on.

[264½]The Encyclopaedia Britannica says: "The ethnological
composition of the population is most mixed: in the two northern
provinces the population is essentially Galician, but further south
the mixture becomes obvious; not only did the conquering Portuguese largely intermarry with the Arabs, but in the places where
they exterminated them they replaced them by colonies of cru-
saders of all nations, chiefly French, English, Dutch and Frisian,
who have left their mark on the features and character of the
nation, and they also largely intermarried with the Jews. No
Jews were so wealthy or cultured as those of Portugal, who,
though for many centuries keeping strictly apart from the Christians, yet after their forced conversion or expulsion by King
Emmanuel largely intermarried, especially with the people of Lis-
bon. Further south an African physiognomy appears, derived
from the thousands of Negro slaves imported to till Alemptejo
and Algarve, from the days of Dom Henry till the decline of the
Portuguese power."

The situation is surely grave enough as it stands, and, in the world-wide awakening of the colored races, demands for its solution concerted, sympathetic and intelligent action on the part of all white peoples. Under such circumstances, it comes with ill grace that one who purports to speak with the authority of exhaustive research and, therefore, with full information, should slur the blood of any people by declaring them largely Negroid when history and scientific research not only fail to justify such assertion, but proclaim the contrary.

No one has a greater regard than I for the Nordic character as typified in the old Norseman with his magnificent physique, courage, daring and other admirable traits of character, or that of the fearless Teuton who made raids upon the Roman power. However, whatever classification one may adopt, we cannot escape from the fact that the brunette type played the most important part in the earliest civilizations, and that the Bronze Age was ushered in by the brunette in all probability, a people with small hands as shown by swords and other implements found. Any extreme laudation of the Nordic, accompanied with corresponding deprecation of other branches of the race, should be met with widespread condemnation in the face of a situation that requires concerted action on the part of all members of the race to keep the race white, not to mention the need for preserving to the White race areas now under its control and not now white, but capable of being made so. However much I may admire the Nordic character and glory in the gallant part played by him in history, I cannot subscribe to the doctrine that the cultural future of the race or its grim continuance as a reality rests alone with the Nordics. Just as the surroundings and the physical and mental condition of the individual are reflected in his activities, so, with a creative race endowed with immortality unless surrendered in amalgamation on the altars of an inferior race, will its achievements reflect the surrounding circumstances in which it finds itself. To-day in a torper of inactivity, it may tomorrow astonish the world by renewed activity in the march of progress, arising from psychic impulse or some change in surrounding circumstances. But these potentialities must be in the blood of the people, and that they are inherent in the White race in all its branches is indubitably attested by its record of events—history —which with equal emphasis points to their absence in the Black race.

In our efforts to arrive at a solution of the race problem that will at the same time save us from the destructive and degrading effects of amalgamation and conform most nearly to basic principles of justice and equity, we find in opposition to us: (1) The facetious monogenetic evolutionist with an axe to grind; (2) A large part of the Christian Church, particularly the missionary element, with its teaching in regard to the brotherhood of man; and (3) Big Business joins the hosts of opposition on alleged economic grounds.

Fortunately all who adhere to the monogenetic theory of evolution or of creation do not fail to appreciate the fact that race means something more than color. Those who disregard this utterly fail to heed the teachings of history in the pursuit of their pet theory.

Big Business must learn that it is neither patriotic nor good business to jeopardize for all time the future of a people in order that a small number of the elect may reap a temporary advantage. What advantage is it to us that this generation or the following may lead the world industrially and have the world at its feet financially, if in the accomplishment of this there is added the last straw that will send the race on the toboggan slide into the black cesspool of amalgamation? This is not exaggeration. Big Business coddles the Negro for the temporary advantage that may come from the use of his cheap labor, and is not interested in the fact that white labor is being destroyed in so doing, and that cheap labor is often the most expensive kind.

CHAPTER VII.

SOLUTION.

When it comes to any serious consideration of the solution of our race problem, we find what amounts to a general pubic indifference, even though in private conversation the practically unanimous opinion expressed is that the problem is one of first magnitude and requires something be done immediately if anything is ever to be done. At the same time, there is an all prevailing belief that solution is a hopeless impossibility. On the other hand, if a labor agent appears in Atlanta, Georgia, Wilmington, North Carolina, or Newport News, Virginia, and begins to send Negro laborers to industrial centers in the North, the powers that be, fearing a labor shortage, demand, and subservient and shortsighted city councilmen or state legislators pass or enact, ordinances or legislation that in effect prohibit the operation of such agencies. Enormous license fees are required and heavy penalties inflicted for operating without a license. This is, of course, stupid, shortsighted, and against the public good; but employers of labor are often stupid in such matters even working against their own interest in the end, and are indifferent to the fact these migratory movements would tend to impress upon the people at large the need for solution of the problem.

Every effort to awaken interest in a solution is squelched as a dangerous agitation or disturbance of an absolutely essential body of labor, and there is a persistence in that long-exploded and ridiculous contention that the Negro is the only source of labor for use in certain sections of the South and in certain occupations.

Nevertheless, since emancipation, there has been a constantly recurring agitation on the part of the Negro himself in connection with the repatriation of his people in Africa, and this should indicate that a well considered movement of this character, fostered by the government, would be popular among the Negroes and secure a large and spontaneous following. However, all movements of this kind are frowned upon and obstacles placed in their way.

Referring to some migratory movements, or tendencies toward this, manifested by the Negro after Reconstruction, Clinton Stoddard Burr says: "But the most significant of all, the Liberian Exodus Stock Company was formed by Negroes in the year 1877, for the purpose of sending Negro emigrants to Africa, and to establish a regular line of steamers between Monrovia and Charleston to bring African products to the United States. It is to the everlasting disgrace of the white people of Charleston that they, in their great greed, resented any loss to the supply of Negro labor, and induced custom house officials not to grant clearance papers until a new copper bottom had been built on the ship '*Azar*'; which brought the cost of the ship from seven thousand dollars up to nine thousand. It was even more disgraceful that the '*Azar*' was stolen and sold in Liverpool, through the connivance of her captain and prominent business men of Charleston; and, what is more, the United States Circuit Court in South Carolina refused to entertain the suit brought by the Negroes."[265]

The same author says: "What is our policy with regard to the Negro? The English have definite policies with respect to their colored populations in South Africa and India. But America appears to have no policy whatsoever. With her fears for her race and civilization, can America afford to let the Negro problem drift along?"[266] And further on he says: "We are willing to fight great wars and sacrifice our young blood to keep out the foreign hosts of destruction; and yet we are unwilling to renounce luxury and the cheap labor of the alien invaders in order to protect the race purity and hereditary genius of future Americans!"[267] If it be a matter of vital importance to discriminate between different types of European immigrants in the interest of American homogeneity, can we fail to pay regard to the greater evil we have with us in the Negro?

W. Laird Clowes, an English writer, says: "And while the armchair theorist of the North is easy in his mind with regard to the race question, concerning which he knows practically nothing, the Southern white man, who ought to know all the dangers of the situation, is, I am obliged to admit, strangely indifferent to

---

[265]"*America's Race Heritage*," pp. 150-1, National Historical Society, N. Y.
[266]Ibid., p. 153.
[267]Ibid., p. 176.

them. His idea seems to be, 'There are dangers in the future; but the present situation will probably last as long as I live, and so I have no need to greatly worry myself about it. I do not fear the negro; I do not believe in his power of organisation; and if he were to rise we could crush him into resignation.' He seems to be unmindful of the fact that the existence of the Black Belt in the South paralyses his material progress and fetters his whole action as a citizen. Capital does not go Southward in search of an investment, or, if it go, it goes seldom, and it goes with hesitation. It has no confidence in a country which may any day fall again under the rule of a black majority, and may then drift back into the anarchy of the Reconstruction period. And, although the white man does not personally fear the negro, he so much fears him corporately that all his political principles and leanings have vanished in face of the one great question, Shall the white rule or the black?"[268]

In view of recent industrial developments in the South, particularly in the textile industry and the manufacture of furniture, there may be some who will say the foregoing picture as to the timidity of capital is overdrawn and that there is no menace from the Negro in this respect. The truth of the matter is that the natural advantages of the sections affected, none of which is in the "Black Belt" territory, induced these industries to go South despite the Negro's presence in large numbers in parts of the States; and but little Negro labor is employed in these industries.

At the same time, it is manifestly apparent these new industrial forces in the South have come to exercise a controlling influence upon the policies of these States in respect to the Negro. Looking at the matter from the sole point of view of benefit to industry, as they see it, the net result is a policy in which the satisfaction and contentment of the Negro is sought, and the welfare of the State lost sight of entirely.

In another place in his work, Clowes remarks: "And here let me say at once, deliberately and without hesitation, that if the racial crimes and outrages which are of daily occurrence in the Southern States were taking place in a semi-civilized part of Europe, and were only half as well advertised as the events in Bulgaria were, the public sentiment of Europe would at once insist

---

[268]*Black America,*" pp. 143-4, Cassell & Company, Limited, London.

upon, and would within six months secure, reform, even at the cost of war. Such a situation as sullies the South is disgrace to the fair name of Anglo-Saxon civilisation. It is not for me to attempt to apportion the blame. Doubtless there are grave faults on both sides. As an unprejudiced observer, I can merely declare generally that the condition of affairs is not only a scandal so far as the United States are concerned, but also a matter of which all civilised humanity has cause to be ashamed."[269]

This is not a captious criticism directed at the people of the South for their treatment of the Negro, but rather one directed at all of the people of the United States because of their failure to take steps to solve the problem. Both Mr. Clowes and Mr. Archer came to this country to study our race problem and, after doing so, wrote about it. It appears that each of these gentlemen came in an open frame of mind and were seeking after the truth. They sought information from the Negro himself and those who were openly recognized as his friends, as well as from sources supposedly inimical to him; and under such circumstances the views of these two writers as to the solution of the problem should be of special interest to Americans, North and South. Each writer seems to be astonished that we should be content to drift along without any effort to solve the problem; and Mr. Archer sums up the situation as follows:

"We have seen that the negro race is not dying out, or that, if it does die out, it can only be, so to speak, at the cost of Southern civilization—through the indefinite continuance of insanitary and barbarous conditions. We have seen that the Atlanta Compromise is illusory and impracticable, that there is no reasonable hope that the two races will ever live together, yet apart—in economic solidarity, yet without social or sexual contact. We have seen that the essence of the whole situation lies in the negro's inevitable ambition (even though it be unformulated and largely unconscious) to be drawn upward, through physical coalescence, into the white race, and the white man's intense resolve that, on a large and determining scale, no such coalescence shall take place. Now this state of war—for such it undoubtedly is—will not correct itself by lapse of time. It will continue to degrade and demoralize both races until active measures are taken to put an end to it. Though I sympathize with the white man's

---

[269]"*Black America*," pp. 130-1, Cassell & Company, London.

horror of amalgamation, I neither approve nor extenuate the systematic injustice and frequent barbarity in which that horror expresses itself. The present state of society in the South is as inhuman as it is inconsistent with the democratic and Christian principles which the Southern white man so loudly, and in the main sincerely, professes. The Jim Crow car, and all such discriminations in the system of public conveyance, are, I believe, necessities, but deplorable necessities none the less. The constant struggle to exclude the negro from political power is at best a negative and unproductive expenditure of energy, at worst a source of political dishonesty and corruption. The wresting of the law, whether criminal or civil, into an instrument for keeping the negro in a state of abject serfdom, is a scandal and a disgrace to any civilized community. The constant resort to lawless violence and cruelty in revenge for negro crime (real or imaginary) is a hideous blot upon the fair name of the South, if not rather an impeachment of her sanity. The truth is, in fact, that constant inter-racial irritation leaves neither race entirely sane, and that abominable crime and no less abominable punishment are merely the acutest symptom of an ill-omened conjuncture of things, which puts an unfair and unnatural strain upon both black and white human nature. The criminal stupidity that brought the negro to America cannot be annulled by passively 'making the best of it.' If its evil effects are to be counteracted, corrected, and wiped out, it must be through an active and constructive effort of large-minded statesmanship."[270]

Professor Dowd seems to accept it as conclusive, or at least that the preponderance of evidence points in that direction, that in accordance with the principles of biology and psychology amalgamation between closely allied races is advantageous, while that between widely divergent races is injurious; and "The namby-pamby religious zealot who," says he, "would solve the race problem by urging, or compelling by law, the indiscriminate social intermixture of races is like the man who would bring about harmony in the feline world by tying together peaceful cats by their tails and hanging them over the clothes line."[271]

His views as to the danger of amalgamation are disclosed in the following quotation:

[270]Taken by permission from William Acher's *Through Afro-America*," pp. 233-5, copyright by E. P. Dutton & Co., Inc.
[271]"*The Negro in American Life*," pp. 443-4, The Century Co.

"Viewing the subject of racial contact from every conceivable psychological aspect, I find no ground for believing that the Caucasian and the Negro will ever amalgamate while they co-exist in large numbers."[272]

With these views as to the situation, he believes "the problem is simply this: To find a means of harmonizing two races as unlike as the Negro and the Caucasian in the same territory and under the same government."[273]

He does not believe that segregation meets the requirements of the situation in view of the fact that, "no matter how earnestly both races may coöperate to make it work satisfactorily, it will always be a source of racial jealousy and friction . . "[274] He thinks the "welfare of the Negro and the whites of the United States is inseparably bound together . . ."[275]

He believes that "both races need a unity of spirit, a hunger for the higher things, a disposition to help each other and to rejoice in each other's triumphs. The white man should be able to say to the black man: Friend, come up higher . . . . But no matter how sincerely both races may desire to promote each other's welfare the problem of racial contact will always call for the highest wisdom of both races in safeguarding their respective interests, and in bringing about equitable and amicable adjustments."[276]

In view of the fact that a superhuman wisdom is required to direct and control the relations of the races as long as they jointly occupy the same territory, why cannot sane statesmanship solve it for once and for all by common sense methods? In view of conditions that have existed in Europe for centuries, and exist to-day in her territories jointly occupied by closely related races on the same cultural level, is it not simply madness to imagine the blacks and whites in a utopian state that could be arrived at only through the attainment of perfection by both races?

The education of our youth should be as appropriate, complete, and universal as the State can make it; and it is only now, when we are beginning to understand that instruction by the same methods and in the same subjects may not produce the

---

[272]"*The Negro in American Life*," p. 423, The Century Co.
[273]Ibid., p. 361.
[274]Ibid., p. 476.
[275]Ibid., p. 549.
[276]Ibid., p. 548.

best results even among members of the same family at all times, that a conception of what is meant by appropriate dawns upon us. When once the South became interested in education, the movement was greatly accelerated as time passed and drew to its ranks some enthusiasts who were not always wise in what they advocated. This wave of enthusiasm swept with it many who were engaged in industrial enterprises in the South and mistakenly, as I believe, thought they saw a great opportunity for promoting good relations between the races by education of the Negro. The methods used and subjects handled were the same for both races, and it seems this cannot be deviated from to any great extent on account of the ironclad provisions of the War Amendments that take from the States all discretion needful to meet the situation properly. This enthusiasm for uplift of the Negro by education on the part of those engaged in industry finds expression through our chambers of commerce; and our race relations are now in the hands of the chambers of commerce, educators, and churchmen, particularly the missionary element among the last. The statesman and the practical hard-headed voter seem to have no interest in the question, or are excluded from participation in matters of racial interest. No attempt to handle the matter as a practical civic question has been made since the failure of Reconstruction based upon the fallacy of racial equality embodied in the War Amendments.

Professor Dowd says he has devoted twenty years to the study of the Negro, and his book contains an enormous amount of information showing long and painstaking research. For these reasons, his conclusions will be influential in shaping those of others who read his work; and it is unfortunate he could not see his way to the one definite final solution. In reading his work I find, as I believe, an explanation of his final conclusions: He is an enthusiastic educator and cannot rid himself of his belief, though it may be partly unconscious, in the potency of education to bring all people to the same level despite their antecedents and hereditary racial traits; and his pleasant memories of the good-natured and loyal Negro of the Civil War period, or the traditions about this character to which he proved receptive, have blinded him to the actual situation and to the consequences of this policy of drift and inaction as embodied in uplift work.

To sum up: Professor Dowd seems to think that, while amalgamation would be a calamity, the danger of its realization is remote; that the Negro question has no solution other than recognition of the finality of his presence with us and molding anew our life, political, civil, religious, and in other ways to further the parallel development of culture of two races so divergent in every respect. Even if we forget the danger of amalgamation for the moment, or assume that it will never occur, can we contemplate with any pride the future State in which there shall be two States or two Nations? Such solution as that proposed by him seems to me to be more replete with obstacles impossible to overcome and more beset with dangers than the solution which he lightly dismisses as impossible. His economics, in dealing with this matter throughout, seem to be based on the assumption that, from now until the arrival of that time when America will be densely populated, there will be a dearth of labor, and that the Negro can fit himself for admission into all positions where skilled labor is required and apparently without injury to the white man. This appears to be an extravagant hope for continuous future prosperity without any solid basis of fact for its foundation, and also unsound race economics.

In the face of a racial situation deemed serious by all and regarded as desperate by some, I am more interested in the hope of an eventual solution than in an aimless, ill-directed uplift movement, experimental in its nature and involving the neglect of my own people.

One solution of the race problem is amalgamation. The acceptance of this method of solution wipes out at once the race problem. This, as repeatedly stated before, was the final solution, whether intentional or not, in Peru and Mexico, where the resultant was a mixture of whites and Mongoloids or Indians of an inferior type; in India, where it was a mixture of whites, blacks and browns; in Egypt, North Africa, and parts of Arabia, where it was a mixture of whites and blacks with some primitive Mongoloid stock in all probability.

This same process is going on amongst us; in some cases, deliberately and with the sanction of the law; in some cases, with the active support and encouragement of religious sects, societies or associations; and that it continues is due to our lack of appreciation of the situation, our indifference or lack of courage—in other words to our *laches*. The process of amalgamation that goes on outside of legal marital ties that are recognized in some localities, while generally so confined, is not necessarily confined to the usually recognized criminal classes, but may be engaged in clandestinely by some who should not be so included except in so far as this particular act makes it necessary. Amalgamation is, it sems, the penalty that follows the joint occupation of a country by the two races.

If there is no difference between the white man and the black; if amalgamation results in no injury to future generations, to civilization, to the progress of the human race—then should we throw down all barriers at once and accept the Negro as one of us. If, on the other hand, there are the vital differences that have been pointed out and amalgamation means race suicide and decadence—then, if we are worthy of survival, we should be interested in the solution of this problem.

It may be solved, outside of amalgamation, by:

(1)   The destruction of one or the other of the two peoples;

(2)   By sterilization of one race or the other;

(3)   By segregation through the removal of one to a separate geographical area.

The first mentioned solution is one that no member of the White race will think of seriously, and may, therefore, be dismissed from consideration at once. However, the mulatto element, through the agency of the N.A.A.C.P. and its misguided but zealous friends, is striving manfully and with some success to bring about a situation in which there are but two alternatives—amalgamation by eventual lawful process or war.

The second is a method to be used in moderation, keeping pace with our advance in knowledge respecting hereditary transmission of mental infirmaties, disease and criminal tendencies; and may be used as an alternative in the application of the third remedy—segregation by removal of the Negro.

Segregation by removal is the remedy in keeping with the humanitarian instincts that should control in such matters. Three great beneficial results will accrue from this solution:

(1)   The integrity of the White race in America will be preserved and this people will thus be made free to fulfill its destiny in due course, and maintain its rightful place in the hosts of marching civilization.

(2)   It will place the Negro in a country all his own, in which his government, his civic and social institutions—in short, his civilization—will be in his own hands, respond to his own efforts.

This perfect freedom of action, uninfluenced or touched by outside pressure, can be assured him by us.

(3)   It will enable us to preserve our democratic institutions.

This solution must of necessity extend over a considerable period of time during which the Negro is gradually removed to his new home.   As removal goes on he should be replaced by selected immigration; and, as a final measure of necessity, those who insist on staying should, as a condition precedent to so doing, be required to submit to sterilization unless beyond the age of reproduction.   The reference here made to selected immigration does not have in view a comparison of Europeans to determine any relative worth as civilized people or people of culture.   The sole thought in view is that of securing homogeneity of the body politic in America; and with this purpose in view replacement immigration should be confined to those elements that will most readily fuse with the previous elements that have come to us and blend into that homogeneous body in which democratic institutions may thrive.

When this replacement has taken place our doors should be closed to immigration, and every effort made to direct the surplus white population to South American and African and Asiatic areas that may be reclaimed and held as the home lands of the race.

Forcible transportation seems a harsh procedure in some respects and should be applied only as a last resort.   However, if the matter were handled in a statesman-like manner, it would seem that the opportunity for repatriation might be gladly seized by the Negro, with the exception of some incendiary mulattoes, as the only chance for development in keeping with his awakening national consciousness, the ultimate fruits of which cannot be realized in America.

First of all, do we owe the Negro anything?   There need be no apology for that application of the law of self-preservation which manifests itself in a determination to maintain racial integrity.   He who would carp at this is beyond the pale of reason.   If we do owe the Negro anything, we cannot, consistently with the preservation of racial integrity, repay him while he remains amongst us; for, as long as he is with us, racial integrity can be preserved, if at all, only by harsh and cruel measures arising of necessity from such contact.   If we do owe anything, we are in honor bound to pay it in a manner that will be for the good of these people and influence for the good their future welfare as a people.

We do owe the Negro something. This is simply elemental, and needs no discussion or demonstration further than a statement of the circumstances under which he was brought to our shores. He has been repaid this debt in a small measure by the progress imposed upon him during the period of slavery, even though his uplift may have been foreign to the motives controlling and directing the institution of slavery. The instruction given the Negro since Emancipation, despite the grievous mistakes made and injury done, has helped further to fit the Negro to work toward the realization of his dreams brought about by an awakening national consciousness, though inimical to peace between the races occupying the same territory. The sum total of the uplift work done for the Negro in America places him in a position far in advance of the Negro elsewhere in the world or at any time within the historic period. But there has been infused into the body of the American Negro a great amount of white blood. This uplift by fusion is not fair to the Negro race and degrades the whites. Are we to stop here?

"First," says Clowes, "let me premise that the United States, as a whole, and not merely the South, owes an enormous debt to the negro race. Everyone admits that the institution of slavery was a crime against humanity; but everyone does not remember that for a century and more the North was *particeps criminis*. Some aspects of her responsibility will be found dealt with in the Appendix on Slavery in the North. It is too often forgotten that Southern slavery, up to the time of emancipation, existed under and was protected by the laws of the Union."[277]

"The debt owing to the blacks is manifold. Something is due to those who, against their will were dragged from their homes, subjected to the untold horrors of the middle passage, and forced to labour, unrequited, for strangers. What the horrors of the middle passage were is hinted at rather than told in the log-book of Her Majesty's ship *Skipjack*, which, in 1835, captured the Portuguese slaver *Martha*, with 447 slaves on board. The *Martha* had left Loango forty-three days before for Brazil with a freight of 790 slaves, of whom 353, or nearly 45 per cent., had perished from the tortures and miseries of the voyage. These

---

[277]*"Black America,"* p. 185, Cassell & Company, London.

tortures and miseries were not less, we may be sure, fifty or one hundred years earlier. Something, again, is due to those who, in the land of their captivity, were deprived by law of education, of the privilege of marriage, and of the guardianship of their children. More, perhaps, is due to those who, in support of the triumphant principles of the land of their captivity, shed their blood. As many as 300,000 people of colour took arms during the Civil War. And thankful recognition, if nothing beyond, is owing by the South to the subject race which, in the hour of national adversity, instead of rising to complicate the troubles of the Confederacy, was loyal, and even helpful, to the dominant class. There are other grounds of indebtedness, but they have been so fully indicated in the course of this work that I need not again specify them. My only objects here are to insist upon the fact that a heavy debt has been incurred, and to point out that the time has not yet come when the United States can say, 'We are doing something tangible towards paying it off.' "[278]

"One cannot foresee, but it is quite certain that it is not yet too late for it to be voluntarily tendered in cold blood, and to be gratefully accepted; and it is reasonable to suppose that delay in payment will not lessen but rather increase the amount—be it of treasure, blood, misery, or unrest—to be ultimately paid."[279]

"It would seem, therefore, that principles of ordinary economy, as well as of common justice, indicate that an effort should be made to pay off the negro as soon as possible."[280]

There can be no doubt the attempts of the Negro to demonstrate his ability to govern himself in reasonable conformity to civilized standards have proved miserable failures in Liberia and Haiti. These failures do not, however, preclude all hope that the American Negro may yet realize his national aspirations in Africa and there establish and maintain a State in keeping with civilized standards, which shall be an inspiration and example to his brother natives. This is certainly the greatest ambition within possible realization open to the race as a race. They cannot accomplish it alone and unaided, but only with the aid and under the protection of the American Government.

The erection of a Negro State in Liberia was not attempted

---

[278]"*Black America,*" pp. 185-7, Cassell & Company, London.
[279]Ibid., pp. 205-6.
[280]Ibid., p. 206.

on such scale or under such auspices as would justify one in looking for any measure of success. The missionary element can play an important part in such movement, but that missionaries should bring success out of sporadic efforts at colonization is simply preposterous.

When Haiti was abandoned to its fate, and it secured its independence because of this and not on account of success of the Negro in arms, the Negro was not in any respect fitted for self-government in this island. The condition of the American Negro now places him in a far superior cultural position than that enjoyed by the Haitian at the time of independence or at any subsequent period.

Referring to Liberia, Burr says: "One very interesting plan to solve the Negro question has been vaguely contemplated, in a more or less visionary manner, for years. It dates back to the year 1792, when twelve hundred Negroes, who had escaped from the United States to Canada, were transported to the British African colony of Sierra Leone. Then again, in 1822, the American Colonization Society was formed, which eventually founded Liberia. Although, in those days of difficult transportation, the trials were too great and the project at last proved a failure, yet the little Republic of Liberia survives to the present day in the hands of the descendants of American Negroes, and as a sovereign member of the League of Nations; and under the sphere of American influence this little Negro nation may take on a new lease of life. To-day American naval engineers instruct the populace in sanitary measures and improve the welfare of the little Negro republic."[281]

In regard to the groping of the Negro for expression of national consciousness, Stone, a very painstaking investigator, wrote in 1908 as follows: "The white man deceives himself if he cherishes the idea that this universal human impulse is not latent in Negro life. The Negro has not yet developed a race consciousness, and he is still very far removed from anything approaching a national life. But in both Africa and America the dawn of the first is beginning to be seen. And in South Africa he is groping, more or less blindly and awkwardly perhaps, but still groping, toward the light of possible nationality. Their ancient continent is the only place on the globe where a national life is possible—

---

[281]*"America's Race Heritage,"* p. 155, National Historical Society, New York.

if indeed it prove to be possible there. It is the only place where the experiment may be even tried. We need not stop to so much as consider the artificial travesties erected upon the blood-stained ruins of white civilization in Haiti and Santo Domingo. They will sometime disappear in a night, when the American white man wants another island for some real or fancied use, even as the 'Republic of Panama' was born in a day after a similar conception. In America, and this is all, we may see the Negro instinctively striving after identity with the national existence of which he forms an artificial and unassimilated part. Back of this lies the same impulse of awakening racial life. What the movement here may be, no man may say, nor how it will manifest itself from time to time. Having here no possible separate national life of his own, his developing instinct manifests itself in an effort toward equality of opportunity and place in that of the white man who surrounds him and hems him in. Every step toward such fancied equality is hailed as a mark of racial progress."[282]

There has been a persistent interest among the Negroes in the subject of Liberia in the face of lack of encouragement and direct opposition from many whites and the mulatto element that now speaks through the obnoxious and dangerous N.A.A.C.P. of growing power.

When this interest manifested itself in the "Liberian Exodus Stock Company," composed of its own people, the movement was defeated, in accordance with Burr, through the chicanery, deceit, and downright fraud of the whites—and Southern whites at that.

What has been the reception of the Garvey movement? The despatches sent through the country as news in regard to this movement led one to believe that a bountiful source of amusing news, rivalling the comic section of our news sheets, was being exploited to the limit. The mulattoes, through their organization, held it up to ridicule and abuse; and when the whites finally chose to give it any serious regard they seem to have viewed it in the light of a menace to the peace of Africa and the powers there holding colonies, and Garvey as a person too dangerous to be at large. He was soon confined in the penitentiary for fraudulent use of the mails.

Assuming Garvey's efforts to carry out his program to have been

---

[282]*"Studies in the American Race Problem,"* pp. 332-3.

honest and sincere, the ramifications of his numerous operations soon become so multitudinous that it would have been surprising had he not become involved in some technical violation of the Federal law. He and his followers were left to themselves. The guiding hand of the white philanthropist and the fostering care of the government were noticeably absent; and it is not to be marveled at that pitfalls were not avoided and extravagant incongruities indulged in. A people who are so indifferent to their own real interest, or so wrapped up in their petty affairs of the moment, as to fail to see the urgent necessity of encouraging movements of this kind, are deserving of nothing better than that all Negroes should become bitterly opposed to any scheme for separation.

Clinton Stoddard Burr emphasizes the urgency of solution in the following words:

"However much our conscience is concerned for the Negroes, we cannot blind ourselves to the serious situation created by the presence of some ten million of them here.[283] Are we Americans of this generation losing the genius to face the greatest problems frankly and fearlessly? A preceding generation took up its responsibilities in bringing the question of slavery to a settlement. Is it not our duty to force a reconstruction that will benefit both the Negro and future generations? Unheard-of treasure would yet be cheap if by its payment we might free the nation of the dread incubus of miscegenation."[284]

Professor Dowd regards the transportation of the Negro to Africa as impracticable, and, referring to the scheme of Marcus Garvey, he says:

"The Garvey movement is regarded generally, especially by the whites, as a mere chase after the rainbow, but I consider it a matter of serious import, in every respect creditable to its leader, and to all who are backing it. Garvey's dream will never be realized, but his effort may result in providing a refuge for his people when they come to feel the struggle for existence here too unequal and too cruel."[285]

---

[283]There were 7,000,000 when Stanley wrote, 10,000,000 when Burr wrote, and there are about 12,000,000 now. As we drift along the number grows, adding difficulties to eventual solution.

[284]*"America's Race Heritage,"* pp. 154-5, National Historical Society, New York.

[285]*"The Negro in American Life,"* p. 466, The Century Co.

"Up to the present time all of the efforts at Negro colonization have been signal failures, and I see no ground for hoping
that Cox's scheme or any other will ever succeed. I think the
time is coming, however, when our country, like the old countries
of Europe, will have an overflowing population, causing the
Negro to feel more sharply than now the pressure of competition
with the whites and then, not unlikely, the states having a large
Negro population may offer transportation to Negro citizens who
may wish to migrate to some other country."[286]

The average American does not seem to regard the fact that
Jefferson and some of the elder statesmen and the martyred
Prsident, Lincoln, were favorable to colonization as having any
bearing upon the race problem at this time. Their views are regarded with good-natured tolerance and are considered of interest
only historically and as an incident in the life of these characters.
But when disinterested, modern English writers, such as Archer
and Clowes, see the only solution in territorial segregation; when
a man like Stanley, with an intimate knowledge of the American
Negro and an explorer's knowledge of the African continent, sees
solution in colonization of the Negro in Africa; and when there
persists in a large body of the American Negro a yearning for
national expression in Africa—when we consider all this it seems
to me it is time we should conclude that Jefferson and Lincoln
advocated the statesman's solution of our problem and that of
the humanitarian as well.

Referring to colonization of the Negro, Burr says: "However,
it was the general view of the American public, during the period
leading up to the World War, that it would be utterly impossible
to transport so large a multitude of our Negroes to Africa, albeit
over a long term of years. At that time the world did not know
that over two million American soldiers would someday be con-
veyed across the ocean to France, through the submarine blockade and the mine fields, in the short space of twelve months;
and that they would be set down in a land 'milked dry,' so that
of necessity they would be forced to take most necessities with
them. The world did not know that it would be startled by the
virtual cities, railroads, ports and institutions that would spring
up in France. But we know this to-day; and we know, too, that,
if our idealism is great enough, we can transport millions of blacks

---

[286]"*The Negro in American Life*," pp. 468-9, The Century Co.

abroad, colonize them in self supporting communities under United States jurisdiction; and have wealth and resources to spare. As a matter of fact, we could make such a scheme self-supporting by utilizing the labor of the Negroes to improve regions with vast resources still untouched. The scheme is not visionary if the nation is big enough to carry through a settled policy which might be fulfilled only after many years of self-abnegation, but whose final results would be as great a benefit to future generations as reforestation or any system of conservation of our national resources."[287]

In regard to the same subject, W. Laird Clowes, an English writer, says:

"This solution is one which, I admit, I almost despair of seeing carried out. The peaceable removal of the negroes from the United States, and their establishment across the ocean in a country and in circumstances that would be propitious not only to their own development but also to the development of their barbarous kindred, are measures which would involve very great expense. But it is not, I believe, on the score of expense that the average American is likely to reject the scheme. His great inheritance provides him with wealth more than sufficient to enable him to pay all his debts, including those huge ones which he owes to the black. He is much more likely to adopt a characteristic attitude such as he has adopted in the past towards many other threatening questions. One of the most distinguished of living American statesmen said to me in November last: 'If my country should ever come to frightful disaster, it will be, I am convinced, because it is the incurable habit of my countrymen to cherish the belief that they are so much the special care of Providence that it would be superfluous, on their part, to take even simple and ordinary precautions for their own protection.' "[288]

"It looks now as if the moment were about to arrive when either the question must be peaceably settled or it will settle itself by violence; and it is, therefore, worth while to consider whether the most radical and permanent solution of the difficulty

---

[287]*"America's Race Heritage,"* pp. 155-6, National Historical Society, N. Y.

[288]*"Black America,"* Introduction, pp. xii-xiii, Cassell & Company, London.

is practicable, and, supposing it to be so, how it may, even at this late hour, be accomplished without force and injustice."[289]

"If my contentions be sound, it results that the experiment of the future must be conducted with due regard to the following conditions:—

"1. The emigrating negro must be offered a country in which he may pursue high aims, enjoy a prospect of improved political, social, and financial *status,* and find climate and employment suited to his needs.

"2. He must not govern, but be governed. At the same time he must not be oppressed, either physically or morally; and there must be no restraint upon his improvement and advancement.

"3. His emigration must be assisted, either by those who owe him a debt or by those who will benefit by his migration, or by both."[290]

"If the American negro were shown, as he easily might be shown, first, that his exodus to Africa would result in vast good to his race, and would open to him an honourable mission as civiliser; next, that the proceeding would result in a general amelioration of his own condition; and finally, that in Africa he would escape from the discomforts and persecutions that hem in his career in America; and if, at the same time, he were offered aid to enable him to migrate to and establish himself on the soil of his fathers, I do not doubt that he would leave America, not merely in his thousands, but in his millions. He desires, above all things, a country and an aim in life. Give him those, and he will seize them gladly. But it is useless to counsel him to go to Africa, or elsewhere, unless you also hold out to him an object to be attained. And even a grand object will not alone induce him to move. He is, as a rule, poor. His investments, such as they are, are all in America. It is necessary not only to assist him to move and settle, but also to pay him generously for the little that he must surrender."[291]

"Even in a greater degree," says Clowes, "than in the African possessions of Great Britain, Germany, and France does there appear to be a career for the American negro in the Congo Free

---

[289]"*Black America,*" p. 185, Cassell & Company, London.
[290]Ibid., p. 200.
[291]Ibid., pp. 204-5.

State. The author of 'An Appeal to Pharaoh' has indicated that State as the American Negro's promised land. A copy of the book was recently given to Mr. H. M. Stanley, a man who, having spent parts of his life not only in the Dark Continent but also in Louisiana, knows the negro both in America and in Africa. The volume drew from the traveller a very interesting letter, from which I extract the following:—

'There is space enough in one section of the Upper Congo basin to locate double the number of the negroes of the United States without disturbing a single tribe of the aborigines now inhabiting it. I refer to the immense Upper Congo forest country, 350,000 square miles in extent, which is three times larger than the Argentine Republic, and one and a half times larger than the entire German Empire, embracing 224,000,000 acres of umbrageous forest land, wherein every unit of the 7,000,000[292] negroes might become the owner of nearly a quarter square mile of land. Five acres of this, planted with bananas and plantains, would furnish every soul with sufficient subsistence—food and wine. The remaining twenty-seven acres of his estate would furnish him with timber, rubber, gums, dye-stuffs, for sale. There are 150 days of rain throughout the year. There is a clear stream every few hundred yards. In a day's journey we have crossed as many as thirty-two streams. The climate is healthy and equable, owing to the impervious forest which protects the land from chilly winds and draughts. All my white officers passed through the wide area safely. Eight navigable rivers course through it. Hills and ridges diversify the scenery and give magnificent prospects. To those negroes in the South accustomed to Arkansas, Mississippi, and Louisiana, it would be a reminder of their own plantations without the swamps and the depressing influence of cypress forests. Anything and everything might be grown in it, from the oranges, guavas, sugar-cane, and cotton of sub-tropical lands to the wheat of California and the rice of South Carolina. If the emigration were prudently conceived and carried out, the glowing accounts sent home by the first settlers would soon dissipate all fear and reluctance on the part of the others. But it is all a dream. The American capitalists, like other leaders of men, are more engaged in decorating their wives with diamonds than in busying themselves with national questions of such import as

[292]Since Stanley wrote, this number has increased to about 12,-000,000.

removing the barrier between the North and the South. The "open sore" of America—the race question—will ever remain an incurable fester. While we are all convinced that the Nessus shirt which clings to the Republic has maddened her, and may madden her again, it is quite certain that the small effort needed to free themselves for ever from it will never be made.' "[293]

"Lastly," says William Archer, "we have to consider the fourth conceivable eventuality—the geographical segregation of the Negro race, whether within or without the limits of the United States."

"This is usually ridiculed as an absolutely Utopian scheme, and at the outset of my investigation I myself regarded it in that light. But the more I saw and read and thought, the oftener and the more urgently did segregation recur to me as the one possible way of escape from an otherwise intolerable situation. Not, of course, the instant, and wholesale, and violent deportation of ten million people—that is a rank impossibility. Between that and inert acquiescence in the ubiquity of the negro throughout the Southern States, there are many middle courses; and I cannot but believe that the first really great statesman who arises in America will prove his greatness by grappling with this vast but not insoluble problem. And, assuredly, the sooner he comes the better."[294]

Mr. Archer did not support the colonization of the Negro in Africa, but rather Lower California, a part of the South American continent, or segregating them in one or more States of the Union. Perhaps, if he were writing now, he might, in view of the lessons learned during the World War and of the existing conditions in Africa, advocate African colonization.

When any serious measures deemed necessary for self-preservation are undertaken, whether private or national, the costs of the undertaking are left for consideration until the inevitable day of reckoning. When American public opinion was prepared for entry into the last war, we did not refer the matter to experts for the ascertainment of costs. We plunged in: the costs were left for consideration at a later period when hostilities had ceased. If the evils of amalgamation and the inevitable certainty of its occurrence under existing conditions are conceded, we are then

---

[293]"*Black America,*" pp. 211-2, Cassell & Company, London.
[294]Taken by permission from William Archer's "*Through Afro-America,*" p. 233, copyright by E. P. Dutton & Co., Inc.

threatened with an imminent danger far beyond any that might result from a World War against us at this time. Under such circumstances no cost is too great to pay. However, it is essential that some view of the cost should be had.

During the ten years prior to the World War about 14,000,000 immigrants came to this country from Europe.

It cannot be conceived that the burden of transportation of 12,000,000 Negroes, and the transportation of a much less number is involved in actual solution, extending over a period of, say, fifty years, would be one appreciably felt by the United States, when 14,000,000 immigrants paid their own transportation during a period of ten years.

During the last war, under extraordinary conditions, we carried across the Atlantic in a short period of time, *one way across*, over 4,000,000 men.

Real property purchased from the emigrant body at full value could be resold to the selected replacement immigrants, or otherwise disposed of, and thus expense of administration would practically be the only one involved in this item.

Little expense other than transportation would be involved in the case of the non-property holding class. But, in order to work no injustice and insure the success of the undertaking, these should be moved only as provision is made, in employment or by small holdings, for them on the other side; and this would involve an initial capital investment in the new land.

Clowes, whose work was published in 1891, makes the following comment in regard to cost of colonization: "It is calculated that an annual sum of twelve or fourteen millions sterling might thus, without undue pinching, be diverted from the annual revenue of the United States; and this represents a very large capital amount—an amount which would probably be quite sufficient, with a certain quota of aid from outside, not only to decently transport, but to comfortably establish in Africa, every pure-blooded negro now on United States territory."

"It might not be also sufficient to buy out the negro; but that might justly be assigned as a duty, in whole or in part, to the individual States concerned, seeing that they are more immediately interested than is the nation at large in getting rid of him, and that the expenditure to be incurred would sooner or later be returned to the States in the shape of payments on the re-sale of lands and buildings now belonging to the negroes."

"That the United States have not already entered upon some such course is rather remarkable; for they have spent scores of millions in the payment of debts which are less pressing, and they have, indeed, been so generous in certain directions as to have incurred the reproach of unwarrantable extravagance. They have over half a million names on their pension-roll, and they pay the pensioners more than twenty millions a year, in spite of the fact that most of the persons who benefit had no legal claim upon the country at the time when the services in respect of which pensions are now paid were rendered. The pensions are not, as pensions are in England, deferred pay; they are compensations and gratuities. The Union has been lavish with them; but the Governments which have granted them have always looked forward to a return in the shape of political support, and so the sums disbursed have been regarded as profitable investments."[295]

"Hitherto, there is no doubt, American politicians as a body have not discovered that any profit can result from the payment of the nation's indebtedness to the negro; and that is the reason why they have not dealt with the negro as they have dealt with the soldier."

"But will there be no profit? The South is now stagnant under the incubus of the negro."[296]

Clowes also indicated that the American Negro had been and would be welcomed in African colonies. The time when he wrote was, of course, before the World War. He says: "If America would do its duty by the negro, those civilised nations which have established themselves in Africa would, in pursuance of their own interests, aid her. Great Britain, Germany, and France would each and all welcome the immigration to their African possessions of large and leavening bodies of American blacks. Not long ago Sir Alfred Moloney, Governor of Lagos, received a deputation from 'the Brazilian and Havannah repatriates in the colony of Lagos,' and was assured that all the negroes of Brazil wished to return to the country of their ancestors. In reply, Sir Alfred Moloney said that he had induced the commercial world to take an interest in the project, and that the African Steamship Company had engaged to provide improved and cheaper facilities for negro immigrants from Brazil. He welcomed the

---

[295]"*Black America*," pp. 207-8, Cassell & Company, London.
[296]Ibid., p. 208.

idea of 'repatriation,' and would encourage it. Much more, no doubt, would he welcome the idea of the 'repatriation' of the immeasurably more civilized and less debauched American negro. The black, it is true, will not do much good for himself anywhere without white superintendence, but there is no reason why such superintendence as is necessary should not be forthcoming, and, if it be once understood that the salvation of Africa lies with the negro even more than with the white, there is every ground for believing that the American negro will rise bravely to the occasion."[297]

Political contentment and social peace and the increased values and greater industry, resulting from homogeneity of population due to replacement of the Negro by selected immigration, would make the investment desirable and the burden small.

Clowes describes the blessings to follow solution, either in the negativing existing evils or the production of positive good, in the following terms:

"The Union is divided, and it is the presence of the negro that causes the division. Nearly one-eighth of the population of the Union is of alien race, and, besides being hopelessly alien, is oppressed, discontented, and dangerous. These are evils which might be abolished to the general profit. And worse evils lurk in the future. The prosecution of a race war would not be cheaper than the promotion of a negro exodus. The severance from the Union of six or eight States would be vastly more weakening to the nation as a whole. In some form the debt must be paid. Nature has never yet admitted the plea of any Statute of Limitations in cases like the one under discussion. It were well, then, to make a settlement while it can still be made peacefully and, comparatively speaking, cheaply."[298]

"I have discussed this great subject copiously, but very inadequately. No question at present before the world has so many aspects; and to America no question is equally important. The solution which I have advocated is costly; but it is, I believe, the only one that promises a permanent and honourable settlement of the difficulty. Any other must be imperfect, or must involve wholesale bloodshed. Until something of the kind is put into practice, the dearly bought union must remain a nominal

---

[297]"*Black America*," pp. 210-1, Cassell & Company, London.
[298]Ibid., pp. 209-10.

one, and North and South must continue to cherish different aims, and to be, in effect, separate nations. Only when the negro shall have departed will the name of the United States truly represent anything more than a magnificent aspiration."[299]

"And what of the South," says Mr. Archer, "when this act of justice to the negro shall have been performed? It will awaken, as from a nightmare, to the realization of its splendid destiny. No longer will one of the richest and most beautiful regions of the world be hampered in its material and spiritual development by a legacy of ancestral crime. All that is best in the South— and the Southern nature is rich in elements of magnanimity and humanity—abhors the inhuman necessities imposed upon it by the presence of the negro. The Southern white man writhes under the criticisms of the North and of Europe, which he feels to be ignorant and in great measure unjust, yet which he can only answer by an impotent, 'You do not know! You cannot understeand!' He has to confess, too, that there is much in Southern policy and practeice that even the necessities of the situation cannot excuse—much that can only be palliated as the result of a constant overstrain to which human nature ought never to be subjected. Remove the causes of this overstrain, and a region perhaps the most favored by Nature of all in the Western Hemisphere will stand where it ought to stand—in the van—not only of civilization, but of humanity."[300]

It would seem not at all improbable that an intensive campaign for solution of the problem, carried on in the right spirit and under proper leadership, should receive a tremendous amount of support in the North, and it would be more spontaneous possibly than what might be given in the South. This view is not without justification when we consider the array of Northern men who have in recent times freely expressed themselves in regard to the race problem after first informing themselves about it. We, in the South, are so accustomed to the Negro that it would seem a strange land without him; and we are so obsessed with the idea of his necessity to us in our economic life that we are blind to the real dangers. This last obstruction to a proper realization of the situation does not exist with the Northern man.

That long-continued familiarity with our surroundings renders

[299]"*Black America,*" p. 214, Cassell & Company, London.
[300]Taken by permission from William Archer's "*Through Afro-America,*" pp. 243-4, copyright by E. P. Dutton & Co. Inc.

us insensible to the magnitude of the problems with which we are confronted, is frequently illustrated by changes in opinion when some phases of these problems are impressed upon us by being seen in new and unfamiliar surroundings. This was the experience of Charles Francis Adams on his visit to the Sudan country of the White Nile. "Far removed from that American environment to which I have been accustomed," says he, "the scales fell from my eyes. I found myself most impressed by a realizing sense of the appalling amount of error and cant in which we of the United States have indulged on this topic. We have actually wallowed in a bog of self-sufficient ignorance,—especially we philanthropists and theorists of New England. We do so still. Having eyes we will not see."***

Further along, he remarks, "Nevertheless, it is not easy for one at all observant to come back from Egypt and the Sudan without a strong suspicion that we will in America make small progress towards a solution of our race problem until we approach it in less of a theoretic and humanitarian, and more of a scientific, spirit. Equality results not from law, but exists because things are in essentials like; and a political system which works admirably when applied to homogeneous equals results only in chaos when generalized into a nostrum to be administered universally. It has been markedly so of late with us."301-302

As applied to the race problem, the motto of the politician and the economist of Big Business, is, "Let sleeping dogs lie." In other words, their advice is to temporize in the face of a dangerous situation when time is an important element in the solution.

The time to solve our race problem is not when some untoward circumstance has thrown everybody into a frenzy of passion; but when we are moving along in the even tenor of our ways and can in cool deliberation justify the procedure to be adopted. Simply because one may realize there is a race question, maintain the white man is superior to the black man, and wish to live separately from him, does not mean that passion controls and the

---

301"*Light Reflected from Africa,*" Century Magazine, May, 1906, Vol. 72, pp. 105-7.

302Mr. Adams referred to the culture of the Sudanese as being the most advanced yet attained by the "African race." This culture is that resulting from the fusion of Semitic blood (that of the Arab) with that of the Negro, and is not that of the full-blooded Negro.

Negro is the recipient of hate. Far from it! Not only do we not entertain any ill will toward the Negro, but we have for him a friendly feeling and kind regard. He is not responsible for the situation and his position is understood and appreciated. We wish to deal fairly with him as well as with ourselves. In all probability his most vociferous leaders, nearly all of whom have white blood in them, could be taken from him by the admission of these leaders into the social and political world of the whites. They would then be no longer interested in the race problem. Of course there may be some exceptions; there are some Negroes who are working for the good of their race. The position of the educated Negro of mixed blood is an unenviable one, but the State can no more be sacrificed in his interest than in that of any other unfortunate individual.

The difference accentuated herein is one of race, which renders occupancy of the same territory by the two races incompatible, and not that of the individual. Some of the most degraded, repulsive human characters have been members of our own race, and some individual Negroes have advanced far in many lines of endeavor. Perhaps, some of the Negroes are equal, if not superior, to some of the whites; but this does not affect the race. Race accomplishment does not depend upon the criminal or degenerate that may be found within it, or upon the erratic genius that may appear occasionally; but upon the average of the blood of the race.

Even should we admit there is no danger whatever from amalgamation and take the most optimistic view of the situation, we must nevertheless conclude that the presence of the Negro amongst us, even though he may not control, is a serious menace to the future welfare of the United States of America; and that our future must inevitably be one of retarded progress and eventual feebleness. There can be little doubt, even among the least informed, as to what the situation would be if control passed to the Negro. Contrast both of these situations with that in which there would be independent development of each in accordance with its own genius, as there would be upon the transportation of the Negro to Africa. If this be done, the question is solved forever. No one can deny this. The spectacle of a great people making reparation to another people, who had been formerly held in slavery, by educating them and returning them to their former home under conditions most favorable to independent progress

in civilization and in an improved material state, would be one,
the like of which, the world has never seen, and would render
puny the efforts of the fanatical churchman and others engaged
in the present uplift movements. It would be a spiritual movement of the highest order; and its realization depends upon
whether or not the white man of America measures up to that
small degree of sacrifice that will be required in the end to avoid
the discord and anarchy of the continued presence of the Negro
with us and eventual corruption of blood and degradation. With
this solution assured, all could join whole-heartedly in helping
prepare the Negro for his independence.

FUNDAMENTALS INVOLVED IN SOLUTION.

If we have enough energy and ambition to consider practical
measures that should be adopted for the solution of our problem,
it would seem that we should, in the first place, proceed on the
assumption that any scheme of colonization based upon a proper
conception of the Negro's interest and what is justly due him,
would appeal to the Negro and become immensely popular. Thus
the question of the application of force may be entirely avoided
in the interest of both parties.

In view of the fact that the African continent is now completely parceled out among the European powers with the exception of Liberia and Abyssinia, the last mentioned being in fact
divided into three spheres of influence under agreement between
England, France and Italy, the good offices of the United States
are essential to secure territory in Africa of the right kind and
in sufficient area. In the next place, an undertaking of this kind,
aside from the primary requisite of obtaining a territorial foothold in Africa, is one of such magnitude and of such delicacy in
carrying out the details essential to its success, that it is beyond
the effort of individuals and must be carried out, if at all, under
the supervision of our government. This does not mean that we
propose to establish a Negro colony in Africa to be administered
as such by the government of the United States. It merely means
that the government, without which the end desired could not
be accomplished, must control and advise until the Negro State
is a going concern with the work intended accomplished. This
also means that, from the initiative until the State is an accomplished fact, the wishes, practical aid, and advice of the accredit-

ed representatives of the Negro will be utilized to the fullest extent possible in the administration of affairs consistent with government supervision and direction until the task is done. Even then we shall afford that protection necessary to prevent spoliation of the State by any power or interference with its natural rights.

In continuation of the assumption with which we have begun, it sems that the first practical step naturally requires a full and complete survey of the possibly available territories. This means a survey as to climate, soil, natural products, etc., agricultural products and industries that might be introduced profitably, and all else essential to a realization of the character of the country and its possibilities for development.

The survey should include Liberia, and an understanding should be arrived at with the Liberian government for the purpose of colonization and the development of its industries to the extent that the survey of its resources justifies.

We should obtain the best territory possible for the Negro and, if a survey of Liberia and the territory to the east of it toward the Niger River, in what was formerly called Upper Guinea, discloses this as a desirable country, the problem might be much simplified by securing an extension of the borders of Liberia to the eastward as far as necessary. However, should other available territory be more desirable, it should be acquired independently of Liberia and the two areas colonized and developed independently.

In our dealings with the European powers interested in Africa for the purpose of obtaining concessions for the colonization of the American Negro, an attempt should be made to induce these powers to consider the matter of pooling interests in Africa (this matter is taken up in the third or concluding part of this work) in consideration of a reopening of the debt question; and at the same time the South and Central American powers should attempt to strengthen their position as white powers (this also is gone into in the concluding part of this work) by an understanding with the European powers in regard to emigration that would relieve their overpopulation and would be received in the Americas under the most favorable possible conditions.

When the preliminary surveys are completed and the necessary authority acquired in the areas desired, capitalists should be invited to invest in the development of industries and the natural resources of the country to the extent justified by the report, and all these undertakings should be open to investment by Negroes in a position to do so.

Steamship lines should be established by the government and transportation furnished the Negro to his African home land; and the United States should offer to each American Negro emigrant a certain holding in land subject to certain conditions in his own interest, including a reasonable equipment and provision with which to start in business, or place him in a situation where remunerative employment may be had.

Each State in the Union should authorize a bond issue or otherwise finance the purchase of the holdings of such Negroes as wish to go to Africa; and, at stated intervals, the appropriate State officer should through the Secretary of the State, or other Federal officer designated, make arrangements for the transportation of emigrants to Africa at such season as is to their advantage.

The State authorities should likewise, through the same channels, be authorized to enter into contractual relations with European authorities or persons for the importation into the State of selected immigrants in numbers equal to the emigrating Negroes.

These immigrants should be financed by the States within limits and for a definite period under a flexible administration in which equitable considerations should take precedence over the technical application of the law. These immigrants, if introduced to replace emigrating Negroes who were engaged in a certain character of work, as, for instance, agriculture, should be under a restriction equitably applied to engage in agriculture for a certain definite period; and, except as required in such respects in order to avoid disturbance in some line of production, no restriction not common to all should apply. In order that this may be accomplished fully and injustice done no one, immigrants should be permitted to come in prior to and in anticipation of the departure of American Negroes for whom provision had been made in the matter of transportation where deemed necessary.

This immigration should be in excess of the quota allowed annually under the immigration law. However, should we exclude all immigrants except those coming under contract with the respective States to replace Negro emigrants, an impetus would be given to the whole movement; we would secure immigrants of the character desired for replacement; and, for the time being at least, Japan would have no reason to complain of any discrimination against her in the Federal law.

Much that is here proposed lies within the authority of the Executive, or with him in conjunction with the Senate under its right to advise and consent to treaties.

Much of what might be gained from a commission appointed to make a preliminary survey, if not all essential information, might be compiled from consular reports, or gathered from special reports to be made by our consular officials in African localities.

Any understanding with Liberia in regard to colonization and development of its resources, must be undertaken by the Executive under his treaty-making power.

The acquisition of African territory for colonization of the American Negro clearly comes under the same treaty-making power lodged in the Executive; and our position as a creditor nation makes the present time a particularly appropriate one for its undertaking, if it is ever to be done.

Capital is already finding its way into Liberia, and, if the practical aid and support of the capitalist seeking investment is to be had for this movement, some definite stand must be taken at once; for, if delayed, the capitalist will find his own way into these regions and will not take kindly to any provisions in the interest of the migrating Negro.

It seems that there is no need for any constitutional amendment to authorize the repatriation of the Negro along the lines proposed, the whole scheme being based on the voluntary migration of the Negro. A resolution by the Congress approving some such course as that outlined, would justify the Executive, who might hesitate to take the initiative otherwise, to proceed at once; and time is an important element in the situation.

Too great emphasis cannot be placed upon the fact that the preservation of our democratic institutions and the future of America depends upon our becoming a homogeneous people. Rome was ravaged by the discord of factions due to dissimilar elements within her borders, none of which reached the extreme range that exists between us and the Negro, and fell an easy prey to pressure from without.

The international aspect of the race problem is of the greatest importance and should impel us to shape our European relations with a view to bringing about white solidarity, and this, of course, involves the avoidance of any shadow of suspicion of partisan action in such relations.   An effort will be made in the concluding part of this work to direct attention to this view of the situation. It is useles, however, for us to interest ourselves in the international aspects of the race situation unless we are determined to adopt that domestic policy which will result in preserving future generations in America to the White race.

PART III

PART THREE.

CHAPTER I.

GENERAL SURVEY OF RACE NUMBERS.

First of all, let us see what are the total numbers of mankind on the earth and the division amongst the races. Doubleday, Page & Company's Atlas for 1917 gives the population by continents as follows: Asia, 850,000,000; Europe, 446,800,000; Africa, 140,000,000; America (North and South), 196,000,000. The same authority gives the following division by races: White (Caucasic), 865,800,000; Yellow (Mongolic), 581,000,000; Black (Ethiopic), 175,000,000; Red (American), 27,000,000.

In accordance with this division of the races, considerably more than one-half of the earth's population belongs to the White race. If this be true, it would be interesting to find where they dwell. If we concede all the inhabitants of Europe to be white, and this would be an asumption contrary to facts, we have accounted for 446,800,000 whites, and we must look elsewhere to find 419,000,-000 white human beings. In accordance with the census of 1920 there were in the United States and its dependencies 94,820,915 white inhabitants. Assuming all the inhabitants of Canada, Chile, Argentine, Australia, New Zealand, and South Africa to be white, and adding them to the number of whites in the United States and its dependencies, we arrive at a total of about 130,497,635. If we add 33 1/3% of the population of North and South America outside of the United States, Canada, Argentine and Chile, as representing the white population in these sections, which is extravagant, we have the grand total of 157,097,635. If we deduct this number from 419,000,000 there will remain 261,902,365 whites to be found outside of Europe and the other areas mentioned. If we assume all the inhabitants of Persia, Asiatic Turkey (this refers to the pre-war area), and Arabia to be white, we should make a further deduction of 31,882,000, leaving 230,020,-365 to be yet accounted for. Making the further assumption that all the people of Algiers, Tunis, Morocco, Tripoli, and Egypt are white there should be deducted 27,170,000, leaving 202,850,-365 whites still to be located. These, it seems, must be located either in Asiatic Russia or India. Assuming all Asiatic Russia to be white, we should deduct 20,876,000, leaving 181,974,365 white people in India.

To speak of 181,974,365 white people being in India is not one whit more absurd than to describe the Chinaman as a man with a white skin, blue eyes, and flaxen hair. In arriving at this final conclusion later figures than those considered by Doubleday, Page & Company have been used in every instance except that for Asiatic Russia, and, therefore, the final numbers would be greater still if the census as to numbers had been accurate in each case. Furthermore the assumption as to the numbers of whites in the various areas considered is incorrect. The figures for the United States are supposed to represent correctly the population in 1920. Canada has a small Negro population and a large Asiatic population in British Columbia. Chile and Argentine are white with the exception of a small Indian element and probably a small Asiatic element. Australia is white to all intents and purposes like Chile and Argentine, though there are still some aborigines within its borders. New Zealand has a number of the aborigines—the Maories. South Africa has a large Negro population, and Cape Colony has a large number of mixed breeds resulting from the fusion of whites and blacks. The original stock from which the Turk was derived is classed as Turanian or Mongoloid, but the European Turk has absorbed so much white blood for centuries past that he may be regarded racially as white. There is a mixture of Semitic, Aryan and Turanian blood throughout Asiatic Turkey, and along the border line of the Brown peoples, themselves Negroid to a large extent, there has been a fusion of blood with them. The general statements made about Asiatic Turkey apply to Persia, and it is unfortunately true that parts of Arabia are largely Negroid. North Africa (Morocco, Algiers, Tunis, Tripoli) was white until the breaking up of the Roman Empire, since which time it has become largely Negroid. Egypt, once the seat of an empire founded by white people, is now the land of the brown race with all of North Africa to the west of it. Throughout this region the number of pure whites is very small. In India, typically the home of the Brown race, there is scarcely a white man aside from the recently arrived European. The Brown race, stretching throughout South Asia and North Africa, contains, aside from any true evolutionary Brown type that may be included within its numbers, the present-day representatives of former white peoples who established ancient civilizations that were lost in the amalgamation of its founders with the surrounding Brown or Black peoples.

In the South we regard any one as a Negro who has any Negro blood in him, whereas those who disseminate knowledge to the youth of the land through textbooks in use in the schools seem to think all are white who have any white blood in them. Though they may be classed as white, neither the Hindu nor the Egyptian nor the North African regards himself as such. It is certainly time this delusion was being suppressed and correct information given out as to race distribution. A conception of this kind once fully accepted and finding its way into text books and current literature is difficult to get rid of, however false it may be shown to be. It seems the philologists, when they made their first great finds as to kinship between Sanskrit and other Aryan tongues, concluded that all Hindus using the tongue must be Aryans; and, in order to explain the change that had been wrought in these people, it was alleged their new complexion was brought about by the hot and sultry climate of India. This theory is considered no longer tenable; and, while the majority of well informed and thoughtful persons recognize it as a fact that the ancient Aryan of India, the ancient white of Egyptian civilization, and the ancient Hamite or Semite of the southern littoral of the Mediterranean, have all disappeared in amalgamation with the Black or Brown races, or with some indigenous Mongoloid type, and that these people are properly included as members of the Brown race, yet the false classification is still persisted in and the uninformed are deluded into the belief in the numerical superiority of the White race.

The true situation seems to be that, of the total number of human beings alive to-day, about 1,700,000,000, only 550,000,000 of them are white, and the remaining 1,150,000,000, colored. Thus the whites instead of comprising over one-half of the earth's population include but one-third of it; and this one-third of the human race has opposed to it the remaining two-thirds of mankind, among whom there is a growing hostility to the whites which manifests itself in every phase of intercourse with these people—commercial, industrial and religious. These colored people have been furnished by us with all the inventions that enable a people to wage a successful war; that make life more comfortable; that lessen the ravages of disease—in fact, all modern knowledge that goes to the uplift and improvement of organized society, thus making the situation worse than it might otherwise have been. We face this situation with a disorganized white world in which hate, greed, and jealousy bid fair to further weaken us and increase, if possible, the existing demoralization. It is surely, therefore, time that we took stock of our situation with a view to reconciling our differences and facing the facts as becomes white men.

This disparity in numbers would not be of such momentous import provided a reasonable degree of harmony could be brought about amongst the white powers, and a concerted action established in world affairs. If this might be done, it would unquestionably be of the utmost benefit to the White race, as a whole, and to the individuals thereof, and without any curtailment or loss to the natural and legitimate aspirations of the political entities or nations included within the race. These adjustments would involve the surrender of the ambition of some individuals among the statesmen and politicians, but would, in the end, involve the surrender of no right by any nation that is not artificial in character, or enjoyed at the expense of injury to some one else.

Prior to the Russo-Japanese War, White Solidiarity was a fact with which all others had to reckon, whatever the situation might be between the white powers themselves. The conflicting ambitions between Russia and Great Britain resulted in the Anglo-Japanese Alliance; and further conflicting ambitions shattered the last remnant of White Solidiarity in the shambles of the World War.

CHAPTER II.

THE COLORED WORLD.

THE AMERICAS.

Canada.—Canada is the white man's land. She was threatened with inundation from Asiatic immigration, but saw the menace and acted in time to save herself.

The United States.—We, likewise, were threatened with inundation from Asiatic immigration, but have adopted the necessary measures to avert it. On the other hand, we lent ourselves to the introduction of the Negro amongst us in great numbers as a slave; and we refuse to solve the problem thus brought about in a manner conducive to the welfare of both races and just to all, the while nursing him to our bosom to our own destruction, to his injury, and to the injury of mankind. He does not yet so weaken our power, however, as to seriously affect our standing as a world power at this time.

Argentine.—In the early days there was some fusion of Indian and a small amount of Negro blood with that of the whites, but this has been rendered of little importance on account of the small numbers affected and the recent large immigration from European centers, and, therefore, the colored races may be said to have no foothold in this country.

Uruguay.—The comment made about Argentine applies generally to Uruguay.

Chile.—Chile is preeminently white, though there may be some slight fusion with Indian blood.

From the northern boundaries of Chile, Argentine, and Uruguay, in the South, to the southern border of the United States, in the North, lies the home of the colored world in America. Within these limits the southern part of Brazil is white, containing a large number of Italian and German immigrants; but from Rio north there is in Brazil a fusion of bloods, white, black, and Indian, and also a large number of Negroes and Indians. Costa Rica also has a very large white population considering its small territory.   Throughout this section the control of affairs was, at the time the provinces revolted from Spain, in the hands of a white ruling caste.   This class has grown less in numbers as time passed, many having been killed in revolutionary battles or lost in amalgamation with other mixed bloods or Indians.   As this class disappeared their place was taken by the mixed bloods, and now in many places the Indian is forging to the front.   The Negro element in this section is confined principally to Brazil.   From the earliest days the Spaniard did not come to these sections in any great numbers as a colonist seeking a home for himself and family, but rather as an adventurer or conqueror looking for booty.   The country was conquered, Spanish authority completely established over the Indian, and fusion of the blood of the conquerors with that of the natives and of the Negro imported from Africa began with the earliest invasions.   The former rulling caste still holds out in some places within this area; but in many sections the mixed breeds or Indians are in the ascendancy and in control of governmental affairs.   This is very evidently the case where revolution and turmoil are the rule and not the exception in the conduct of public affairs.   The only way out of this situation, in the interest of the White race, is the stiffening of control in the hands of the white minority until European immigration in their support insures continued white control.   If this element is so small as to be helpless, the only solution then is control by some outside powers that will direct a wholesome immigration into these sections and thus preserve the Americas for the White race.   This is a matter for consideration by Canada, the United States, Chile, Argentine, Brazil, and such other States in the Western Hemisphere as can be brought in concert with this end in view.

EUROPE

Europe is usually considered solidly white, but it is not altogether so as a matter of fact.   The Basques in Spain and the Finns and some other remnants around the Baltic are almost unanimously conceded to be the descendents of an aboriginal Mongoloid type that at one time occupied the whole of Europe. Neither of these people are, however, an obstacle to the White Solidarity of Europe—certainly they would not be antagonistic to it in any racial sense.   The Hungarians are classed as of Tu-

ranian or Mongoloid origin, but they have long since been regarded as European. There is a very considerable amount of
Turanian or Mongoloid blood in Russia, particularly among the
people usually designated as Tartars. The European Turk of
Turanian extraction now should be unquestionably classed as
white. Thus, it seems that throughout all Europe there is no
people who would side against the white on racial ground that he
is white It might appear at first blush that this is not true as
applied to the Turk, but upon investigation it will be found that
his antagonism is based rather in religion or in grievances arising
at the hands of the major powers, though it seems that there has
been recently an effort among the Turks to awaken sentiment in
behalf of the Turanians—Pan-Turanism. The weakness of the
whites in Europe does not arise, however, from any anti-white
sentiment among any of its peoples, but from the antagonisms of
conflicting selfish ambitions of peoples and men.

AFRICA

Africa is one of the strongholds of the colored world. Here we
find the Black race in its home, and the Brown race in possession
of the whole northern part of the continent. The whites in Africa
south of the Sahara, outside of the South African States, are the
few engaged in colonial offices or held there by commercial enterprises. In the South African States there are about a million and
a half whites, but in Cape Colony there is a large black and white
mixture. In North Africa about 1,000,000 Europeans have settled, and there still remain in this section some white Berbers
(Moors) and some pure blooded Arabs. In Egypt nearly all the
people except the European residents should be classed as members of the Brown race. In Abyssinia they are either members
of the Brown race or distinctly Negroid, and the same classification applies to the Soudan country. Aside from some of the
Abyssinians and a sect in Egypt, who are nominally Christians,
and a few Negroes in South Africa, Christianity is confined to
Europeans. All the Brown race in Africa and many of the blacks
are united in the bond of brotherhood that goes with the profession of the Islamic Faith, and included in this bond are such
pure Arabs as there may be in Africa and the Berbers. Thus Islam places the few whites that may be native to Africa in the
ranks with the colored world.

Stoddard numbers the Brown race at about 450,000,000, but he apparently includes in these numbers all the Islamic whites, such as are native to North Africa and Southwest Asia, and also the Turks. It is erroneous, as I believe, to include the Turk and the whites among the Persians, Arabs, Syrians, and the inhabitants of Asia Minor—all in Southwest Asia, and the Berbers and white Arabs in North Africa, as members of the Brown race. However, in view of the fact that the great majority of these peoples profess Mohammedanism, Christians among them being few in numbers, they act with the Brown race because of the bond of Islam, and for other reasons, and are, therefore, properly classed as anti-white under existing conditions. The actual number of native whites in all this section is a matter of difficult determination as it stands and one requiring a careful survey for ascertainment. Stoddard gives the total black population, including Africa where are its principal numbers, at about 150,000,000.

ASIA.

It is folly to talk of a white man with a climatically acquired black skin. At some remote period in the past, far antedating the remotest historic period, man may have perceptibly changed his color in the process of evolution; we have no knowledge of any way in which color of skin has changed during the historic period other than by amalgamation in which conflicting hereditary traits brought about compromises in color. There are in India near-whites, near-blacks, and numerous browns, and to all intents and purposes, therefore, the 315,000,000 in India may be classed as members of the Brown race; for they so regard themselves and are all anti-white in sentiment. The inhabitants of the peninsula to the east of India are of like character with the exception of a mixture of Mongoloid into which the inhabitants gradually merge toward the north.

To the north and east of India we come upon the Mongoloid type; and when we reach China and Japan we find a pure fixed-type of Mongoloid with a national consciousness, with traditions reaching back into the dim past, with a common type of civilization, with similar views and sentiments in religious and social matters. Particularly is this true of China. China is known to have existed as a political entity for over 4,000 years. Situated in the southeast of Asia, the southern and western borders were protected from invasion by high mountain ranges, the southeast and east by the ocean itself. Thus the only point of attack lay in the north; and here, in order to protect herself from invasions by kindred Tartars or Turanians, a wall 1,500 miles in length was completed over 2,000 years ago. Toward the end of the 15th century China was awakened from her long sleep by European assaults from the ocean front, and found her dream of security rudely shaken. From then till now China has been distraught and the easy prey of European greed. She seems now to be going through the last throes preparatory to the resumption of her poise or stability—a much marked characteristic of the race. For four thousand years or more within the historic period there has been in making a Chinese type with its peculiar civilization; and these people, despite such differences as may be found among them, constitute the most homogeneous body to be found anywhere on the face of the earth under one government; and this homogeneity extends not only to blood but to customs, manners, religion, language, and common hopes and fears. That these people so much asleep, so utterly indifferent to the rest of the world, so contemptuous of Europeans in particular—that these people should have been deeply touched in the hidden depths that affect the destinies of peoples, is the only explanation of the civil war that has been continuously going on for 15 years. That the climax approaches and the hidden future will soon be disclosed to us in its hideousness or pleasing lines seems a foregone conclusion.

We may see a new China discarding her old garments and fitting herself with new ones with which to find her place by peaceful methods in the commerce and industry of a world made new by modern invention. On the other hand, we may see a militant power indignant over the wrongs she has suffered for three centuries and filled with desire for revenge upon the white world.

The Chinamen, disciplined by adversity for thousands of years and thus endowed with the ability to survive under harsh conditions that would eliminate other races, possessed of homogeneity and stability of purpose and traditions upon which to build for the future, will, in view of his vast numbers, become a formidable antagonist should he choose to place himself athwart the path of progress of the White race.

The white man can doubtless compete with and down any other race under conditions of environment favorable to the development of the best there is in him; but, subjected to the harsh conditions of life and privations under which the Chinaman might survive, he would be eliminated from the earth.

When the catch phrase "survival of the fittest" came into current use, there came with it, in explanation of its use, the idea that "fittest" and "best" were synonymous and we being the best were foreordained to survive; and this persists even now with some people. The tumblebug survives in the manure pile, and the vulture on the field of carnage. The white man survives and develops the best in him under the most favorable conditions, which are now largely of his own making. "The white man's burden" is not the elevation of the Black or other races, but the preservation of conditions and areas favorable to his own survival and development.

CHAPTER III.

THE COLORED WORLD CONTINUED.

SUMMARY.

The Mongoloid Powers in Asia.—There are two great Mongoloid powers in Asia, Japan and China. Japan defeated Russia in war in 1904 and served notice on the white world that Asia was for Asiatics. Since that time Japan, by every public act of responsible parties in control of governmental affairs, has shown it to be the universally accepted opinion of all Japanese, that they are unjustly restrained from relieving the economic pressure due to overpopulation by the restrictions of white powers which forbid their entry into countries under white control, particularly in the Western Hemisphere. They further conceive that these restrictions act as an effective bar to the realization of their legitimate national aspirations.

As a result of this there has been a growing sentiment in Japan antagonistic to and contempuous of all white powers. Particularly did they hold us in utmost contempt up to the time we took part in the World War. Their success against Russia, the strategic position they held in Asia early in the war when they had taken over the German holdings in China, their contempt for us as a cowardly lot of mongrel traders who were only interested in making money, led them to believe the time was about ripe for them to realize their greatest dreams of world conquest as the directors or representatives of the Mongoloid peoples in which China would be joined to them under their leadership. These dreams of world empire always had in view the colonization of the Western Hemisphere and making it a dependency of theirs. They also had in view the control of the 315,000,000 inhabitants of India, whose people, although incapable of carrying out any definite program of their own making requiring cohesion of the whole, would fill their armies and replenish its depleted ranks in case of necessity. When we entered the war and demonstrated that we were not quite altogether lacking in what are considered military virtues, these ambitions received somewhat a check, but they have not by any means been abandoned. Even now, there is in Japan an influential minority that still urges war with the United States, as is evidenced by writings that appear from time to time in periodicals and elsewhere, in order to have free entry into the United States and the rest of the Western Hemisphere. This is the fixed, definite, determinate policy of Japan, the fruition of which—that is, if it can be carried through—depends largely upon the future policy of China when she assumes her proper role as a world power and fixes her national policies, as she surely will in the near future.

That China will, in the near future, reconcile her internal differences and formulate and support such definite internal and international policies as she deems to her interest, cannot be seriously questioned. Should she adopt an aggressive, militant policy, she might lend herself to the furtherance of the Japanese program, which, to us in America, means the erection of an Asiatic dependency extending from the southern boundary of the United States to the northern boundary of Chile. This might be accomplished through the combination of commercial enterprise, peaceful penetration, and conquest by war. The combined resources for this purpose would be those of about 500,000,000 people, aside from any aid that might be drawn from India and other sources; and included in this plan is that of making the Pacific an Asiatic body of water, which it is now in so far as the population of its islands is concerned.

Should China be content with the pursuit of its destinies in its Asiatic home-land and frown upon the extravagant schemes of Japan, the plans of the latter might receive a serious setback, if not complete checkmate. However, we should not depend upon a possible future act of China as a safeguard to our interests, particularly when there is equally a possibility that her future policy may be directed to our injury, and we are supposed to be free agents competent to plan for our own protection. The maxims we have come to regard as fundamental in the determination of right and wrong in our relations with one another and with other peoples are such as are applicable only to a homogeneous people in a body politic, and possibly to an outside people of the same characters as ourselves. Certainly such maxims should not be allowed to blind us to our true interests and our real position in a world filled with peoples whose mental attitudes and general

views as regards religion, civil rights, politics, and all that goes
to make life are a mystery to us, and whose international acts
are all a part of ambitious world-wide schemes in the furtherance
of what they conceive to be their own interests.

The Brown Race.—Of these people India contains about 315,-
000,000, and the only sentiment common to all this number is
that of dislike for and opposition to the white man and all white
powers. The 70,000,000 Moslems included in the above numbers
are bound together with all other peoples of the same Faith in
the common cause of Islam, which, aside from any definite religious program, has for its principal object at this time opposition
to all white powers, and includes unfortunately some white people within its ranks.

Many of the brown people are found in the peninsula to the
east of India and in Arabia to the west of it and throughout North
Africa. The Brown people of India consist principally of the
Dravidians, Arab Mohammedans among whom there is little
pure Arab blood, and the great body of Hindus the result of fusion of blood between the former Aryans and the aborigines. On
the whole there seems to have been such a fusion of extreme
bloods among these people that the resultant body has been left
devoid of fixed racial traits that make for stability and the pursuit of some fixed purpose in the common good. They therefore
form a great body of people, who, purposeless in their aims when
left alone, could be utilized by the Mongoloid powers or a rejuve-
nated Islam in its wars against the white powers.

Into this brown belt that extends across South Asia and North
Africa there is driven a wedge, the apex of which lies in Arabia
with its body in Southwestern Asia, and which contains quite a
numerous white people—pure blooded Arabs and other Semites,
Persians and some other white peoples. These whites are gradually becoming less and less in numbers through fusion with the
brown peoples along the border line between them; and the religion common to most of these peoples, Mohammedanism, hastens this, in that the bond of brotherhood in this sect entirely ignores race lines. These people are enlisted in the Islamic campaign against white domination; and although there may be a
slight awakening of race consciousness among the Arabs, as there
undoubtedly is among the Turks, both are anti-European on account of treatment they have received at the hands of European

powers, and through the bond of Islam they readily act with the Brown races in their opposition to the European powers.

Throughout North Africa, particularly in Egypt, the great body of the people are of that intermediate race that makes for instability of character and renders them a sort of jelly-like political protoplasm rather than a vertebrate organization that might develop into a nation. But like the people of India they may be utilized in an anti-white movement under the direction of competent leadership. Islam under the Turk or the Arab with other whites of the Faith, may be able to join all brown peoples in the serious and dangerous experiment of expelling all Europeans from areas in which the browns are dominant in numbers. It is, of course, possible that circumstances may arise in which we would find the Brown races allied with the Mongoloid peoples as represented in the Chinese or the Japanese or a union of the two. Independently of leadership of the Turks or of the Arabs and other white Mohammedans, or of the Chinese or Japanese, it does not appear that concerted action to a common end against the whites could be brought about among the multitude of brown people.

The immediate menace to Europe seems to arise from the possible union of all the brown peoples with the bulk of the blacks in the common cause of Islam for the expulsion of the Europeans from India, the Near East, and North Africa; that to America comes from the desire of Asiatics to make a large part of the two Americas into an Asiatic colony.

The danger from the blacks in Africa arises from their acceptance of Islam and their organization for war purposes under its banner. The conversion of the natives of Africa to Mohammedanism is going forward rapidly, and the natives, particularly those bordering on the south of the Sahara, make good soldiers and they would be most effective under the banner of Islam that knows no race or color in its application to human affairs. This fact alone has worked a great injury to Islam, and indirectly to mankind, in that, while it may have directly added many numbers to the hosts, it lost through amalgamation its most virile and energetic blood.

The inanity displayed by us in failure to solve our race problem, to intelligently handle our immigration problem, and in the constant assertion of the equality of the races and the "melting-pot" theory of America's destiny, amply justifies the Japanese opinion of us and that of many Europeans. The mere fact that the virile old stock is yet sufficient in numbers to leaven the whole body politic and assure us our position at the present time, does not mean that this foreign opinion of us may not be the only one to be drawn from future actual conditions that must be brought about unless we take steps to avert them. The error of this foreign opinion is in assuming that results which must inevitably follow our persistence in the course we are pursuing have already arrived.

CHAPTER IV.

THE MENACE.

That the Mongoloid menace to America is not imaginary but real may be seen if we examine into the situation candidly. Mexico to the south of us enjoyed a comparatively long period of peace and seeming prosperity under the rule of Porfirio Diaz, himself partly Indian; but since he was deposed Mexico has been in a constant state of revolution. His administration seems to have been the one quiet period since Mexico revolted against Spain. In fact, it appears that but one President prior to the regime of Diaz finished his term of office without the tumult of revolution. If the inhabitants of Mexico were the only ones affected by this perennial banditry and revolution to the south of us, we should quietly leave them to themselves. But this is not the case. The Mexican seems to be possessed with a peculiar and deep-seated animosity toward Americans and everything American. This may be partially due to resentment towards some American capitalists who may have used corrupt methods in procuring concessions for purposes of exploitation; it may be partially due to slumbering resentment, having its origin in the Mexican War and feeding upon hope of revenge; but, in the main, it is due to the unstable character of the Mexican himself, which is the result of fusion between the ancient Atlantean, the Indian, and the Spaniard of the Conquest. The characteristics of this combination manifest themselves in a restless discontent of the kind that forbids constructive work and lends itself to continuous unrest and disorder —plottings and counter-plottings, revolutions and insurrections.

"Japanese activities in Mexico," says Stoddard, "are of especial interest. Here Japan has three strong strings to her bow: (1) patriotic dislike of the United States; (2) mestizo[303] hatred of the white 'gringo'; (3) the Indianista movement. In Mexico the past decade of revolutionary turmoil has developed into a complicated race-war of the mestizos against the white or near-

---

[303]A mestizo is the result of mating between a Spaniard and a native Indian woman.

white upper class and of the Indian full-bloods against both whites and mestizos. The one bond of union is dislike of the gringo, which often rises to fanatical hatred. Our war against Mexico in 1847 has never been forgotten, and many Mexicans cherish hopes of revenge and even aspire to recover the territories then ceded to us. During the early stages of the European War our military unpreparedness and apparent pacifism actually emboldened some Mexican hotheads to concoct the notorious 'Plan of San Diego.' The conspirators plotted to rouse the Mexican population of our southern border, sow disaffection among our Southern negroes, and explode the mine at the psychological moment by means of a 'Reconquering Equitable Army' invading Texas. Our whole Southwest was to be rejoined to Mexico, while our Southern States were to form a black republic. The projected war was conceived strictly in terms of race, the reconquering equitable army to be composed solely of 'Latins,' negroes, and Japanese. The racial results were to be decisive, for the entire white population of both our South and Southwest was to be pitilessly massacred. Of course the plot completely miscarried, and sporadic attempts to invade Texas during 1915 were easily repulsed."[304]

"Nevertheless, this incident reveals the trend of many Mexican minds. The framers of the 'Plan of San Diego' were not ignorant peons, but persons of some standing. The outrages and tortures inflicted upon numerous Americans in Mexico during recent years are further indications of that wide-spread hatred which expresses itself in vitriolic outbursts like the following editorial of a Mexican provincial paper, written during our chase after the bandit Villa in 1916: 'Above all, do not forget that at a time of national need, humanity is a crime and frightfulness is a virtue. Pull out eyes, snatch out hearts, tear open breasts, drink—if you can— the blood in the skulls of the invaders from the cities of Yankeeland. In defense of liberty be a Nero, be a Caligula—that is to be a good patriot. Peace between Mexico and the United States will be closed in throes of terror and barbarism.' "[305]

"All this is naturally grist for the Japanese mill. Especially interesting are Japanese attempts to play upon Mexican Indianista sentiment. Japanese writers point out physical and cultural

---

[304]"*The Rising Tide of Color*," pp. 132-3, Charles Scribner's Sons.
[305]Ibid., pp. 133-4.

similarities between the Mexican native races and themselves, deducing therefrom innate racial affinities springing from the remote and forgotten past. All possible sympathetic changes were rung during the diplomatic mission of Señor de la Barra to Japan at the beginning of 1914. His reception in Tokio was a memorable event. Señor de la Barra was greeted by cheering multitudes, and on every occasion the manifold bonds between the two peoples were emphasized. This of course occurred before the European War. During the war Japanese-Mexican relations remained amicable   So far as official evidence goes, the Japanese Government has never entered into any understandings with the Mexican Government, though some Mexicans have hinted at a secret agreement, and one Mexican writer, Gutierrez de Lara, asserts that in 1912 Francisco Madero, then President, 'threw himself into the arms of Japan,' and goes on: 'We are well aware of the importance of this statement and of its tremendous international significance, but we make it deliberately with full confidence in our authority. Not only did Madero enlist the ardent support of the South American republics in the cause of Mexico's inviolability, but he entered into negotiations with the Japanese minister in Mexico City for a close offensive and defensive alliance with Japan to checkmate United States aggression. When during the fateful twelve days' battle in Mexico City a rumor of American intervention, more alarming than usual, was communicated to Madero, he remarked coldly that he was thoroughly anxious for that intervention, for he was confident of the surprise the American Government would receive in discovering that they had to deal with Japan'."[306]

There is scarcely a Congress to go out of existence that does not, some time during its life, have its attention called to some concession or alleged concession to Japan, or to some body of the Japanese, in Lower California or on the west coast of Mexico.

Even Brazil seems to be flirting with the Japanese in connection with what is termed a limited immigration of Japanese to that country for settlement in its Northern States.

The Literary Digest for January 8, 1927, under the caption "Booming Brazil in Japan," quotes from and comments upon an address by Mr. Shichita Tatsuki, late Japanese Ambassador at Rio de Janeiro, as published in the Tokyo *Trans-Pacific*. The

---

[306]*"The Rising Tide of Color,"* pp. 134-5, Charles Scribner's Sons.

Trans-Pacific says, in part: "A native Brazilian may be anything from a man of mixed Portuguese, Indian and Negro blood to a blond whose forebears lived in Holland. Color to him means little, as he has found men of all shades of skin may live peacefully together, speaking the same language and cooperating for the welfare of the country."

"In general the tendency has been for Nordics to settle in the southern States of the Republic—where there are many Germans and Poles—and for Latins to settle in the Central States. Asiatics, therefore, would seem to have the best opportunity in the north, where there is less competition and where their racial strains will be more readily accepted."

"São Paulo, the great coffee-raising State, for example, is predominantly Italian and probably would not offer as advantageous a home for Japanese as Maranhão in the north. The present Japanese colony in São Paulo has been successful, but large numbers of emigrants from this country probably would not be."

"Recent efforts for Japanese expansion in Brazil generally are reassuring in that they show an intelligent appreciation of the problems involved."

"Plans for a Japanese colony in Paraná recently were announced with the backing of the South American Enterprise Association with a capital of 1,000,000 yen. The Association is reported to have purchased 10,000 acres in Brazil as an initial homesite for the colony. This holding will be increased to 100,-000 acres if the scheme works out successfully. Mr. Reizo Yamashina, former vice-president of the Tokyo Chamber of Commerce, is reported to be one of the chief spirits in the enterprise."

"We are further informed by *The Trans-Pacific*, an American-owned journal," says the Literary Digest, "that the Japanese Brazilian Association of Hyogo Prefecture agreed at a meeting at Kobe to plans for the formation of a company with a capital of 3,000,000 yen to encourage Japanese activity in the Latin-American countries. One of the features of this scheme would be to instruct Japanese emigrants in the Spanish and the Portuguese languages, as well as to give them financial aid until they were established in their new country. Big Japanese silk and cotton interests, it seems, have representatives in Brazil and are said to be ready to invest considerable capital in an effort to fix the silk industry in that country, and to open cotton plantations to provide an additional source of supply for Osaka's mills.

All these plans would seem logically to point to the expansion of Japanese activity in Latin America in the next few years, says *The Trans-Pacific,* which adds:

'Shipping connections are excellent owing to the direct lines from this country to Brazilian ports and return. Brazil has just started a new Presidential administration under the able Dr. Washington Luis, which promises much for the prosperity and development of the country, and the Brazilian diplomatic and consular representation in Japan is active in explaining the situation by contact with the leaders of the Japan-Brazil movement to improve trade.'

'With intelligent cooperation and understanding on both sides there seems no reason why Japan and Brazil may not become of vast importance to one another in the next decade. Brazil has in superabundance the raw materials this country needs, and in turn can use much that is produced in Japan, provided Japanese products are able to hold their own in a highly competitive market now dominated by the United States and Britain with all the European countries striving for a foothold.'

'It is doubtful whether any of the other Latin-American countries offers as attractive a field for Japanese investment and limited emigration as Brazil, primarily because none of them has anything like so vast a domain or so urgent a need of capital and labor. Argentina is largely an all-white nation, and probably would not look on any Asiatic penetration with favor. Chile is small in area, dominated by aristocratic descendants of the Spanish Conquistadores, and her resources already fairly well organized for production. Peru, while rich in raw materials, has not the advantage of the excellent shipping connections which favor Brazil. The same argument applies to the northern countries of South America and to the small Central American States'."

What has been quoted should enable us to form some conception of the menace, to the nations of the extreme north and the extreme south of the Americas, from Asiatic immigration into the territories between them. The people in these territories include about 40,000,000 full-blooded Indians and mixed-bloods; and in addition there are several million Negroes and people with more or less Negro blood, the most of whom are located in Brazil. The Indian and the near-Indian types readily respond to overtures from the Asiatic as an alleged kindsman derived from a common ancestry in the remote past; and they fall in with any scheme that is based upon antagonism to or injury of the whites, particularly those of the United States of America. Japan with her fecund people, having unrestricted access to this section of America, would convert it into a Japanese possession or Asiatic colony within half a century. China, great and powerful, is in a transitional, revolutionary period, and it is probable she will shortly emerge from this period ready to assume her proper place among the nations of the earth. In what direction her great energies will be exerted no one knows, but this is sure—China must be taken seriously and no longer considered as a mere shadow of a power. If, when she takes her place as a power, the Americas from the United States to Argentine are open to emigration from her shores, China could easily convert this region into an Asiatic province within twenty-five years. It would probably take twice this period to consolidate and organize in an efficient way; but in all probability fusion between the Indian element, dominant in most of this section, and the Japanese or Chinese, would proceed without any racial antagonism—without jar or clash of any kind. Thus free access to this section by immigrants from China and Japan will thrust an Asiatic wedge between the United States in the north and Argentine in the south, whose people would have the backing of the hundreds of millions in China and Japan across the Pacific. The position of the white man in America would then be precarious, indeed.

In what has gone before in the concluding part of this work there has been indicated briefly some of the possibilities in a conflict between the colored and the white world. That these possibilities should become realities, needs but sufficient justification on the part of the aggressor together with reasonable belief in success. Anything desired by one people and denied to them by another may be deemed a sufficient cause for war, depending upon the confidence of the former in its results. One who intensely desires a thing may become so obsessed with this desire as to imagine conditions most favorable to the accomplishment of what he desires, when the actual facts of the situation are directly the opposite. The same psychological condition applies to nations in international affairs at times, and leads them to take a plunge that proves fatal.

The ambitions of Japan to expand in the Western Hemisphere, their dealings with Mexico, their efforts toward the colonization of Brazil, and their opinion of us have already been indicated. However, some of the extravagant ambitions of the Japanese imperialist may be gathered from a Japanese Opinion written in October, 1916, and published in "The Military Historian & Economist" ior January, 1917, a part of which is as follows:

"Fifty millions of our race wherewith to conquer and possess the earth! It is indeed a glorious problem! Rome built an empire with less; Napoleon nearly did it with less; and England will have done it with less, if she wins,—if she wins! And therefore I ask, shall we let her win? Need we with any one divide the earth? And if needs be, shall it be with England? The matter must with care be weighed."

"To begin with, we now have China; China is our steed! Far shall we ride upon her! Even as Rome rode Latinum to conquer Italy, and Italy to conquer the Mediterranean; even as Napoleon rode Italy and the Rhenish States to conquer Germany, and Germany to conquer Europe; even as England today rides Wales, Scotland, Ireland, her Colonies and her so-called 'allies' to conquer her robust rival, Germany,—even so shall we ride China. So becomes our fifty million race five hundred millions strong; so grow our paltry hundreds of millions of gold into billions!"

"How well have done our people! How well have our statesmen led them! No mistakes! There must be none now. In 1895 we conquered China;—Russia, Germany and France stole from us the booty. How has our strength grown since then,— and still it grows! In ten years we punished and retook our own from Russia; in twenty years we squared with and retook from Germany; with France there is no need for haste. She has already realized why we withheld the troops which alone might have driven the invader from her soil! Her fingers are clutching more tightly around her oriental booty; yet she knows it is ours for the taking. But there is no need of haste: the world condemns the paltry thief; only the glorious conqueror wins the plaudits and approval of mankind." . . . . . .

"As for America,—that fatuous booby with much money and much sentiment, but no cohesion, no brains of government, stood she alone we should not need our China steed. Well did my friend speak the other day, when he called her people a race of thieves with the hearts of rabbits. America, to any Warrior race, is not as a foe, but as an immense melon, ripe for cutting. But there are other warrior races,—England, Germany,—would they look on and let us slice and eat our fill? Would they?"

"But, using China as our steed, should our first goal be the land? India? Or the Pacific, the sea that must be our very own, even as the Atlantic is now England's? The land is tempting and easy, but withal dangerous. Did we begin with India, the coarse white races would too soon awaken, and combine, and forever immure us within our long since grown intolerable bounds. It must therefore be the sea; but the sea means the Western Americas and all the islands between; and with these must soon come Australia, India. And then the battling for the balance of world-power, for the rest of North America. Once that is ours we own and control the whole,—a dominion worthy of our race!"

"North America alone will support a billion people; that billion shall be Japanese, with their slaves. Not arid Asia, nor worn-out Europe (which, with its peculiar and quaint relics and customs should, in the interests of history and culture, be in any case preserved) nor yet tropical Africa, is fit for our people. But North America, that continent so succulently green, fresh and unsullied,—except for the few chattering, mongrel Yankees,—should have been ours by right of discovery: it shall be ours by the higher, nobler right of conquest." . . . . .

"Every hour, every day, every month, every year, by leaps and bounds, our strength increases; America to us is as helpless as the jelly-fish stranded upon the sand is helpless to the dragon! Only another hand can save her, and what hand is there? England cannot now stop us as she did before, but,—if we pluck the fruit now, Germany wins; and, having won, will she not once again take our well-earned prize away from us, unless she first consents? Yet, if we wait, England will retain her mastery of the sea, and so the opportunity, for a time, will pass."[307]

The same issue of this publication, referring to Japanese demands, comments editorially as follows: "When, at the beginning of 1915, she thrust her demands upon China, she knew that the Allies were helpless, but she did not know what we would do about it, nor was it possible, indeed, to guess what we would do about it. What happened then? The *Asama* was gently run into a mud bank in Magdalena Bay, and while our fleet was in the Atlantic and our diplomacy floundered at Pekin, Japanese

---

[307]Pp. 43, 44, 45.

help gathered about the *Asama*. In other words a Japanese fleet was kept within striking distance of Panama, for nearly six months, until our State Department finally decided to accept, under a cloud of words, the predominance of Japan in China. Nor was this enough. In the following autumn we were visited, in unofficial guise, by the Japanese financier Shibusawa, who did not hesitate to warn us in a banquet at New York that we had best beware lest 'our activities in China might lead to hostile competition, mutual distrust, and bitter animosity, which may be disastrous'."[308]

It is worthy of note that Japan, although she rendered but little aid to the cause in behalf of which she is supposed to have enlisted, received as a reward at the close of the World War a confirmation of her title to the possession of the Pelew, Caroline, Marianne, and Marshall Islands. These island-groups in the hands of an enemy constitute a direct menace to the Philippines, Guam and the Hawaiian Islands, and to communication between them and the United States. It should also be borne in mind that our sugar planters have converted the Hawaiian Islands into a Japanese colony so far as population is concerned. It may be that the four-power pact in relation to the Pacific has removed in a large measure the menace indicated, but there is involved in this the matter of good faith of all the parties interested.

Furthermore we should not forget when considering the islands in the Pacific that Japan protested against our annexation of the Hawaiian Islands; and it might be well to refresh our memory as to the incidents connected with their acquisition in a brief manner. Ridpath says: "In June of 1897 President McKinley sent to the Senate, from the Department of State, a treaty providing for the annexation of the Hawaiian Islands. Japan protested against this measure. It was claimed that that power had planned to seize upon Hawaii, a charge that received a certain plausibility from the fact that the number of Japanese in the Republic was far beyond the number of any other one nationality, and also from the fact that Japan, on account of the refusal of the officials at Hawaii to allow a large number of recent Japanese immigrants to land, had sent two warships to the harbor of Honolulu. On the other hand, Japan declared that the shutting out of the immigrants was contrary to her treaty with the

[308]Pp. 53-4.

Hawaiian Republic, and that the warships had been sent to the island merely in support of her claim for damages."

"The rumors of a possible Japanese uprising in the island, while largely credited in the United States, were not trustworthy, owing to the essential minority of numbers on the part of the Japanese as compared with all others in the territory. Of the native Hawaiians of pure blood there were, at this time, at least thirty-seven thousand, with an additional ten thousand of mixed descent. Of the Chinese, the natural enemies of the Japanese, there were fifteen thousand, while the nine thousand Portuguese, two thousand Americans, fifteen hundred Englishmen, and twelve hundred Germans, made the total much too great to overcome."[309]

Viewed more critically in the illumination of subsequent events, the conduct of Japan in relation to the Hawaiian Islands appears now to have been in pursuance of a definite policy in regard to the islands of the Pacific that met with a partial reward at the close of the World War.

"Whatever may be its ultimate goals," says Stoddard, "Japanese foreign policy has one minimum objective: Japan as hegemon of a Far East in which white influence shall have been reduced to a vanishing quantity.   That is the bald truth of the matter—and no white man has any reason for getting indignant about it.   Granted that Japanese aims endanger white vested interests in the Far East.   Granted that this involves rivalry and perhaps war.   That is no reason for striking a moral attitude and inveighing against Japanese 'wickedness,' as many people are to-day doing.   These mighty racial tides flow from the most elemental of vital urges: self-expansion and self-preservation. Both outward thrust of expanding life and counter-thrust of threatened life are equally normal phenomena.   To condemn the former as 'criminal' and the latter as 'selfish' is either silly or hypocritical and tends to envenom with unnecessary rancor what objective fairness might keep a candid struggle, inevitable yet alleviated by mutual comprehension and respect.   This is no mere plea for 'sportsmanship'; it is a very practical matter. There are critical times ahead; times in which intense race-pressures will engender high tensions and perhaps wars. If men will keep open minds and will eschew the temptation to regard

[309]*"Library of Universal History,"* Vol. XVII., pp. 83-4.

those opposing their desires to defend or possess respectively as impious fiends, the struggles will lose half their bitterness, and the wars (if wars there must be) will be shorn of half their ferocity."[310]

The Japanese do not regard their exclusion from this country by legislative enactment as final. On the contrary, they regard the matter as a pending issue, one which they will urge for settlement favorable to them when the conditions are propitious. The substitution of legislative exclusion for the "gentlemen's agreement" is deeply resented by all Japanese writers; for they insist the question of race equality is involved and look upon the "gentlemen's agreement" as less offensive than legislative exclusion. These are the views of the moderate, temperate school of writers among the Japanese. Mr. K. K. Kawakami, Washington representative of the Osaka Mainichi Publishing Company, in a recent article, "Japan Looks to America," states the Japanese view-point to be in effect that given; and he further alleges that the United States has fostered an All-American policy of Asiatic exclusion, which, while it has borne fruit in the case of Panama, has encountered opposition among some of the "Latin American" States, who are unwilling to hazard the good will of the Orient.[311]

The facts are that the exclusion of Asiatics is an economic question; that the "gentlemen's agreement" had the same end in view as does legislative exclusion, but that the former was far more prolific of troubles than the latter can possibly be. The danger in the "gentlemen's agreement" came from the fact that whenever a question arose under it, there was involved the past, present, or future conduct of the respective parties to the agreement, in which might come to the front the good faith and fairness of the parties, and such a situation was filled with all sorts of disastrous possibilities. On the other hand, legislative exclusion clearly defines the situation and leaves no room for doubt. It becomes simply the execution of a municipal law.

Clinton Stoddard Burr comments on the "gentlemen's agreement" as follows:

"It is most illuminating to observe the figures for the Japanese immigrants both before and after the passport agreement of 1908. As a matter of fact, Japan appears in the immigration

---

[310]"*The Rising Tide of Color*," pp. 41-2, Charles Scribner's Sons.
[311]*Harper's Monthly Magazine*, March, 1927, pp. 448, 451.

statistics for the first time as early as 1861, but from that year up to 1890 only a few hundreds entered the country. But this number constantly grew through net immigration and a prolific birth rate. For a time after the 'gentlemen's agreement' went into effect, it appeared that the plan was successful, for emigration of Japanese from the United States was comparable to the number of arrivals into the country, but the recent rapid increase of Japanese in the country during the decade from 1910 to 1920, and, above all, the considerable movement of so-called picture brides, proves that the Japanese government is either unwilling or is powerless to live up to the terms of the agreement. For which reason the grievance of the Californians and other Western Americans is a most just one. The agitation of the State of California over the matter of Japanese immigration led the Japanese government to acquiesce in a compact to prohibit the further importation of Japanese women, but the Californians are now sceptical, with good reason, as to the future intentions of the Island Kingdom, and are now advocating a drastic law to include Japan within our barred zones."[312]   This last sentence relates to the immigration act of February 5, 1917, under the provisions of which the inhabitants of certain zones or geographical areas are not permitted to enter the United States as immigrants.

"One of the most unreasonable features of the Japanese objections to what they term 'race discrimination' is the fact," says he, "that they erected precisely the same kind of laws in Japan against the Koreans and Chinese, when the latter threatened the standard of living in Japan by their greater thrift and inferior living conditions. Yet the Japanese are akin to the Koreans, and far less remote from the Chinese than the Americans are to the yellow races. Furthermore, the Japanese do not in general allow foreigners to hold land in the Japanese Empire."[313]

If we insist, as we should, that the two Americas shall in fact become and remain a white man's land, we should, on the other hand, avoid all appearance of aggression within the limits of properly recognized Asiatic spheres; and our policy as regards the Philippines should be shaped solely and entirely with a view to the interests of the peoples of these islands, though it may in-

[312]*"America's Race Heritage,"* pp. 159-160, National Historical Society, N. Y.
[313]Ibid., p. 164.

volve complete independence, provided there are guarantees they may not become a menace to white Australia. Our interests in Asia should be confined to such as are concerned with trade and commerce as distinct from political control, spheres of influence and special concessions.

The fact that China made a formal declaration of war in behalf of the Allied Powers against the advice and urgent pressure brought to bear by Japan, indicates clearly the awakening national sentiment in China. The interests of both China and the United States were sacrificed in the Versailles Treaty to the advantage of Japan. The United States was, of course, in a position to look after its own interests; and if these were neglected we cannot shift the burden of blame on any one else. Furthermore, the fact that we did not look for reward in the acquisition of territory for our participation in the war does not make any less inexcusable our acquiescence in the distribution of spoils in such way as to menace us. In the case of China, however, the situation was quite different. When she entered the war she entrusted her interests unreservedly to the Allies, and these were shamefully neglected in the final treaty. However, China has received so many injuries and insults within the last four centuries that it is difficult to estimate the effect of this last upon her future conduct, or how much it contributed, if at all, to the shaping of her conduct in the present situation. In fact, although we may have a quite definite idea as to the policy of Japan, it is futile to indulge in guesses at this time as to what China's future policy may be. We can, however, see that a militant China trained in modern warfare through civil strife and utilizing to its full extent all modern inventions, would be a foe to give us cause for many anxious moments.

In the early period of Mohammedan expansion there was a marked spirit of tolerance on the part of the followers of the Prophet for both the Jew and the Christian, all three after a manner having a common ground of belief in the acceptance of the Old Testament, but this degree of tolerance was then altogether lacking in their dealings with the peoples of all other beliefs. However, the fear and hatred of the white world was such at the time of the Russo-Japanese War in 1904, that the Japanese success was hailed with delight throughout Islam. Former tolerance of the Christian West had been forgotten and the Islamite was willing to enter into alliance with Idolaters (so regarded by the Islamite) in order to compass the designs of their white oppressors. The Sultan of Turkey went so far as to send a warship to Japan on a visit of courtesy, with the hope evidently of securing Japanese adhesion to Islam; for there was on board an Islamic Mission. The intense satisfaction of the colored world over the defeat of Russia showed itself in expressions of satisfaction and rejoicing even in the darkest corners of Negroid Africa.

When the World War broke there was great glee throughout Asia and Africa over the fact that the White races were at last at each other's throats and destroying themselves in internecine warfare. This satisfaction over the situation extended even to some of our own colored population and to that of some sections of Central and South America. There was revolt in Tripoli, Egypt, and the Indian Northwest Frontier, and unrest throughout the rest of the brown world and Africa. But for the whole-hearted action of the Arabs in revolting against Turkish authority and waging relentless war against it, Egypt, India, and North Africa might have been lost. The Arabs were led into doing this by promises, on the part of Great Britain, of independent control in certain areas, which promises were incompatible with definite secret arrangements between herself and France in regard to division of the territory in question.

The occupying of one's territory, the displacement of native by foreign control, and the exploitation of the resources and the people of the land by a foreign power, is a situation of affairs that must engender the most deep-seated and lasting hatred for the conqueror, irrespective of any blessings, from his point of view, conferred by an advanced civilization upon a backward people. It is simply human that this should be so. This is an unvarnished statement of what has occurred in Southwest Asia as far to the eastward as Persia, inclusive, and in North Africa, in which areas, particularly in Asia, there is a large white population. The same condition as to occupation holds true in India and Egypt.

The propaganda put forth by the Allies during the war in regard to self-determination of peoples and other kindred subjects naturally led these people to believe, if language means anything at all, that they might look forward to a considerable degree of self-government, if not actual independence, at the close of the war. When the Arab found that the promises made to him were but "scraps of paper," and other peoples found themselves more firmly in the grasp of foreign control than ever, their passionate hate became a frenzy. The Mussulman Hindu became a comrade of the Brahmin in the common cause against the whites, though heretofore they had been unrelenting foes. The growing union of sentiment against all white people, among the non-white and the Islamic people, is a matter of the gravest concern; and many are now trembling lest Bolshevik Russia, white though she be, may make common cause with China and lead Europe again into the shambles.

CHAPTER V.

THE WHITE WORLD.

When America was discovered the population of Europe was about 70,000,000, and these people were situated between the Turanian peoples, by whom they had been hard pressed from the East for more than a thousand years, and the Atlantic Ocean. Attila and his Huns were defeated at Chalons by the combined power of the Romans, Goths and Franks in A. D. 451; and the Turks, another branch of the Turanian family, were not stopped in their aggressions upon Europe until their defeat under the walls of Vienna in 1683, seventy-six years after the settlement at Jamestown, Virginia. Not only were the Europeans threatened by the Turanians on the East, but on the South and Southwest by the Saracens during the ascendency of Mohammedanism; and the Arabs or Moors held sway in Spain for several centuries, the last Moorish stronghold being taken in 1491. The conquests of the Arab in southwest Europe were halted between Tours and Poitiers where they were decisively defeated in battle by Charles Martel in 732, after which they withdrew behind the Pyrenees. Sardinia, Southern Italy and Sicily felt the ravages of the Saracens who obtained footholds in these sections.

The terrors of the ocean having been dissipated by the discoveries of Columbus and of the Portuguese navigators who preceded him, the people of Europe found new pathways over the ocean belonging to no man and merely awaiting use by adventurous spirits who were willing to accept the ordinary hazards of the sea. Soon India, the coasts of age-long known Africa, the new continents of North and South America, and innumerable new islands became known to the world.

The Dutch, English and French seemed to acquiesce for some time in an arbitrary division of the newly discovered world between the Spanish and the Portuguese by grant of Papal authority; and the Spaniards had established themselves in some of the principal islands of the West Indies by 1500, while the Portuguese had reached Calicut in India in 1498, and on the capture of Goa in 1511 made it the capital of their possessions in this land.

Spanish authority had been firmly established for a number of years by 1600 in Florida, Mexico, Peru, and Buenos Ayres of Argentine of to-day, and in other parts of so-called Spanish America; and, in fact, became and remained supreme throughout Mexico, Central and South America, with the exception of Brazil, until her colonies revolted and obtained their independence early in the 19th century.

The first Portuguese Governor for Brazil was appointed in 1549 and Rio de Janeiro was founded in 1567.

England was slow to take advantage of the new situation, and this was probably due in some degree to regard for Papal authority; but after Henry VIII. broke off relations with the Roman Church, and particularly after the defeat of the Invincible Armada of Spain, the English began to realize the peculiar significance to them of seaborne power and became aggressive navigators and colonizers. In 1607 the English established their first permanent settlement in America, but it was not until toward the end of the 18th century that she became firmly fixed in India.

In 1800 Canada was in possession of the English, the United States was an independent power, and practically all of the Americas to the south of her, with the exception of Portuguese Brazil, were in possession of Spain. England was at this time firmly lodged in India and had taken Cape Town from the Dutch and thus come into possession of Cape Colony.

The comparitively small number of whites who were in Europe in 1492, had in 1914 increased to about 550,000,000; had partitioned Africa amongst themselves, with the exception of Abyssinia and Liberia; had brought under their control all of India, the peninsula to the east of it with the exception of Siam, all of Asia north of the Chinese Empire, Mongolia, Afghanistan and Persia, and Persia itself was, to all intents and purposes, under their sway. During all this time the only check to white aggression was that received by Russia at the hands of the Japanese in 1904, but signs were not wanting, toward the end of this period, of a nascent resentment on the part of the Chinese that might find effective expression against the overlordship of the white powers.

Western Europe, arising slowly from the sloth and gloom of

the Middle Ages, began to see the light of modern times under the stimulus of discovery and the revival of learning during the 15th century. The discovery of America and new pathways across the sea freed the mind of the race from the shackles of sloth, ignorance, and bigotry in which it had been entombed during the Middle Ages, and gave an incalculable stimulus to mental, moral and material progress. With these discoveries the European world seemed to emerge from darkness into daylight, and the results following have simply been immeasurable in their benefits to the race and to mankind. The wealth obtained from the New World in gold and silver was so vast that, until very recent times, it formed the basis of the monetary systems of Europe; and this vast increase in wealth was reflected in more comfortable living conditions among the people. "In the course of twenty-five years after the Conquest the Spaniards sent from Peru to Spain *more than eight hundred millions of dollars of gold,* nearly all of it taken from the Peruvians as 'booty'."[314]

---

[314]Ignatius Donnelly's *"Atlantis: the Antediluvian World,"* p. 395, Harper & Brothers.

CHAPTER VI.

THE WHITE WORLD CONTINUED.

England, France, and Spain were evolved from a congeries of petty feudal domains; and by 1500 the power of the Feudal Lords had been much abated, certainly to the extent that the primacy of the Monarch was recognized in all matters pertaining to the people among whom there was developing a national consciousness. The Dutch, too, were beginning to feel that national consciousness which arises from occupancy of the same territory, the use of the same tongue, and joinder in kindred pursuits, as were also the peoples of the present Scandinavian Powers, whereas Germany and Italy were yet, as they would be for many years to come, mere geographical expressions without unity among their peoples; Russia was in her nascent state, and Hungary and Poland were striving to preserve some sort of national expression.

A review of the wars in which the European Powers were engaged from 1500 to 1870, discloses much heroism, a great amount of military genius, and a deplorable sacrifice of good white blood as a result, in most cases, of the pride, jealousies or ambitions of the ruling monarch, or their religious bigotry and intolerance. This, of course, does not mean the body of the people were less bigoted or intolerant. Charles V. of Spain, Francis I. of France, and Henry VIII. of England, seemed to regard their realms as personal estates in which the nobility were a sort of superior stewards, and the ordinary person little, if any, better than a serf.[315] International affairs were matters strictly personal to the Monarch, who engaged in war or other undertaking as prompted by his fancy, prejudice or ambition, with the sole

---

[315]There is a considerable amount of liberal and constructive legislation dating from Henry VIII, particularly relating to estates. He undoubtedly favored this character of legislation as a necessary step in breaking the power of the Nobility.

qualification, if he were wise, that he would not press beyond the limit of endurance.

This absurd personal view of the Monarch's position seems to have persisted in England even with William III., who, upon the death of Mary in 1694, was left to rule alone. "This he did," says Swinton, "by prudently conceding a good deal to the Parliament, provided that they gave him money to carry on the war with Louis XIV."[316]

The religious wars that devastated Germany, the excesses indulged in by both sides, the cold and calculating greed displayed by some of the major powers, and the petty politics played by rulers of some of the minor states in the struggle, make a page in history we seldom wish to consult.

Of course these struggles brought to light the great qualities and the magnificent heart of some peoples and men; and one of the outstanding characters for all times is William of Orange, known as William the Silent. A Roman Catholic before he became a Protestant, he was, from the time he began to take interest in public affairs and during both periods of his religious affiliations, a devout believer in Christianity and in religious freedom, when intolerance was the open sesame to wealth and power. When it was the fashion among his contemporaries to sell their sword to the highest bidder and to transfer sword and influence from one cause to another, as personal interest seemed to require, and even during hostilities, he remained steadfast to the cause of religious freedom and the liberties of his people, and could not be diverted from the persistent and diligent pursuit of these ends by threat of the assassin's dagger, to which he finally succumbed, or offer of reward. Under the greatest adversities he displayed many of the admirable traits that at a later day were found in the make-up of the Great Washington and placed them both among the Immortals. Should the Netherlands never again produce a great man, she may feel she has done well in contributing this great character to the world's history.

During this period, when Peacock-Monarchs were leading peoples into wars because they did not like the plumage worn by some other bird and offensively asserting the Divine Right of Kings, the sober common sense of the English people, acquired in adversity, began to assert itself, and the Iron Cromwell,

---

[316]*"Outlines of the World's History,"* p. 363.

though there may have been little in him that appealed to the heart, led them by the stern and rough paths of a tyrannical Puritanism—the only ones open to such a character and the only ones that could provide an effective remedy under the circumstances—to that proper conception of Parliamentary control that enabled the English to demand the Bill of Rights from William and Mary on their accession to the throne. Any candid observer must concede the necessity for and the effective manner in which Cromwell did his work; and it, therefore, comes with ill-grace from our English cousins that they should condemn the conduct of the Bolshevik in unmeasured terms, when, in the excess of their zeal over the return of the Royal Prerogative, the sober Conservatives lent themselves to the execution of ten so-called regicides, and, not content with this, went even so far as to condemn the dead Cromwell, exhume him from his honorable resting place, hang him on a gallows, and bury him under it after having exposed his head at the gateway of Westminster.

Some of these struggles were justified on the part of one or more of the contestants, as a just resistence to wanton aggression; and, in these turbulent times, a ruler who wished to bring about a union amongst his people and place them in a position in which they might be free to develop and progress without being buffeted around by surrounding powers, must have the praise of the candid historian. Among the people of this character is to be found Frederick II., known as Frederick the Great, whom Carlyle regarded as a hero because "he managed *not* to be a liar and charlatan, as the rest of his century was."

The later Franco-Prussian War was of like character, and resulted in the union under one government of all German States outside of Austria, many of which had been kicked and cuffed about for centuries by the greater powers of Europe. This union met with the approval of the enlightened opinion of all mankind. It was only when it was recognized by some of the great powers that a powerful rival state had taken the place of the petty principalities of Germany that regrets over the situation began to be expressed in some quarters. The Mountebank-Napoleon gave ample justification for this war in so far as the standards for justification in the past are concerned; and this was never seriously questioned except by war-propaganda during the World War. "Louis Napoleon, said a member of his family, deceived Europe twice: first when he succeeded in passing off as an idiot, and next when he succeeded in passing off as a statesman."[317]

The campaigns that led to a United Italy likewise form a bright spot in history, the pages of which give account of so many gloomy, senseless wars.

"When the Russian Revolution broke," says Frank H. Simonds, "the Western world turned instantly to the parallels of the French Revolution, and particularly in Great Britain—that nation which had fought the French Revolution because of principles which Time has approved—sought to invest this new upheaval with virtues which Englishmen had rejected in that other earthquake a century and a quarter before."[318] If, in course of time, there has come a justification of the assaults upon France by the united European Sovereigns in the early days of her Revolution, this justification is one that is not commonly accepted. It seems to be the almost universal opinion, and this appears to be in accord with facts in so far as facts can be had out of the situation, that the early concreted action on the part of the Sovereigns of Europe united against France arose from an inherent desire on the part of these personages to stifle the liberties of the people wherever they were manifested, as the most deadly enemy to their well being. Doubtless had they scrupulously permitted France to look after her own affairs from the very beginning, and had the French Nobility showed the courage of real men and remained with the distracted Ship of State, the duration of the Revolution and its blood letting would have been much less than it was. Attack from without did nothing but more firmly knit together the revolutionary forces and increase their frenzy. That this should have been so is elemental human nature; but the civilized world seems to have failed to profit by the example of France and apply the lessons there learned in its dealings with Russia. Of course, when Napolean, the Emperor, appeared upon the scene with his inordinate ambitions, the situation had become complicated because of the action and reaction resulting from the conduct of the different powers, and the last of this struggle was doubtless a national one between England and France. Russia, now the Bête Noire of Europe, obtained a foothold upon the shores of the Baltic early in her national evolution as a European power. This outlet be-

---

[317]McCarthy's *"History of Our Own Times,"* Vol. I., p. 402.
[318]*"History of the World War,"* Vol. 4, p. 175, Doubleday, Page & Company.

ing entirely inadequate to her needs, both on account of the inhospitable shores of this region and the enormous extent of her empire, desire on her part for expansion through the Black Sea to the shores of the Mediterranean should have been regarded as a legitimate national aspiration that was of no concern to any one other than Russia, on the one hand, and Turkey with her mixed population, on the other. However, every step taken by Russia in this direction was not only grudgingly allowed by England, France and other powers, but most frequently arrested or limited by war against Russia on the part of these powers. In other words, because of alleged fear of Russian power they were determined that she should remain without an adequate outlet to the sea; that incidentally Christian peoples should remain subject to Turkish rule, and the Turkish Empire remain inviolate. This situation in which the Christian peoples of Turkey in Europe were encouraged in their aspirations for freedom by Russia, on the one hand; and Turkey was encouraged in looking forward to the continuance of her power by England and France, on the other hand, led inevitably to continuous unrest, revolts, plottings, murders and massacres.

Balked in his efforts to obtain an outlet on the Mediterranean, the Russian turned his eyes toward the Persian Gulf, and here again he found himself opposed by Great Britain on the ground that he threatened her possessions in India. Further to the East went the Russian and found lodgment on the Pacific in the port of Vladivostok where the waters were frozen in winter and could be kept open only by the use of stoutly built ice breakers, if at all. Russia still yearning for sea outlets open all the year around, there was continued with greater intensity than before a series of plots and counter-plots, secret treaties and alliances; and the climax of these, which broke White Solidarity in world affairs, was the Anglo-Japanese Alliance.

It is idle to conjecture what might have happened had there been a little more frankness in dealings between these powers, and had there been a little more candid admission of the legitimate aspirations of the Russian people. Probably somewhat more abrupt in their dealings and somewhat more open in avowal of ultimate objects and somewhat more venal in dealing with public matters than were the other Europeans, yet the Russians were but little less given to sharp practices, evasions and falsehoods of diplomacy than were the others with whom they dealt; and we cannot but speculate as to what might have been the outcome had they realized some of their ambitions in seeking open ports. A more intimate acquaintance with the more cultured people and an increase in commerce and trade and facilities of communication, might have placed the Russian people so far along the path of progress as to have avoided the pitfalls that led to the World War.

CHAPTER VII.

INDUSTRIALISM.

Industrialism, in its intense form an evolutionary development of finance, trade, commerce, manufacturing and the corporation, combined, has had a marked effect upon all civilized peoples—upon the peoples themselves physically as distinctive types within the white family, upon the policies of these peoples as political entities or nations, and consequently their views in international affairs. Particularly has this been true of the principal European powers for the quarter of the century prior to 1914.

The change wrought in industry within this time has been marvelous. New machinery and new methods brought into coordination in large corporate bodies have greatly multiplied the output of human labor in the necessities and luxuries of life, and thus rendered the sustenance of a much increased population not only possible but desirable in accordance with the ethics of Industrialism. Under the stimulus of these forces the population of the principal foci of industry in Europe, Great Britain and Germany, had so greatly increased before 1914, that the matter of markets for manufactured goods and supply of cheap raw materials from which to make these goods, was becoming more and more a matter of vital importance. This was true not only from the point of view of profits to the manufacturer, but also from that of the sustenance of the population which had increased by leaps and bounds under modern conditions of industry and sanitary control. These conditions existed in an intense form also in Italy where an increase in industry was hoped for in their amelioration; in a less degree in France; in a minor degree in the United States and other parts of the white world. It can be readily seen that when the markets become glutted with manufactured products or the sources of supply for cheap raw materials become restricted, a condition of intense competition and rivalry is brought about.

Just as the white world was emerging into the dawn of an enlightened future through the education of its peoples and the adoption of democratic principles in government in recognition of the rights of man as an individual in the body politic, and the Peacock-Kings were giving place to enlightened Ministries in which the individual seeking personal renown could do so only in pursuit of the common good—just as this was coming within our grasp, the baneful effects of modern industrialism began to manifest themselves. With a keener competition in the markets the Ministries began a search for exclusive markets and exclusive sources of supply for raw materials. These were essential if the populations were to be maintained in a sufficient degree of comfort to carry on the work; and their importance was impressed upon the people and their Ministries when it was realized that support of a population that had reached the point of industrial maximum depended upon holding the markets and sources of supply already had or increasing them. Thus as time passed there was brought about an intenser competition and the mad race was on. Alliances were hawked about and disposed of to the best industrial advantage. Irrespective of the form of government or the character of titles of the persons engaged in this contest among the respective powers of Europe, the objects in view were the same for each and the same methods were employed in carrying them through.

It was this mad race that largely contributed to the World War; and, if any informed person could ever have doubted this, the conduct of the respective powers from the time they first sat at the peace table till now conclusively shows this to have been the case. It is as clear as the nose on one's face that, England, France, Germany, and Italy cannot each maintain a population far in excess of what it can support upon its own natural resources, and each, at the same time, maintain the advantageous position of leadership over the others in the exploitation of backward peoples, exclusive markets, and exclusive sources of supply for raw materials. The backward peoples for exploitation are growing less and less likely to remain content under exploitation, and, in the face of a divided white world, this becomes more and more apparent. If the leadership in industrial Europe is to be determined from time to time by resort to arms, there will not be many repetitions of this act in the face of a hostile colored world; and rather than continue this it might be better to return to the period of the Peacock-Kings. However, the education we have had and the knowledge we have accumulated means retrogression instead of progress unless we can find some more intelligent solution; and this seems to lie in the pooling of interests by all white peoples in all backward countries outside of areas peculiarly fitted for colonization and for that purpose properly included within the body politic of the power controlling.

CHAPTER VIII.

EUROPE FROM 1870 TO THE WORLD WAR.

In the preceding chapter it was pointed out that the growth of modern industrialism with its materialistic views caused a far keener competition between the European Powers than formerly existed, and led eventually to the World War, in which the guilt for its occurrence must rest, if not equally, then in some measure at least, on each and every one of the participants.

Competition between the Powers in the exploitation of backward peoples and the race for exclusive privileges and special concessions among these people, together with the imperialistic program of Russian leaders and the ambitions of some other leaders, brought about the pre-war situation in which each power was struggling under a back-breaking burden of armament in preparation for war. The form of government of the different powers did not in any way affect the object sought or the methods employed. Each Power used any and every means within its reach to bring about a Coalition of Powers favorable to itself. Prejudice, passions, self-interest, and greed were appealed to, and behind closed doors representatives of the various Ministries planned and plotted in secret and entered into all sorts of agreements, some of them highly inconsistent, for the aggrandizement of their people or some of them and in the furtherance of their personal ambitions.

East of Italy in the Mediterranean lies that section of Europe in which strife between its peoples and war are perennial. Here Russia has been plotting since the time of Peter the Great with the eye on Constantinople as its future Capital; and here England has entered into counter-plots to defeat this Russian ambition, believing that a Russia in the East Mediterranean would menace her occupation of India. Never did the two join in war single-handed, on the contrary, there was always dragged in some other power or powers not directly involved in the issues of the war. Just as England feared Russia as a menace to her continued occupation of India, so did Germany fear her as a menace to her national existence. The industrial expansion of Germany found an outlet in the Balkan States and Turkey, and it soon became apparent that British industry and political influence were being displaced in this region by those of Germany. When German concessions were obtained for railroads heading towards the Euphrates valley and the Persian Gulf, Germany, in the English mind, assumed the position of menace toward India formerly occupied by Russia, which last power had been defeated by Japan in 1904 as a result of the Anglo-Japanese Alliance. In the meantime Russia saw the possibilities of her future possession of Constantinople disappearing in the growing influence and power of Germany in Turkey; and plotting and counter-plotting, prompted by self-interest, political ambition, and race prejudice, were given a greater intensity. Although there had been brought about a more friendly relationship between Germany and France not so long after the War of 1870, there nevertheless arose in time an intimate understanding between Russia, England, and France that had definite objects in view. French passions were reawakened and hopes of revenge for 1870 renewed; England saw a trade rival laid low; and Russia indulged again in her visions of Constantinople. Of course Germany did all she could, employing the same methods as the others, to hold the Triple Alliance together, weaken the union against her, and strengthen her own position. One Balkan State was played against another, and there were doubtless dreams of a powerful central empire reaching not only to the Mediterranean but possibly to the Persian Gulf. However, Italy had become so detached from Germany and Austria that no one seriously thought she would be aligned with them in war. As a matter of fact it is difficult to conceive of a more cold-blooded sale of a country's support in war than is disclosed by Italy in the diplomatic correspondence published by her own authority and relating to her entry into the World War. Italy having been detached from her allegiance to her former associates —and this was in evidence before the war began—there remained in support of Germany only Austria, disorganized and weak—a discord of races. It seems to have been the commonly accepted opinion throughout the world at this time that the Austrian Empire was crumbling and that the slightest pressure from without would complete this disintegration. There is not the least doubt that Serbian officials in the pay of Russia were doing all in their power to instigate revolt in Austria and were implicated in the

murder of the Hereditary Archduke. We must remember that
the Serbians were the most turbulent people in the Balkans, outside of the Albanians, and that but a few years before they had
changed rulers by spectacular murders which one might regard as
appropriate to the forcible deposition of an African Chief in some
bedchamber plot—one entirely out of place among a civilized
people.

No member of our race should find it in his heart to fail to
sympathize with any of the peoples who suffered because of this
war; and nothing here said is with the intention of giving expression to harsh feelings which do not exist, but rather with the intention of trying to lay bare the truth and clarify the situation.

We have heard so much about the violation of the neutrality of
Belgium it would be well to examine into the practical effect heretofore given this guaranteed neutrality not with a view to excus-
ing Germany's entry into Belgium, but to gain some insight into
the real magnitude of the alleged crime, because of which Britain
is said to have entered the war.

The treaty of 1839 is the fountain head of all that has been
said or written about the guaranteed neutrality of Belgium. In
this treaty (it was rather a number of treaties), the States, Austria, France, Holland, Prussia and Russia, agreed that Belgium
should be perpetually a neutral State, and each power agreed or
bound itself not to violate this neutrality. Each of the signatory
powers agreed to abstain from violation of Belgium neutrality,
but none took upon itself the obligation to enforce this neutrality.
This was recognized to be a fact by Lord Palmerston and others,
including Gladstone who secured the consent of both France and
Prussia, under threat of intervention, to a new treaty in 1870, by
which each power bound itself to abstain from violation of Belgian neutrality during the war in which they were then engaged.

The British Government had incurred certain obligations by
secret understanding with France through which she was bound,
at least morally so, to come to the aid of the latter in case of war
with Germany; and, therefore, the Belgian episode was the pre-
text upon which Parliament was induced to enter the war.

Russia, France and England had understood for years that in
case of war with Germany the first shock of troops would come in
Belgium, and the two latter powers had an agreement as to the
number of forces to be placed by Britain on the Belgium frontier,
or in Belgium, if necessary, with or without her consent. Belgium

had been importuned to become a party to this understanding, and, as a matter of fact, the Belgian King, in the spring of 1914, expressed himself as more fearful of a French than of a German invasion. The fact that the French did not rush forces into Belgium and that they issued an order for the withdrawal of French troops ten kilometers from the frontier, was out of deference for British opinion, and to enable the British Ministry to present to the Parliament a complete case of German aggression.

Of course the British Ministry believed that the interests of Great Britain would be served by following France into the war; but, under the circumstances outlined, and in view of England's treatment of Greece, and of the fact that she refused to remain neutral provided Germany did not pass through Belgium, it appears that the Allies had little justification in magnifying the guilt of the Belgian invasion.

It has been abundantly and conclusively shown[319] that from 1891 to 1914, the officials of Russia (this seems to have included the most prominent, if not all) and some of the officials of France, using the original treaty of 1891-94 as a basis, conspired to crush Germany in order that France might regain Alsace-Lorraine and otherwise weaken Germany on the left bank of the Rhine, while Russia acquired Constantinople and the Straits and was to be given a free hand in fixing the eastern frontier of Germany. Russia, under the agreement, was to be given a free hand in the Balkans, and, should some one of the Central Powers, Austria for example, mobilize her troops as the result of Balkan conditions, Russia and France were to mobilize at once and attack, mobilization meaning war.

It is simply childish to talk of excessive German preparation, on the one hand, and lack of preparation and surprise on the part of the Allies, on the other. Each and every one of them had done all it could in the matter of expenditure for war purposes and in hard work toward the creation of an efficient war machine. A simple recital of the numbers, resources and expenditures made in behalf of preparation for war on the part of all the powers involved, should have indicated with reasonable certainty the success of the combination of England, France and Russia in war against that of Germany and Austria. In 1912 Poincare informed

---

[319]See Professor H. E. Barnes' *"The Genesis of the World War,"* and Senator Robert L. Owen's *"The Russian Imperial Conspiracy."*

Izvolski, Russian Ambassador to France, that in the opinion of French military authorities the chances for victory in a war waged by France and Russia alone against Germany and Austria were favorable to the former; and Sir Edward Grey says that it was the opinion of French and British military experts in the spring of 1914 that France and England together could withstand the Central Powers.[320]

The Allies had every reason to believe that a war with the resources of Russia, France and England on one side, against Germany and disorganized and tottering Austria on the other, would be of short duration. The surprise with which the Allies were confronted was that resulting from the underestimation of the efficiency of the German forces, and the strategic advantage they enjoyed because of their geographical position and the equipment they possessed for transportation toward enemies on either flank. This and the fact that England's energies were for a long time employed largely in colonial and other operations rather than along the front in France, together with the corruption and inefficiency of the ruling classes in Russia, came near bringing defeat in a situation in which victory without much delay was a reasonable expectation from outward appearances.

France and England came to depend, it seems, upon the ready sacrifice of men on the part of Russia as a matter of course; and this attitude of mind probably led to an earlier collapse of Russian resistance, after the Revolution, than might have been the case otherwise. Had the Allies shown a more sympathetic understanding of the real difficulties of the Russian situation they would not have insisted that Russia make another aggressive campaign. Doing this doubtless hastened the eventual collapse. *It is possible* that the adoption of a more sympathetic attitude on the part of the Allies toward Russia would have resulted in the maintenance for some time on the East Front of a sufficient body of men to have diverted considerable German forces from the front in France and Belgium This was not done and it is useless to speculate as to what might have happened. The final result was that the newly liberated Russian could see no difference between the ruling classes they had deposed and the representatives of the Allied powers with whom they were formerly associated. They were put in the same class and further aid was refused.

---

[320]See Professor H. E. Barnes' *"The Genesis of the World War,"* pp. 402, 438.

It is true that civilization seems to have been at stake in this struggle, and we cannot feel positively assured that it is yet safe; for the world is still in a chaotic condition from wars now in progress in some places and inability to resume the orderly pursuits of peace and progress in others. This civilization, which is yet on trial and the fate of which is not yet definitely determined, is not French civilization, or that of England or Germany, but the civilization of the White Race; and it has been put in jeopardy not by the aggressions of any one power, but by the short-sighted selfishness of all the principal white powers, some of whom were willing to risk an exhausting war for a temporary commercial or industrial advantage, or the realization of an imperialistic dream, even though it endangered the safety of the whole white world. We may have been accessories, for the course we pursued may not, after all, have been the best in the end. Certainly we do not see any great benefits, either to ourselves or to the white world as a whole, on account of our participation in this war. Had we, immediately after the war began, adequately increased our capital naval forces and added to them the necessary auxiliaries, aircraft and submarine vessels, and made a small effective addition to our army, we would have been in a position to have enforced our demands as to neutral rights *with all ease,* and we would have had a clean and consistent slate conforming to our historic attitude in this respect. Furthermore, we would have been in a position to have intervened in the interests of peace long before exhaustion had arrived and intense hatred awakened; and we could have done this effectively and at less cost than that in which we find ourselves involved in the end. When the war had been carried into the period of exhaustion, a session at the peace table, to which all powers would come with depleted manpower and wealth consumed, was dreaded but little less than a defeat on the field of battle.

AMERICA.

CHAPTER IX.

The early settlers of America came from the best stock in Europe. Among them were the forward looking people who refused longer to submit to the cramped and discouraging surroundings in which they found themselves in Europe, when by going to America their condition could be bettered economically and a greater religious liberty and political freedom there awaited them. Joined with them were adventurous spirits who enjoyed the excitement and uncertainties of existence in a new land in which they hoped fortune would smile upon them. The characters of the Revolutionary period were from these people or their descendents. They had been winnowed from the human chaff and flotsam under the adversities incident to hewing their way in a new land peopled with savages; and they were pre-eminently leaders among men, whose work will ever stand as a monument to their greatness.

The line of descent of these people traced back to home-lands leads us to England, Scotland, Ireland, Germany, Holland, Norway, Sweden, Denmark and France; and these strains continued to come to our shores for many years afterward while the vast territories of the country were being reclaimed for agricultural purposes, and commerce and trade were expanding in a healthy, normal manner. However, with the introduction of modern industrialism and concentration of population in cities, there has come into the country many elements that are undesirable under existing conditions; and this situation, together with the enfranchisement of the large Negro element in the country, compels any thinking person to concede that the American character of to-day is not in any sense comparable to that of Revolutionary times and for many years after, and that the future holds promise of a further lowering of the standard. However, this is not what we are concerned with at present. We are here interested in the fact that we are still, as a people, of European extraction and a powerful nation, and are concerned in our relations to the European world as it bears upon White Solidiarity in the face of a hostile colored world

Early after our Independence and the organization of our government under the Constitution, there was in process of formation two hostile parties in America due to the wars that raged in Europe for many years, and in which the principal actors on the opposite sides were the English and the French. One of these parties was the English party, always ready with excuses for violations of our neutrality by England and anxious to make war on France; on the other hand was the French party, entertaining Genet, Minister from France, and condoning his insolence toward our government, proclaiming all French violations of our neutrality as the just indignation of true Republicanism against the monarchial English in America, and urging war against England. These divisions continued to the great injury of America until we had passed through the War of 1812. The position of America would have been sufficiently trying during this period had there been no dissensions whatever among our people; for throughout the struggle between France and England, both belligerents were highly contemptuous of all our rights and did not give as much attention to our protests as we would now to those of Liberia. Not only was this true as to neutral rights we claimed as a power among the nations of the earth, but the contempt of both powers for us was shown in insults to our citizenry and officials by accredited officials of these powers and the officers of their war vessels visiting our ports. The tribes on the African coasts and their chiefs never received more insulting treatment than did our citizens and government during this period of our infancy.

Yet, throughout this period, our official utterances were persistently and consistently in support of that enlargement of neutral rights that received the approval of our Supreme Court during our Civil Strife, and found lodgment in the accepted principles of International Law prior to 1914. Thus our attitude as to neutral rights became fixed and historic.

The climax of dissension was reach during the War of 1812, when these divisions resulted in lack of support for the government in the prosecution of the war, particularly in New England; in the Hartford Convention; and, at various times, in intrigues on the part of government officials and public characters for the purpose of defeating government policies by unauthorized correspondence and undertakings with representatives of the enemy.

This tendency on the part of Americans to insist that we shall be interested in the affairs of European States to the extent even of dragging us into their wars when we have no interest whatever in them, is an evil persisting to this day; and, in consequence of this, it is essential that we busy ourselves to the end that immigration in quality and in numbers shall be limited to that which is *readily* assimilable and will lend itself to the production of an American type and eventually to homogeneity in our people. Even then we shall have to fight the tendency to meddle in European affairs in behalf of England, which arises from a continuous flow of propaganda that comes in our own tongue through the various channels of publicity used in the dissemination of news, and seems to be a part of our daily life. The dissemination of matter that inevitably leads in this direction must be carried on by powerfully organized forces, and it bears fruit among that class of Americans who believe our destinies lie in the acceptance of England's leadership in world affairs. It seems, however, that this attitude of mind can arise only from the fact that such Americans as support these policies are inflicted with an inferiority complex in the presence of the English. An example of what we get from time to time, and somewhat typical, may be found in the Literary Digest for February 5, 1927, under the heading, "What We Must Do about China." The Digest quotes from numerous newspapers in regard to the Chinese situation and, among others, from a metropolitan newspaper of the great Northwest in which we are cautioned to ponder well the situation before we proceed to act alone without the concert of other Powers. The same editorial suggests, in view of the fact that China is incapable of governing herself and is a menace to the world, she be annexed to the British Empire so that order may be brought out of chaos and peace restored. It seems astonishing that any American editor should give expression to such sentiments as these unless he has learned nothing from history and is totally ignorant of the trend of current affairs in the world. It does not at all follow that resentment over a situation of this character means hostility to England or is prompted by enmity toward her in any degree. Nothing is more natural than that we—the great body of our people, irrespective of particular racial antecedents—should have the kindest feelings for a people who speak the same tongue with us and whose methods of thought and institutions are kindred to our own, and that we should gladly cooperate with them when there is any common, reasonable ground upon which we may do so; but I do resent the attitude of mind that seems to regard us as still in swaddling clothes and unable to go abroad unless under the protection of leading strings in the hands of a stepmother.

"Europe has a set of primary interests, which to us have none, or a very remote relation. Hence she must be engaged in frequent controversies, the causes of which are essentially foreign to our concerns. Hence, therefore, it must be unwise in us to implicate ourselves, by artificial ties, in the ordinary vicissitudes of her policies, or the ordinary combinations and collisions of her friendships or enmities." This admonition of Washington is as much applicable to our dealings with Europe of to-day as it was during our infancy as a nation, when England and France were waging their destructive wars.

We are happily situated in America as compared with the European powers. We are not congested with a dense population and suffering from limited resources; for the latter are sufficient to provide the needs of our increasing population from natural causes for many years to come without our being compelled to seek raw materials and exclusive markets elsewhere. The pressure of necessity does not drive us to these things, and therefore leaves us in a favorable situation to judge dispassionately and impartially of European conduct in this respect, and enables us to form an accurate judgment of the consequences brought about by what may be called competition from population pressure.

Furthermore, we should be able to dispossess ourselves of the evils incident to the prejudice and bitter hatred that persists among the different peoples of Europe, in the interests of our own welfare and possibly that of Europe as well; for collectively we come from Europe—from the several European countries, and not from one of them alone—and should be able to estimate accurately the evils of European discord. Let us hope we shall not again permit them to lead us into the shambles of a war in which we have no vital interests. It is the most natural thing in the world that each of us should have a particular regard and affection for the European country from which our forbears came; and this fact alone should put us on our guard against the advocacy of any partisan intervention on the part of America in any struggle between whites in Europe, which must of necessity be injurious alike to us and them in the long run.

The great destiny of America in view of the advantageous position we enjoy—the exalted duty required of her, spiritual in its nature, as I see it—demands that we shall for all time avoid any and all partisan action in affairs between European powers; and that we shall lose no opportunity to aid in bringing about White Solidarity in world affairs. But as a necessary preliminary to any effective action in these directions, it is absolutely essential we take definite and final steps that will insure our becoming and remaining a homogeneous white people with a distinctive American type.

CHAPTER X.

AMERICAN NEUTRALITY.

When the World War began in 1914, certain definite principles and rules had been accepted in the International Code—that is, if there existed such a body of law—and the following comment is made on the assumption of its existence at that time.

As an incident to carrying on war, the parties thereto, the belligerents, could legally capture neutral goods and neutral ships attempting to violate a legally established and maintained blockade, and also articles contraband destined for the enemy together with the ship carrying them. It is, therefore, of vital importance to know what constitutes a blockade and what makes an article contraband.

The rules established are premised upon the assumption of an impartial conduct on the part of the non-combatant powers, or neutrals.

BLOCKADE

Custom, as evidenced by our practice during the Civil War, as stated in the Declaration of Paris, 1856, and as finally codified under the direction of expert representatives of the Powers taking part in the Conference resulting in the Declaration of London, required that the blockading force should be sufficient to prevent ingress or egress to or from the port, river, harbor, or coast blockaded; and that it should not "extend beyond the ports and coasts belonging to or occupied by the enemy," and "must not bar access to neutral ports or coasts."

CONTRABAND

The same sources declare certain articles used solely for purposes of war, such as ships of war, cannon, and things of like character, to be absolutely contraband, which can, during a war, be captured by either belligerent when destined for the other, either

directly or indirectly; certain other articles are declared to be
conditionally contraband, and may, therefore, be captured when
bound to an enemy's country for use of its armed forces or to an
enemy government for use in the prosecution of the war. The
Declaration of London also contained what is called a "free list"
—a list of articles not to be declared contraband.

It may be candidly admitted at the outset that the World War
was fought under conditions quite different from those encountered in any other war. Some of the old authorities in International Law have insisted that, when actual war began, each and
every individual of one belligerent was at war with each and
every individual of its enemy belligerent. This was true in theory
only, actual operations being confined to the armed forces, though
in certain matters of minor import the individual not connected
with the armed forces had to regulate his conduct with reference
to an actual, existing state of war or suffer the consequences.
With the increase and improvement in means of communication
and transport, bringing distant peoples closer together, and the
development of modern industrialism, there has been brought
about a much wider scope of coordination and inter-dependence
amongst the peoples in all nations; and there has been, therefore,
an increased number of its people directly affected by and included within the governmental operations in war, and an increasing difficulty in determining, during a period of war, what articles going into a belligerent country were for use in carrying on
war and what for the ordinary peaceful pursuits not connected
with the war.

Another new phase of this war resulted from the introduction
of the submarine and aircraft for the first time as weapons of war.
Thus, at the outset, we were confronted with conditions that were
going to make our position as a neutral a difficult one; and it is
interesting to note dispassionately the complications brought
about by the conditions above mentioned and our final reaction
to them. An understanding of the actual facts, and a candid
statement of them, may result in clarifying the situation to a
certain extent and be helpful in bringing about a better understanding.

The English and French ships in the several seas, particularly,
the English, busied themselves from the declaration of hostilities
in clearing the seas of German cruisers and raiders. This was
eventually done in the manner in which such things are usually

done, and we were not involved in any questions of consequence in connection with these operations. However, from the beginning, our rights as a neutral were immensely affected by the conduct of the belligerents in respect to blockade and contraband.

Owing to the fact that the Germans had developed the submarine and made it into an effective war weapon, it was natural to assume they would use it to the fullest possible extent in order to lessen the disparity between the belligerent fleets and win the war. The English at once realized that a blockade of the enemy's ports, as required by usage and International Law, would be accompanied with many hazards; and, in fact, it is doubtful if any sort of effective blockade could have been maintained in the face of hostile submarines. Nor could a blockade be maintained, on the other hand, in the face of superior naval forces of any other type; and, therefore, the inability to establish a legal blockade in the face of hostile submarines and hostile aircraft would not in any sense justify the establishment of an illegal blockade, or resort to other illegal measures in order to compass the inability to establish a legal blockade.

The final outcome of the situation was that England and her allies sowed the North Sea and the English Channel with mines as a protection against the depredations of the submarine upon her commerce, and required all neutral shipping entering either of these bodies of water to call at certain ports, irrespective of the neutral destination of these ships and the character of the cargo. This was, in effect, establishing a blockade by mines; and, if neutral vessels did not come in voluntarily, they were brought in as prize for adjudication on the ground of suspicion that they were carrying contraband to the enemy, England having extended illegally the list of conditional contraband to include practically all articles of commerce. All previous practice on her part in the observance of the rules of International Law in regard to contraband and her obligations under the Declaration of Paris were thrown to the winds. Her own fleet was safely housed in harbor from attack by submarine, and the patrol of her waters was in the hands of minor cruisers, small craft, submarines and aircraft. Eventually every neutral power in Europe was placed upon a ration in violation of International Law and on the assumption that, if these countries had anything in excess of their minimum national needs, this excess in goods or supplies might find its way into the enemy country. All seaborne trade was taken into her hands and no country could trade with any other except by permission of England, if the communication was by water; and she would not permit any goods or supplies to go into the neutral countries of Europe, except upon her own terms as to their disposition and assurance to her satisfaction that they would not reach Germany or her allies. The merchants or manufacturing concerns of our own country who desired to import wool, rubber, or tin were required to enter into formal agreement, under oath, as to the disposition of the crude material received, the manufactured articles made therefrom, and other matters; our merchants, manufacturers, and shipping people were blacklisted if they did anything contrary to the wishes of English representatives swarming on our coasts. This blacklisting went even so far that, before we entered the war, Austrian and German merchant ships interned in some of our ports were compelled to obtain supplies for the ships and the men on board of them surreptitiously from dealers, who would not supply them openly for fear of being blacklisted. English consular offices were X-raying the packages in all cargoes, sealing hatches, and furnishing certificates to avoid seizure and detention of cargoes; but it seems to have been seldom that this accomplished the purpose for which it was intended, practically all vessels being taken into port, detained, and put to heavy expense, irrespective of what may have been done previously under direction of English authority. Cotton was by the Declaration of London on the free list—not contraband, but by illegal practices and intimidation on the part of England (she finally put cotton on the contraband list), together with non-support of our own cotton people in their rights by our government, the market for about one-third of the cotton crop was cut off and the resulting losses from the drop in price below the cost of production were heavy and much felt. England, taking advantage of the situation brought about by her illegal practices, appears to have overstocked in cotton at a low price and to have taken over the cotton trade with neutrals in Europe.

This is borne out by statistics obtained from the official journal of the Manchester (England) Cotton Association. The cotton year, it seems, ends on the Friday nearest to July 31. In 1911-12 the total imports of cotton in bales were 605,962 (American cotton, 466,264), whereas the total exports were 507,000 (American, 315,000); in 1912-13, imports 578,020 (American, 397,935), exports 429,000 (American, 233,000); in 1913-14, imports 907,562 (American, 614, 682), exports 342,000 (American, 177,000); in 1914-15, imports 1,505,500 (American, 1,197,650), exports 519,000 (American 249,000).[321]   When, upon the outbreak of the war, we acquiesced in the closing of the ports of the Central Powers and those of European neutrals as well, the result was a great slump in the price of cotton. That England, under the circumstances, should have stocked up in low-priced cotton and have taken over our cotton trade with European neutrals is not surprising in the least. It would be difficult to imagine her, or any other nation for that matter, doing otherwise as long as we quietly submitted to a situation we could have terminated any time by firmly making known our intention to do so.

As the war proceeded, neutral rights became of less and less consequence to the belligerents on either side in view of the fact that, as it must have appeared to them, we were willing to submit rather than insist upon our rights with our might. The English established a war zone that shut off communication with neutrals of Western Europe via the north coast of Scotland and the North Sea, and advised neutrals to route their vessels by way of the English Channel, thus facilitating taking them all in for such disposition as they saw fit; some months later Germany established a war zone that included the English Channel and surrounded the British Isles, and advised neutrals that the only safe route was that north of Scotland and along a strip of sea not far from the coast of Norway.

Germany's activities in submarine warfare were extended until she finally interdicted all communication with Great Britain under threat of sinking any and all ships found within certain limits around the British Isles. The final situation was this: Our seaborne commerce with any and all peoples was interdicted by both belligerents. That on the part of Great Britain was carried into effect without loss of life, except in cases where it may have occurred through contact with British mines with which she largely carried out what was in effect a blockade, because of the fact of her overwhelming seaborne power that enabled her to cover the seas with her war vessels of some character; that of Germany did result in loss of life in her use of the submarine against merchant ships.

The United States Government was at all times in a position to

---

[321]*"American Rights and British Pretensions,"* pp. 27, 30.

require both belligerents to observe scrupulously our rights as a neutral; but it did not do so. When we tacitly acquiesced in the illegal supervision and control of all neutral trade by Great Britain, we were, in effect, aiding the cause of the Allies and injuring that of Germany; and we thus gave the latter cause for complaint. This was fully appreciated by Mr. Bryan when Secretary of State[322] and seems to have been realized by our Executive. "My frank criticism," says Joseph P. Tumulty, "deeply aroused him. Replying to me he pitilessly attacked those who were criticising him for 'letting up on Great Britain.' Looking across the table at me he said: 'I am aware of the demands that are daily being made upon me by my friends for more vigorous action against England in the matter of the blockade; I am aware also of the sinister political purpose that lies back of many of these demands. Many senators and congressmen who urge radical action against England are thinking only of German votes in their districts and are not thinking of the world crisis that would inevitably occur should there be an actual breach at this time between England and America over the blockade.' Then looking squarely at me, he said: I have gone to the very limit in pressing our claims upon England and in urging the British Foreign Office to modify the blockade. Walter Page, our Ambassador to England, has placed every emphasis upon our insistence that something be done, and something will be done, but England, now in the throes of a great war crisis, must at least be given a chance to adjust these matters. Only a few days ago Mr. Page wrote me a most interesting letter, describing the details of a conference he had had with Sir Edward Grey, the British Foreign Secretary, to discuss our protest against the British blockade. Mr. Page described the room in which the conference was held, on the wall of which was hung as a memorial the fifteen-million-dollar check with which Great Britain paid the *Alabama* claims in the Civil War. Mr. Page pointed to this *Alabama* check and said: "If you don't stop these seizures, Sir Edward, some day you will have your entire room papered with things like that." Sir Edward replied: "That may be so, but we will pay every cent. Of course, many of the restrictions we have laid down and which seriously interfere with

---

[322]See Mr. Bryan's letter to the President, dated April 23, 1915; Professor H. E. Barnes' *"Genesis of the World War,"* pp. 599-601, taken from *"The Memoirs of William Jennings Bryan,"* pp. 396-7.

your trade are unreasonable. But America must remember that we are fighting her fight, as well as our own, to save the civilization of the world. You dare not press us too far!" ' Turning to me, the President said: 'He was right. England is fighting our fight and you may well understand that I shall not, in the present state of the world's affairs, place obstacles in her way. Many of our critics suggest war with England in order to force reparation in these matters. War with England would result in a German triumph. No matter what may happen to me personally in the next election, I will not take any action to embarrass England when she is fighting for her life and the life of the world. Let those who clamour for radical action against England understand this!' "323

Each belligerent, from the time the war began in Europe, exerted itself to the utmost to secure the goodwill and sympathy of the United States, the two principal actors in this respect being Great Britain and Germany. Neither hesitated to advance the most preposterous falsehoods with the minutest details of description, some of which were based upon occurrences scarcely justifying mention and others without any justification whatever in fact.324 We were again divided into two camps in a manner similar to those existing for a long time after the Revolution. In this latter case, however, one camp contained the German sympathizers, the other, that of the French and English. Soon after the war began the German propaganda sank into insignificance in comparison with that of the English; for, with the isolation of Germany, *all foreign news came to us censored by British or French officials*, and it was always colored with an account of some alleged German atrocity or cruelty. It was only a question of time, under the wearing away of opposition by this constant stream of propaganda, when the American public would be ready, even anxious, to enter the war in behalf of the Allies.

In the mean time America had become a veritable arsenal for the Allies. Nominally we were neutral, but it is doubtful if we can be considered to have been so upon any critical or, for that matter, even any honest, superficial examination of the actual

---

323"*Woodrow Wilson As I Know Him*," pp. 230-1, Doubleday, Page & Company.

324See Professor H. E. Barnes' "*The Genesis of the World War*," and Senator Robert L. Owen's "*The Russian Imperial Conspiracy of 1892-1914*, in regard to propaganda by the Allies.

situation. Soon after the slump due to the cotton situation, re-ferred to above, things began to pick up in a business way; for the Allies were in need of all we could send them in the way of both ordinary provisions and supplies and war materials and munitions. These Powers did not, at that time, find any objec-tion to the fact that business was brisk with us, and we were ap-parently making money out of the necessities of their situation. They knew full well that our neutrality was most benevolent so far as they were concerned. The ordinary business affairs of the country were disarranged to the extent found necessary to ac-commodate ourselves to the production of all the needs of the Allies, including munitions of war. When necessary to do so, money was found for the purchase of magazines and papers for purposes of propaganda, or to establish or aid in establishing mu-nitions plants, and this money came from the Allies or their Amer-ican friends. Every rule of International Law that has any rela-tion to the right of neutrals to deal in contraband of war, cer-tainly has in view, as a foundation premise upon which these rules are postulated, a situation in which the ordinary commercial and manufacturing interests of the community shall not be replaced entirely, or even largely, by one in which the energies of the peo-ple are devoted to the supply of warlike materials. This situation may certainly raise the question of neutrality, if the party ad-versely affected is in a position to do so.

Furthermore, our treatment of the submarine issue is open to question of fairness under the circumstances of professed neu-trality. We should not have done less than insist upon protec-tion of American vessels from attack by submarine. But when we went to the extent of declaring that an American citizen on board of a belligerent merchantman should serve to protect it from attack by an enemy submarine, we were establishing a prec-edent that may some day be brought home to us to our own in-jury; and, when we, under the circumstances failed to insist upon our rights from both belligerents, we laid ourselves open to the charge of observing a partial neutrality.

In the early case of the Nereide it was strongly urged that a neutral, placing himself and his goods aboard an armed British merchantman under charter to seek British convoy, had so adopted the enemy character as to bring the consequent penalties upon himself and his goods when this merchantman was captured by an American vessel, we being then at war with Great Britain.

This view was held by Justice Story, the leading authority of his time in all the world in the matter of "Prize," captures at sea in time of war, and he was supported in this view by one other member of the court. The decision in this case partook of one new in its nature and arising for the first time, as there seem to have been no authoritative decisions purporting to bear directly upon the matters in issue. Chief Justice Marshall and, it seems, three other members, one member being absent, concurred in the opinion that an association of the character mentioned did not operate to infect the neutral goods with penalty of forfeiture. (9 Cranch, 388). There is a vast difference, however, between holding that the presence of a neutral's goods on board of an armed enemy merchantman taking convoy with an enemy warship does not subject such goods to condemnation as prize, and holding that the presence of a neutral on a belligerent merchant ship protects such ship from attack by a submarine of the enemy.

We certainly gave the Allied Powers no cause for complaint as to our conduct; for our neutrality was extremely benevolent towards them in its partiality from the beginning. They were allowed to secure any and all kinds of essential supplies, war materials and munitions; were supplied with funds with which to meet the situation from American sources when necessary; were not only permitted to carry on a campaign for our entrance into the war in their support but received much encouragement and help in this direction, and were aided in disseminating propaganda to the effect that they were fighting our battles in behalf of civilization. With the active aid of sympathizers for the Allied cause, this campaign was continued until we finally went into the war on their side and cast that final, decisive power and strength in the conflict, however small or however great it may have been, that rescued the Allied cause from certain defeat and turned it into victory. This we did in behalf of a people engaged in a war with the origin of which we had no connection of the remotest kind, and in the result of which we had no direct interest whatever, other than what would necessarily follow from the dreadful loss of white blood, the weakening of the white world, the shattering of White Solidarity, and the exhaustion of the world. That this is true, should be apparent from all that went before and from all that has been done since the Allied powers sat at the peace table and found there were not spoils enough for all, and that even victors cannot always escape the penalty attached to waging war.

Now, it seems, we are execrated by all; held up to the world as a selfish, material people, who are interested in nothing but making money and parading our wealth before a poverty stricken and exhausted world from whose people we are incidentally exacting the Shylock pound of flesh; we are told they fought our battles for us while we were making money by manufacturing contraband of war for them and gathering in their reserves of wealth; and that when these reserves were exhausted we finally went into the war to save their debts to us. This comes with ill-grace from a people who have for centuries been engaged in commerce, trade and manufacturing; who, through shrewdness and sharp practices, have for many years exploited the exploitable world; and who have maintained their commercial and financial ascendency, thus gained, by crushing any people that threatened this supremacy, playing one combination against another, and striking relentlessly at the proper moment to accomplish this. With all our shortcomings we have no such unenviable record as this. This does not mean that we are in possession of any innate qualities that place us above such conduct; but it does mean that we are so situated that we do not of necessity, in any sense of the word, have to join in this mad competition that, as it is now practiced, inevitably leads to war. If we should do so now, it will be because we deliberately will it so, and we shall be unable to justify it by reference to any measure of necessity. Nothing offensive is intended by this; but it does seem rather strange, however, that we, who have heretofore been noted for staying at home, attending to our own busines, and trying to be just and fair in all our international dealings, should be accused of a greedy materialism by peoples who have for centuries been venturing over the wide world in search of material fortune and taking it when opportunity presented without much regard to the ethics of the situation.

CHAPTER XI.

PEACE.

With the Powers situated as outlined in the preceding chapters it would, indeed, have been a miracle if a constructive peace had resulted from the gathering at Versailles; and yet our President went to it with the expectation that this might be done. As a matter of fact, at the time of our entry into the war exhaustion had gone so far that the only hope held out by victory was relief in such compensation as might be had from the defeated and yet, reading his war message in the light of subsequent events, it is seen that he had in mind at that time the League of Nations that he subsequently advocated with all his strength. "Our object now, as then," said he, "is to vindicate the principles of peace and justice in the life of the world as against selfish and autocratic power, and to set up among the really free and self-governed peoples of the world such a concert of purpose and of action as will henceforth insure the observance of those principles . . . We are at the beginning of an age in which it will be insisted that the same standards of conduct and of responsibility for wrong done shall be observed among nations and their governments that are observed among the individual citizens of civilized States."

The treaty that terminated hostilities for the time being was not a peace attained by mutual concessions in instances where the path of justice was not clearly marked out for perception by all; but one exacted by conquerors—weary and exhausted conquerors, who were in a bad humor and seeking compensations for losses in a war-weary distracted world.

Surely any one who imagined that a new era was ushered in by the plenipotentiaries at Versailles, when they produced the League of Nations with its Covenant and the Treaty which was to be enforced by the League, should not be able to persist in this delusion in the light of subsequent international events. The treaty was simply an old type, old style treaty in which the conquerors, after much debate and much delay, formulated certain demands as to indemnities in money and cessions of territory and presented them to the conquered for formal acceptance. There was no negotiation with the conquered, the only negotiation being that between the Allies in regard to the reconciliation of their several demands for indemnities and cession of territories. The treaty showed much evidence of good will and unselfish generosity where this could be had at the expense of the conquered and without interference with appropriate indemnities and cessions of territory to the conquerors; but there was no evidence whatever of generosity or the existence of an era of good will when it came to sacrifices being made by any of the conquerors. As a matter of fact, it is only in recent months that conflicting contentions in regard to mandates, spheres of influence, or territorial control in the Near East have been settled between some of the principal powers; and this was not finally done until they had actually engaged in war by proxy through Greece and Turkey. The treaty inflamed anew old sores, and introduced many new elements of discord in the European situation as potential causes of war. The straw thing created to carry into effect this iniquitous treaty that was to end war—the League of Nations— served merely the purpose of giving a euphonious designation to the concerted action of the principal Powers when they could bring themselves into a concerted action of any kind in carrying out the provisions of the treaty. It is folly to regard the League of Nations as an instrumentality of peace resulting from a new conception of international duty and regard for right, when its practical workings depend upon the Principal Powers who are yet struggling one with the other for exclusive rights, concessions, or advantages of some kind among the backward peoples to a greater degree possibly than in the times preceding the World War.

The League of Nations does seem to perform a useful function of a kind—that of a clearing house in which some of the quarrels between the victors and others are threshed out. A degree of publicity is given these matters which must have a wholesome effect in the long run; but it is doubtful as to how far this procedure has replaced direct negotiations and secret understandings in important matters.

The second feature that may eventually prove of some value is that relating to Mandatories; for this, after a manner, touches upon that most prolific source of troubles leading to war—the exploitation of backward peoples by means of concessions, exclusive privileges, and direct political control. The provision for Mandatories was included in the Covenant upon the insistence of our President at the Peace Conference in lieu of direct acquisition as a colony by one of the Allied Powers. It is doubtful if any of these Powers imagined that the provision relating to Mandatories, contained in Article 22 of the Covenant, would do anything other than bring about a theoretical condition which would, in practice, amount to the direct political control of the mandated territory as a colony. The provision may prove to be the entering wedge that will in the end lead to a more cordial solidiarity among the white powers than has ever existed before.

CHAPTER XII.

SOLUTION.

The solution had in view, to state it in general terms, involves the pooling of interests among backward peoples by the principal White Powers; and this, in turn, involves distinguishing between colonial areas capable of being converted into a home-land for members of our race by colonization, and such areas as are held solely for purposes of exploitation. The areas affected are Africa, Europe, and parts of Asia; and parts of North and South America should be considered in connection with colonization.

The term "Exploitation" has come to be used in such a way that it has an offensive sound to many of us; but if we confine it to the development of the natural resources in backward countries with a due regard to the interests of both the backward peoples in these areas and to a common right of enjoyment on the part of all white peoples, it will cease to be an evil and become a positive good. The evils appear when competition for the industrial advantages of exploitation become keen. Under these conditions all sorts of plots and conspiracies are brought into play by the parties interested; methods are used without hesitancy by representatives of the Powers interested that would be resented with indignity if imputed to them in private transactions; chaotic disorder is introduced among the exploited peoples, and eventually war results. A development of the natural resources of a backward country with the introduction of modern means of communication and transportation and modern conveniences that make life more comfortable, will, if the people in these areas are treated with justness and given opportunities to enjoy some of these advantages, be more effective in impressing upon such people the true worth of Christianity, as represented in the colonial authority, than the preachings of all the missionaries that might be crowded in the area—provided there be firmness and justice and lack of bickering amongst the exploiters themselves.

If white civilization is to be preserved there must be established a *modus vivendi* under which the good of the race as a whole is sought, and under which we can gradually adjust ourselves in accordance with a deliberately planned campaign for the relief of pressure from overpopulation in certain centers; and, as stated above, this involves the pooling of interests in backward areas and colonization.

No power has any particular right, by conquest or otherwise, to the exploitation of specific backward areas from which all others shall be excluded, if it is to involve us in additional wars amongst ourselves to determine who shall enjoy it for a period of years in the future. Under such circumstances all White Powers become vitally interested in safeguarding themselves against future conflicts.

France and England possess enormous areas on the face of the earth which they have acquired by numerous wars, much of which is held for purposes of exclusive exploitation and incapable of being colonized and made a home-land for members of our race. Some of these areas contain colonists, others without them may become the home-land for white colonists so far as climate and natural conditions are concerned, but neither England nor France has the population to convert these areas into the land of the white man. England it is true has a greater population than she can support upon her own natural resources, but it may not be greater than she can support for some years to come because of her industrial position. But even if this view should be wrong, she has not that excess population that would properly take care of the colonization areas within her domains. France, on the other hand, with her enormous domains, some of them fit for colonization, cannot reclaim and hold them for the white world simply because she has no excess population to send to these lands.

England has held sway in India for many years, and her continuance in possession during this time has led to several wars in which other white powers were involved. This possession of India does not benefit the white world in the least aside from the direct benefit to the English who profit by commerce and trade and such indirect benefit, if any, as may come to the rest of the white world through this; for India is not and can never be made a white man's land otherwise than by wholesale extermination of its inhabitants. This occupation has been beneficial to India in accordance with modern industrial ethics. Under her regime peace has been preserved in a country formerly turbulent and incapable of preserving peace; the lower strata in the caste system have had dealt out to them a measure of justice to which they were strangers before; many of the people have been dragged from the depths of ignorance and superstition; and the population has been trebled, though this last may be considered a doubtful blessing. It may be even doubted if this uplift work, largely incidental to exploitation, has been beneficial to either the people or the world at large. If these people are not capable of carrying through, by cohesive purpose and constancy in action, some of the legitimate aspirations that have been developed as a result of this uplift work, then they have become a dangerous disorganized element, which, incapable of direct aggression themselves, may become a positive menace in the hands of ambitious foes. Under existing conditions, therefore, no one who has the best interests of the White race at heart would advocate the policy of "scuttle" in India. It is to our interest that India remain in the control of the White race; but this retention should cease to be the central policy in England's world affairs involving herself and other white powers in war.

North Africa and South Africa, Southwest Asia, and all of North and South America should be and remain not only areas of white political control, but the White man's home to the same extent as is Europe. This can be done only if the white powers come together and agree as to some colonization scheme and some scheme for pooling interests in the exploitation areas that exist outside of the sections to be devoted to colonization.

Any scheme of colonization naturally divides itself into two spheres of operation, one having to do with the New World, the other with the Old World. In the former America is jointly interested with Europe, in the latter it is a matter that directly concerns Europe alone. Canada, with Argentine, Chile, and other South and Central American countries should join together with us for the purpose of framing some policy in the encouragement of immigration to those sections in which the need therefor is most urgent. When a policy satisfactory to the Americas is arrived at in this manner, then Europe should be consulted in order to come to an understanding for drawing from her several Powers the white immigrants desired. This should be undertaken jointly by the several Powers; and would serve to relieve the pressure of over-population where it exists and bring a much needed population to areas which will become Asiatic unless this be done or the threat averted by war.

The situation in Africa involves not only the question of colonization but that of exploitation areas in which Europe alone is concerned, except in so far as the peace and welfare of the whole white world is bound up in that of Europe to a large degree. The first step in the right direction would appear to be a division of the areas under political control into those which are properly considered areas for colonization and those which are held for purposes of exploitation. The latter should be held open alike to all the nationals of the White Powers under identically the same conditions; and the areas which are retained by the respective Powers for colonization purposes should be thrown open to colonists from the other White Powers under the same favorable conditions as their own nationals enjoy unless the Power in control can supply all the immigrants desired, which is a condition hardly likely to occur in any case. In places where there is an indigenous white population in these backward areas, every effort should be made to awaken their race pride and every encouragement given for their education and advancement as is afforded the nationals of the power in control, and every cause for complaint as to discriminations in administration and general control removed. Of course, it cannot be expected that a thing of this kind should be accepted in its entirety at once and applied in its perfection. It would be a matter of growth, but we can, at least, hope for an adoption of some such scheme in principle.

The matter of the administration of the so-called Mandatories has already come up for serious discussion in the Council of the League and has been the subject of comment by spokesmen for the various Cabinets. Germany is now a member of the League of Nations, holds a permanent seat in the Council and a place on the Mandates Commission formerly held by a Spanish member; and she will undoubtedly press the issue in relation to the Mandate for her former colonies at a convenient time. Germany, like the other parties, is not here working for any altruistic purpose, but there are possibilities of good in the situation.

There has been a continuation of the former colonial parties in Germany and they are still working with the hope of regaining their lost colonies. They hold to the view that the mandate, so far as relates to these colonies, was temporary in character and instituted to bridge over the transitionary period antecedent to her taking her place in the League and assuming her former place among the powers.

The Mandates Commission seems to have taken its duties as something more serious than the mere formal and perfunctory acquiescence in the wishes of the Mandatory Powers; and issues have already arisen in connection with the duties of this body. Sir Austin Chamberlain has resented criticism of the British policy in Palestine by the Commission, and the suggestion by the Commission that it should make investigations directly in its own behalf in certain cases has encountered opposition. The British Premier and Colonial Secretary seem to hold to the view that Britain received the Mandates from the League but holds them in her own right. This is, of course, an open avowal that these are British colonies and that Great Britain does not look with favor upon meddling with them by the League. Recently the Governor of Tanganyika (formerly German East Africa), in his address to the Legislative Council, affirmed the permanency of the British mandate and stated the declaration was made with full authority of the British Government.[325]

Katharine J. Gallagher, Professor of European History, Goucher College; Instructor, Johns Hopkins University, in an article in Current History for February, 1927, entitled, "The Problem of the Former German Colonies," says, among other things: "There seemed to be three main parties in the congress (referring to the meeting of German colonial societies in Hamburg from July 31 to August 4, 1926): (1) The extremists, who demanded the return of the colonies intact; (2) those who felt that negotiations could be carried through with France and England for some special colony or mandate, or, at least, for economic opportunities in the mandates, and (3) those who hoped for the opening up of new colonial opportunities. Among these latter the pamphlet of Dr. Schacht, entitled *The New Colonial Policy*, was very influential. Dr. Schacht advocated the revival of chartered companies (some modern form of the London or Virginia Company of hallowed memory), which, with the aid of American and British capital, should undertake the exploitation of colonial resources. He suggested the empty spaces of Canada or Australia as desirable sites for the experiment. His main contention, however, was in regard to Germany's need of colonies.

---

[325]*Current History*, March, 1927, p. 924.

'The fight for raw materials,' he declared, 'plays the most important part in world politics, an even greater role than before the war. The problem of surplus population, though not now acute, will soon become the spectre it formerly was. The only solution of these problems is the acquisition of colonies.' Without the continuous commerce which only colonies can give he did not see how Germany was to secure the favorable balance of trade which alone could make certain her contributions under the Dawes agreement." (Pp. 667-8)

"In the Reichstag itself the political parties of the Right and Centre are favorable to the colonial movement, but not pledged to it. The Government group will not even push it until word is given from headquarters. Even the Socialists support it, though the Communists, under Bolshevist influence, are opposed. In view of the general opinion, Herr Stresemann would be singularly unresponsive to national interests if he failed to push colonial claims. . . . . The colonial question should be considered in a large way. Italy is sadly in need of fields of expansion. Italy and Germany are confronted with the same necessities. It is a little unfortunate that Italy's ambitions appear to lie outside of the mandate system, and a mere adjustment of mandates will not solve the whole question. The sudden capitulation of Turkey on the subject of Mosul, and her unexpected application at the last session of the League of Nations for admission into the League are probably not unrelated to the question of Italy's colonial ambitions. A new distribution of colonial territory would have to include Italy and Spain, as well as Germany. It is to be doubted whether France and Great Britain are yet large-visioned enough to realize that this might well be thoroughly considered before it becomes a dangerous necessity." (P.668).

As has been already stated the matter of spheres of influence, concessions, colonies, and mandates of European powers among the backward people of Africa and Asia is one in which we have no direct concern; but we nevertheless have European affairs thrust upon us in connection with debts due us by European powers as a result of the World War. Not only are these matters thrust upon us by the Europeans themselves, but by many of our own people who insist the Allied powers were fighting our battles before we entered into the war. It is not to be wondered at, therefore, that the Powers indebted to us should hasten to assert the same matters, and contend that the debts due should be cancelled in payment of these services in our behalf. The Americans who are lending themselves to a campaign of this character are injuring their own countrymen and are not helping Europe in any way. The truth of the matter is that this war arose from circumstances which were the logical consequences of the pursuit of selfish ends by all the Powers involved and which formed a continuous chain of inter-related events that led inevitably to war. With these events we were in no manner concerned or in any way connected. Neither England, nor France, nor Russia, nor Italy, nor Belgium nor any other country, fought any battles for us or protected us in any way either prior or subsequent to our entry into the war. Our fate as a power was at no time, either prior or subsequent to our entry into the war, compromised or endangered in the sense in which the propaganda was carried forward. No single one of the belligerents was fighting for the preservation of its civilization or any particular type of it. All were engaged in a war, in the condemnation for which all should have been included; and to attempt to shift the major burden of guilt on any particular power or powers on some technical ground is as barren of useful results as would be a discussion as to how many angels may stand upon the point of a needle. When the war was finally launched in its frightfulness, all were hard put to survive under the drains of life, culture, and treasure that were being exacted each day of its continuance. Doubtless the nationals of each belligerent were led to believe that they were engaged in a holy cause; that they were fighting for the preservation of civilization; and for the purpose of outlawing war. This certainly was the prevailing idea in the American mind when we entered into the struggle; and, since the most of us are no longer suffering from this delusion, there seems to be no reason why we should make any further sacrifices that will not be productive of any results toward the attainment of White Solidarity or anything else for the good of the race. Unless we can see our way clear to bring about accord and understanding among the European powers by doing so, there exists no equitable consideration that might urge a cancellation of European indebtedness. This we have already done to a very considerable degree, although there is every reason why we should refuse to forgive one penny unless in so doing it will prove helpful in bringing about a mutual understanding for the common good and promote concord and solidarity among the White race.

If the European nations will come to a common understanding in regard to emigration into colonization areas to be reclaimed for the White race and held by them, and also come to an understanding in regard to pooling interests in exploitation areas among the backward peoples, the surrender by us of their total indebtedness to us would be a small price to pay as our contribution to this desirable end. But to cancel these debts merely as a matter of grace to the debtor nations would not elevate our character in their opinion, in which it could not sink much lower judging by the constant stream of abuse that reaches us, and would brand us a people without intelligence—one suffering from an inferiority complex as well.

From the view-point of the industrial economist large areas in Southwest Asia, the African Continent, and Central and South America have been but scratched upon the surface in so far as relates to the development of natural resources and the building up of industries appropriate to these areas. The intelligent direction to these areas of the excess numbers of Europeans from overpopulated centers and the adoption of labor saving devices in the countries from which the emigrants go, will result in an increased demand for articles of trade or commerce in the newly developed areas and a stimulus to industry in the migratory centers free from the deadening effect in these communities of large numbers of unemployed. Such procedure would help bridge over the period of readjustment without disaster.

If there is any possibility of the development of the Negro, the location of a Negro State somewhere in Africa between the Sahara and the Union of South Africa under the auspices of the United States, and in which the superior American Negro might be given an opportunity for work in his own behalf, would result in the development of Africa, and world trade and industry would be much stimulated.

If, in connection with what has just been outlined, there could be brought about an understanding of some sort under which all White Powers should receive some recognition in exploitation areas not appropriate for colonizatin by the whites, a long step toward White Solidarity would be brought about.

At the same time the nationalist aspirations of China and

Japan as Asiatic Powers should be given fullest recognition as such.

God knows there is every reason why the differences between all members of the White race should be compromised in seeking the common good, but this will never be accomplished through hypocritical pretense that matters are otherwise than they are. Good can come only through the association of the principal White Powers in an honest endeavor to compromise their conflicting interests in a manner that will actually be in the interest of all in the end. This will of necessity involve the sacrifice of some grandiose ambitions that could not, any how, have been realized in the end; but it will enable these Associated Powers eventually to bring all white peoples into a unity of action when the welfare of all requires that this be done. If these Powers cannot see that their real self-interest lies in the direction of mutual concessions in the interest of peace and the strength of union in world affairs, it is presumed America will be able to survive as long as the others do unless we deliberately and with our eyes open permit our land to become a second Egypt or India.

BIBLIOGRAPHY

A

Adams, Charles Francis, *"Light Reflected from Africa,"* Century
    Magazine, Vol. 72.
Allen, Stephen Haley, *"The Evolution of Governments and Laws,"*
    Princeton University Press, 1916.
Archer, William, *"Through Afro-America,"* E. P. Dutton & Co.,
    1910.
Army and Navy Register, *"The Color Line in the C. M. T. C."*
    Issue for April 9, 1927.

B

Barnes, Professor H. E., *"The Genesis of the World War,"* Alfred
    A. Knopf.
Bjorkman, Edwin, *"The Search for Atlantis,"* Alfred A. Knopf.
Brawley, Benjamin, *"The Negro in Literature and Art,"* Duffield &
    Company, 1918.
Bryce, James, D. C. L., *"The Relations of the Advanced and Back-*
    ward Races of Mankind," Oxford at the Clarendon Press,
    London, Henry Frowde, Amen Corner, E. C., 1903.
Burr, Clinton Stoddard, *"America's Race Heritage,"* The National
    Historical Society, 1922.

C

Catlin, George, *"North American Indians,"* Chatto & Windus, Lon-
    don, 1876.
Carroll, Chas., *"The Negro a Beast or In the Image of God,"* Amer-
    ican Book and Bible House, St. Louis, Mo., 1900.
Caucasian, *"Anthropology for the People: A Refutation of the*
    Theory of the Adamic Origin of All Races," Everett Wad-
    dey Co., Richmond, Va., 1891.
Clowes, W. Laird, *"Black America,"* Cassell & Company, Limited,
    London, 1891.
Cooley, Judge Thomas M., *"Principles of Constitutional Law,"* 2nd
    ed., by Alexis C. Angell, Boston: Little, Brown, and Com-
    pany, 1891.
Cox, Earnest Sevier, *"White America,"* White American Society,
    Richmond, Va., 1923.
Crozier, Dr. John Beattie, *"Sociology Applied to Practical Politics,"*
    Longmans, Green and Co., London, 1911.
Current History, *"Tanganyika,"* issue for March, 1927, and *"The*
    Problem of the Former German Colonies," by Katharine J.
    Gallagher, issue for February, 1927.

D

Darwin, Charles, *"The Descent of Man,"* D. Appleton and Company, 1895.

Daily Press, Newport News, Va., June 27, 1926, *"Campaign to Raise a Million to Fight 'Jim Crow' Law Is Started in Chicago,"* by National Association for the Advancement of Colored People.

Donnelly, Ignatius, *"Atlantis; The Antediluvian World,"* Harper & Brothers, 1910.

Dorsey, Professor George A., *"Why We Behave Like Human Beings,"* Harper & Brothers, 1925.

Dowd, Professor Jerome, *"The Negro in American Life,"* The Century Co., 1926.

DuBois, Dr. W. E. Burghardt, *"Darkwater,"* Harcourt, Brace and Howe, 1920, and *"The Souls of Black Folk,"* A. C. McClurg, & Co., 1903.

E

Encyclopædia Britannica.

G

Gallagher, Katharine J., *"The Problem of the Former German Colonies,"* Curren History for February, 1927.

Grant, Madison, *"The Passing of the Great Race,"* Charles Scribner's Sons, 1921.

H

Hale, William Bayard, *"American Rights and British Pretensions on the Seas,"* Robert M. McBride & Company, 1915.

K

Kawakami, K. K., *"Japan Looks to America,"* Harpers Magazine for March, 1927.

L

Literary Digest, *"What Must We Do About China?"* February 5, 1927.

Living Age, *"An Ethnological Potpourri,"* Arnold Hollriegel's *"The West Indian Pepperpot,"* January 1, 1927.

Lull, Professor Richard Swan, *"The Way of Life,"* Harper & Brothers, 1925.

M

McCarthy, Justin, *"A History of Our Own Times,"* Merrill & Baker.

McMaster, John Bach, "*A History of the People of the United States*," D. Appleton and Company, 1888-1913.

Mecklin, Professor John Moffatt, "*Democracy and Race Friction*," Macmillan Company, 1914.

Military Historian and Economist, "*A Japanese Opinion*," (October, 1916), Harvard University Press, January, 1917.

Mulhall, Marion McMurrough, "*Beginnings or Glimpses of Vanished Civilizations*," Longmans, Green and Co., London, 1911.

N

Neame, L. E., "*Oriental Labor in South Africa*," p. 181, Annals of the American Academy of Political and Social Science, Vol. XXXIV, No. 2, September, 1909.

O

Owen, Senator Robert L., "*The Russian Imperial Conspiracy*," Albert and Charles Boni.

P

Patterson, Raymond, "*The Negro and His Needs*," Fleming H. Revell Company, 1911.

Payne, Rev. B. H., "*The Negro: What Is His Ethnological Status?*" "Ariel."

Plecker, Dr. W. A., "*Virginia's Attempt to Adjust the Color Problem*." Paper read before the American Public Health Association at Detroit, October 23, 1924.

R

Ridpath, John Clark, "*Universal History*," The Jones Brothers Publishing Company, Cincinnati, and Merrill & Baker, New York, 1899.

Ross, Professor Edward Alsworth, "*The Old World in the New*," The Century Co., 1914.

S

Shaler, Professor Nathaniel S., "*The Neighbor*," Houghton Mifflin Co., 1904.

Shannon, Rev. A. H., "*Racial Integrity*," Publishing House of the M. E. Church, South, 1907. (Printed for the author).

Short, John T., "*The North Americans of Antiquity*," Harper & Brothers, 1879.

Simonds, Frank H., "*History of the World War*," Doubleday, Page & Company, 1917.

Smith, Professor G. Elliot, "*The Influence of Racial Admixture in Egypt*," Eugenics Review, October, 1915, Vol. 7.

Spence, Lewis, *"The Problem of Atlantis,"* William Rider & Son, Limited, London, 1924.

Stoddard, Lothrop, *"The Rising Tide of Color,"* Charles Scribner's Sons, 1920.

Stone, Alfred Hart, *"'Studies in the American Race Problem,"* Doubleday, Page & Company, 1908.

Swinton, William, *"Outlines of the World's History,"* Ivison, Blakeman & Company, New York and Chicago, 1874.

T

Tatsuki, Mr. Shichita, *"Booming Brazil in Japan,"* Literary Digest for January 8, 1927.

Termier, Pierre, *"Atlantis,"* Annual Report of the Smithsonian Institution, 1915.

Tumulty, Joseph P., *"Woodrow Wilson As I Know Him,"* Doubleday, Page & Company, 1921.

V

Virginian Pilot, *"The Jim Crow Law,"* January 24, 1927.

W

Walton, Lester A., *"Congregational Church Mother of Negro Schools,"* N. Y. World, May 30, 1926.

Westermarck, Edward, *"The History of Human Marriage,"* Macmillan and Co., 1891.

Winchell, Professor Alexander, *"Preadamites,"* S. C. Griggs and Company (Scott, Forseman and Company) Chicago, 1880.

INDEX

A

Accad, Cushite or Semitic civilization near Turanian Shumir, 47.

Adams, Charles Francis, Found light on American Negro question in Egypt, 294-5.

Amalgamation, Wendell Phillips on, 116; Bishop Gilbert Haven, 116-7; Rev. B. H. Payne, 119-21; Marriage and illicit cohabitation between the races, a Negro author's views in regard to, 192-3; In Virginia (Dr. Plecker), 196-9; Archer, 205, 219-20; Some of the mixed-bloods in Virginia (Estabrook and McDougal), 219; Rev. A. H. Shannon, 220-5; If consummated future generations will have less white blood than an octoroon, 225.

Africa, Prehistoric man in (Lull), 164.

America, Professor Ross' conception of her destiny, 192; W. Laird Clowes as to effect of Negro's presence on America's destiny, 192; Dissensions among our people when the principal European powers fight among themselves, 353-7; Neutrality of, during World War, 358-67; Cotton situation and Great Britain during World War, 361-2; The President's views as to the enforcement of neutrality against Great Britain, 363-4.

America, Prehistoric. Prehistoric man in North America (Richard Swan Lull), 43; Popular conception as to Indian type, 51; Matters to be considered in the peopling and development of prehistoric America, 51-2; Glacial Period, 52-3; Isolation of Americas, 53-4; Production of American type and development of civilization, 54; Conditions on discovery by Columbus, 54-5; Civilization could not have been indigenous with the Indian, a Metal Age preceding the Rough Stone Age in the Mississippi Valley, 55; Antiquity of man in America indicated by skeletal remains and domestication of Flora and Fauna, 55-6; Mound-builder civilization, 56-7; Copper mines, trade and sculpture of Mound-builders, 57-8; Nahaus connected with Mound builders, 58-9; Cliff-dwellers, 59-60; Nahuas in Oregon country, 60; Legend of Moquis, 60-1; Complexions of Indians, 61-4; Menominees, 62; Tlinket or Koloshian family, 62-3; Mandans, 63-4; Zuni Indians, 64; Caucasian and Negro types shown in monuments and sculptures of Central American civilizations, 66; American civilization not due to Japan, 67-8; Any Asiatic connection with American civilization must have been Aryan and not Mongoloid, 68; Not to be attributed to Egyptians, 68; Languages found in